High-Integrity Software

Software Science and Engineering

Series Editor: **Richard A. DeMillo**
Purdue University, West Lafayette, Indiana

High-Integrity Software
C. T. Sennett

A Continuation Order Plan is available for this series. A continuation order will bring delivery of each new volume immediately upon publication. Volumes are billed only upon actual shipment. For further information please contact the publisher.

High-Integrity Software

Edited by
C T Sennett
Royal Signals and Radar Establishment
Malvern, UK

Plenum Press · New York and London

ISBN 0-306-43552-7
Library of Congress Catalog Card Number 89-043671

PLENUM PRESS
A Division of Plenum Publishing Corporation
233 Spring Street, New York, NY 10013

© Chapters 1, 2, 3, 6, 9, 12: Crown Copyright 1989
© Chapters 5, 7, 8, 10, 11: Pitman Publishing 1989

First published in Great Britain 1989
by Pitman Publishing
A Division of Longman Group UK Limited

Printed in Great Britain at The Bath Press, Avon

Contents

1 Introduction

C. T. Sennett, Royal Signals and Radar Establishment

The requirement for highly reliable software increases with every year. The benefits from the use of computers are so great that applications multiply to the extent that large sectors of modern society are totally dependent on their use. This dependence brings with it a vulnerability to serious damage if the software should fail: we are now entering an era in which software failures could have life-threatening consequences. This vulnerability compels the use of software techniques which will largely eliminate errors and it is the purpose of this book to describe some of these techniques and to set them into the context of the procurement process.

The awareness of the need for high-integrity software has arisen in three different communities, the avionics industry, the defence industry and the large-scale procurers of software who are growing less and less tolerant of current standards of software reliability. The avionics industry has been the leader in the field of safety-critical applications, partly because of the need for airworthiness certification but also because of the generally high awareness of the need to consider safety requirements in the industry. The use of "fly-by-wire" systems in which computers are interposed between the pilot and the control surface actuators has brought this problem to a head, but there are other applications, such as the use of computers to produce synthetic displays, where software failures could have intolerable consequences. Other safety-critical applications occur in software used for the fuzing and arming of munitions, where safety-critical functions are now under software control. Nor are the safety-critical applications all confined to the military field. One can cite the cases of process control, including control of nuclear reactors, and railway signalling where systems are being designed which are vulnerable to software failure. Even in such apparently low-technology industries as water supply, computer-controlled systems are being considered whose failure could lead to large-scale water pollution.

The defence community has of course a keen awareness of the need for security and the need for security accreditation has focussed on the criteria which software must satisfy in order to be trusted to process classified data.

In the past, the degree of trust required has not been great as such cases have been confined to isolated systems. Now, however, there is an increasing necessity to link systems, and the operational needs are such as to require the placing of trust in the software. Typically, one can envisage the secure software as being used for an operational command and control system, for which the security needs are fairly obvious. However, the question of security also arises in the non-operational ADP systems which are used for the normal administrative purposes, because of the inferences it is possible to make from the administrative data.

The defence community is also very much aware of the possibilities for denial of service. A software failure may be such that it renders a system unavailable at a time of crisis, when it is most needed. It is possible that this failure could be engineered deliberately, a possibility which is not confined to defence systems alone. The jargon of computer viruses and logic bombs indicates that there are many individuals who, from a variety of motives, are interested in subverting computer systems. This is a typical hazard for computer networks, but it is also experienced by computer-controlled telephone exchanges which are vulnerable to abuse. Telephone exchanges are also vulnerable to sudden unexpected increases in demand. The integrity requirement here is that the emergency services are not denied as a result of a sudden upsurge of demand caused by, say, a phone-in programme.

The other thread to the demand for high-integrity software has been cost. Software errors are costly to correct but their occurrence can give rise to substantial losses. In the financial sector, computers control immense resources and their failure can give rise to substantial losses simply from loss of service, quite apart from actual errors. A recent example is the case of a US bank which suffered an error in its computer system which gave rise to directly attributable losses of $9 000 000, even though the fault was cured within one day. Similarly, satellite launch vehicles are controlled by computers and their failure can put at risk an extremely valuable payload as well as the vehicle itself.

The three threads of safety, security and cost have given rise to different emphases and techniques for addressing the integrity issue, all of which have something to offer. From the safety field emerged the ideas of fault tolerance and N-version programming. Fault tolerance has proved to be a very fruitful idea with techniques ranging from defensive programming to the use of system designs in which the trusted components constrain the behaviour of the untrusted ones. This has led to an emphasis on the quality of the design and the use of the best available techniques from the rest of the software industry.

The security field has been marked by an emphasis on the use of formal methods, in particular on the use of formal proof of software. This stems partly from the early interaction with the academic community, but also from the fact that security requirements are easier to specify than safety requirements. Security requirements are simply concerned with information flow and so are easily formalized and the result will fit a whole class of problems. Another contribution from the security world stems from the realization of the importance of evaluation. This is because the problem is not so much one of writing secure systems as of demonstrating to an accreditor that the system is trustworthy enough. In other words, it is not enough for a system to be secure, it must also be seen to be secure. This emphasis on the procedural aspects and evaluation criteria is a distinguishing feature of the security world.

The cost driver in high-integrity software has always been a problem as the high-integrity techniques are themselves costly to apply: in some cases very much so and only warranted for situations where failure might lead to loss of life. The contribution here has been in an understanding of the way in which the procurement process has a role to play in producing reliable software. This covers issues such as risk analysis to ensure that procurement specifications accurately capture the integrity requirements, through management tools and on to an understanding of the importance of balancing the costs throughout the life-cycle of the software. Thus there is an increasing realization of the importance of producing valid specifications. A good programmer can cause difficulties by correcting a poor specification, but a good specification can be implemented by a poor programmer. A good specification is cost-effective because it is easy to implement and meets all the operational needs. A bad specification can increase implementation difficulties and result in the wrong system being produced.

In gathering together the topics for this book I have drawn on techniques from each of these fields. I have concentrated specifically on the requirements for high-integrity software, so the general need for quality assurance, project control and the use of structured methods of design should be taken as read. Although the topics cover advanced techniques, I have also tried to ensure that they are immediately applicable. In almost every case, the techniques are usable and supported by tools which are commercially available now, or will be shortly.

Chapters 2 to 4 deal with specification and design issues. Chapter 2 is an introduction to formal specification and implementation, using the specification language Z. There is undoubtedly a tendency for non-mathematicians to recoil from a formal language such as Z. This tendency should be resisted as a formal specification has benefits both to procurers and to implementors. For procurers, the advantage is in the precision which the formal specification offers. It is both possible and desirable to go through a formal specification with the users of a system to ensure the specification accurately captures the user's requirements. Without this phase, the specification may give rise to more difficulties than it solves. For implementors a formal specification language also has benefits. By working at an abstract level it is possible to design software very rapidly, postponing implementation decisions to the most appropriate time. Design using an implementation language has the tendency to become lost in implementation detail.

The theme of design is taken up in chapter 3 which deals with techniques for fault tolerance, the detection of errors and the treatment of recovery. Chapter 4 reverts back to formal methods again to cover the topic of proof of correctness. This chapter helps to give a feeling for the process of formal proof with a theorem prover. This is another of those human activities like programming which really has to be experienced to be understood properly. It is clear that our current experience with theorem proving is rather like that of programming in the early days of computers. At present, theorem proving requires mathematical understanding, just as the early computers were programmed by mathematicians. One may expect that, as with programming, the techniques will become accessible to the normal professional software engineer.

The next two chapters deal with implementation languages. This is rather a vexed question because there are so many human issues associated with it: everyone has a favourite programming language. But this is where the trouble lies, for in their desire to provide attractive language features language designers introduce complexities with unexpected error conditions and exceptions. These in turn give rise to failures which may escape normal testing. There are two possible approaches to this problem: one is to take an existing programming language and prune it of undesirable features and the other is to design a language from scratch with the needs of high-integrity software in mind. Chapter 5 describes the first approach, chapter 6 the second, from which the relative merits of each approach may be seen.

The next three chapters deal with software analysis and the integrity of the compiled code. This stage in the development process is often neglected in discussions on high-integrity software, but in fact it is a very important part of the whole. Surprisingly often, software bugs arise from such simple errors as numerical overflows, or accessing an array outside its bounds or overflowing a field of a record. Faults such as these simply do not appear in the specification or design stages and can only be found by analysing the implementation itself. Analysis is a general evaluation technique. The problem of being given a few thousand lines of code and then being asked to find unexpected features of it is intractable without some method of probing the code. Analysis may be used, as described in chapters 7 and 8, to measure test coverage, information flow and to verify properties of the implementation by the use of assertion statements and the propagation of the resulting conditions. Indeed the analysis techniques are so useful that the algebraic ideas which underly them have been used to define a common target language for use by compilers. This exciting approach is described in chapter 9 and its use will allow the formal verification of implementations, various forms of analysis and the possibility of correctness preserving transformations.

The book finally concludes with a group of chapters which are concerned with the procurement process, rather than software development. Chapter 10 deals with the concept of *assurance*. This is the word used for the measure of confidence that a procurer may have that the software is correct and has the properties desired. A high level of assurance gives trustworthiness, but is costly to attain. Consequently the specification of an assurance level is an important part of the procurement document. Assurance on its own is of course meaningless. Assurance can only apply to a specification which states which functions are trusted. This raises the very important question as to whether the trusted functionality matches the threats to the system and whether all the vulnerabilities have been reduced to an acceptably low level. This is the topic of risk analysis and is the subject of chapter 11, which deals not only with the software but also with the human and physical environment in which the software runs. Finally, chapter 12 deals with the writing of the procurement specification itself. Here again, human and external issues dominate. In a procurement specification it is useless to say "the system shall be reliable" or "it shall fail no more than once in a thousand years." These statements are simply not testable for compliance. There is a considerable art in specifying the requirement in a manner which is testable for compliancy and does not led to excessive costs.

The technique for producing and specifying high-integrity software described in this book are of concern to all who are involved in specifying and implementing software. Knowledge of these techniques will help reduce programming errors; actual use incurs costs which must be balanced against the long-term reduction in costs brought about by having more reliable software, so the techniques must be chosen accordingly. For some safety and security critical applications the most exigent techniques must necessarily be employed.

2 Formal specification and implementation

C. T. Sennett, Royal Signals and Radar Establishment

2.1 Introduction to formal methods

The production of high-integrity software is a matter of engineering. Bridges, buildings, cars, television sets, and well engineered artefacts generally, are all produced to quantifiable standards of reliability. It is possible to step into a lift, for example, with no qualms about its safety simply because the engineering requirements for its production are both well understood and enforced by society. To achieve a similar state of affairs in software engineering requires a similar discipline but absolutely fundamental to any engineering discipline must be its scientific basis and the mathematical tools and techniques which support it. The safety of a bridge depends critically on an ability to calculate stresses and decide on the strength of materials and, indeed, the whole basis of engineering is dependent on the ability to calculate performance and build a product to quantifiable standards. By these criteria software is poorly engineered: all too often the performance and reliability is assessed by building the product and patching deficiencies as they occur, so for high-integrity software the science behind software engineering must be both understood and practised. Broadly speaking, formal methods may be equated with this scientific basis. Professional software engineers should have a thorough understanding of the subject, and production methods for high-integrity software should be marked by extensive use of mathematical tools based on this science.

The word formal for a mathematician is applied to symbolic notations whose meaning is defined in terms of transformation rules which convert strings of symbols into simpler ones, ultimately ending up with terms whose meaning is self-evident. An example is a proof system which may be used to convert a logical formula into the truth symbol as a result of applying transformation rules corresponding to the laws of deduction. The scientific basis for software engineering is provided by the observation that computer languages form just such a formal system and consequently that the idea of correctness could be linked to the idea of proof. Without this fundamental idea, the only meaning which could be given to the word "correct" as applied to a computer program is that the program should work in practice, and this meaning cannot form the basis of an engineering approach. The word "proof" on its own is not enough as it is always necessary to have something to prove. Consequently a specification is required, itself written in a formal language, and the idea of correctness is now quite simply that the program, considered as a formal statement, should provably satisfy the specification.

In many cases, one will be content with a formal proof of quite simple properties of the program, such as the absence of overflow, rather than with the full specification itself. This is usually established with an analysis tool, rather than with a formal proof, but the tool itself is still based on formal methods and the algorithms used need to be proved to be correct. Techniques of analysis are discussed in Chapters 7 and 8, so in this chapter I shall only be concerned with formal specification and the transformation of a specification into an implementation while preserving correctness. The intention is to give a view on the state of the art in what is still a very new discipline, concentrating on the requirements for the use of the methods in an engineering context. To give a concrete form to the discussion I shall be using the specification language Z [Sufrin1983, Hayes1987, Spivey1988] as an example of an advanced notation which supports the use of formal methods. However, before going into this, it is necessary to introduce the notation and set the scene with a brief outline of the mathematical notions of formalism, proof and logic.

The simplest form of logic which almost everyone is familiar with is the propositional calculus. In this, the logical connectives $\land, \lor, \neg, \Rightarrow$ and $\Leftrightarrow$ (and, or, not, implies, and if and only if, respectively) may be combined with terms represented by symbols to form formulae such as $(A \lor B) \land (\neg A \lor B)$. The formalism of the propositional calculus enables one to reason about the truth of such formulae. Adding structure to the terms, allowing them to be drawn from predicates, or truth values, over sets, together with the quantifiers $\forall$, for all (members of a set), and $\exists$, there exists (a member of a set), gives the predicate calculus. Within these simple bounds one can prove certain tautologies such as de Morgan's rule

$$\neg(A \lor B) \Leftrightarrow (\neg A \land \neg B)$$

or the properties of the quantifiers such as

$$\forall x \bullet A \Leftrightarrow \neg \exists x \bullet \neg A$$

which are both formulae valid for all A and B.

The tautologies may be used as a basis for proof: an expression of the form $\neg(A \lor B)$ may be replaced by $(\neg A \land \neg B)$ as one proof step or rule of deduction aimed at demonstrating that a given formula is a tautology. This is an entirely symbolic process which is the essence of what is meant by calling a calculus a formal system. A proof system therefore consists of the syntax for the formulae together with rules of deduction enabling one theorem to be developed from another. The proof consists of the application of the rules to a given statement to show that it is a tautology. As the use of the deduction rules is symbolic, it has the property that it may be carried out mechanically and this is the basis for the mechanical aids to proof. The proof itself cannot be carried out mechanically as, except for certain simple though important situations, the decision about which deduction rule to employ cannot be made automatically. However, mechanical aids are a very important part of the proof process. This is because the actual carrying out of a formal proof for even a medium-sized program may involve millions of proof steps. Not only is this number quite beyond the capabilities of a human, the symbolic manipulation involved is very error-prone, so that detailed formal proofs which have not been checked by machine are not particularly credible.

Mechanical theorem proving and checking is a field of software development which may be equated with compiler writing in terms of extent and activity. It is possible to develop simple theorem checkers quite quickly, just as it is relatively easy to develop interpreters for simple languages. An industrially useful theorem proving aid on the other hand will be a much larger project, comparable with a full-scale Ada compiler. It will pay attention to performance and have extensive libraries of heuristics to help search for proofs; it will itself be a high-integrity program, based on sound mathematical principles, and it will be usable from a human point of view having an acceptable interface to the user and a module system suitable for use with a large team of programmers. Unfortunately, technology at this scale of utility does not exist at the moment although there are hopeful signs that the issues are being addressed, and chapter 4 describes experience with one of the more powerful systems currently available.

The proofs which may be developed using the predicate calculus as described above are not very interesting from a specification point of view as they can only depend on the properties of the logical connectives. Application details are introduced in the form of axioms, that is true statements about the properties of the system under study. The requirements for the system may then be expressed in this logic, say as a relation on the set of inputs and outputs: the implementation should also be expressed in this form and the basis of the formal proof of correctness is that the one conforms to the other, a logical statement which is susceptible of proof. Bearing in mind the difficulties of carrying out formal proofs with a mechanical aid, it is often necessary to use informal techniques in which the proofs are justified in natural language. If carefully done, this may result in no great loss of rigour; sometimes it may actually improve the situation as the formal system may introduce so much detail as to obscure what is going on. A typical example could be a graphical routine which depended on two numbers being co-prime. The proof which simply states that this algorithm works because 512 and 127 are co-prime is much more convincing than any amount of machine manipulation to establish this fact, so it will be a necessary requirement for mechanical aids to support informal as well as fully formal reasoning.

Regardless of the technique for carrying out the proof, the property to be proved should always be identified and understood for any high-integrity software. Consequently, the specification language should be understood first and foremost as a vehicle for displaying this property in a manner which the user may readily understand; but secondly and almost equally important, the specification language is an input to tools which will assist in the checking and carrying out of the proof and it is on the basis of the ease with which these aspects may be supported that the pros and cons of specification languages in general, and Z in particular, will be discussed.

2.2 Formal specification using Z

To the programmer, the very idea of a special-purpose specification language can seem unusual. After all, the programming language can be regarded as a mathematical statement and programming languages often provide procedure specifications and so on which capture quite a lot of the requirement, so why develop a special language? To show the benefits which a special-purpose language can give, the specification for a sorting routine may be considered. This will simply say that the input to the routine consists of a sequence of numbers and the output should be the same numbers in an increasing order. The specification is entirely without algorithmic elements and simply states a relationship between the input and the output; any attempt to do this in a programming language has to be done algorithmically and amounts to an implementation of the requirement. In addition, the programming language will be concerned with extraneous detail such as sizes of arrays, reading input values and so on, which is a necessary part of the implementation, but which obscures the specification. A special-purpose specification language allows the specification to be written at an abstract level, so that it can be easily understood. Because it is a specification, there is no need to use particular constructs provided by the implementation language, such as arrays and lists, but instead the specification may be expressed in the abstract language of sets.

Quite apart from these considerations of expressive power, the specification must serve the purposes of proving correctness and this is concerned with the formal properties of the language. If the implementation language is to be considered as a formal mathematical statement, it is a complicated object expressed in a logic in which it is hard to carry out proofs. This brings us to what should be the first consideration in discussing specification languages, which is the logic on which it is based: there should be one. But the choice of the logic for a specification language is affected by a number of conflicting considerations including the field of application, the clarity of user understanding, the ease with which the logic may be handled by machine, and the ease with which the specification may be translated into implementation language terms.

A typical way in which the field of application affects the logic is in the decision as to whether parallel processing is an important aspect or not. An extreme example of this is in formal specification of hardware. For software, temporal logic or a formalism such as CSP, which both provide means for reasoning about processes and concurrent events, may be used. For sequential software, special-purpose logics are not necessary but where a specification system is associated with a particular theorem prover, the needs of the latter have tended to dominate the other factors. In fact the objectives of a language for input to a theorem prover and a specification language are quite different as the former will be concerned with the soundness of the logic and the ease with which it may be mechanized, together with the requirements for steering and directing the proof itself. Consequently one may expect that specification languages and proof languages will also become specialized for their particular requirements with the specification language logic being implemented in the theorem proving logic.

As discussed below, the objectives of specification and implementation languages are also different and lead to the ability of implementation languages to express certain mathematically undefined concepts such as unterminating programs and exceptions. The logic for dealing with this uses domain theory [Scott1976, Stoy1977] which if employed in a specification language would allow the use of constructs which may be readily implemented. This approach is typified by VDM [Jones1986] which pioneered a rigorous approach to the development of software and the use of formalism in specifying the semantics of programming languages. The advantage is bought at the cost of difficulty in carrying out the proofs and a certain loss in clarity as the domain theory logic is not quite so intuitive as ordinary set theory.

The main motivation in the design of Z has been ease of user understanding, which is the reason for the adoption of set theory, supplemented by a simple type system, for the basic logic for Z. Surprisingly enough, the language may be developed, as will be shown below, to have a rich expressive power even though it is based only on the simple notions of set membership and equality. Thus the logic is simple and one may expect that it will be capable of being handled by mechanical means, although a mechanical theorem checking aid for Z has yet to be made widely available. Apart from the intuitive nature of the logic, the main problem for comprehensibility which a specification language must tackle is concerned with imposing structure on predicates which may contain hundreds of terms. For this the characteristic feature of Z, namely the schema notation, is brought into play as it provides a means of structuring the specification at a similar level of granularity to that provided by a procedure in an implementation language. Preliminary work on tool systems for Z has also resulted in the definition of a module system for Z which enables large-scale structure to be imposed on specifications.

The language itself has a fairly long history, dating back to 1979 with early work by Abrial while at Oxford. This has been developed by a number of researchers at Oxford so the language now has some maturity from the user point of view. A particularly useful feature, which has grown during the course of this evolution, is the mathematical toolkit, in which the basic set-theoretic expressions are developed into operators, relations and sets of particular usefulness for forming formal specifications of software. The other characteristic feature of the language is the use of graphical features exploiting the capabilities of modern workstations, including a full set of mathematical symbols and the indication of structure by lines, boxes and layout, rather than the more traditionally oriented use of keywords.

The expressive power of Z is built from simple logical foundations. To show how this is done and to relate the set-theoretic concepts to those of programming languages I shall give a very brief survey of the Z language. For more details the best starting point is the book of specification case studies [Hayes1986]. Initially, the best way of approaching Z is to regard it as a notation for writing set-theoretic expressions. For this, the most primitive terms are the given sets which are introduced by enclosing the identifier which stands for the given set in square brackets as follows:

$$[T]$$

The recommended style for writing Z, which will be followed here, is to intersperse fragments of specification with the English language explanation. This is a very simple innovation but one which adds considerably to the readability of a Z document. Given sets are treated as unique within a document but they may be instantiated when the document is imported into another one. A member of this set is indicated by

$$x : T$$

which recalls programming language declaration conventions and also serves to indicate the type of the identifier. The set of numbers $\mathbb{N}$, tends to be built in to the tools which support Z, but technically it is also treated as a given set. From any set, the powerset may be formed, indicated by the special symbol $\mathbb{P}$. This is often used in declarations so that

$$n : \mathbb{N}; \; ns : \mathbb{P}\,\mathbb{N}$$

means that n is a number whereas ns is a set of numbers. Tuples, corresponding to the programming concept of records, may be formed from a series of sets. For example for a pair, the notation is (x, y) which is a member of the Cartesian product set $(X \times Y)$, given that x and y belong to the sets X and Y respectively. A labelled, disjoint union corresponds to programming concepts such as Pascal enumerated types or Algol68 unions.

It is formed by means of a *datatype* declaration as follows:

$$Tree ::= leaf\langle\!\langle T\rangle\!\rangle \mid node\langle\!\langle (Tree \times Tree)\rangle\!\rangle$$

The angle brackets enclose the domains of the constructor functions *leaf* and *node*. The declaration means that the set *Tree* is made up of either leaves or nodes constructed from the arguments of the constructor functions.

Sets may also be constructed; for example the set of the first 10 squares is written

$$\{x : \mathbb{N} \mid 0 < x \leq 10 \bullet x^2\}$$

A set of pairs is equivalent to the set-theoretic concept of a relation. Relations are indicated using the $\leftrightarrow$ symbol, so that a relation on the integers, say, is written

$$\_<\_ : \mathbb{N} \leftrightarrow \mathbb{N}$$

where the underlines indicate the parameter position and consequently confer infixed status on the symbol $<$. The relation symbol itself may be defined with the very useful Z feature of a generic syntactic definition as follows:

$$
\begin{array}{|l}
\hline\!\!=\!\!= [X, Y] =\!\!=\!\!=\!\!= \\
\; X \leftrightarrow Y \triangleq \mathbb{P}(X \times Y) \\
\hline
\end{array}
$$

This construction defines the relation symbol $\leftrightarrow$ in terms of the two generic parameters X and Y. The box drawn round the definition indicates the scope of the parameters while the double line indicates a definition which uniquely defines each instance of the symbol.

A function is a special case of a relation in which each element in the domain of the relation is uniquely related to an element in the range. For example the function delivering the square of an integer could be explicitly constructed as follows:

$$square \triangleq \{x : \mathbb{N} \bullet (x, x^2)\}$$

and considered either as a set of pairs or a relation. To draw attention to the fact that a construction is actually a function the more suggestive notation

$$square \triangleq \lambda x : \mathbb{N} \bullet x^2$$

may be used.

A partial function on two sets is a (functional) relation whose domain may be a subset of the first set. It is indicated by drawing a vertical bar through the function arrow and may be defined using another generic construction as follows:

$$
\begin{array}{|l}
\hline
[X, Y] \\
\hline
X \nrightarrow Y \triangleq \{f : X \leftrightarrow Y \\
\qquad | \, \forall \, x : X; \, y_1, y_2 : Y \\
\qquad \bullet \, (x, y_1) \in f \wedge (x, y_2) \in f \Rightarrow y_1 = y_2 \\
\qquad \} \\
\hline
\end{array}
$$

Another example of a generic construction is given by the set of sequences of a given set, say X. These are defined as those finite partial functions (indicated by two bars through the function arrow) whose domains are the initial segments of the non-zero natural numbers:

$$
\begin{array}{|l}
\hline
[X] \\
\hline
seq \, X \triangleq \{f : \mathbb{N} \nrightarrow X \mid dom \, f = 1 \, .. \, \#f\} \\
\hline
\end{array}
$$

As well as infixed symbols, the syntax allows for pre- and post-fixed and distributed symbols, which enables most standard mathematical notations to be supported and built up from relatively primitive foundations.

Predicates similarly are built up from the concepts of set membership, $\in$, and equality, with extra syntax for the infixed relations and combinations with the logical connectives. Local definitions and declarations and the μ clause (that x such that...) may then be derived from this. For example a local definition is written

$$
\begin{array}{ll}
P & \qquad \text{equivalent to} \qquad \exists \, x : T \mid x = E \bullet P \\
where & \\
\quad x \triangleq E &
\end{array}
$$

while that x satisfying the predicate P is written

$$
x \triangleq \mu \, t : T \mid P(t) \bullet t
$$

which satisfies

$$
P(x) \wedge \forall \, t : T \mid t \neq x \bullet \neg P(t)
$$

The combination of these structures gives an extensive and powerful notation for terms and predicates built up, within the language itself, from a very small number of primitive concepts.

The new and characteristic feature introduced in Z is the schema, standing for the combination of a signature and a predicate, but treated as an entity in itself. Schemas may be named and used in other constructions. As an example, we shall consider the specification of an operation to extract an integer square root, given by the following schema:

$$\begin{array}{|l}
\hline
\text{\textit{Square\_root}} \\
r, s : \mathbb{N} \\
\hline
0 \leq s \wedge r^2 \leq s < (r+1)^2 \\
\hline
\end{array}$$

As usual, the box delimits the object being named which is an entity in which values r and s, drawn from the integers, are such that the predicate applies. The schema is not a procedure but is more closely analogous with a macro; the precise semantics of schemas may be found in [Spivey1988]. Its use may be illustrated by the following examples:

$\exists\, r : \mathbb{N} \bullet Square\_root$

The predicate asserting the existence of the square root for a given s.

$Square\_root \vdash r > 1 \Rightarrow r \neq s$

A simple theorem on square roots.

$\{Square\_root \bullet (r, s)\}$

A set of pairs of integers representing the square root relation.

$\lambda\, s : \mathbb{N} \bullet \mu\, r : \mathbb{N} \mid Square\_root \bullet r^2$

The function giving the nearest perfect square less than or equal to s.

The schema is a very powerful structuring device. One of the most important aspects is that schemas may be included in other schemas, allowing a complex specification to be built up gradually by the addition of predicates representing extra constraints. As the schema definition is assembled the accompanying text allows the meaning of what is being specified to be made clear in a step-by-step fashion. Apart from inclusion, schemas may be combined together using logical operators so that, for example, the schema expression $A \wedge B$ represents the schema in which the signature parts of A and B are merged and the predicates conjoined. This is particularly useful for specifying error cases: for example the error case for the square root operation could be specified as

$$
\boxed{
\begin{array}{l}
\text{\textit{Root\_error}} \\
\hline
s : \mathbb{N}; \; reply : seq\ Char \\
\hline
s < 0 \wedge reply = \text{"Invalid value for square root"}
\end{array}
}
$$

Now the specification for the total operation is

$$\textit{Square\_root} \vee \textit{Root\_error}$$

The final notational apparatus is designed for the specification of operations and is used to represent the values of state variables before and after the operation and to distinguish values which represent inputs and outputs. This is done very simply by allowing identifiers to be decorated: ' represents a value after an operation, ? an input and ! an output. This is entirely a notational convention so no extra semantics are required, but it allows other schema expressions to be defined such as a schema operator to represent the composition of two operations.

This is clearly only a cursory description of Z, but it is enough to show that the notation provides a pleasant environment for mathematical reasoning, with most of the standard notations of mathematics being represented within a syntax which is capable of being processed by machine. That this is expressive enough to allow most software specification problems to be expressed can only be found by working through specification case studies, given, for example in [Hayes1986], but it should be clear that the express-iveness is greater than that of the languages provided by existing verification systems. This expressive power has not been bought at the cost of a complicated logic as all the constructions in Z have been based on the primitive axioms of set theory and therefore rest on firm foundations. The question of the suitability of those foundations for mechanical theorem proving aids has not yet been extensively addressed although enough work has been done to indicate that no substantial problems should be encountered.

The main objective of Z has been to provide understandability without compromising rigour and it is worth concluding this section with some remarks on the difficulties this presents for the implementors of tools to process the language, based on work at RSRE on a type checking tool for Z [Sennett1987]. The difficulties are not severe, but it is necessary to use advanced techniques. The full character set requires a graphics workstation if editing is to be in terms of the symbols themselves rather than graphics control sequences. The symbols do not exist on the keyboard so it is necessary to have various ways of calling them up; we have found three techniques to be useful, namely the use of the CTRL key to act as a special shift to allow the mathematical characters to be typed directly from the keyboard, the use of a pop-up menu of all the characters, and finally a pop-up menu of certain sequences of characters which occur together (for example ∀ | •). Special shifts are useful for the commonly occurring characters such as ∧ and ∨, but it is difficult to remember more than a half a dozen or so of these combinations, so this is something which is left as an option to the individual programmer. The menu of character groups is not only useful for getting several of the special characters in one interaction it also provides a primitive structure-editing capability by gathering together all the key symbols for a syntactic unit which can be arranged into horizontal or vertical forms according to taste.

Structure editing is a useful technique for drawing the various types of Z box and for delimiting the Z text from the surrounding documentation and in this the Flex structure editing feature has been found to be useful [Core1987]. With this feature it has been found possible to draw the boxes and change their shape dynamically to accommodate the effects of editing the characters within. The existence of the defined structure allows for a simple syntax to be provided for tools and gives an easy strategy for syntax recovery on error as the structure editor delimits and guarantees the major syntactic units. Lexical analysis on the other hand does present some rather tiresome challenges. Certain questions about differentiating fonts and character modifications (bold, underlined, subscript, superscript, etc.) must be settled at the outset and one of the tricky points in this area has been the correct treatment of superscripts to allow for their use to indicate exponentiation and for symbols such as transitive closure. Similarly a scheme of lexical analysis which is relatively easy to implement and understandable by the users is quite hard to develop bearing in mind the need for user-defined characters and the routine use of the Greek alphabet. The question of whether these characters are alphabetic or symbolic illustrates the kind of decision one has to take in lexical analysis, which although basically trivial may, if mistakenly taken, mar the user interface.

Specifications must be capable of modularization so a suitable system has been developed, based on the syntax of [King1987], but developed to include export clauses to allow the module specification to hide internal structure. The actual "code" of the module will be determined by the type of theorem proving tool to be used, but the specification of the module simply provides the types of the identifiers defined in the module, allowing for its incorporation in other modules of specification without explicit imports lists.

In terms of specification writing, such a system provides almost all that is necessary, as the main requirement for theorem proving arises when specifications are refined into implementations, as described in the next section. With this approach the specification is presented in a concise and consistent manner with most of the trivial mistakes being caught by the type checking; the module system provides for suitable cross-referencing between documents while the Z style of mixed English and mathematics supports well documented and understandable specifications.

Apart from these assurance building aspects, the notation has a use simply as a production tool. This is because the features of the language are such that a large specification may be produced quickly, which makes it possible to understand the problem as a whole and design appropriate module and data structures. A standard trauma in program development is to discover that the data structure one has been successfully using for the last twenty modules does not have the capabilities required to implement some feature required by the twenty first, leading to massive re-compilations. By having a complete specification of the problem the capabilities required of the data structures can be made visible at the outset of the implementation. The notation is also a good means of communication between specifiers and implementors. The underlying set theory is easily understood and the notation is compact enough not to obscure the overall structure with excessive syntactic detail.

Finally Z does provide a pleasant medium to work with. The success of any formal specification technique in practice depends to a large degree on its acceptability to the normal industrial programmer.

2.3 Formal implementation from Z

The process of transforming a high-level specification into an implementation is called *refinement*: it is the creative, human, activity of software design and within the context of high-integrity software the problem is to carry it out in such a manner that the assurance given by the formal, high-level specification is not lost. As usual with assurance, the problem is not so much a question of carrying it out correctly as of *demonstrating* that it has been carried out correctly. Consequently the problem with refinement is to develop a notation which adequately demonstrates that an implementation satisfies its specification.

The target for the refinement process is a text capable of being mechanically translated into an implementation, in other words an implementation language. The source of refinement is the specification language and there is a strong case for arguing that the two languages should be different, largely because the objectives they must satisfy are different: the specification language is designed for abstraction; it will manipulate concepts such as infinite sets and relations on those sets without thought for implementation considerations. Note that this remark is addressed to the form of the specification language itself, rather than the act of specification which should take place with at least some consideration being given towards the implementability of what is being defined. The requirement is that the implementability should not constrain the expression of the specification. The implementation on the other hand must be very much concerned with the finite size of the machine, for example the range of implementable integers and the need for repetitive constructs to terminate. It must inevitably be concerned with efficiency: the increase in the demands made on computers has exceeded the increase in the capabilities of the hardware and there seems to be no reason why this should not always be the case. Finally, the machine itself must constrain the implementation language, which must be concerned with questions of storage layout, environments and the necessity for sequential operation.

Given a separate implementation language, the question arises as to what form it should take. An obvious candidate is to use a standardized language such as Algol, Pascal, Ada or whatever is currently preferred but this raises the problem of lack of assurance in going from a formal specification statement to an informal implementation language. Clearly one has to give up the formal chain of reasoning at some point in the transformation of the specification into software running on an actual machine, but it is desirable that, at this point, the problem should be stated in intuitively understandable and less complex terms than the preceding phase of the transformation. A formal specification of the target language undoubtedly improves matters, but it is important to realize that unless the specification is used within the rules of refinement and the compilation process the transformation is still only informal. To have a formal refinement of a specification into Ada, it is necessary to use the formal semantics of the Ada language in the refinement and the Ada compiler must realize those semantic definitions in its translation to the target machine. Ideally, the machine itself should also be formally specified, but it is plain that this is beyond the bounds of what is practical for any large-scale system. Nevertheless, a critical requirement on an implementation language will be its simplicity and the extent to which the compiling system is supported by informal but rigorous methods.

Apart from lack of formality, existing implementation languages have been designed without the requirement for refinement being taken into account. Refinement is concerned with reasoning about fragments of program with respect to fragments of specification, and the module system should support this use so that one can have refinement modules dealing, say, with the general properties of arrays or references and be able to incorporate these generic fragments into differing implementations. This use of modules tends to be incompatible with the normal implementation language concepts of a module which may be restricted to procedures, say, and contain no specification aspects.

These objections may be countered by the use of a special-purpose language designed to support all aspects of specification, refinement and implementation. In this case a different set of problems is encountered. A major one is the question of the integrity of the compiler: while the special-purpose language itself may have formal semantics, it is rarely the case that the compiler for it will be developed rigorously. A standard language, on the other hand, will have validated compilers which even if not rigorously developed have probably been extensively tested in use. Current special-purpose languages are very simple and have limited expressive power; this may make it difficult to produce anything other than the simplest programs. They may have pitfalls in user understanding and one will not be able to count on readily available programming expertise or the ability to port implementations between differing computers. This is an important consideration for high-integrity software: a formally verified program represents a substantial investment of resources and it is legitimate to expect a return in the shape of trustworthy implementations on a number of systems.

It is clear that one may argue the case in either direction and the choice may depend on the requirements of a particular project; unfortunately, in practice, the choice is likely to be determined simply by the availability of tools as currently there is only a limited number of formal verification systems, each with their special-purpose language. For the purposes of illustrating this exposition of refinement I shall be using as an implementation language the Ten15 notation, the salient features of which are described in chapter 9. However, as far as the examples are concerned, a limited subset of the notation is employed whose meaning should be fairly obvious and which is common to nearly all languages. In many ways Ten15 might be regarded as a compromise between the two approaches answering the objections to both. Although a special-purpose language, translators may be defined algebraically and implemented with a high degree of rigour; the language is portable and as it is the target language for compilers for standard languages one may produce mixed language systems allowing the most trusted component to be verified, with the untrusted software being produced by standard means and the whole being integrated at the Ten15 level. The language is comprehensive enough to implement a program as complex as an operating system, so the limitation for formal verification is not on the expressive power, but on the complexity of the theorems to be proved.

Given that the problem is to transform a specification, written in a language such as Z, into an implementation written in a language such as Ten15 notation, the next step is to decide how to go about it. One could simply write down the program and then prove that it satisfied the specification, but this is unlikely to be satisfactory. The verification conditions which assert the conformity will be very large and it is unlikely that the structure of their proof will be related to the design; consequently carrying out the proof will not lead to a greater understanding of the program and this should be a property of all assurance building techniques. Consequently the desirable way to carry out a refinement is to proceed by small stages in which a specification is gradually transformed into an implementation with a large number of small proofs of conformity, rather than complete the implementation in one step with a small number of large proofs.

This carries with it the necessity of reasoning and processing a notation which encompasses both the specification language and the implementation language, in this case Z and Ten15. No such notation currently exists, so I shall be using an *ad hoc* notation based on the work at Oxford and Malvern [refinement in Z is described in Morgan/Robinson1987, Morgan1988, based on the work of Dijkstra1976]. This notation will demonstrate that machine assistance to the process of refinement is feasible as well as indicating the qualities which a refinement language should display.

The mathematics of refinement are relatively well understood and are based on the various techniques for proof of correctness [see for example Gries1981, while a practical exposition from the programmers point of view may be found in Jones1986]. The fundamental concept for the purposes of refinement is that of an *operation* whose specification is to be implemented by a fragment of program. Consider the fragment $x := x + 1$; the semantics of this statement express a transformation from a state of affairs in which the variable x has one value to a state in which the value is incremented by one. The fragment therefore brings about a transformation of state and it is this which an operation represents; the state consists of the variables which are used in the operation, in this case the single variable x. It is clear that any program fragment may be represented as a transformation on states and that any operations which have the same relation of state before to state after are equivalent as far as questions of implementing a specification are concerned.

There are two varieties of refinement; one in which an operation is shown to have the same effect as a number of smaller operations combined together using the combining operators of the implementation language (semi-colons, if-statements, etc); and the other in which the representation of the state variables is changed. The first is called operation refinement, the second data refinement. Operation refinement is relatively easy to understand; an operation containing a disjunction will frequently be implemented by an if-statement and a composition by a sequence. However it does not always follow that the structure of the specification predicates will be reflected in the structure of the program as the structure may be chosen to clarify the specification rather than model the implementation. This typically occurs in error cases where, for example, a predicate contains a function application and the error test is that the parameter should lie within the domain of application of the function. The implementation will nearly always supply a total function with the error being reported in the body of the function. This is an example of the general requirement in implementation of the need to arrange the order of execution and this may result in the structure of the implementation being quite different from the structure of the specification.

Data refinement is a different process. It is used when the specification is written in abstract terms, say relations on abstract sets, and it is necessary to realise these in terms of programming constructs, linked lists or arrays for example. In this case the implementation is simulating the behaviour of the abstract specification, so the requirement is that it should be possible to say at any point what abstract state corresponds to what implementation state:

in other words it should be possible to provide a function from the implementation state variables to the abstract state variables. Similarly there should exist a correspondence between the abstract and implementation operations which should take corresponding states through similar transitions. This is usually shown by a commutation diagram similar to Figure 2.1.

Fig. 2.1

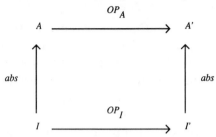

In this diagram, an abstraction function *abs* gives the abstract state A corresponding to the implementation state I. An operation OP_I takes I to I' which must correspond to the abstract operation OP_A taking *abs(I)* to *abs(I')*.

Note that the implementation state can, and usually will, contain more information than the specification state; for example, if the specification is for an ordered sequence and the implementation is in terms of binary trees, many binary trees will correspond to a given sequence. It is possible for the converse to be true, namely for information to be present in the abstract state which is not defined by the specification state. This is allowable if none of the abstract operations can be used to detect the presence of this information. This situation is termed bias in the specification and may arise when one implementation is transformed into another one rather than being refined from a specification. Note also that data refinement is different from instantiation, in which an operation, generic in some term T, is converted into its applied form by supplying the actual term to be used for T. In this case it is in the nature of instantiation that nothing may be deduced about T; this is different from the abstract state in data refinement which contains structure used by the abstract operations.

2.3.1 The refinement notation

The purpose of the refinement notation is to exhibit the steps by which a given implementation may be shown to satisfy a specification. The basic notion of refinement is that an operation is defined by its pre- and post-conditions. The pre-condition expresses what may be assumed on entry to the operation, the post-condition what must hold true on exit from the operation. Any way of meeting the post-condition given the pre-condition is a possible implementation. In terms of the Z notation an operation would be represented by a schema such as the following:

$$
\begin{array}{|l}
\hline
OP \\
\hline
s, s' : STATE \\
\hline
P(s, s') \\
\hline
\end{array}
$$

where P is some predicate expressing the change of state from s to s'. Given that this is a specification of the operation to be performed, the weakest pre-condition which may be assumed for the use of this operation is

$$\exists\, s' : STATE \cdot P(s, s')$$

while the post-condition is simply $P(s, s')$. Note that the pre-condition depends on the values of the state variables before the operation and the post-condition, in general, depends on the values both before and after.

In an implementation language, the types of the variables are usually declared at the start of their scope of validity, forming an environment, rather than being carried around implicitly as with Z schemas. Following this convention, the basic notation for an operation can simply be given as $[\phi, \psi]$, where ϕ and ψ represent predicates in the Z notation expressing the pre- and post-conditions respectively. The Z specification for the operation will be a schema definition containing identifiers related to the identifiers in the environment by the following obvious rules:

- *id* and *id'* in the specification refer to the variable *id* in the environment; *id'* in the specification refers to the value after the operation.

- *id!* refers to the value of the variable *id* after the operation and the pre-condition does not depend on it

- *id?* refers to the value of *id* in the environment, which is not changed by the operation.

With this convention, any Z schema operation may be transformed into the new notation.

As the operations are broken down into simpler sub-operations, each one alters less and less of the environment, so it is useful to prefix the operation by the variables which are altered, thus avoiding the need to specify that the rest of the environment is unchanged. This is indicated as follows: $\Delta x, y\,[\phi, \psi]$, where x and y are the only variables changed by the operation. With this notation one can now write down some simple rules of refinement. In developing these rules it is useful to bear in mind that the requirement is to provide an implementation for an operation which satisfies the condition that what holds true in the state before the operation, the pre-condition, is transformed by the operation into what holds true afterwards. It is required therefore that the semantics of the implementation language be given in the form of predicate transformers in accordance with the Hoare logic on which this refinement process is based. In addition to these rules, which may be regarded as introduction rules for the various elements of the implementation language, there are two fundamental rules expressing the idea of satisfaction of a specification. These may be given as follows:

$$\Delta \, \zeta \, [\varphi, \psi] \sqsubseteq \Delta \, \zeta \, [\chi, \psi], \text{ provided } \varphi \vdash \chi$$

and

$$\Delta \, \zeta \, [\varphi, \psi] \sqsubseteq \Delta \, \zeta \, [\varphi, \chi], \text{ provided } \varphi, \chi \vdash \psi$$

In these two rules, the symbol $\sqsubseteq$ is to be read as "is refined by" and indicates that the operation on the right-hand side of the symbol is a possible implementation for that on the left. ζ stands for the set of changing variables and the theorem signs indicate side conditions which must be proved. In the first one, for example, the requirement is to prove χ, given ϕ.

The first rule expresses the fact that the pre-condition may always be weakened: the refinement satisfies the post-condition of the specification and the pre-condition is true at least as often as the pre-condition for the specification. The second rule is the converse of this in which the implementation strengthens the post-condition; the refinement does at least as much as the specification but may also fix some options. Note that the inclusion of the pre-condition in the assumption list of the theorem to be proved allows the post-condition to be simplified on the basis of what held true in the initial state. These two rules express the idea of the "correctness" of the implementation. The process of verifying the refinement therefore consists in using these rules until the operation is of a form which will match one of the introduction rules to be given below. Some examples of the process will be given later.

For an imperative language, the simplest construction is the assignment operator, for which the introduction rule is

$$\Delta \, x \, [\varphi_{[E/x']}, \varphi] \sqsubseteq x := E$$

The subscripted expression $[E/x']$ indicates a substitution of the expression E for the Z value x', the value of the variable x after the assignment. This rule (and the others also) may be derived in terms of the weakest pre-condition semantics for assignment [see Morgan1988], but it may be motivated informally by noting that, after an assignment to x, everything which held true at the start of the operation must hold true at the end, except that x now has the new value given by E. This introduction rule may only be used for very simple operations: only a single variable is changed and the expression E must be in implementable terms.

An operation may be implemented as two simpler operations by the use of Ten15 sequential composition, indicated by a semi-colon. The introduction rule is

$$\Delta \, \zeta \, [\varphi, \psi] \sqsubseteq \Delta \, \zeta \, [\varphi, \chi]; \, \Delta \, \zeta \, [\chi, \psi]$$

The composite operation clearly establishes ψ given ϕ, so there are no proof obligations. However, in many cases the post-condition will depend on the initial values and as, in the second operation, the state ζ corresponds to ζ' at the end of the first operation, a separate identifier is needed to represent the initial value. This value can be named with a *logical constant* which may be introduced to simplify any operation. For the particular case of retaining an initial value, it may be introduced with the keyword *con* as follows:

$$\Delta x [\varphi, \psi] \; \sqsubseteq \; con \, X \bullet \Delta x [\varphi \wedge x = X, \chi]$$

Informally, the meaning of the rhs of this refinement is that the identifier X, not present in either ϕ or ψ, stands for the initial value of x. This can now be used to form a sequential composition rule for the case where the post condition is a function of the initial and final states of the variable x as follows:

$$\Delta x [\varphi(x), \psi(x, x')] \; \sqsubseteq \; con \, X \bullet \Delta x [\varphi(x) \wedge x = X, \chi(x, x')]; \; \Delta x [\chi(X, x), \psi(X, x')]$$

Note that the scope of *con* extends far to the right. Logical constants do not exist in implementations so they must be eliminated if the refinement is to be productive. In many cases, the intermediate state χ will be such as to define X in terms of x: it may then be substituted into the post-condition and eliminated from the operation.

There are various forms of conditional constructions in Ten15: for the simplest the introduction rule is

$$\Delta \zeta [\varphi, \psi] \; \sqsubseteq \; \textbf{\textit{if}} \, G$$
$$\textbf{\textit{then}} \, \Delta \zeta [G \wedge \varphi, \psi]$$
$$\textbf{\textit{else}} \, \Delta \zeta [\neg G \wedge \varphi, \psi]$$
$$\textbf{\textit{fi}}$$

Note that the Ten15 notation adopts the rather endearing convention of indicating the termination of a construct by the keyword reversed. The predicate G is usually termed a guard after [Dijkstra1976]. There are no proof obligations, although there is not much point in introducing the conditional construct unless the post-condition is a disjunction involving G.

The simplest loop is the while-loop which may be introduced as follows:

$$\Delta \zeta [I, \neg G \wedge I] \; \sqsubseteq \; \textbf{\textit{while}} \, G$$
$$\textbf{\textit{do}} \, \Delta \zeta [G \wedge I, I \wedge V]$$
$$\textbf{\textit{od}}$$

The operation must be cast into a form in which the pre-condition expresses the invariant, I, which will be maintained by the loop, and the post-condition must contain the loop termination condition in the form of the negation of a guard, G. The termination of the loop itself is guaranteed by the variant, V, which is defined in terms of a measure function, M, on the state variables and which delivers decreasing values bounded from below for each iteration. In many cases the measure function will simply be an integer value and in the simplest possible case will be a loop counter. Typically, for these cases, V would have the form $0 \leqslant M(\zeta') < M(\zeta)$. Unlike G, M need not be an implementable expression.

It is always possible to introduce a local variable into the state; Ten15 requires such variables to be initialized, so it is convenient to define the introduction rule in the following form:

$$\Delta \zeta \, [\exists \, x \bullet \varphi \wedge x = E, \, \psi] \sqsubseteq \textbf{\textit{var}} \, x := E$$
$$\textbf{\textit{in}} \, \Delta \, \zeta, x \, [\varphi \wedge x = E, \, \psi]$$
$$\textbf{\textit{ni}}$$

As usual, E must be implementable. A variation of this construction uses *let* instead of *var* and = instead of := to define a local constant. To give a motivation for the choice of this form, one may observe that schema operations frequently take the form

$$
\begin{array}{|l}
\hline
S \\\hline
s, s' : STATE \\\hline
\\
P \\
where \\
\quad x \triangleq E \\
\hline
\end{array}
$$

which corresponds to

$$\Delta \, s \, [\exists \, x \bullet \varphi \wedge x = E, \, \psi], \text{ where } \varphi \triangleq \exists \, s' : STATE \bullet P \text{ and } \psi \triangleq P$$

Once the variable has been introduced into the enclosing state, it may be included in the Δ part of the operation, leaving x' undefined. In cases where the operation is not defined in terms of a where-predicate, it may still be cast into this form provided ϕ does not depend on x.

This completes the description of the operation refinement rules for Ten15 as far as is required for the examples which follow. Apart from the parallel processing operations, which will not be discussed here, the refinement rules for other structures within Ten15 are for the most part generalizations and variations on the ones given above. The remaining structure given by the various ways of constructing procedure values and applying them can be considered to be variations and generalizations of the local variable rule. However, the most general forms of control structure allowed by Ten15 would probably not be used within a formally verified implementation, because of the difficulties of carrying out the proofs required. Implicitly, the use of exceptions has also been discounted: "implementable" in the rules above implies that exceptions will not be raised and this has many consequences for data refinement.

Most of the implementation problem therefore consists in carrying out the data refinement, that is finding a representation of the specification objects in terms of the values manipulated by the Ten15 machine. There is only one data refinement rule and this is common to all implementation languages. To express this within the notation one needs some means of specifying the signature of the abstract state, the signature of the concrete state which will be used to implement it, and the abstraction invariant which relates variables defined according to the two signatures. The later will be a Z schema defining a relation from the concrete state to the abstract state; the relation will be a function in the usual form of data refinement. The actual data refinement rule is expressed as follows:

$$\Delta \, \alpha, \zeta \, [\varphi, \psi] \preceq \Delta \, \gamma, \zeta \, [\exists \, \alpha \cdot I \wedge \varphi, \exists \, \alpha' \cdot I' \wedge \psi]$$

In this rule α represents the abstract variables which are implemented by the concrete variables γ, ζ represents the variables unaffected by this step of data refinement and the $\preceq$ symbol is used to indicate data refinement. In the case where the post-condition depends on the initial values of the abstract state, logical constants will be necessary to express the refined operation. In the usual case, the abstraction invariant I will allow the logical constants to be eliminated on the right-hand side as I defines α in terms of γ, which allows for substitution in ϕ and ψ.

To show how these rules may be used to demonstrate the correctness of an implementation and to show the kind of difficulty which is encountered in practice two examples will be considered, the first of which is a simple problem in integer arithmetic. In this case the problems arise with the data refinement when it is used to represent the unbounded integers of the specification language by the bounded values of machine arithmetic. For the purposes of this example it is necessary to start with a Z specification of the arithmetic operators: a simplification of the treatment of integer values within Ten15 has been made which retains the salient features of the problem but without overwhelming detail; in particular, we shall work in terms of the positive integers.

From a machine point of view, the difficulties arise from the fact that the arithmetic operations may overflow and this will be represented as the calculation of an exceptional value. Consequently machine integers will be represented by a Z datatype derived from the mathematical integers as follows:

$$N ::= exception \mid num \langle\!\langle \mathbb{N} \rangle\!\rangle$$

The maximum integer value is left unspecified, and the machine plus, times and divide operators are defined in terms of it as shown in the specification positioned at the top of page 27, with a similar definition for *times* and *div*. The Ten15 comparisons do not raise exceptions (this is not true for some implementations of some languages) and so the same symbols will be used for comparisons of machine integers.

For the example the extraction of an integer square root will be taken, as described in [Dijkstra1976]. The specification for this problem will be developed from the version given previously by allowing for a maximum

$maxint : \mathbb{N}$

$(\_plus\_), (\_times\_), (\_div\_) : (N \times N) \rightarrow N$

$\forall i, j, k : N$

• $i \ plus \ j = k \Leftrightarrow$

$\qquad (i = exception \lor j = exception) \land k = exception$

$\qquad \lor$

$\qquad\qquad i \in rng \ num \land j \in rng \ num$

$\qquad\qquad z \leq maxint \land k = num \ z \lor z > maxint \land k = exception$

$\qquad where$

$\qquad\qquad x \triangleq num^{-1} i$

$\qquad\qquad y \triangleq num^{-1} j$

$\qquad\qquad z \triangleq x+y$

---

value of the input:

$\qquad max : \mathbb{N}$

Square_root

$r', s : \mathbb{N}$

$0 \leq s \leq max \land r'^2 \leq s < (r'+1)^2$

The refinement problem could be considered as a calculation of *max* in terms of *maxint*, or in other words what the specification must be in order for it to be implementable in the chosen algorithm.

The algorithm to be used is quite straightforward, and may be described in terms of the loop invariant which will be used in the refinement given below:

Loop_Inv

$r, s, u : \mathbb{N}$

$0 \leq r < u \land r^2 \leq s < u^2$

$0 \leq s \leq max$

The algorithm works by introducing a variable u whose square is greater than s and initialising r to zero. Any number between r and u will have a square which is either greater or less than s, and, depending on the case, this number is used as a new value for u or r respectively and the calculation repeated. The loop terminates because r increases towards s, while u decreases and stops when they differ by one. Thus a simple measure function is $u - r$, which gives a form for the loop variant as:

$$
\boxed{
\begin{array}{l}
\textit{Loop\_Var} \\
\hline
u, r, u', r' : \mathbb{N} \\
\hline
0 < u' - r' < u - r
\end{array}
}
$$

The data refinement invariant expresses the fact that the machine representation must not involve overflowed values:

$$
\boxed{
\begin{array}{l}
\textit{Data\_Inv} \\
\hline
r, s : \mathbb{N} \\
rt, sq : rng\ num \\
\hline
rt = num\ r \wedge sq = num\ s
\end{array}
}
$$

The pre-condition and post-condition for *Square_root* may be simplified, and the data refinement rule invoked, to give

Square_root
⊑
$\Delta\ rt\ [\exists\ r, s : \mathbb{N} \bullet \textit{Data\_Inv} \wedge 0 \leq s \leq max,$
$\qquad \exists\ r', s' : \mathbb{N} \bullet \textit{Data\_Inv}' \wedge r'^2 \leq s < (r'+1)^2]$

It is perfectly clear that the abstract variables may be eliminated from this operation, but any attempt to expand the data invariants results in such a complicated expression that clarity is lost which destroys some of the point of presenting the refinement argument in this way. This is an annoying feature of machine arithmetic. Arithmetic exceptions rarely happen, but their complete elimination causes endless complication in any formal treatment. For high-integrity applications, it is not acceptable to ignore this problem but data refinement does not appear to be the best way forward. This problem will be discussed in more detail later on, but for the moment it will be ignored in the formalism and the specification integers treated as directly implementable. For each step in the refinement an informal description of the requirements for unexceptional evaluation will be given.

The proof now proceeds using steps of operation refinement and this clearly demonstrates the advantages of the technique in relating the proof steps to the structure of the implementation. In the first step, declarations are introduced for the variables r and u:

$\sqsubseteq$ **var** $r := 0$ & $u := s + 1$
in $\Delta\ r, u\ [0 \leq s \leq max \wedge r = 0 \wedge u = s + 1,\ r'^2 \leq s < (r'+1)^2]$
ni

This step needs some justification. First of all two declarations have been introduced in one step. In the first, r has been taken from the global state into a local declaration and the fact that the result of the operation, r', will actually appear as the result of the Ten15 **var** clause will be glossed over. Clearly some extra syntactic sugar will fix this up. The pre-condition does not depend on r, so it is possible to choose any value and the denotation 0 is clearly implementable. The second declaration causes more of a problem because incrementing s must not raise an exception. This requires *max* to be less than *maxint*. Apart from this, the pre-condition cannot depend on u, so we are free to give it any value.

To introduce the loop, the introduction rule requires the internal operation to be cast into the form

$$\Delta\ r, u\ [Loop\_Inv,\ u' = r' + 1 \wedge Loop\_inv']$$

and this follows from the basic refinement rules and the two theorems

$$0 \leq s \leq max \wedge r = 0 \wedge u = s + 1 \vdash Loop\_Inv$$

and

$$u' = r' + 1 \wedge Loop\_inv' \vdash r'^2 \leq s < (r'+1)^2$$

Consequently

$$\Delta\ r, u\ [0 \leq s \leq max \wedge r = 0 \wedge u = s + 1,\ r'^2 \leq s < (r'+1)^2]$$

$\sqsubseteq \Delta\ r, u\ [Loop\_Inv,\ u' = r' + 1 \wedge Loop\_inv']$

$\sqsubseteq$ **while** $u \neq r + 1$
  do
    $\Delta\ r, u\ [u \neq r + 1 \wedge Loop\_Inv,\ Loop\_var \wedge Loop\_inv']$
  od

The implementability question here is concerned with the expression $r + 1$ which, as $r \leqslant s < maxint$, will not overflow. The loop body is implemented with a local declaration for the trial value for the square root:

$\Delta\ r, u\ [u \neq r + 1 \wedge Loop\_Inv,\ Loop\_var \wedge Loop\_inv']$
$\sqsubseteq$ **var** $t := (r + u)/2$
  in $\Delta\ r, u, t\ [t = (r + u)/2 \wedge u \neq r + 1 \wedge Loop\_Inv,\ Loop\_var \wedge Loop\_inv']$
  ni

The overflow condition is $r + u \leq maxint$; it is possible to establish that $r + u < 2s + 1$, which makes max less than half $maxint$. For the next stage, we have

$$\Delta\, r, u, t \; [t = (r + u)/2 \land u \neq r + 1 \land Loop\_Inv, Loop\_var \land Loop\_inv']$$
$$\sqsubseteq if\ (t{*}t) \leq s$$

$$then\ \Delta\, r\ [Loop\_inv \land t^2 \leq s \land r < t < u, Loop\_inv' \land r < r' < u]$$

$$else\ \Delta\, u\ [Loop\_inv \land t^2 > s \land r < t < u, Loop\_inv' \land r < u' < u]$$
$$fi$$

Several proof steps have been combined here in order to get the operations in each arm of the conditional into a form suitable for applying the assignment rule. Taking the first operation, the pre-condition has been weakened using the theorem

$$t = (r+u)/2 \land u \neq r+1 \vdash r < t < u$$

and the post-condition has been strengthened by holding u invariant; this allows the variant condition to be simplified and u to be dropped from the Δ part of the operation. A similar transformation is applied to the other operation. The calculation in the guard is guaranteed to be unexceptional so no further constraint on the range of max is incurred. It is interesting to note that if, in an endeavour to overcome the restriction on max, r and t are divided by 2 separately and then added, the algorithm loops in the case when $r = s - 1$ and $u = s + 1$ and both are odd. This is actually picked up by the formal method as the conjecture

$$t = r/2 + u/2 \land u \neq r+1 \ ?\!\vdash r < t < u$$

cannot be proved.

Implementing the two assignments gives the following composite refinement rule:

$$Square\_Root$$
$$\sqsubseteq var\ r := 0\ \&\ u := s+1$$
$$in\ while\ u \neq r+1$$
$$do\ var\ t := (r+u)\ /\ 2$$
$$in\ if\ (t{*}t) \leq s$$
$$then\ r := t$$
$$else\ u := t$$
$$fi$$
$$ni$$
$$od$$
$$ni$$

with the additional constraint that $2s < maxint$. The advantages of the method should now be apparent. As with any formal proof, the proof steps appear to be incredibly small but the development of the proof has been closely related to the implementation. More syntax is needed than has been given here but it is clear that the notation could be supported by tools for type checking and computation of the proof obligations, and indeed it seems likely that many of the proof steps could be mechanised. The problem remains however, what to do about the integers.

The standard approach, adopted by most verification systems, is to ignore the issue. This is not at all satisfactory as overflow errors and the related problem of indexing outside an array are very common: they are data sensitive and can escape even quite rigorous testing. An alternative suggestion is to implement unbounded integers, with a representation which expands to accommodate the integer values required. But this too is bounded by the total store of the machine and a runaway loop will simply take longer to report an error. It is obviously slightly less efficient too, but of more importance is the fact that programmers writing formally verified, and possibly safety critical, software ought to have an understanding of the numerical operations they are using in the implementation.

Treating the implementation of integers as data refinement on the other hand really does lead to large quantities of tedious and obscure detail which has a number of drawbacks. The solution seems to be not to use explicit data refinement but to generate the numerical proof obligations automatically. For the most part these are relatively simple and it may well be the case that they can be simplified automatically. An alternative, and presumably equivalent approach, is to refine to the language NewSpeak (see chapter 6) and allow the NewSpeak compiler to sort out the numerical constraints.

The next example is concerned with the use of anonymous references which again brings notational difficulties. Such computations are a common feature of practical high-integrity computing which, because of the interaction with the real world, will require list processing and other forms of non-numerical computing. As a typical example of this, operations for adding and removing objects from a queue, defined in terms of the Z sequence operators, will be refined into an implementation using linked lists. The linking will be carried out by using Ten15 reference values, so before going on to the refinement it is necessary to provide a Z specification of the properties of memories and references. For the purpose of this example a simplification of the Ten15 treatment of reference values has been made which again captures the salient features of the problem without overwhelming detail.

The example will be generic in the type of the objects to be queued, so this will be introduced as a Z given set, T:

[T]

Reference values are generated within the Ten15 algebra and are again indicated by a given set, with a distinguished value, *nil*:

[*Reference*]

nil : Reference

Memory is represented by generic functions from references to values:

$$
\begin{array}{|l}
[X] \\\hline
\textit{Memory} \triangleq \{f : \textit{Reference} \nrightarrow X \mid \textit{nil} \notin \textit{dom } f \bullet f\} \\
\end{array}
$$

The particular portion of memory of concern to a specification will be given by a declaration such as

$@ : Memory$ $\mathbb{N}$

Given a reference *r* to this memory, the integer it refers to is given by $@r$. For the current case, the linked list will use pairs of values and references and all such references must be in the domain of the memory under consideration. This is expressed by the following schema:

$$
\begin{array}{|l}
\textit{Pair\_ref} \\\hline
@ : \textit{Memory } (T \times \textit{Reference}) \\
r : \textit{Reference} \\\hline
r = \textit{nil} \vee r \in \textit{dom } @ \\
\forall \textit{ pair} : \textit{rng } @ \\
\bullet \quad rp = \textit{nil} \vee rp \in \textit{dom } @ \\
\quad \textit{where} \\
\quad\quad rp \triangleq \textit{snd pair} \\
\end{array}
$$

The dereferencing operator, @, and Ten15 reference values are both implementable and references on the Ten15 machine are defined to satisfy the constraint in the schema *Pair_ref*, which ensures that if a reference is given then a memory exists which holds the value referred to.

To give a realistic slant on the implementation of queues, the linked lists will be formed into rings. This is a standard programming technique in which, if the queue is not empty, the reference will point to the last object on the queue, which in turn points to the first, which points to the next, and so on. The empty queue is represented by *nil*. This representation leads to a fast implementation of the operation for adding to the end of a queue without substantially slowing down the one for taking from its head. With this representation, the abstraction invariant is as follows:

$$
\begin{array}{|l}
\hline
I \underline{\hspace{10cm}} \\
s : seq\ T \\
Pair\_ref \\
\underline{\hspace{11cm}} \\
s = \langle\rangle \Rightarrow r = nil \\
s \neq \langle\rangle \Rightarrow \\
\quad ringlist(snd(@\ r)) = s \\
where \\
\quad\quad ringlist : Reference \nrightarrow seq\ T \\
\quad\quad \underline{\hspace{8cm}} \\
\quad\quad \forall\ ref : Reference;\ st : seq\ T \\
\quad\quad \bullet\ ringlist(ref) = st \Leftrightarrow \\
\quad\quad\quad st = \langle\rangle \wedge ref = r \\
\quad\quad\quad \vee \\
\quad\quad\quad hd\ st = fst(@\ ref) \\
\quad\quad\quad \wedge ringlist(snd(@\ ref)) = tl\ st \\
\hline
\end{array}
$$

The projection operators for pairs, *fst* and *snd*, have exact analogies with the more general tupling structures in Ten15, so these will be assumed to be implementable without further refinement.

The first operation, to take from the head of the queue, is simply written down and refined by this abstraction invariant as follows:

$$\Delta\ x, s\ [s \neq \langle\rangle, s' = tl\ s \wedge x' = hd\ s]$$
$$\sqsubseteq \Delta\ x, @, r\ [\exists\ s : seq\ T \bullet I \wedge s \neq \langle\rangle, \exists\ s' : seq\ T \bullet I' \wedge s' = tl\ s \wedge x' = hd\ s]$$

This presents the first notational difficulty inasmuch as the dereferencing operator $@$, appears among the state variables. This is unexpected from a programming point of view as it tends to be thought of as a constant operator. However, in operations of this nature the memory, whose value is given by $@$, is a natural part of the state of the machine.

It is useful to introduce local constants for the head of the list and the result, *x*, as follows

$$\sqsubseteq \textbf{\textit{let}}\ head = snd(@r)\ \&\ x = fst(@head)$$
$$\textbf{\textit{in}}\ \Delta\ @, r\ [r \neq nil,$$
$$\quad\quad\quad\quad (r = head \wedge r' = nil \vee r \neq head \wedge$$
$$\quad\quad\quad\quad r = r' \wedge @' = @ \oplus \{head \mapsto @snd(@head)\})]$$
$$\textbf{\textit{ni}}$$

Again, a number of proof steps have been combined together, mainly because of the amount of space required to display the abstraction invariant at various stages of the simplification. First of all, the pre-condition for the implementation and the new value of *x* follow directly from the specification and the abstraction invariant. Secondly, the case for a single element on the queue corresponds directly to the first arm of the disjunction in the post-condition; however, the second arm corresponds to the more difficult case of more than one element on the queue. The $\oplus$ operator is a relational override and represents the memory changes brought about by shortening the ring by one element. Proof that this gives a stronger post-condition than the specification is a fairly simple proof by induction.

This operation is now refined into an if-clause using $r = head$ as a guard. The first arm of the if-clause is refined into an assignment in a straightforward fashion, but the second arm may also be refined to an assignment. This requires a generalization of the assignment introduction rule for operations which change memory in such a way that only one value referenced is altered:

$\sqsubseteq$ **let** $head = snd(@r)$ & $x = fst(@head)$
  in if $r = head$
    then $r := nil$
    else $head := @snd(@head)$
    fi
 ni

The second assignment is somewhat surprising as *head* has been defined to be a constant: however, the assignment is to the memory referenced and the reference value itself does not change.

Before discussing these somewhat alarming developments, the full picture on computing with references will be filled in by giving an example of heap generation in the operation to add to the end of a queue. The specification is as follows

> ┌─ *Add_to_queue* ─┐
> $s, s' : seq\ T$
> $x : T$
> ─────────────
> $s' = s\ snoc\ x$
> └──────────────┘

where *snoc* is the append element operator (the reverse of *cons*). For the implementation we need the operation to generate a new reference:

> ┌─ *New_ref*[X] ────────────┐
> $@, @' : Memory\ X$
> $ref : Reference$
> $val : X$
> ─────────────────────
> $ref \neq nil \land ref \notin dom\ @ \land @' = @ \cup \{ref \mapsto val\}$
> └───────────────────────┘

Rather than enter the refinement notation directly, it is helpful to work at the Z level and define the implementation as follows:

$$\boxed{\begin{array}{l} OP1 \\[4pt] \hline Pair\_ref \\ New\_ref_{[(T \times Reference)]} \\ x : T;\ pair\_ref,\ last\_ref : Reference \\ \hline pair\_ref = ref \wedge val = (x?,\ nil) \\ r = nil \wedge last\_ref = pair\_ref \vee r \neq nil \wedge last\_ref = r \end{array}}$$

$$\boxed{\begin{array}{l} OP2 \\[4pt] \hline \Delta Pair\_ref \\ pair\_ref,\ last\_ref : Reference \\ \hline @' = @ \oplus \{last\_ref \mapsto pair'\} \\ r' = pair\_ref \\ where \\ \quad pair \triangleq @\ last\_ref \\ \quad x \triangleq fst\ pair \\ \quad pair' \triangleq (x,\ pair\_ref) \end{array}}$$

The first operation creates the space for a new pair to hold the element to be queued; it will be the last element and so the new queue pointer will refer to it. The value *last_ref* is the reference which must be altered in order to join up the ring and this is done in the second operation. In fact, for efficient implementation, we need a reference to the second element of the pair to be altered rather than to the whole pair, but the formalism developed for this example does not allow us to do this. The problem is not so much a question of specifying the effect required, but of specifying the property provided by Ten15, that given a reference to a tuple it is possible to derive a reference to one of the constituent elements of the tuple, in a sufficiently general manner.

We have to show that

$$OP1 \,\S\, OP2$$

is a data refinement of *Add_to_queue*. Using the data refinement and implementation rules gives the following theorems to be proved:

$$x : T;\ s : seq\ T;\ pre(OP1 \,\S\, OP2) \vdash I$$

$$x : T;\ I;\ I' \wedge s\ snoc\ x = s' \vdash OP1 \,\S\, OP2$$

The proofs of these theorems are tedious rather than difficult, so they will not be given here. Similarly, the implementation of *OP1* and *OP2* is straightforward and given, with some more extensions of notation, by

> *Add_to_queue*
> ≙ *let pair_ref = New_ref(x, nil)*
>   & *last_ref = if r = nil then pair_ref else r fi*
> *in snd @ last_ref := pair_ref; r := pair_ref*
> *ni*

These two examples indicate both the splendours and miseries of formal implementation with references. The first point to make is that it is impressive that the formalism can tackle this subject at all: most formal verification systems apply to implementation languages using static storage allocation, or, at the most, functional implementations of list processing. This latter approach is attractive but leads to implementations in which list structures are copied rather than altered and this may critically affect the storage requirements and speed of the implementation. In addition, one may make the criticism that by treating the list structures as primitive the problem is simply being swept under the carpet as the compiler will certainly implement them using references, so the problem should be tackled at some stage.

The proofs given above also have the air of being cumbersome, particularly when expanded into the kind of detail necessary for formal verification. The difficulty is partly in the nature of the problem and partly in the understanding. Treatment of lists will almost inevitably involve a proof by induction: this proof is not trivial because the operation brings about changes to the list. List structure is also not so intuitive as the structure of the integers. This is simply a question of familiarity, but the effect is that theorems involving lists appear harder to prove than corresponding theorems about integers, which is not the case.

A more serious criticism is that the formalism does not model the intuitive ideas of reference provided by programming languages. Ideally one would like a generic set *Ref T*, giving the type of objects which referred to *T*, with corresponding generic operators @ and *New_ref*. Unfortunately, references cannot be treated in this way as it would imply that references to the same value were the same, which is not the case. It seems that the introduction of memory, in some way similar to that given above, is inevitable given a model-based approach to specification. If theorems are to be proved about references it is necessary to have a formal model of their behaviour and this implies some treatment of memory.

This makes one turn towards the algebraic approach in which the memory is hidden behind the algebraic properties of the operators such as $@(New\_ref\ x) = x$. This is certainly worth investigating, but the model-based approach does seem to be almost inevitable when building a large specification. The algebraic approach is powerful for expressing properties about the implementation but user requirements are defined in a more intuitive way by using models and this inevitably leads to data refinement. In a way, model building can be equated with a top-down approach, algebraic methods with a bottom-up approach, and it is clear that the examples given above require techniques which are transitional between the two. However, given a model-based approach, the technique given above has advantages as the type structure and the schema structure both partition the memory into that part relevant to the particular problem, and hence proof, in hand.

2.4 Conclusion

Enough has been said to indicate that an understanding of formal methods is an essential part of software engineering. Given this, the question is: to what extent to they contribute to software engineering practice? The answer to this question depends on the tool support for the formal method as it should be clear that pencil and paper will simply not do in an industrial environment. But such tool support need not be complex: much of the power of formal specification comes from the clarity of expression which a formal notation encourages and from this point of view, much of the benefit of formal methods can be obtained with simple editing and type-checking tools.

But formal specification should be supplemented by some way of refining to an implementation. The advantage of the approach described here is not so much its utility in building an implementation as in structuring the demonstration of compliance in a way which is related to the structure of the implementation. The approach also allows an incremental style of presentation and the possibility of breaking up proofs into logical steps. As with Z, the technique could be regarded simply as a notation and in due course, when mature, it will have much to offer from this point of view. However, an industrial use of formal methods will require tool support and a large scale structure in the form of a module system for refinement documents.

Theorem proving is an essential part of the refinement process, so mechanical aids for this are desirable and their use will lead to a higher level of assurance. They are not however mandatory; formal refinement is of value even when the proofs are given informally and it is probably better to spend effort in increasing the range of the assurance building techniques to cover the whole of the implementation process than to concentrate on mechanical proof of one part of it. This is because the mechanical aids have a very large effect on the production process itself and it is not clear exactly how they ought to be deployed. At the moment theorem proving aids are research tools and their use has to be very carefully controlled if they are not to use up large amounts of project resource. Nevertheless, formal methods, given current levels of tool support, raise the reliability of software; future levels of tool support, using mechanical proving aids, offer the possibility of very high levels of trustworthiness, but obtained at some cost.

References

[Dijkstra1976]   Dijkstra E. W., *A Discipline of Programming*, Prentice Hall (1976).

[Core1987]   Core P. W., *User-extensible Graphics Using Abstract Structure*, RSRE report 87011 (1987)

[Gries1981]   Gries D., *The Science of Programming*, Springer (1981).

[Hayes1987]   Hayes I., *Specification Case Studies*, Prentice Hall (1987).

[Jones1986]   Jones, C. B., *Systematic Software Development Using VDM*, Prentice Hall (1986).

[King1987]   King S, Sorensen I. H., Woodcock J., *Z: Grammar and Concrete and Abstract Syntaxes*, Programming Research Group, University of Oxford (1987).

[Morgan/Robinson1987]   Morgan C. C., Robinson K. A., "Specification statements and refinement", *IBM Journal of Research and Development*, **31**, 5 (1987).

[Morgan1988]   Morgan C. C., The specification statement (private communication, to appear in TOPLAS).

[Scott1976]   Scott, D. S. "Data types as lattice", *SIAM Journal of Computing*, 5, pp. 522–587 (1976).

[Sennett1987]   Sennett, C. T., *Review of the Type Checking and Scope Rules of the Specification Language Z*, RSRE report 87017 (1987).

[Spivey1988]   Spivey, J. M., *Understanding Z: a Specification Language and its Formal Semantics*, Cambridge University Press (1988).

[Stoy1977]   Stoy, J. E., *Denotational Semantics: the Scott-Strachey Approach to Programming Language Theory*, MIT Press (1977).

[Sufrin1983]   Sufrin, B., "Formal system specification: notation and examples", in *Tools and Notations for Program Construction* (Ed. Neel), Cambridge University Press (1983).

3 Designing for high integrity: the software fault tolerance approach

M. R. Moulding, Royal Military College of Science

3.1 Introduction

Traditional software engineering approaches for highly reliable systems are aimed at *avoiding* the introduction of faults into the software, and at *removing* faults during subsequent verification, validation and testing. Collectively, these approaches attempt to *prevent* software faults from existing in the operational system, but for realistic systems they are unlikely to be totally successful and a number of residual faults will remain. Consequently, in the cost-effective engineering of reliable software, it can be appropriate to supplement fault prevention with design approaches which attempt to suppress the effects of residual faults. Such *fault tolerance* approaches are the subject of this chapter and the major schemes which have been devised to achieve this will be investigated and some associated design and implementation issues will be discussed. However, the chapter will commence with an overview of software fault tolerance and in so doing uncover some important concepts and terms. The chapter as a whole has been written primarily for software developers, but software managers are invited to read the overview and summary sections in order to gain an understanding of this technology.

Before commencing with the technical material of the chapter, it is important to understand that, although the suppression of residual software faults has been introduced as a primary objective of software fault tolerance schemes, it must not be considered as the only objective. Such schemes must be careful not to compromise the structural quality of the software since this plays such an important role in fault prevention approaches. Indeed much of the research in this topic has been directed towards the architectural issues of software fault tolerance designs and this is reflected in the treatment of the subject here.

3.2   Overview of software fault tolerance

In order to discuss the basic principles of software fault tolerance, it is first necessary to obtain a simple abstract model to describe software systems. Such a model is illustrated in Figure 3.1. This portrays a software system as a number of components which cooperate under the influence of a design to service the demands of the environment with which the software system communicates. The design can be considered as the algorithm which is responsible for defining the interactions between components, establishing connections between components and the system environment, and for providing any supplementary processing for the system to achieve its required behaviour. The components, which themselves may be viewed as systems in their own right, may be categorized as being either *synchronously* or *asynchronously* related to the design which employs them. Synchronous components are passive and, when invoked by their calling environment, will complete before the environment may resume, whereas asynchronous components are active and, once invoked, will operate asynchronously with their environment. The top-down decomposition of a sequential program into a hierarchy of procedures is a common form of design using synchronous components. The design of the system is embodied in the algorithm of the program main body which invokes the individual procedures and passes data between them. A structure chart, as illustrated in Figure 3.2, is often used to describe the procedure hierarchy and identify the communication which takes place between a procedure and its calling environment. In contrast to this, program designs utilizing asynchronous components are often expressed in the form of a network of communicating parallel processes, as illustrated in Figure 3.3. Here, the role of the program main body, which embodies the design of the system, is to construct the network and, in frozen systems [MASCOT1980] where the network is static, the main body algorithm plays no further part in the operation of the system. Once activated, the processes will instigate their own communications and the design notation concentrates on explicitly defining their connectivity.

Fig. 3.1 Abstract model of a software system

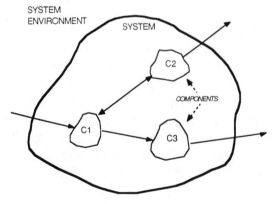

SYSTEM
ENVIRONMENT

SYSTEM

C2

COMPONENTS

C1

C3

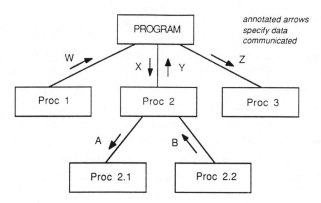

Fig. 3.2
Hierarchical structure chart for a sequential program

The choice of procedure-hierarchy and process-network representations to illustrate synchronous and asynchronous component designs reflects a traditional *functional* view of software design. However, the simple abstract design model is equally appropriate for the object-oriented approach to software design. Under such circumstances the individual components will be objects which offer synchronous interfaces via their procedure operations. The internal design or realization of an object is hidden by these interface operations and, consequently, decisions regarding the selection of the object as a synchronous or asynchronous component can be deferred. For example, an object employed by a design may initially be implemented as a synchronous object such that an invoked operation only returns to the calling environment when all processing associated with that operation is completed. However, after system performance considerations, the object could be re-implemented to run on separate hardware as an asynchronous component which continues to process certain aspects of the invoked operation after this operation has returned to the calling environment. The actual design of an object-oriented program can be very similar to that of the procedure-hierarchy program, described above, in that the main body algorithm could be responsible for invoking various object operations and, consequently, effecting the transfer of messages between objects. In such cases, a structure chart can be used to define the object hierarchy.

From the simple abstract design model it can be established that a design has associated with it two separate specification stages. The first stage of

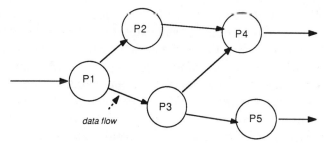

Fig. 3.3 Network of processes

specification defines the system requirements which the design must satisfy; the second stage defines the properties of the components which are identified by the design. Clearly, the model is recursive in that each component can itself be considered as a system in its own right and thus may have an internal design which can identify further sub-components. The recursion will continue until, at the lowest level, a design is purely algorithmic, or employs re-usable software components of pre-defined specification. This separation of *design* from *specification* is an important issue in software fault tolerance and must, in any case, be considered as good software engineering practice. It is most regrettable that the specification of components is often carried forward implicitly in the designer's head and that the only description of a component is its design at the next level. In many respects the need for explicit component specifications outweighs arguments concerning whether such specifications should be mathematically formal or not. However, the adoption of any technique which will draw attention to the role of specifications and improve their quality is strongly supported here.

So far, the simple abstract model of software systems has been used to describe the static architectural features of such systems. Before discussing software fault tolerance with respect to this model, it is necessary to extend it in order to describe the dynamic behaviour of software systems and, in particular, the sequence of events that leads to the failure of these systems. Classically, the failure of a system is considered to occur when the external behaviour of the system first deviates from that defined in its specification. Such a definition ignores the difficulty of producing a specification which correctly, completely, consistently and unambiguously defines the software system's required properties and thus may always be used as an authoritative test for failure. Practical specifications are likely to be imperfect in some way and this must be accounted for in any notion of failure. However, for the time being, the imperfections of software specifications will be ignored and this issue will be revisited when the dynamics of software failure have been investigated.

The dynamic behaviour of a software system is characterized by the series of *internal states* which the system adopts during its processing. Certain elements of an internal state will coincide with the interface between the system and its environment, and these form the *external state* of the system through which its external behaviour is realized. Each internal state will comprise the set of data values within the scope of the design: output values produced by the components (their external states) and the values of any variables maintained directly by the design such as the variables used by the main body algorithm of a sequential program. Under normal processing conditions, the system will advance from one valid internal state to the next by means of a *valid transition*. However, if a *fault* is encountered in the software during its processing, an *erroneous transition* may occur which transforms the system to an invalid internal state containing one or more defective values or *errors*. Once the system state is damaged in this way, subsequent invalid states can be produced from valid transitions. Alternatively, if the natural processing repairs the damage, for example by overwriting an incorrect variable with a new correct value, then the system can revert to a series of valid internal states. If an error in an internal state maps on to the external state, for example when an incorrect value is output, then a failure of the system will result. Consequently all system failures can be attributed to errors in the internal state of the system but not all errors need result in failure. All errors and, therefore, all failures are attributable to faults in the system.

Within the context of the simple abstract model of software systems, faults may be categorized, at any level of abstraction, as either design faults or component faults. To illustrate this point, consider that the system of Figure 3.1 has failed during its operation. This may have resulted from the failure of the system design algorithm to perform its intended function (a design fault) or, alternatively, may derive from the failure of a system component to operate according to its specification (a component fault). Of course, all software components can be considered as systems in their own right and, due to the abstract nature of software, will eventually decompose purely into a set of designs. Therefore, all software faults can be considered as design faults at some level of abstraction within the software system. Nevertheless, the concept of software component faults is valuable when discussing the deployment of software fault tolerance within a software system, and is likely to gain in significance with any trend towards re-usable software components.

The object of software fault tolerance is to prevent software faults from causing system failure. A general arrangement for achieving this for the abstract model of a software system is illustrated in Figure 3.4. In order to allow the system to operate successfully in the presence of a system design

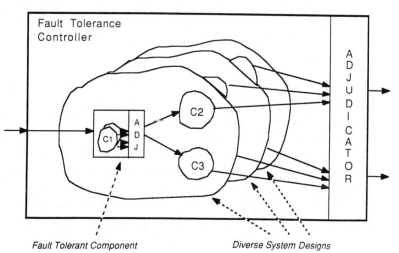

Fig. 3.4 Abstract model of a fault tolerant software system

Fault Tolerant Component   Diverse System Designs

fault, the software must be constructed from a number of diverse system designs which have a low probability of exhibiting common-mode failure; that is, the production of similar erroneous output for the same processing conditions. A fault tolerance controller can then be used to organize the execution of the various designs and, with the aid of an adjudicator function within it, to determine the overall system output. Redundancy applied at this level can also give protection against component faults if different components are used by the various diverse system designs. Alternatively, protection against the failure of individual components can be provided by having diverse component designs which can be organized by a fault tolerance controller in the same way as at the system level. The precise way in which the controller operates is a function of the particular fault tolerance scheme which is employed. Nevertheless, there are four major activities which will be performed by any such scheme:

1) *Error Detection* When a diverse design executes, it is necessary to determine whether a fault has been encountered. Faults are not directly detectable but the effects of a fault, namely one or more errors in the internal state of a system (or component), can be used to identify the presence of a fault. In order to avoid system failure, it is important that such internal errors are detected before they can propagate to the external state of the system, and the most obvious way of achieving this is for the adjudicator to vet the output of an executing design.

2) *Damage Assessment* When the internal state of the system (or component) contains one or more errors, the extent of this damage must, in general, be assessed. Often this is achieved by having damage confinement structures present within the system which limit the propagation of errors.

3) *Error Recovery* Having assessed the extent of the damage to the internal state of a system (component), this damage must be repaired so that failure of the system (component) can be averted.

4) *Fault Treatment* Allowing the fault to remain in the system following recovery can lead to further errors. Removing the fault will require the offending software design to be configured out of the system for some processing period.

The foregoing discussion of software faults implicitly assumes that software specifications at both the system and component level are perfect and, consequently, can always be used to define system or component failure. In reality this will not be so and greater insight into software faults can be gained by considering the fallibility of specifications. At the system level, the specification may contain errors; it may not accurately reflect the requirements which the environment places on that system. Consequently, behaviour which is correct with respect to the specification may be viewed as a perceived failure in terms of the *expectation* of the environment. Furthermore, incompletenesses, inconsistencies and ambiguities in the system specification are likely to cause the specification to be interpreted in a way which does not reflect the true requirement, thus resulting in additional, perceived failures. By applying these arguments to both the system and component specifications of the simple abstract model of a software system the following origins of software faults can be derived:

> *System Specification Faults:*
>> *Errors*
>> *Misinterpretations*
> *System Design Faults*
> *Component Faults:*
>> *Component specification faults:*
>>> *Errors*
>>> *Misinterpretations*
>> *Component design faults*
>> *Sub-component faults*

Consider first the application of software fault tolerance to the system level. This will not deal with system specification errors but may provide some protection against misinterpretations since these may not be common to each of the diverse system designs. The use of diverse system designs will strive to protect against system design faults, and component faults (whether they be specification, design or sub-component) should not cause common-mode failure between system designs which employ different components. Correspondingly, fault tolerance applied at the component level will not cope with erroneous component specifications but may cope with component specification interpretation problems. Similarly, the use of diverse component designs employing different sub-components will strive to protect against component design faults and sub-component faults. Thus the higher the level at which fault tolerance is applied, the greater the range of faults that are addressed and, in particular, the greater the potential protection against specification faults, but the higher the cost in terms of software redundancy. However, no protection can be provided against an erroneous system specification; a deficiency which software fault tolerance shares with other specification-driven techniques such as formal verification.

3.3 Towards an implementation framework for software fault tolerance

In the preceding overview discussion, the adjudicator function within the software fault tolerance controller has been introduced as the main method of achieving error detection. In practice, adjudicator checks will not detect all errors and, consequently, should be supplemented with:

1) Error detection *measures* within a software design which will check for

anomalous data values. Assertion statements are a common form of error detection measure. These attempt to demonstrate that certain properties of the software design hold during its execution.

2) Error detection *mechanisms* provided by the underlying virtual machine upon which the design executes. These will attempt to ensure that the software design does not attempt to use the virtual machine in an invalid way. The most powerful forms are those associated with the hardware; for example, memory protection mechanisms which will detect an invalid memory access by the software.

Clearly such measures and mechanisms must be able to indicate the presence of errors to the fault tolerance controller so that the remaining phases necessary for fault tolerance can be instigated. Exception handling provides a way of achieving this: the controller will provide an exception *handler* which will be automatically invoked when a measure or mechanism *raises* an exception to indicate the detection of one or more errors. A major benefit of this approach is that the abnormal processing of the fault tolerance controller following error detection is clearly separated from the normal processing associated with a software design.

Within the simple abstract model of Figure 3.4, there will exist two levels of exception handler: one at the component level and one at the system level. If a fault tolerance controller at the component level cannot continue correct operation following the detection of an error within the component, then it itself may raise an exception to the system level controller. Generally, exceptions propagated in this way may be categorized as:

- *Interface Exceptions* These indicate that a software design is being used incorrectly; for example, it may be asked to process data which it does not expect. At the component level, this would indicate that a design fault exists at the system level, or that the component specification is faulty (does not reflect the way in which the component is required to be used). At the system level, an interface exception would be indicative of a system specification fault, or the misuse of the system by its environment (e.g. operator abuse).
- *Failure Exceptions* These indicate that the fault tolerant system or component has failed due to an internal fault which it cannot mask.

Evidently, the goal of software fault tolerance is to prevent the propagation of failure exceptions. Nevertheless, their identification is useful since they can be used to instigate fault tolerant actions at a higher level, or at the system level they can be used to raise an alarm condition to the system environment. Interface exceptions raised from the component level are also of value since they provide error detection to the design level which utilizes the component. They are very similar in nature to the exceptions raised by error detection mechanisms since both indicate that the design at a certain level is misusing the facilities which are provided for it. Logically, the components of a design could be viewed as an extension to the virtual machine on which the design executes and, continuing this rationalization, suggests that the virtual machine should also be capable of raising failure exceptions. This is indeed the case and, in particular, is the way that tolerance to hardware faults may be organized. However, in the remainder of this chapter, the fallibility of the virtual machine will not be considered further but, instead, emphasis will rest on the way that software fault tolerance may be applied to the applications software.

When an exception is handled by a fault tolerance controller, in general, damage assessment and error recovery will follow. An important dynamic structuring concept which assists in these activities is the *atomic action*, defined as follows [Anderson1981]:

> "*The activity of a group of components constitutes an atomic action if there are no interactions between that group and the rest of the system for the duration of the activity*"

If the system is known to be in an error-free state upon entry to an atomic action, and an exception is raised during its execution, then only those components which have participated in the atomic action need be recovered by the fault tolerance controller. However, it is important that such atomic actions are enforced by the underlying virtual machine since the errant applications software cannot be trusted to adhere to this planned dynamic behaviour. The recovery itself can be categorized as:

- *Forward Recovery* The system is returned to an error-free state by applying corrections to the damaged state. Such an approach demands some understanding of the errors which exist.
- *Backward Recovery* The system is recovered to a previous error-free state. No knowledge of the errors in the system state is required.

Software faults, whether they be design faults or specification faults, are by their very nature unpredictable, as are the errors which they introduce. Consequently, backward error recovery provides the most generally applicable approach for software fault tolerance. However, for those limited cases where the characteristics of a fault are well understood, forward recovery can provide a more efficient solution. Moreover, the two techniques can be viewed as complementary and their combination will be discussed later in this chapter.

When error recovery is completed, the fault treatment phase of software fault tolerance will normally be carried out, and this will usually involve the use of one or more diverse designs in order to obtain continued correct operation. However, some limited form of software fault tolerance can be possible without the use of diverse designs; for example, by detecting and recovering an error, and either ignoring the operation which generated it, or by providing a pre-defined and heavily degraded response to that operation. In such cases the software cannot be considered as truly fault tolerant since some perceived departure from specification is likely to occur. However, this approach can result in software which is robust in the sense that catastrophic failure can be averted. In the following section of this chapter, robust software will be discussed in the context of the exception handling facilities provided by the programming language Ada. The remaining sections will then concentrate on the two main comprehensive software fault tolerance schemes of N-version programming and recovery blocks, both of which include diverse software designs for fault treatment.

3.4 Robust software using Ada's exception handling facilities

It has long been recognized that a major source of unreliability in software is the inability of a software design, whether it be at the system or component level, to cope with invalid inputs. Over the years, this realization has led to a software design style known as *defensive programming* in which the software is required to perform extensive checks on its input so that invalid values can be identified and remedial action taken, such as informing the calling environment that the required operation has been denied. The overall defensive programming strategy is to attempt to enumerate all the things which can go wrong and include features within the software design to deal with these. Importantly, a software design might also need to deal with errors detected by the underlying hardware; for example, overflow or underflow during arithmetic operations.

Inevitably, the programmed validity checks of the defensive programming approach will result in run-time overheads and, where performance demands are critical, many checks are often removed from the operational software; their use is restricted to the testing phase where they can identify the misuse of components by faulty designs. In the context of producing complex systems which can never be fully tested, this tendency to remove the protection afforded by programmed validity checks is most regrettable and is not recommended here.

Using the software fault tolerance terminology introduced above, defensive programming requires the inclusion in a design of error detection measures to check for invalid inputs, and forward recovery handlers to remove the predicted errors detected by either programmed measures or hardware mechanisms. Of course, such an approach will provide very limited protection against residual design faults since errors introduced by these will be hard, if not impossible, to predict; backward recovery would be more suitable here. Moreover, the absence of any diverse designs means that an operation cannot be completed successfully in the presence of a software fault; either a failure exception must be raised or a heavily degraded response for that operation must be pre-programmed as part of the recovery handler. Nevertheless, the defensive programming approach will help to ensure that software behaves in a robust fashion when predictable errors occur.

One of the major difficulties of conventional defensive programming is that the fault tolerance actions are inseparably bound in with the normal processing which the design is to provide. This can significantly increase design complexity and, consequently, can compromise the reliability and maintainability of the software. Modern programming languages with strong data typing like Pascal, Modula-2 and Ada do much to reduce the need for programmed validity checks. By carefully selecting data types to reflect the range of values which a variable may hold, and the permissible operations which are available to it, much of the run-time checking previously performed in untyped languages can now be conducted at compile time. Where run-time checks are still needed to enforce the data typing, these can be automatically included by the compiler, thus not compromising the complexity of the software design. The compiler essentially supports the abstraction of a strongly-typed virtual machine which raises some (interface) exceptions at compile time and the remainder at run-time—by virtue of embedded run-time checks. Of course, if the hardware supports data typing, then the compiler can map many of the run-time checks directly on to hardware instructions and significantly reduce their overheads. Consequently, when compared with conventional defensive programming, a strongly typed language can not only reduce the complexity of the software but also improve its run-time performance.

The Ada language distinguishes itself from Pascal and Modula-2 in that it defines how run-time exceptions may be handled by the applications software. The other two languages make no such provision but instead allow the particular virtual machine implementation to control this. In fact, Ada's exception handling facilities closely model those introduced for the software fault tolerance implementation framework, discussed above. In broad terms, each program block may declare one or more exception handlers to service particular exceptions raised during the execution of that block. If no exception handler exists in a block for a particular exception, then the exception is propagated out to the enclosing block (which caused the inner block to be executed) and a handler is sought for it there. This outward propagation continues until either a handler is found or the exception is propagated out of the program to the environment. If a suitable handler is found, it is executed and then control is transferred out of the block where the handler resides to the enclosing block, that is, an exception results in a premature exit from the block. A number of pre-defined exceptions are provided in Ada and result from the Ada virtual machine run-time checks. In addition, applications software may declare other named exceptions which error detection measures within the software may explicitly raise. The simple program of Figure 3.5 illustrates how these facilities may be used to provide a robust program which is resilient to certain predictable errors.

The purpose of the program of Figure 3.5 is to calculate the real roots of a

```ada
with FLOAT_IO, TEXT_IO;
procedure REAL_ROOTS is

    A,B,C, TEMP, R1,R2: FLOAT;
    IMAGINARY_SQ_ROOT, SQ_ROOT_FAILURE: exception;

    function MULT (X, Y: FLOAT) return FLOAT is
    begin
        return X*Y;
    exception
        when NUMERIC_ERROR =>
            if (X<0.0 and Y<0.0) or (X>0.0 and Y>0.0) then
                if (X<1.0 or Y<1.0) then
                    return FLOAT'SMALL;
                else
                    return FLOAT'LARGE;
                end if;
            else
                if (X<1.0 or Y<1.0) then
                    return -FLOAT'SMALL;
                else
                    return -FLOAT'LARGE;
                end if;
            end if;
    end MULT;

    function SQ_ROOT (X: FLOAT) return FLOAT is
        TEMP: FLOAT;
    begin
        if X < 0.0 then raise IMAGINARY_SQ_ROOT; end if;
        -- body of function contains statements which will compute
        -- square root of X and assign this to local variable TEMP
        return TEMP;
    exception
        when IMAGINARY_SQ_ROOT => raise;
        when others => raise SQ_ROOT_FAILURE;
    end SQ_ROOT;

begin
    TEXT_IO.PUT ("Please input coefficients in order A, B, C: ");
    FLOAT_IO.GET(A);   FLOAT_IO.GET(B);   FLOAT_IO.GET(C);   TEXT_IO.NEW_LINE;
    TEMP := SQ_ROOT( MULT(B,B) - MULT(4.0,MULT(A,C)) );
    R1 := (-B + TEMP) / MULT(2.0,A);
    R2 := (-B - TEMP) / MULT(2.0,A);
    TEXT_IO.PUT ("Roots are: ");
    FLOAT_IO.PUT(R1);   TEXT_IO.PUT ("  ");   FLOAT_IO.PUT(R2);   TEXT_IO.NEW_LINE;
exception
    when IMAGINARY_SQ_ROOT => TEXT_IO.PUT_LINE ("ERROR - roots are IMAGINARY");
    when SQ_ROOT_FAILURE => TEXT_IO.PUT_LINE ("SORRY - square root routine has FAILED");
    when others => TEXT_IO.PUT_LINE ("SORRY - unpredicted failure has occurred");
end REAL_ROOTS;
```

Fig. 3.5 Exception handling in Ada

quadratic equation which is specified by an operator in terms of its three coefficients. As is normal practice in Ada, the program is written as a parameterless main procedure. The *with* clause preceding the main procedure heading allows the program to import the library packages FLOAT_IO and TEXT_IO and use their procedures by qualifying the procedure name with the package name (those readers familiar with Ada will note that the *use* clause has been omitted in order to ensure that all references to library package procedures are clearly visible—an approach which is strongly recommended here in order to make the program easier to understand and, hence, contributes to fault avoidance). The two library packages can essentially be considered as input/output extensions to the Ada virtual machine.

The program itself employs two functional components which are declared in the declarative region of the main procedure, along with six floating point variables and two *exceptions*. The first of these functions MULT provides robust multiplication for floating point numbers. The body of the function simply attempts to return with the product of the two operands. If underflow or overflow occurs as a result of this, the pre-defined exception NUMERIC_ERROR will be automatically raised. Consequently, in the exception section of the procedure there is a handler declared for this. Its action is to return a result which corresponds to either the smallest (underflow) or largest (overflow) floating point number of appropriate sign, thus effectively recovering the error with a pre-defined result of degraded accuracy.

The second program function SQ_ROOT provides the square root of a floating point number. For simplicity, the algorithm for this has been omitted but its effect is to compute the square root of the floating point number operand into the local variable TEMP which can then be returned as the function result. Before computing this, however, a measure within the function first checks if the operand is negative and raises the IMAGINARY_SQ_ROOT exception which was declared in the main procedure. The exception section of the SQ_ROOT function contains two handlers: one for the IMAGINARY_SQ_ROOT exception explicitly raised within the function, and one for any other exception raised during the execution of the function such as a computational error in the square root algorithm. The action of the IMAGINARY_SQ_ROOT handler is simply to raise this same exception to the calling program; the other handler explicitly raises the exception SQ_ROOT_FAILURE which was also declared in the main procedure.

It can be noted that the exception handling strategy of the SQ_ROOT function is somewhat different from that employed in the MULT function. No attempt is made to recover from errors within the function but, instead, named exceptions are propagated out to the calling program so that it may deal with them in an appropriate way. One of these exceptions is an interface exception which identifies that the function was called with an invalid (negative) operand; the other is a failure exception which indicates that the function has failed due to some residual fault.

The action of the body of the main procedure is simply to obtain the coefficients for the quadratic equation, compute its roots using the MULT and SQ_ROOT functional components, and output these results. Exceptions raised during the execution of this code are serviced by three handlers: one for each of the exceptions raised by the SQ_ROOT function, and one for any other exceptions which may occur. In each case, the handler provides forward recovery for the program by producing an appropriate response to the operator in lieu of the required computation.

The above example demonstrates how exception handling separates the normal processing aspects of a program from the abnormal actions required to achieve robust operation. However, it is difficult to generalize about the required actions of exception handlers since these will depend very much on the particular application. This is typical of the forward recovery approach. For example, the loss of accuracy when overflow or underflow occurs within the MULT function may be unacceptable in some programs and, instead, a failure exception may need to be raised so that the operator can be informed that a suitably accurate result cannot be obtained. Evidently, the forward recovery action of a software system or component under erroneous conditions is an important aspect of its specification, but often this is not adequately addressed. Ideally, a specification should identify various levels of degraded functionality for predictable errors. Sadly, this is seldom the case and it is left to the designer to interpret what might be regarded as acceptable forward recovery action under such circumstances. The absence of suitable attention to erroneous conditions in specifications is also reflected at the programming level in Ada where a subprogram (procedure or function) heading, which specifies the subprogram interface to a calling environment, does not identify the exceptions which are explicitly raised and propagated out of that subprogram; exceptions form part of the hidden interface along with global variables accessed, and can only be determined by examining the code (design) of the subprogram.

3.5 N-version programming

In contrast to the robust software approach described above, where the presence of a fault will affect the operation of the system, the N-version programming scheme, illustrated in Figure 3.6, attempts to mask software faults so that the system environment is unaware of their presence. This is achieved by utilizing three or more (N) versions of a program, each of which has been independently designed from the same specification and is activated by a *driver* module (D) which provides all versions with read-only access to the same input data. The driver then collects the individual outputs from the versions and, in the simplest case, performs a majority vote in order to

Fig. 3.6 N-version
programming

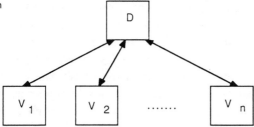

determine the overall output from the N-version program. Consequently, a fault in any one version can be effectively masked.

Relating the N-version scheme to the general principles of software fault tolerance, introduced in the overview section of this chapter, shows the driver module to be a specific implementation of the software fault tolerance controller, and that the voting check provides the adjudication function. In principle, there is no reason why the N-version scheme cannot be applied at both system and component levels, thus providing various nested levels of fault tolerance. However, as suggested by its attendant terminology, the application of N-version programming is normally limited to the outermost, system level of the software.

In terms of the four major activities which must be performed by a fault tolerant system, detection of errors in the state of the system is provided by the voting check which, by virtue of the disparity of an erroneous output, also locates the faulty version. Damage assessment is based on the premise that each version executes as an isolated atomic action and thus any damage must be confined within it. This atomicity can be achieved physically by running each version on dedicated hardware or, logically, by sharing one or more computers between versions and using appropriate protection mechanisms. It is important to recognize that atomicity is not simply concerned with preventing the versions from communicating with each other. It also means that the failure of a version must not affect the operation of the other versions, and the virtual machine which supports the operation of the various versions must provide this insulation. With atomic execution, error recovery is achieved by the driver ignoring the output values identified by the voting check as erroneous. Fault treatment can be considered as simply ignoring the results of the version identified as being faulty.

When an N-version program is invoked, all versions are normally executed. Consequently, each version can retain data between calls and, therefore, can be designed as an *object* which hides its internal structure. This has the advantage of increasing the design independence of the versions and reduces the data which must be passed to a version upon invocation. However, if the versions do retain data, then a driver will not be able to re-use a version which has produced an erroneous output since its internal state might have become inconsistent with the other versions. If the fault tolerance properties of the N-version system are not to be degraded under these circumstances, it will be necessary to provide some form of recovery of the internal state of a faulty version. One simple method of achieving this would be for each version to offer a *recover-last* operation which rolls it back to the state that it was in prior to its last operation. However, in order to ensure that all versions are in a consistent state, the driver must recover not only a faulty version, but all others, thus losing some of the previous history of the system. If this is not acceptable, then a more elaborate recovery strategy will be required which will recover the internal state of the faulty version to one which corresponds to those of the other up-to-date versions. This is a difficult task since the versions are of independent design and their internal data structures will, in general, be different. Essentially, a translation algorithm is required which will map from the internal state of one version to that of another.

The success of the N-version programming approach critically depends upon the voting check identifying the erroneous output of a faulty version. In order to increase the effectiveness of the voting check, it is normal practice to include in the specification for the versions intermediate cross-check values which will be delivered to the driver module together with the output results. By using these cross-check values, the voting check can now detect errors in the internal states of the versions as well as in their external states. The cross-check values will, of course, limit the design independence of the various versions since their internal processing must converge at these points, and an engineering trade-off must be made to determine the degree to which they are employed.

The voting check itself must be simple in order to minimise the possibility of design faults within it but, unfortunately, the design of voting checks may not be trivial. One complication occurs when the results involve non-discrete values such as real numbers, since different algorithms may produce slightly differing correct results. Consequently *inexact* voting is required which partitions the output from the various versions into equivalence classes prior to voting. Provided there are more than $N/2$ outputs in the largest equivalence class, then any of these could be used as the system output; alternatively, the median of the largest equivalence class could be adopted. The inherent difficulty with such an approach, however, is defining the class boundaries, since the normal variation in results from the versions will, in general, vary from one computation to the next.

Practical considerations can also serve to complicate the voting mechanism. For example, the driver module will, in general, have to time-out versions which do not produce their output within a specified time period and, in real-time systems, it may be necessary to compute the voting check on-the-fly, as results emerge from versions, so that a majority result can be output before all versions have completed. Of course, majority voting may not be suitable for all applications. For example, in safety critical systems, a unanimous voting strategy may be needed; if all versions do not produce the same, or equivalent, results then a failure exception must be raised so that the system can be placed in a fail-safe state. In summary, the type of voting check employed in an N-version programming scheme will depend very much on the particular application and will, in general, require careful consideration.

When implementing N-version programming for real-time systems, it is attractive to use a multiprocessor configuration where each version runs on its own dedicated hardware. This reduces run-time overheads and provides physical separation for atomic execution. Moreover, if different processor types are used in each case, then this overall design diversity can provide protection against both hardware and software design faults. Such a mapping approach would, however, limit the degree to which N-version programming could be applied to various nested components within a system, since each fault tolerant component would then require its own set of (N) processors. Of course, this limitation does not concern those applications where N-version programming is used only at the outermost level of a program.

3.6 Recovery blocks

The recovery block approach, like N-version programming, attempts to prevent residual faults from impacting on the system environment but, unlike N-version programming, it is aimed at providing fault tolerant functional components which may be nested within a sequential program. The basic features of a recovery block are illustrated in Figure 3.7.

A number of software modules of different design are produced from the same specification. There will exist a primary module which represents the preferred design and a number of other alternate modules which, for the time being, can all be considered to offer the same functionality. On entry to a recovery block, a recovery point is established which allows the program to restore to this state, if required. The primary module is executed and an acceptance test checks the state of the program for successful operation. If the acceptance test fails, then the program is restored to the recovery point taken on entry to the recovery block, the first alternate is executed and the acceptance test applied again. This sequence continues until either an acceptance test is passed or all alternates have failed the acceptance test. If the acceptance test is passed, then the recovery point taken on entry is discarded and the recovery block is exited. If all alternates fail the

Fig. 3.7
Recovery
block structure

ENSURE	acceptance test
BY	primary module
ELSE_BY	first alternate
ELSE_BY	second alternate
:	:
ELSE_BY	n^{th} alternate
ELSE_ERROR	

acceptance test, a failure exception will be raised. Since recovery blocks can be nested, the raising of an exception from an inner recovery block would invoke recovery in the enclosing block. Generally, any exception raised during the execution of an alternate will indicate premature failure of that alternate and thus instigate the same recovery action as for acceptance test failure. Run-time assertion statements within a module and hardware error detection mechanisms can be used to raise exceptions in this way.

In the context of the general principles of software fault tolerance, previously discussed, the recovery block structure itself defines the actions of the fault tolerance controller and the acceptance test provides the adjudication function which is the primary method of error detection. Ostensibly, damage assessment is not required because backward error recovery will eliminate all damage to the program. However, in a multiprocessing environment, backward recovery will only be applied to a single process (or at most a defined set of interacting processes, as discussed in a following section) and thus practical schemes will require protection mechanisms within the machine to confine the damage to that part of the system which will be backward recovered. This constitutes implicit damage assessment. Fault treatment within a recovery block is achieved by the execution of a new alternate following recovery.

Although recovery blocks are based on the notion of backward error recovery, forward recovery techniques can also be used in a complementary way. If, for example, a real-time program communicates with its (unrecoverable) environment from within a recovery block then, if recovery were invoked, the environment would not be able to recover along with the program and the system would be left in an inconsistent state. However, if appropriate forward recovery action were applied at the environmental interface, for example by sending the environment a message informing it to disregard previous output from the program, then the system can be returned to a consistent state.

It should be noted that not all modules will be executed each time the recovery block is invoked. Consequently, they must not retain data locally between calls since they could become inconsistent with each other; they must be designed as memory-less functional components and not objects.

3.6.1 Recovery block acceptance tests

The overall success of the recovery block scheme rests on the ability of the acceptance test to detect errors. There are a number of distinct approaches which can be adopted, including:

1) *Reversal checks* The acceptance test takes the results from a module and attempts to calculate what input values should have been applied. These are then compared with the true input values to determine whether the results are acceptable. For example, if a recovery block

provides a square root function, then the acceptance check could square the result and compare this with the input value.

2) *Coding checks* Consider a database system in which data records carry a checksum of the data contained within the record and this is to be maintained by the software as the data is updated. Re-computing the checksum after a module had completed its processing could provide the acceptance test with a means of detecting corruptions to data in a record. This is an example of a coding check.

3) *Reasonableness checks* The purpose of this type of test is to determine whether the state of the system following the execution of a module is consistent with the designer's view of the system. The acceptance test for the aircraft tracking recovery block of the following section is an example of a reasonableness check. Often, such checks will require access to the values of variables prior to the execution of a module so that they can be compared with their corresponding values after execution. The virtual machine which supports the execution of recovery blocks should normally provide this facility.

4) *Structural checks* Consider the situation where a recovery block maintains a chained list of data which is linked in the forwards direction only. If the list is enhanced to a doubly-linked list with backward, as well as forward, pointers, then an acceptance test can check whether there has been corruption to the list structure by reading the list in both directions. Thus structural redundancy [Taylor1980] within the list has allowed structural checks to be performed.

As with the voting check in N-version programming, an acceptance test must be simple otherwise there will be a significant chance that it will itself contain design faults. Moreover, the acceptance test will also introduce a run-time overhead which could be unacceptable if the test is complex. In summary, the development of simple effective acceptance tests is a difficult task. Most tests (with the possible exception of reversal checks) will not provide a guarantee of correct execution, and so it is important that they are supplemented with assertion statements within the modules in order to provide additional error detection capabilities. Equally important is the provision of a strongly-typed virtual machine which is capable of detecting errors via run-time checks.

3.6.2 Recovery block alternates

In a recovery block, all modules are available on entry to the block, regardless of previous faults, and they are always executed in the strict sequence defined by that block. The rationale for this is that a design fault will only be uncovered by a rare combination of processing conditions which are unlikely to recur when the recovery block is next executed. The sequential nature of the execution of primary and alternate modules gives rise to three basic strategies for providing design diversity within a recovery block:

1) *Equally weighted, independent designs*   Each module is designed to provide exactly the same functionality, in the optimum way, and diversity is achieved by having independent developers (ideally using different development methods and tools) for each module. In this case, the sequence in which the modules are executed is arbitrary and the design approach is the same as in the N-version scheme.

2) *Prioritized, fully-functional designs*   Each module provides the same functionality but there is a strict sequence in which their execution is preferred. For example, the alternates may be older, less-refined versions of the primary and, consequently, uncorrupted by faults which may have been introduced during such enhancements. Alternatively, the alternates may be deliberately designed using less-efficient, but perhaps more robust, algorithms. The fact that these alternates should rarely be executed mitigates their inefficiencies.

3) *Functionally degraded alternates*   The primary module will provide full functionality, but subsequent alternate modules will offer progressively degraded functionality. The alternates may be older versions of the primary which have not been corrupted by functional enhancements or they may be deliberately degraded to reduce software complexity and/or execution time. Note that the use of degraded alternates must weaken the acceptance test. However, the effect of improved acceptance testing for primary and high functionality alternates can be provided by adding assertion statements to these modules.

Functionally degraded alternates are particularly useful in real-time systems since there may be insufficient time available for fully-functional alternates to be executed when a fault is encountered. An example of a degraded alternate recovery block is illustrated in Figure 3.8 where the recovery block provides a simplified radar tracking function for aircraft. Upon invocation, the recovery block will be passed a track record containing the track parameters of an aircraft (e.g. last smoothed position at time, smoothed velocity, etc.) and a plot record indicating the latest measured position of the aircraft from the radar at a certain time. In its primary module, the aircraft's new smoothed position and velocity will be calculated from its last smoothed position and velocity, and the radar-measured position. The acceptance test

Fig. 3.8 Recovery block with functionally degraded alternates		
	ENSURE	changes in aircraft smoothed position and velocity are within physical limits
	BY	Smoothed Tracking Algorithm (track data, plot data)
	ELSE_BY	Prediction Only Algorithm (track data, current time)
	ELSE_BY	Null
	ELSE_ERROR	

which is then applied will check whether these smoothed position and velocity results are reasonable within the physical velocity and acceleration constraints of the aircraft. If this test fails, the first alternate provides degraded functionality in that it simply calculates the current predicted position of the aircraft from its last smoothed position and velocity, assigns this to the current smoothed position, and leaves the smoothed velocity untouched. Further failure of the acceptance test results in the second alternate simply leaving the track record in its initial state.

The degenerate case of degraded alternates corresponds to a recovery block which contains a primary module and a null alternate. Under these conditions, the role of the recovery block is simply to detect and recover from errors, and to ignore the operation which uncovered the fault. Of course, this approach means that the occurrence of a fault will result in a loss of service to the environment, as in the case of robust software, discussed above. The important difference is that forward recovery employed by the robust software approach can only remove predictable errors from the system state whereas backward recovery used in recovery blocks can cope with the unpredictable errors caused by residual design faults.

The decision where to use degraded alternates can be based on the identification of high- and low-integrity data paths in a system [Moulding1987]. For example, the passage of radar data through an aircraft tracking program can be considered as a low-integrity high-volume data path; degraded alternates would be appropriate here since the loss of an individual radar plot is unlikely to have a long-term effect on the system. On the other hand, aircraft positional information input by a pilot would correspond to a high-integrity low-volume data path; each item of data is important and thus every attempt to process it correctly must be made. Consequently, full-functionality alternates should be used. Where data integrity and volume are inversely related, as above, the alternate choices are sympathetic to run-time performance constraints; high-volume paths will have reduced alternate execution overheads because the alternates will be degraded, and the run-time overheads of full-functionality alternates are mitigated by the low data rates associated with this processing.

3.6.3 Recovery blocks in concurrent systems

When a regime of communicating processes employs recovery blocks, each process will be continually establishing and discarding recovery points, and may also need to restore to an established recovery point. If recovery and communication operations are performed in an unco-ordinated fashion, then it is possible that the *domino effect* [Randell1975] will occur. This is illustrated in the first diagram of Figure 3.9 where the horizontal lines describe the process in time of two processes P1 and P2, the vertical lines indicate communication between processes, and the open square brackets correspond to the establishment of recovery points. If, at the most advanced

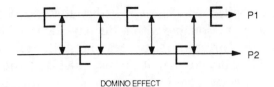

Fig. 3.9 Backward error recovery in concurrent systems

DOMINO EFFECT

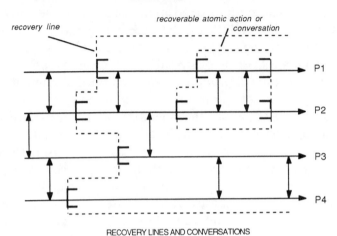

RECOVERY LINES AND CONVERSATIONS

stage of its progress, P1 wishes to recover to its last recovery point, then this can be achieved without affecting P2. However, if process P2 wishes to recover to its last recovery point, then this will cause recovery beyond a communication with P1. In general, this communication must now be considered invalid (e.g. P2 may have passed P1 erroneous data) and so P1 must recover to its penultimate recovery point. In so doing, this invalidates further communication and causes P2 to recover to its penultimate recovery point. This sequence will continue until either a consistent pair of (possibly ancient) recovery points are found, in which case the system may proceed, or the processes will be left in an inconsistent state when all recovery points of one or both processes have been used up.

One simple solution to the domino effect is to prevent processes from communicating with each other when they are in a recovery block. However, this can be unacceptably restrictive and a more general solution is to establish *recovery lines* in the system, as illustrated in the second diagram of Figure 3.9. A recovery line connects a mutually consistent set of recovery points and can be achieved by the insertion of additional pseudo-recovery points [Shin1984] which do not correspond to the recovery blocks of the individual processes but are forced on a process by the run-time virtual machine in order to guarantee consistent recovery. Such an approach will, of course, add significant complexity to the virtual machine, and also result in a recovery structure which is dynamically generated and thus lacking in design visibility. An alternative strategy which can provide better design visibility of the intended recovery structure is for processes to co-operate to form recoverable atomic actions called *conversations* [Randell1975].

On entry to a conversation, a process establishes a recovery point and, thereafter, may only communicate with others that have also entered the conversation. If a process wishes to recover whilst in a conversation, then all other processes of that conversation are forced to recover also. When a process wishes to leave the conversation, it must wait until all other processes are ready to leave. This, of course, introduces a synchronization overhead but is the price paid for controlled recovery. Conversations, like recovery blocks, can be nested as illustrated in Figure 3.9. Here processes P1-P4 initially enter an outer conversation. Some time later, P1 and P2 form an inner conversation which, after two communications, completes and returns P1 and P2 to the outer conversation. At some future point in their processing, P1-P4 will synchronize to complete the outer conversation. Note that, for effective operation, the atomic nature of conversations should be enforced by the underlying hardware of the virtual machine.

3.7 Comparison of N-version programming and recovery blocks

In principle both N-version programming and recovery blocks provide the basis for achieving software fault tolerance. In practice, a software designer must make an objective decision as to which technique is likely to be most effective for a particular application. In order to uncover the relative advantages and disadvantages of the two schemes, they are compared below in terms of their ability to detect errors, their propensity to encourage effective diverse designs, and the run-time overheads which their adoption is likely to impose.

Error detection   The practical effectiveness of any software fault tolerance scheme rests critically on its ability to detect errors in the internal state of the system before they can impact on the system environment. The voting check in N-version programming provides a powerful error detection approach where precise results can be specified, but the need for inexact voting in other cases will introduce complexity to the voting check and may, consequently, reduce the effectiveness of this approach. However, acceptance tests for recovery blocks are often much more difficult to devise and, in many cases, they will provide no guarantee that a module has executed correctly. To some extent the fallibility of acceptance tests can be mitigated by the provision of run-time assertions and virtual machine run-time checks, and the use of nested recovery blocks does mean that an error which is not detected at a low level might be identified by an acceptance test at a higher level. Nevertheless, a movement towards acceptance tests which are aimed at establishing the run-time correctness of the software is highly desirable, and the use of formal methods to identify such tests is likely to be of value here [Melliar Smith1983]. Only when acceptance testing is based on such correctness notions can it be considered to rival an effective voting check.

Software diversity   In order to provide a continued service in the presence of residual software design faults, both N-version programming and recovery blocks require diverse software modules. Both schemes can achieve such diversity by attempting to produce independent designs from the same specification, but recovery blocks offer the additional approaches of prioritised fully-functional designs, where diversity is deliberately planned at the expense of design efficiency, and degraded designs where the diversity is achieved at the expense of functionality. In particular, the degenerate case of null alternates in recovery blocks can provide an effective fault tolerance strategy for real-time systems, and this has no counterpart in the basic N-version approach. However, where independent designs are to be produced, recovery blocks do suffer from the limitation that the algorithms for each module must all operate on the same global data structures, and this limits the degree to which such designs can be made independent. The ability of modules of the N-version scheme to retain locally their own data structures allows a greater level of design independence to be achieved, but some loss of independence will result from the specification of cross-check values for voting checks.

Run-time overheads   High software reliability is commonly a primary requirement of embedded computer systems where the need to maintain real-time responsiveness is also critical. In such applications the run-time overheads imposed by both N-version programming and recovery blocks will be an important consideration for the software designer. Where the target hardware for a system contains a single processor, N-version programming will introduce a high run-time overhead since all individual versions must execute serially. However, where separate hardware processors are available to run each version concurrently, the performance of the N-version scheme will correspond to the execution time of the slowest version which is to participate in the voting check (a synchronization penalty), and the duration of the voting check itself. In contrast, the execution time of a recovery block is normally that of the primary module, the acceptance test, and the operations required to establish and discard a recovery point. However, when an error is detected, backward recovery, serial alternate execution and repeated acceptance testing will result in an increased run-time overhead. Thus the overhead of recovery blocks is less predictable than N-version programming and this must be accommodated in time-critical applications by ensuring that there is sufficient slack time in the processing cycle of the system to cope with a worst-case overhead. In fact a special variant of the recovery block, known as the *deadline mechanism* [Campbell1979], has been specifically proposed to address this issue. However, even within the constraints of the general recovery block scheme, much can be done to reduce both the magnitude and variability of the run-time overhead. For example, hardware assistance for the recovery of main memory will reduce the overhead of recovery-related operations; a *recovery cache* [Lee1980] has been successfully developed for this purpose and, more recently, a technique aimed at providing memory devices which are intrinsically recoverable has been devised [Hyland1985]. Furthermore, functionally degraded alternates will reduce execution overheads, and the use of null alternates can be an effective option for real-time systems. However, a more subtle and fundamental run-time overhead of recovery blocks is the synchronization penalty of conversation-type structures used to co-ordinate recovery between concurrent processes. Here, the onus is on the software designer to select conversation structures which map on to the natural synchronization of the design, thereby minimizing the overhead [Halliwell1984].

From these comparisons it is evident that the choice of scheme must depend upon both the characteristics of the application and the hardware configuration on which it will run. Generally, the critical importance of error detection in software fault tolerance would suggest that where voting checks may be easily constructed, and replicated hardware is available to reduce run-time overhead, N-version programming is most appropriate. In contrast, the recovery block scheme is a generally applicable approach which maps naturally onto nested component structures, and is most appropriate for those systems where hardware resources are limited and voting checks are inappropriate [Anderson1981].

In many respects. N-version programming and recovery blocks are complementary in terms of their relative merits. This has led to hybrid schemes which combine various features of each approach [Anderson1985a]. For example, one or more alternates of a recovery block could be run in parallel with the primary (providing their executions were atomic); the run-time overhead of alternate executions would be minimized, and their outputs could be used to support the acceptance test. Alternatively, acceptance tests could be used in N-version programming to assist the voting algorithm, and a version could employ run-time assertions to detect internal errors and signal the driver to disregard its output.

3.8 Practical application of N-version programming and recovery blocks

Although these two basic techniques of software fault tolerance have been available for more than a decade, uncertainties regarding their overall cost-effectiveness have inhibited their widespread adoption in industrial and commercial systems. However, limited forms of N-version programming have been employed in safety-critical systems to provide additional confidence in the light of stringent reliability requirements. For example, dual-version programming (N = 2) is used to provide error detection in computerized point switching, signal control and traffic control in the Gothenburg area by the Swedish State Railways [Taylor1981], and the approach has now been adopted in several railway installations elsewhere

[Hagelin1988]. In these applications, differing outputs from two versions result in the rail network being placed in a safe state (signal lights set at red). Dual-version programming has also found considerable application in the avionics industry [Voges1988] as exemplified by the slat-and-flap control system of the Airbus Industries A310 aircraft [Martin1982]. In this case, two diverse programs are executed on separate diverse computers and their outputs compared to provide error detection which is used to instigate manual backup procedures to ensure safe flight and landing of the aircraft. This approach has been taken one step further for the pitch control of the *fly-by-wire* A320 aircraft [Traverse1988]. Here, four-version software diversity and two-version hardware diversity are combined in a dynamically reconfigurable architecture to tolerate both software and hardware design faults. However, a limited form of mechanical backup is still provided.

In order to understand the key issues involved in the development of software fault tolerance systems, a number of experimental evaluations have been conducted using the two basic schemes. N-version programming has been under investigation at the University of California Los Angeles (UCLA) since 1975. Initial work established the basic principles of the approach and this was followed by an experiment which investigated the impact of specification on residual faults [Avizienis1984]. Recent work has been concerned with the development of a test bed for N-version experiments [Avizienis1986, 1988], and its use to investigate issues such as inexact voting strategies and recovery of failed versions.

Further evaluation of N-version programming has been performed in a project on diverse software (PODS) which has been jointly conducted by the Safety and Reliability Directorate (SRD) and the Central Electricity Research Laboratory (CERL) in England, the Technical Research Centre of Finland (VTT) and the Halden Reactor Project (HRP) in Norway [Bishop1986]. Three versions of software for a reactor over-power protection system were developed independently by CERL, VTT and HRP, and then combined in an N-version configuration to determine the effect on software reliability. Of the nine residual faults detected, six resulted from difficulties with the *customer* specification and two were attributable to modifications made during testing. Two faults were common between versions and, consequently, would have caused the three-version unit to fail, when encountered. All other fault combinations were effectively masked by the majority voting.

The presence of common design faults raises questions regarding the independence of versions and an investigation of this issue [Knight1986a] has demonstrated that in a large-scale experiment, involving a twenty-seven-version program submitted to one million test patterns, common-mode failures of two or more versions were encountered on 1255 occasions. This was viewed statistically as demonstrating that the failures of versions were NOT independent, but care is needed when interpreting this result. It does not mean that the twenty-seven-version program ever failed to produce the correct output since no more than eight versions ever failed at the same time. Nor does it mean that reliability improvements could not be achieved if the versions were grouped into smaller voting units. In fact, in a later experiment [Knight1986b] when three-version programs were randomly constructed from the twenty seven, the average probability of failure for a three-version unit was found to be 19 times less than the average for individual versions. The significance of these results is that reliability prediction calculations for N-version programs based on the assumption that independently designed versions would fail independently is invalid, and that this will result in reliability predictions which are optimistic. However, significant reliability improvements can still be achieved.

Recovery blocks have been the subject of a long-term research programme at the University of Newcastle upon Tyne since the early 1970s, and in 1981 a project was set up to evaluate the cost-effectiveness of applying recovery blocks to a naval command and control demonstrator. The software was based on MASCOT [MASCOT1980] and a scheme was devised to establish conversation-type recovery structures for a regime of communicating MASCOT activities [Moulding1986]. The practical development work of the project included the design and implementation of a MASCOT virtual machine which supported recovery blocks, together with extensions to the CORAL programming language to allow the software fault tolerance applications to be written in this high-level language. The results of experimentation on the completed demonstrator revealed that 74% of potential failures were averted by the software fault tolerance. The price of this improvement was approximately 60% increased development costs, 33% extra code memory, 35% extra data memory, and 40% additional run-time [Anderson1985b]. Research at the Royal Military College of Science has recently extended this work to the design of a demonstrator modelled on functions provided at the London Air Traffic Control Centre, and the results have reinforced confidence in the general applicability of this software fault tolerance approach [Moulding1987]. Continuation of the work is aimed at investigating the use of formal specification techniques to improve the independence of module designs, and for identifying effective acceptance tests and run-time assertions. Future planned work is to integrate software fault tolerance into the methods and tools employed across a typical software engineering life-cycle. This will include extensions to the Ada programming language for both N-version programming and recovery blocks, and the integration of software fault tolerance considerations into conventional software analysis and design methods employed for real-time systems.

3.9 Summary

This chapter has been concerned with explaining the ways in which software may be designed so that it can tolerate its own residual design faults, and so provide high reliability operation. The general principles and terminology of software fault tolerance have been explained within the context of a simple abstract model of a software system and an implementation framework for software fault tolerance, based on exception handling and including the notions of atomic actions and backward and forward recovery, has been identified. The utility of exception handling in separating the abnormal fault tolerance actions of software from its normal processing has been demonstrated with a simple Ada program which uses forward recovery techniques to provide robust operation when predictable errors occur. Such robust software solutions attempt to ensure that the software does not fail catastrophically but they cannot mask the presence of a fault from their environment. In order to provide continued correct operation in the presence of faults, diverse software designs must be employed and the main emphasis of the chapter has been concerned with describing the principles and practice of N-version programming and recovery block schemes which provide the framework for introducing such design diversity.

Over the past decade, a number of experimental evaluations have been made into the utility of software fault tolerance and these have generally shown that such schemes have proved effective in improving the reliability of software. An attendant technology has emerged which is available for practical exploitation and only when this occurs will uncertainties regarding cost effectiveness be resolved. No doubt the provision of re-usable virtual machines to support software fault tolerance schemes would do much to encourage the uptake of this technology and it is hoped that future developments will contribute to this. Of course, as the applications software becomes increasingly reliable through the use of software fault tolerance, then this may expose reliability deficiencies in the design of the virtual machines. Thus the construction of virtual machines to support software fault tolerance may well need to incorporate this technology to achieve the desired levels of reliability [Avizienis1986].

The *achilles heel* of software fault tolerance, which it shares with other specification-driven approaches, is an erroneous system specification since any diverse designs derived from it will be perceived to exhibit common-mode failure by the system environment. Formal specification techniques will do much to reduce the possibility that system specifications are misinterpreted but, since they are merely an abstraction of the real-world problem, they can never be shown to be error free. However, by introducing diversity into the specification process, increased confidence in their correctness can be gained and it is interesting to note that the back-to-back testing of formal executable specifications, which have been independently produced, has been proposed as a way of improving the correctness of specifications [Avizienis1986]. This is one of a number of ways in which formal methods and fault tolerance techniques may be combined to improve the reliability of software, and it is hoped that, in time, the engineering of cost-effective reliable systems will be achieved through a *measured* blend of conventional validation and testing, formal specification and verification techniques, and software fault tolerance approaches. Such would be the hallmark of a mature engineering discipline.

References

[Anderson1981]   T. Anderson and P. A. Lee, *Fault Tolerance: Principles and Practice*, Prentice Hall (1981).

[Anderson1985a]   T. Anderson, "Can Design Faults be Tolerated?" *Software and Microsystems*, Vol. 4, No. 3, pp. 59–62 (June 1985).

[Anderson1985b]   T. Anderson, et al., "Software Fault Tolerance: An Evaluation", *IEEE Trans S/W Eng*. Vol. SE-11, No. 12 (Dec. 1985).

[Avizienis1984]   A. Avizienis and J. P. J. Kelly, "Fault Tolerance by Design Diversity: Concepts and Experiments", *Computer*, Vol. 17, pp. 67–80 (Aug 1984).

[Avizienis1986]   A. Avizienis, "The N-Version Approach to Fault Tolerant Software", *IEEE Trans. S/W Eng*. Vol SE-12, No 1, pp. 1491–1501 (Jan. 1986).

[Avizienis1988]   A. Avizienis et al, "DEDIX 87—A Supervisory System for Design Diversity Experiments at UCLA", *Software Diversity in Computerized Control Systems* (Ed. U. Voges), Springer Verlag (1988).

[Bishop1986]   P. Bishop et al., "PODS—A Project on Diverse Software", *IEEE Trans S/W Eng*. Vol SE-12, No 9, pp. 929–940 (Sept. 1986).

[Campbell1979]   R. H. Campbell, K. H. Horton and G. C. Belford, "Simulations of a Fault Tolerant Deadline Mechanism", *Digest FTCS-9*, pp. 95–101, Maddison (WI) (June 1979).

[Chen1978]   L. Chen and A. Avizienis, "N-Version Programming: A Fault-Tolerance Approach to Reliability of Software Operation", *Digest FTCS-8*, Toulouse, pp. 3–9 (1978).

[Hagelin1988]   G. Hagelin, "ERICSSON Safety System for Railway Control", *Software Diversity in Computerized Control Systems* (Ed. U. Voges), Springer Verlag (1988).

[Halliwell1984]   D. N. Halliwell, *An Investigation into the Use of Software Fault Tolerance in a MASCOT-based Naval Command and Control System*, Reference A049/DD.17/1, MARI, Newcastle upon Tyne (Feb. 1984).

[Hyland1985]   I. Hyland, *A Backward Recoverable MC68000 Microcomputer*, Final-year undergraduate project, The Hatfield Polytechnic (1985).

[Knight1986a]   J. C. Knight and N. G. Leveson, "An Experimental Evaluation of the Assumption of Independence in Multi-version Programming", *IEEE Trans. S/W Eng*. Vol. SE-12, No 1, pp. 96–109 (Jan. 1986).

[Knight1986b]   J. C. Knight and N. G. Leveson, "An Empirical Study of Failure Probabilities in Multi-version Software", *Proc. FTCS-16*, Vienna (July 1986).

[Lee1980]   P. A. Lee, N. Ghani and K. Heron, "A Recovery Cache for the PDP-11", *IEEE Trans. Computers*, Vol C-29, No 6, pp. 546–549 (1980).

[Martin1982]   D. J. Martin, "Dissimilar Software in High Integrity Applications in Flight Controls", *Proc. AGARD Symposium on Software for Avionics*, The Hague, The Netherlands, 1982, pp 36:1–36:13.

[MASCOT1980] MASCOT Suppliers Association, *The Official Handbook of MASCOT*, RSRE, Malvern, U.K. (1980).

[Melliar Smith1983] P. M. Melliar Smith, *Development of Software Fault Tolerance Techniques*, NASA Contractor Report 172122 (March 1983).

[Moulding1986] M. R. Moulding "An Architecture to Support Software Fault Tolerance and an Evaluation of its Performance in a Command and Control Application", *Digest IEE Colloquium on Performance Measurement and Prediction* (Feb. 1986).

[Moulding1987] M. R. Moulding and P. Barrett, *An Investigation into the Application of Software Fault Tolerance to Air Traffic Control Systems: Project Final Report*, Ref. 1049/TD.6 Version 2, RMCS, Shrivenham, Wilts (Sept. 1987) (CAA copyright)

[Randell1975] B. Randell, "System Structuring for Software Fault Tolerance", *IEEE Trans. S/W Eng.* Vol SE-1, No 2, pp. 220–232 (1975).

[Shin1984] K. G. Shin and Y. H. Lee, "Evaluation of Error Recovery Blocks Used for Co-operating Processes", *IEEE Trans. S/W Eng.* Vol SE-10, No 6, pp. 692–700 (1984)

[Taylor1980] D. J. Taylor, D. E. Morgan and J. P. Black, "Redundancy in Data Structures: Improving Software Fault Tolerance", *IEEE Trans S/W Eng.* Vol SE-6, No 6, pp. 585–594 (Nov. 1980).

[Taylor1981] J. R. Taylor, Letter from the editor, *ACM Software Eng. Notes*, Vol. 6, No. 1 pp. 1–2 (Jan. 1981).

[Traverse1988] P. Traverse, "AIRBUS and ATR System Architecture and Specification", *Software Diversity in Computerized Control Systems* (Ed. U. Voges), Springer Verlag (1988).

[Voges1988] U. Voges (Editor), *Software Diversity in Computerized Control Systems*, Springer Verlag (1988).

4 Practical experience with a formal verification system

Paul Smith, Secure Information Systems Ltd.
Nick Bleech, SD-Scicon plc.

4.1 Introduction

This chapter reports on experience gained by the authors with the Gypsy Verification Environment (GVE) over the period 1985 to 1988. The emphasis is primarily on the fundamental approach to verification which Gypsy supports. The goal is to provide the reader with some insights into the practical problems of formal verification. A secondary concern is to show how the design constraints of Gypsy and the GVE in turn impose constraints and restrictions on the activities of specification, proof, and programming. Finally, we offer some observations on likely future directions for program specification and verification systems.

An overview of Gypsy and the GVE is given in the next section. In section 4.3, a simple example program is used to illustrate in more detail the process of code verification, and in section 4.4 the features of Gypsy which might be used for system specification are explored. GVE is the most well developed and deployed verification system in the world. Even so, verification technology is still quite new, and our account identifies some desirable features which we feel are missing from GVE and the language. In section 4.5, our suggestions are discussed, and our experience summarized in section 4.6.

4.2 Background

Gypsy was developed in response to the need for system developers to produce highly assured secure computer systems, that is certified with respect to the highest assurance levels of the DoD "Orange Book" of 1985. It is a fundamental premise of the Orange Book that the degree of assurance increases with the rigour of the life-cycle methods used. For example, a security device that was informally specified in the English language may not be trusted as much as a device that was formally specified using a mathematical notation. As more of the design stages (for example security policy specification and design) are treated formally, the higher the level of assurance rises.

The highest Orange book level is currently A1, which insists that the high-level design satisfies the security policy. Possible criteria for higher assurance than that provided by A1 would include formally verified code. Because of the difficulty of determining the properties of programs that must be proven, and then producing proofs of these properties, mechanical support, especially for symbol manipulation, is required before higher levels of trustworthiness can be claimed. This is where Gypsy, and other program verification environments, are required.

In order to understand the scope of Gypsy in producing high-integrity software, it is necessary to consider it within the context of other formal systems. These provide a spectrum of methods ranging from specification and proof-oriented approaches to those more closely related to normal implementation languages and concepts.

At the one extreme, proofs in constructive mathematics are used to derive (functional) programs. The derived program is known to be correct by the rules of reasoning in the constructive logic [Martin-Lof82]. Less extreme is the use of a restricted (e.g. horn clause) logic which is chosen for the property of being executable [Warren77]. Here, specifications identify with programs. Moving further along the spectrum, we place approaches which use well-known objects from discrete mathematics (e.g. sets, functions) to model systems. Z and VDM are examples of these model-oriented approaches [Woodcock88]. Different levels of abstraction may be represented by different models, which can be proven to be consistent with each other. Usually systems are only described at the highest levels of abstraction, as program verification has not been well addressed by these methods yet, the primary focus being on system design specifications.

Next, wide-spectrum high-level languages, such as CIP [CIP85], combine specification and programming constructs, so as to be able to implement a variety of concepts in an appropriate, problem-oriented way.

Finally, implementation languages which have been tailored and restricted to be sound enough to permit formal reasoning of correctness form the extreme. These languages must have specification constructs. We place Gypsy in this final class, although it does have the potential to be used for modelling systems as well. Gypsy uses an approach based on seminal work by Floyd [Floyd67], where verification conditions are derived from the program and specification, and it is the proof of these that verifies the correctness of a program. Programming logics which can be used to reason about the program and specification directly are Hoare logics [Hoare78], and the (Enhanced) Hierarchical Development Methodology [Crowe86] supports such an approach.

Each of these types of method offer different benefits in terms of expressive power, analytical power, and relative costs. Expressiveness determines the size and complexity of systems that can be addressed, while the analytical power of a method bounds the confidence one has in the end system (see chapter 9). For example, methods from the implementation-oriented end of the spectrum tend to be expensive to apply and low in expressive power, but because of the availability of tools that check static semantics and proof validity, verification systems achieve high levels of assurance. Executable specifications, such as in Prolog, are again low in expressive power, but high in analytical power, because specifications are effectively prototypes, and can be experimented with, using test data to expose operational insights. Set-theory-based models of systems are very high in expressive power, and although there is the potential to reason rigorously about properties of such specifications, they have been analytically weak because of the apparent difficulty in constructing tools for processing the notations.

We know of no reports of the industrial use of constructive methods in the production of high-integrity software, but it seems that these methods would have great analytical power. In particular, programs and their proofs are developed closely, indeed they are not distinguished at all. This contrasts with the approach detailed in this chapter, where the proof activity follows on from program specification and development as a distinct activity. This also applies to the Hoare logic approach where, although proofs relate specification and program fragments, programs are distinct from proofs. It seems reasonable to suppose that a method which not only provides a logic for formal specification and reasoning, but also binds verification with program design, would be analytically more powerful. In the remainder of this chapter, the discussion is confined to Gypsy as it currently exists, or how it might be, and what effect this has on its position in the spectrum.

4.2.1 History and facilities of Gypsy

The Gypsy methodology was developed at the University of Texas at Austin, by Don Good and his many colleagues. The language has undergone continuous development and improvement since the very beginning of the Certifiable Minicomputer Project in 1974, when the definition of Gypsy 1.0 was undertaken. The tools have evolved around successive versions of Gypsy since the publication of Gypsy 1.0 in 1976. The language developed rapidly as more notation was added, although some simplifications had to be made before version 2.0 was published in 1978. By the same process, Gypsy evolved further to version 2.1 in 1984, and then restricted to version 2.05 in 1986 [Good86], which is the version we have used.

The Gypsy project aimed to produce a language that was amenable to program verification. Another language, called Euclid [Lampson77], was developed in the seventies as a derivative of Pascal [Jensen75]. The primary design goal for Euclid was also that it should be more amenable to program proof than its mother language, and this was achieved mainly by restrictions in the static semantics and scope rules. The Gypsy project aimed to develop a restricted Pascal derivative that was similarly amenable to program proofs, additionally providing a specification notation, and a set of tools to support the tedious mathematical proof process.

This emphasis on supporting program proofs left little effort remaining for the development of traditional software engineering tools, such as compilers and runtime testing tools. Prototype source code translators have been built (e.g. Gypsy-to-Ada [Akers83] and Gypsy-to-Bliss [Smith88]), but these only implement subsets of Gypsy.

One of the most significant achievements of the Texas project was the production of a *Verification Condition Generator* (VCG). This tool automatically constructs all the predicates that must be proven to show that a program is "partially" correct, that is, performs the right actions if it terminates. The underlying program logic of Gypsy does not directly facilitate proofs of program termination which is required for total correctness. However, Gypsy does support features that many modern programming languages fail to offer, such as communicating processes, data type encapsulation and exception handling.

It is the provision of mathematical objects, such as sequences, together with these advanced programming language constructs which has enabled Gypsy to be applied successfully to the verification and certification of modest-sized message switching subsystems (approximately 1000–2000 lines of source code) and secure computer systems such as the Honeywell SCOMP.

The tools are all written in Lisp, and have been ported to various dialects, running on various machines such as Sun 3, Symbolics Lisp machines and Multics.

Gypsy was designed as an academic demonstrator, but is now accredited by the US National Security Authority for use in the production of highly secure systems. GVE is now supported by Computational Logic Inc. of Austin, Texas.

Thus, Gypsy is a unified specification and programming language, and the formal verification of Gypsy programs is supported by the *Gypsy Verification Environment* (GVE). The following sections provide an overview of the Gypsy language followed by a description of the GVE. More detail is introduced and explained in the presentation of a concrete example in a later section.

4.3 The Gypsy language

Gypsy being a unified specification and programming language provides both specification and programming operators for each standard data type. Clearly there is an overlap between the two sublanguages, particularly in the use of some standard data types and operators, expressions, and recursive functions.

The programming language is based on Pascal. There are some minor syntactic differences, such as the use of the token = after procedure headers, instead of semicolons. But the more significant departures from the mother language are severe restrictions to the static semantics, and extensions to support data hiding, sequences, mappings, concurrency, and exception handling.

The restrictions are mainly forced from the requirements for program verification. This includes banning global variables, so that a subprogram's only effect on its calling environment is through fully documented parameters, results and exceptions. Procedural parameters are excluded and variable aliasing is outlawed by the language definition. Pure functions (expression abstractions) are a consequence of these restrictions, conjoined with the further restriction that functions may not use call by reference. Variant records are not accommodated by the syntax of the language, which is consistent with the widely held view that these are not "type safe" in Pascal. However, the lack of any type union construct is disappointing in Gypsy.

The specification component is based on first-order predicate logic, except that predicates are boolean valued terms, rather than being syntactically distinct as in classical logic. External specifications may be provided for each procedure and function by using pre- and post-conditions. These are called *entry* and *exit* assertions in Gypsy. A *block* assertion is used to describe the blocking behaviour of (buffered) communicating sequential processes. Internal specifications such as loop invariants often need to be provided for proof purposes, and the *assert* statement enables these to be expressed.

Extensions to the predicate notation permit the specification of exit conditions when the exception handling mechanism is used. Standard (specification) functions for reasoning about communications buffer histories are provided in the specification notation.

Since the only variables referenced by a procedure must be named in the procedure header (recall global variables are not allowed), each unit may be proven independently of any other unit, a feature which greatly simplifies the verification process. This is called the principle of independence.

The namespace of Gypsy unit definitions is quite flat. The *scope* construct is provided to break down the namespace by one level, allowing units to be grouped by a common scope name. A facility is provided for naming units from other scopes to make them visible within the current scope.

4.4 The Gypsy Verification Environment (GVE)

The main attraction of using Gypsy is its tool support for the whole of the formal verification life-cycle, from syntax checkers to theorem provers (see Figure 4.1).

A database lies at the heart of the GVE, providing the basis for integrating

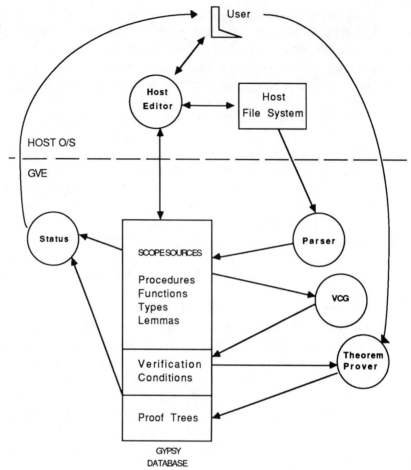

Fig. 4.1 The Gypsy verification environment

User

Host Editor

Host File System

HOST O/S

GVE

Status

SCOPE SOURCES

Procedures
Functions
Types
Lemmas

Verification Conditions

Proof Trees

Parser

VCG

Theorem Prover

GYPSY
DATABASE

the different tools. The database is passive in the sense that the user cannot directly insert, delete or update items in the database. Program units, VCs and proofs enter the database as a side effect of invoking the various tools.

The toolset contains a parser, for checking the syntactic and static well-formedness of Gypsy texts, which are read from a host operating system file. The local editor of the host operating system is generally used to input Gypsy texts, although the editor may be invoked directly from the GVE, to compose or alter definitions of units from the database. The parser inserts a tool-readable representation of a well-formed program unit into the database.

The Verification Condition Generator (VCG) tool is invoked by the user on a program unit. The VCG semantically analyses the code against the specification clauses to yield a set of predicates, the validity of which guarantee the (partial) correctness of the program unit. The effect of the VCG on the database is to associate a set of verification conditions with the program unit. The conditions are notionally tagged with proofs, which of course do not exist initially. It is the task of a further tool, the interactive theorem prover component, to post user-devised proofs of VCs into the database.

Before describing each of the main components of the GVE in turn, mention should be made of the multi-window and menu/mouse-driven user interface supported on the version of Gypsy on Symbolics workstations. All interaction with GVE is conducted via one of two screens. At the "outer" level, GVE tools can be invoked from the GVE screen, which is split into two half-screen panes. One pane permanently displays the status of the units in the GVE database, and even makes suggestions on what the next course of action should be. The other GVE pane is used to enter commands and display results from all the GVE tools, except the theorem prover. The theorem prover tool requires a great deal of interaction from the user, as exemplified in the following section, and so has its own screen. The theorem prover screen replaces the GVE screen each time the theorem prover is invoked, and the GVE screen only returns once the prover session is ended. The theorem prover screen is similarly split into two panes, one of which is for interaction. The other pane permanently displays the current subgoal.

All GVE or Prover commands may be typed at an interaction pane, or can be picked from a context-sensitive pop-up menu. The context-sensitive menu can be used in conjunction with typing to produce a menu which contains all units with particular naming prefixes. We have used this trick along with good naming conventions for units and lemmas, to be able to search quickly for likely lemmas. The interface significantly improves the effectiveness of the GVE by providing a high degree of visibility of a growing database. Also, the luxury of having the current subgoal always displayed in the theorem prover screen provides the effect of complex and tedious symbol manipulations being carried out in front of the user's eyes.

4.4.1   The database

The GVE maintains a coherent view of the database, so that a unit is tagged proven, when all of its VCs have been proven for example. The GVE automatically conducts *proof chain analysis*. This ensures that a unit which depends upon the proof of other units (procedures, functions, or lemmas) is not tagged proven until the requisite theorems have all been proved, in addition to the unit's own VCs.

The database represents the current state of the project, including all program units, lemmas and proof logs, as well as the verification status. A facility is provided for storing the current database in a host operating system file, and conversely restoring a database at the start of a new session.

Facilities are provided to query the database and to view the contents of a unit, or a snapshot of the verification status of a project, scope or unit, including dependency information. The GVE only maintains one database, which is added to as a project develops. Unfortunately, multiple databases cannot be maintained, even by the user, since there is no facility for either directly storing parts of the database to different dump files, or selectively deleting components before dumping the entire database.

4.4.2 Verification Condition Generator

The VCG tool transforms a specification and code fragment into a set of verification conditions, using an extended form of Floyd–Hoare programming logic. A verification condition formalizes the condition that the code between any two adjacent program assertions, executed in a state satisfying the first assertion, yields a state satisfying the second assertion. For a program consisting of a single in-line thread of code, this is quite straightforward. There is only one verification condition which expresses the requirement that the entry assertion, with each variable substituted by the effects of the code on that variable (a process called *forward symbolic execution*), should imply the exit assertion.

Typically, a block of code involves assignments to the main variables, and to temporary variables used to break down a computation into small steps. For instance, to swap the values of the integer variables x and y to achieve the specification

$$x = y' \quad \textbf{and} \quad y = x'$$

the integer variable t is used as follows:

```
t := x;
x := y;
y := t
```

Each time a variable is assigned to during symbolic execution, its value is "frozen" by labelling the identifier with #n, for the nth assignment to that variable, and ' (prime) for the initial value. So the three assignments above yield $t \# 1 = x$, $x \# 1 = y$, and $y \# 1 = t \# 1$. Therefore,

$$y \# 1 = t \# 1 = x'$$
$$x \# 1 = y'$$

The final frozen value is the "current" value, so

$$x \# 1 = x$$
$$y \# 1 = y$$

so the effect of the program is evaluated to

$$y = x' \quad \textbf{and} \quad x = y'$$

which trivially implies the specification of the swap code given above, since they are identical statements.

For a slightly more complex program, containing a single conditional statement, there are two VCs, one for each branch. As an example of this, consider the simple, but common, program which puts the maximum of two numbers x and y in the variable z (we will not be interested in what happens to x and y). The formal specification is

$$(z = x' \ \textbf{or} \ z = y') \ \textbf{and} \ z \ \text{ge} \ x' \ \textbf{and} \ z \ \text{ge} \ y'$$

This is implemented by the branching code:

```
if x ge y
    then z := x;
    else z := y;
end;
```

The VCG's view of this code is manifested formally as

$$y' \ \text{le} \ x' \quad \rightarrow z \# 1 = x' \quad \text{and}$$
$$x' + 1 \ \text{le} \ y' \rightarrow z \# 1 = y'$$

which after renaming $z \# 1$ to z is

$$y' \ \text{le} \ x' \quad \rightarrow z = x' \quad \text{and}$$
$$x' + 1 \ \text{le} \ y' \rightarrow z = y'$$

Note the use of the less than or equal comparator (le) where greater than or equal (ge) is expected. This is because Gypsy uses canonical forms for integer inequalities that involve only le or ne (not equal). This canonicalization seems obscure, but it is necessary so that later on the theorem prover component can automatically reduce assertions about integers, and soon becomes less obscure to the experienced user.

The VC for the branching code example requires that the VCG's assertion of what the code actually does implies the specification assertion, once that too has been canonicalized, giving:

$$y' \ \text{le} \ x' \quad \rightarrow z = x' \ \text{and}$$
$$x' + 1 \ \text{le} \ y' \rightarrow z = y'$$
$$\rightarrow$$
$$(z = x' \ \text{or} \ z = y') \ \text{and} \ x' \ \text{le} \ z \ \text{and} \ y' \ \text{le} \ z$$

which is easily proven by analysis of the complementary cases of $y' \ \text{le} \ x'$ and $x' + 1 \ \text{le} \ y'$.

For the more complex loop programs, there are three verification conditions. These show: that the code between the entry assertion and a fixed point in the loop satisfies a weakened form of the exit condition; that the code between that fixed point and the actual exit condition meets the exit condition; and that the loop round from the fixed point to itself satisfies the weak form of the exit condition. That weakened exit assertion is called a *loop invariant*, because it documents the property of the loop that remains constant at each visit to the fixed point in the programs locus of control.

An example of this is a program which sets all the components of an integer array a, to zero. The specification quantifies over all elements of the array, indexed by the set smallint from 1 to n, say. The universal quantifier is represented by the keyword **all** in Gypsy: **all** j: smallint, a[j] = 0

The following looping program achieves this effect, using the loop counter i:

```
i:= 1;
loop
        if i le n
            then a[i]:= 0;
                    i:= i + 1;
            else leave;
    end;
```

Note that there is only one loop construct in Gypsy, which is used in conjunction with conditional statements and the leave imperative to mimic classical control structures. This simplifies the programming logic, and hence the VCG implementation.

A loop assertion must be supplied with this program, in order for the VCG to be able to generate any of the VCs. If not, the VCG issues a warning, along with a set of unprovable VCs. An accurate loop assertion for the above code fragment must state that, at any iteration, the first i elements of the array have been initialized, thus:

all k: 1..i, a[k] = 0

The corresponding loop VC is then:

$$\begin{array}{l} \textbf{all}\ k:\ 1..i,\ a[k] = 0\ \textbf{and}\ a[i+1] = 0 \\ \rightarrow \\ \textbf{all}\ k:\ 1..i+1,\ a[k] = 0 \end{array}$$

A more complex example including the other loop VCs is introduced in section 4.5. This covers the VCG's handling of imperative control structures, such as loops, but a different set of VCs is generated for recursive programs. Each recursive call of a program unit gives rise to a VC to show that the calling point satisfies its own entry assertion (with calling parameter expressions substituted), and that its exit assertion (again with parameter substitutions) can satisfy itself. Note that, although recursion is another form of iteration, invariant assertions are not needed.

The verification condition generator component of GVE is not formally developed. However, more recently the programming logic of Gypsy has been formally axiomatized. The VCG manifests the GVE's view of the programming logic, and it may be that the formal axiomatization could be used to informally check the correctness of the VCG. The VCG is one of the most impressive components of the GVE, in that it generates VCs that accurately relate control flow and data assignments to specification assertions for most programs.

However there are programming features for which the VCG will generate valid VCs even though the program is nonsense. An example is the use of variable aliasing which is outlawed by the static semantics of the language, but not trapped by the parser. The dynamic semantics of the language prescribes that a standard exception is raised when the potential for aliasing is detected, so therefore a loop-free program would be verified, only to fail at runtime.

Less critical, the VCG has not been programmed to deal with interactions between concurrency and recursion. In this case, a recursive process generates unprovable VCs. Although this is a limitation, it is arguably not a serious problem, because the system will not facilitate the proof of these programs whether they are correct or not. The main point is that now a formal programming logic for Gypsy is under consideration, it is likely that incompletenesses in the VCG will be addressed. Although we do not advocate too much effort being spent on "verified" verification systems, it is clear that the mathematical basis for proving programs, the programming logic, must not only be shown to be internally consistent, but also consistent with the semantics of the language. This is primarily seen as a foundational exercise which should be fulfilled for any new language which claims to have the potential to describe and verify high-integrity systems.

4.4.3   The Interactive Theorem Prover

Having used the VCG to generate a set of VCs for a Gypsy unit, the task of proving that every VC is a theorem lies ahead. The GVE provides an interactive, semi-automatic tool for reducing logical expressions to "true", called the theorem prover.

At the heart of the theorem prover is a simplifier, called SUPINF, which can decide equalities and inequalities for each of the standard data types—hence SUPerior and INFerior values. The supinf values for each variable are recorded at any time in the so-called *typelist*. The simplifier decides whether predicates involving only constant terms are true or false, and is expected to know all about the basic data types. The prover has undergone a fairly ad hoc development over the years, as data types and constructs have been added to the language. This seems to have given rise to incompletenesses in the simplifier, for example it cannot infer that the empty set is of size zero. These problems can be factored out of a particular proof using a standard "assume"ed lemma, and there will be little argument with the evaluator (say) over the consistency of such an "axiom". However, as a general rule, users should be discouraged from introducing axioms on the system data types.

The business of introducing extra axioms on the data types can be a nuisance to the verification evaluators, and it is hoped that support for Gypsy would include fixes to the simplifier for suitably straightforward omissions.

The prover can also attempt to apply a limited number of the interactive commands automatically, in a semi-intelligent manner, using a command called PROCEED. Many VCs are automatically proven in this way, particularly the more trivial entry assertion requirements for called procedures and functions, and entry assertions to loop invariant VCs.

However, for the more complex VCs, involving explicit or implicit induction—from recursive or loop programs respectively—the user will usually need to direct the theorem prover by applying a series of prover commands. Conditional statements and expressions in programs and specifications give rise to case splits in proofs, which logically makes a proof trace a tree. Implications in entry or exit specifications give rise to chaining arguments, which correspond to modus ponens and modus tollens in predicate logic.

Proof management commands are provided to inspect the proof tree as it is developed. The outline structure of the proof may be printed, with command names and proof step numbers indicated for each node. From this information, it is possible to "home in" on particular parts of the proof tree, perhaps inspecting the state of the theorem at that point, or substitutions for quantified variables that were in force when the step was carried out, and the typelist representing the possible range of each variable at that point.

It is possible to structure the proof activity by making lemmas out of theorems using a facility available from within the prover (*makelemma*). This generalizes all the free variables, and inserts the new lemma into the database (to be proven later). One could envisage taking each proof step one or two subgoals further and then making lemmas out of the resulting subgoals, to be proven later. The prover normally transfers the proof session along a depth-first route, but the use of lemmas in this way forces the system to take a breadth-first strategy. This technique allows progress to be made in exploring the proof, without letting difficult details interrupt the overall structure. This also leads to the idea of building "theories" of data types to factor out common properties which might be used in the proofs of several similar programs.

It should be emphasized that program proving is primarily an intellectual activity, rather than a mechanical interaction with the computer. It is the authors' experience that proofs are effected more efficiently if a hand-sketch or proof outline has been constructed on paper before the interactive prover is brought into play. This might encourage the reader to view the tool as a proof-checker, which is not accurate. Since the tool is capable of performing tedious reductions very quickly, it does encourage the user to experiment with alternative proof tactics at the very detailed stages of a proof. So the tool is on the one hand a checker, making sure that the proof is sound, and on the other hand a proof assistant encouraging the user to try out different strategies.

In the next section, the above overview of Gypsy and its toolset is exemplified in detail by a simple, but archetypal, verification problem.

4.5 A simple example

In this section, an informal problem statement is followed by a formal specification and implementation in Gypsy. The details of Verification Condition Generation and interactive proof are then elaborated in tutorial detail. The problem statement is as follows:

> Given an array of some objects of arbitrary type, together with a required object, we require a procedure that returns the position in the array that holds the required object.
>
> Further, if the object is not found, we require the procedure to return some indication.

The example is a very simple programming problem, but adequately serves to illustrate the use of Gypsy, as well as raising wider issues in the solution. Throughout this section an elementary knowledge of Pascal and predicate logic is assumed. The Gypsy constructs that combine these concepts are introduced as they appear.

The following type declarations for the search example should present no difficulties (language keywords are in bolder type):

```
const i : integer := pending;
const j : integer := pending;
type index = integer(i .. j); {implicitly, i < j}
type object = pending;
type obj_array = array (index) of object;
```

Here we declare the necessary constants and types to allow us to talk about objects and **arrays** of objects. The **pending** keyword means "not yet defined". Although we have not completely defined the constants and types there is enough information to reason about them, since the properties of integers and arrays, and the equality of objects of a given type, are known. Note minor variations in concrete syntax compared with Pascal—these should be self-explanatory.

The complete definition of the array searching procedure is

```
procedure search ( a : obj_array;
                   x : object;
              var k : integer ) =
begin
    entry true;
    exit ( a[k] = x or all l : index, a[l] ne x )

    {implementation of the specification}
    k := i;
```

```
        loop
            assert ( all l : index, l < k → a[l] ne x)
            if (k > j or a[k] = x)
                then leave;
                else k := k + 1;
            end;
        end;
    end; {search}
```

Procedure search takes an obj_array (a) and a required object (x), returning the index value of the array position holding the required object. More precisely, the entry or precondition assumes nothing about the parameter values. The exit or post-condition states that either the array indexed by the returned value is x, or that all array positions are not equal to x. Note that variable names are strictly controlled in Gypsy. All external objects are passed to this procedure as parameters.

An immediate criticism (which we do not intend to remedy) is that nowhere in the specification presented so far does one find a clear statement as to how the absence of x in a is signalled. Jumping ahead, one could inspect the code to discover that k will have the value $j + 1$ in this event, and arguably this "looseness" of specification is a problem of validation of the specification rather than verification, particularly given that the original requirement is vaguely worded in this respect.

The goal of the specification annotations is to capture all possible behaviours of the procedure, and the entry and exit statements label the respective start and end of the procedure's set of control paths. The standard requirement of the Floyd–Hoare approach exemplified here is that every possible internal control path between the start and end is either acyclic or, in the case of loops, is cut by a loop invariant. Here the Gypsy assert statement provides such an invariant by stating that every array position below that indexed by k is not equal to x. As explained earlier, the invariant bears a subtle (rather than a direct) relationship to the actual termination condition of the loop itself. In this case either k exceeds the index value or the current position a[k] is x.

The executable code of search comprises all of the procedure text apart from the entry, exit and assert statements. The returned parameter k initially assumes the lower array bound value. The loop (in this case a while .. do equivalent) checks whether the upper bound has been exceeded or the current position is x; otherwise it increments k. Notice the use of what is effectively a conditional-or, since the indexing of a k-value outside the range i .. j is undefined.

To summarize the initial presentation of search, we have seen how a typical procedure is specified and implemented, and explored the composition of the appropriate specification predicates. Now consider the proof that the implementation meets the given specification. Note that in no sense may the above executable fragment of search be passed as a correct implementation of search without reference to the specification, and the Gypsy language and tools do not ameliorate the intellectual effort of formulating the basic specifications.

Verification Condition Generation

It has already been explained that the proof approach in Gypsy relies on the use of a verification condition generator (VCG). The general VCG approach implemented by Gypsy was explained informally in section 4.2, but as real VCs are presented below as the GVE presents them to the user, it will be apparent that the VCG produces dense output that is difficult to understand, particularly for the novice. Unfortunately, the control structure of the program has a considerable effect on the nature of the VCs generated, and therefore the overall structure of the corresponding proof. Consequently it is impossible to carry out the theorem proving activity in isolation from the rest of the program development activity.

Recall that the VCG generates proof obligations (VCs to be proven) in the form of implications. Paths that contain conditional statements give rise to multiple VCs, to break down the size of such VCs. The starting point is control path analysis; in the case of search, there are three control paths: from the entry statement to the assert (loop invariant) statement, from the assert (round the loop and back) to itself, and from the assert to the exit statement. The specification statements themselves do not necessarily emerge unchanged from the VCG, as will be clear from the VCs for search presented below. Before reviewing the VCs it is worthwhile to recall what is to be proved.

We have formulated the procedure in terms of a loop, and the intuitive understanding of the loop's behaviour is specified by its invariant, namely that the segment of the array examined "so far" does not include x. The loop invariant is so called because it represents the property the loop is trying to establish, which should always be true. For any invariant property I, say, the following partial correctness criteria must be proven:

a) I is true before the loop is executed.
b) Given that I is true and the termination condition is not true, a single iteration of the loop leaves I still true.
c) I is true upon termination of the loop.

Generation of the first VC   The first VC for search combines the control path with its starting point at the entry statement, with case *a* of the loop analysis to derive the following VC:

    H1: L # 2 + 1 le I

→

    C1: A [L # 2] ne X

Several conventions need to be explained first of all. As mentioned earlier, the VC is in the form of an implication. Gypsy presents the VC as a conjunction of hypotheses (or antecedents) implying a conjunction of consequents. Here there is only one hypothesis (labelled H1) and one consequent (labelled C1). All variables are in upper case and stand for the values of the program variables at the point under consideration. The presence of the suffix #2 on the logical variable L is due to a process known as *skolemization*, which is explained later; a simplified view is that the name L has been modified to ensure uniqueness across all the VCs associated with this procedure. Finally, the convention among the Gypsy tools is to express integer inequalities in the form exemplified above by the expression

L + 1 le I

rather than

L < I

To understand the derivation of the VC, consider what needs to be proved for this path. This is usually expressed in Hoare logic as follows:

'search entry condition' { k := i } 'loop invariant'

This statement specifies that, in all program states, the entry condition and the execution of the code imply the loop invariant whenever the code actually terminates. Substituting Gypsy text for the informal statements above,

true { k := i } all : l index, l < k → a[l] ne x

which might be expressed as the "pseudo-VC":

H1: true
H2: { k := i }
→
C1: all L : index, L < K → A[L] ne X

(Note that our pseudo-VC notation is not used by the GVE. It is used here purely for pedagogical purposes.) To simplify the hypothesis labelled H2, consider the effect of the code within the braces, a simple assignment. Clearly, under any possible situation the value of k will equal i after the assignment, and, given that i is a constant, H2 can be immediately expressed as

true → k = i

which simplifies the pseudo-VC to

H1: K = I
→
C1: all L : index, L < K → A[L] ne X

The VCG further simplifies this by substituting i for k throughout the conclusion, a move which renders the hypothesis (H1) trivially true, as follows:

> H1: true
>
> →
>
> C1: all L : index, L < I → A [L] ne X

The final step that leads to the real VC presented earlier is skolemization, again mentioned above. The process of skolemization removes quantified expressions in VCs. In this case the quantified expression ranges over all values of L, and implicitly all values of the program variables a and x. But the whole VC is also implicitly "universally quantified" in the sense that it is making a statement about all executions of this program path under the hypothesis. Thus, the VCG drops the quantification to produce

> H1: true
>
> →
>
> C1: L < 1 → A [L] ne X

and finally simplifies this to

> H1: L + 1 le I
>
> →
>
> C1: a [L] ne X

An expression involving existential quantification, or universal quantification, in the hypotheses must be treated differently. In this case substitutable variables are introduced, because it is possible to prove the VC by substituting values as well as by reducing the VC to a formula that is always true.

Generation of the second VC   The second VC corresponds to the path

> all l : index, l < k → a [l] ne x
> { not (k > j or a [k] = x); k := k + 1 }
> all l : index, l < k → a [l] ne x

It might seem as though the code has been changed slightly here, but this is only to emphasize that the loop termination condition is explicitly false for the path in question. Again it is possible to re-express this as a pseudo-VC:

> H1: all L : index, L < K → A [L] ne X
> H2: not (K > J or A [K] = X)
> H3: { k := k + 1 }
>
> →
>
> C1: all L : index, L < K → A [L] ne X

Again, the "effect" of the code is indicated by the dummy conjunct H3 containing the code fragment in question.

There is a need to be more precise about the treatment of the code by the VCG this time, because the VC clearly involves expressions which, given they are true before execution of the code, may or may not be true afterwards. The first VC was less difficult, since the pre-condition was simply true.

The effect of the code fragment can be formulated in terms of the initial value k' as follows:

$$k = k' \{ k := k + 1 \} k = k' + 1$$

Making the appropriate substitutions in the post-condition yields:

C1: all L : index, $L < K' + 1 \rightarrow A[L]$ ne X

where k' is the value of k prior to executing the code; so the variable k in H1 can be replaced by k'. The full VC so far, incorporating these substitutions and applying de Morgan's rule to H2, is

H1: all L : index, $L < K' \rightarrow A[L]$ ne X
H2: K' le J
H3: $A[K']$ ne X
$\rightarrow$
C1: all L : index, $L < K' + 1 \rightarrow A[L]$ ne X

The priming of k will be omitted henceforth, as the VC only depends on k', rather than k and k'. The final step is to consider the effect of skolemization. The quantified expression in the consequent is similar to that in the consequent of the first VC, but to keep the L distinct from that in H1, the GVE labels it as $L \# 2$ again. Taking into account the representation of $a < b$ as $a + 1$ le b and appropriate simplification, this makes the conclusion:

C1: $L \# 2$ le $K \rightarrow A[L \# 2]$ ne X

There is another quantified expression in H1, and this too emerges slightly differently because the GVE allows substitution of values for L in this case. To see why this is possible, consider the simple VC

(all x: T, $p(x)) \rightarrow p(y)$

which states that if p is true for every x, $p(y)$ is true (x and y are of the same type). Clearly, one way to prove this VC is to show that when x takes on the value y, we have $p(y) \rightarrow p(y)$ which is always true. So, returning to the hypothesis, we obtain

H1: $L\pounds \# 1 + 1$ le $K \rightarrow A[L\pounds \# 1]$ ne X
H2: K le J
H3: $A[K]$ ne X
$\rightarrow$
C1: $L \# 2$ le $K \rightarrow A[L \# 2]$ ne X

Here the £ sign denotes a substitutable variable which may assume arbitrary values for the purpose of the proof.

Generation of the third VC   The final VC corresponds to the path from the terminated loop to the exit of the procedure:

> all l : index, l < k → a[l] ne x
> { a[k] = x or k > j then leave }
> all l : index, a[l] ne x or a[k] = x

which appears as

> H1: L£ # 4 + 1 le K → A[L£ # 4] ne X
> H2: A[K] = X or J + 1 le K
> →
> C1: L # 1 le K → A[L # 2] ne X

Once again, distinct names have been allocated in sequence for the logical variable L, and the skolemizer has made L in H1 substitutable. The inequality k > j has also been converted to the equivalent canonical form.

Proof of the first VC   The first VC is re-written below:

> H1: L # 2 + 1 le I
> →
> C1: A[L # 2] ne X

The reader may already have proved this in anticipation, and indeed the VCG is able to do so automatically. The mechanism by which the VCG achieves the proof (the typelist) will be explored in the context of the proof of the third and final VC. It is sufficient for now to note that H1 assumes that L # 2 is less than I. But the declaration of L # 2 (or L as it was in the original program unit) restricts L # 2 to the range I .. J. Hence H1 is always false, so the VC is proved.

Proof of the second VC   The initial step in this first non-trivial proof is to rearrange the VC to make it more manipulable. The key is to exploit the fact that A → B → C is the same as (A and B) → C, so the VC may be transformed into

> H1: L # 2 le K
> H2: L£ # 1 + 1 le K → A[L£ # 1] ne X
> H3: K le J
> H4: A[K] ne X
> →
> C1: A[L # 2] ne X

An insight derived from our knowledge of the program allows us to make further progress. The loop invariant states the property of the array segment examined "so far". It seems profitable to treat this segment in two cases, namely the current, position k, and the prior positions less than k. This strategy is also suggested by H1 and H4. The Gypsy prover tool allows us to replace H1 by the equivalent "claim": $L\#2 = K$ or $L\#2 < K$ (which is itself equivalent to the canonical form $L\#2 + 1 < K$).

The justification for the claim is

    H1: $L\#2 = K$ or $L\#2 + 1$ le K
  →
    C1: $L\#2$ le K

which can be split into

    $L\#2 = K \rightarrow L\#2$ le K and
    $L\#2 + 1$ le K $\rightarrow L\#2$ le K

both of which the prover is able to reduce to true automatically, by its "knowledge" of integer inequalities. Returning to the VC, there are two cases to prove. The first is

    H1: $K = L\#2$
    H2: $L\#2$ le K
    H3: $L\#2 + 1$ le K $\rightarrow$ A[L\#2] ne X
    H4: K le J
    H5: A[K] ne X
  →
    C1: A[L\#2] ne X

The prover allows equality substitution where such a term appears as an assumption. Here we wish to do a global replacement of $L\#2$ by K:

    H1: K le J
    H2: A[K] ne X
  →
    C1: A[K] ne X

(Notice how the prover automatically drops true hypotheses.)

Using the reduction A and B → B to true, the result is proven immediately.

The second case is

    H1: $L\#2 + 1$ le K
    H2: $L\#2$ le K
    H3: $L\#2 + 1$ le K $\rightarrow$ A[L\#2] ne X
    H4: K le J
    H5: A[K] ne X
  →
    C1: A[L\#2] ne X

The hypotheses do not suggest any possible substitutions, which means that the theorem must be suitably transformed. Such a transformation is provided by the BACKCHAIN inference rule, which replaces the form

W   and   (X → C) → C

by the form

W → X

In this case, W is H4 and H5, X is L#2 + 1 le K, and C is A[L#2] ne X. In other words, C1 follows from the consequent of H3. So it is sufficient to prove the antecedent of H3. This inference rule is known as modus tollens in logic. The result of the backchain is

H1: L#2 + 1 le K
H2: L#2 le K
H3: K le J
H4: A[K] ne X
→
C1: L#2 + 1 le K

which leaves H1 the same as C1 and so the second case is proved, and consequently the second VC is proved.

Proof of the third VC   The basis for the proof in program terms is the observation that the range of L#1 is a suitable range for L£#4. This can be justified by considering the segments of the array that may have been examined by the loop: none, some or all. In each case, the range of index values to be considered is the same for both variables. Hence the hypothesis involving the loop invariant can be modified by substituting L#1 without loss of generality. The proof proceeds by considering the alternatives for loop termination in turn. The proof of the VC by the GVE prover follows this scheme. Substituting L#1 for L£#4 results in

H1: L#1 + 1 le K → A[L#1] ne X
H2: A[K] = X or J + 1 le K
→
C1: A[L#1] ne X or A[K] = X

Noting that

[A   and   (B or C)] → D

is equivalent to

[B   and   A → D]   and   [C   and   A → D]

(the ORSPLIT rule) allows the proof to proceed by cases. The first is

> H1: A[K] = X
> H2: L # 1 + 1 le K → A[L # 1] ne X
>
> →
>
> C1: A[L # 1] ne X or A[K] = X

The prover can work out for itself that H1 appears as a disjunct in C1 and automatically simplifies C1 to true, which proves the case.

The second case is

> H1: J + 1 le K
> H2: L # 1 + 1 le K → A[L # 1] ne X
>
> →
>
> C1: A[L # 1] ne X or A[K] = X

Once again the BACKCHAIN inference rule is appropriate. In words, the first disjunct of C1 follows from the consequent of H2, so it is sufficient to prove the antecedent of H2. Hence,

> H1: J + 1 le K
>
> →
>
> C1: L # 1 + 1 le K

The theorem prover can now simplify this formula by applying its SUPINF deduction function. In a data structure called the typelist, the SUPINF mechanism keeps track of the maximum (SUPerior) and minimum (INFerior) values which integer-valued variables in the current theorem can take. As inference rules and simplifications are applied to create new (sub) goals, this typelist is modified to reflect the modified assumptions. In this case, the typelist initially recorded the range $I..J$ for $L # 1$, based on the declaration in the program unit. But the current assumption in H1 is that $K > J$. So C1 reduces to true immediately, completing the proof of the second case and hence the third and final VC.

Observations The proof presented above raises some important questions. First of all, it was shown that it is possible to introduce an unsafe array reference without apparent complaint from the GVE. The more recent Spade and Malpas systems [see chapter 8] are capable of detecting this kind of anomaly. What is needed is a tightening of the static semantics of Gypsy, or a separate VCG mechanism which generates the conditions which must be proven to show that unsafe references are never possible.

Perhaps more striking is the lack of support for total correctness. The additional VCs required would show that k is bounded from above as long as the loop has not yet terminated, and that each loop iteration is guaranteed to increase k, hence confirming that the loop must always terminate. That such a proof is necessary should be apparent to anybody who has debugged a computer program. Fortunately, user-supplied lemmas can be provided which imply total correctness, but adding these as additional assertions or additional conjuncts to the existing assertions is not enforced.

The VCG is undoubtedly the most powerful tool in GVE. The proof steps performed subsequently were all (except where noted) the result of explicit commands to the prover. Hence the main role of the prover is as a book-keeping device. Furthermore, whilst most tactics employed by the proof were justifiable in terms of standard inferences, the simplification and type inferences performed automatically were somewhat "magical", which leads to a problem for someone auditing the proof.

The problem presented in this section is quite typical of the programming level verification to which Gypsy is ideally suited, with its array representation. However, there is a limit to the complexity of problem that can be expressed using low-level machine-oriented data types, without the complexity of the data types themselves becoming dominant. In the next section, the more abstract data types, including a type abstraction mechanism, are discussed.

4.6 Specification data types

So far in this chapter, we have presented an appraisal of Gypsy in the context of program verification. Programs operate on machine-oriented data types such as integers, and arrays, but these are not sufficiently abstract to describe complex systems concisely. In this section, Gypsy's support for problem-oriented data types is discussed, and the suitability of Gypsy for system specification is assessed.

Objects from set theory are usually more suited to problem descriptions than data types which closely model machines such as arrays for linear stores. Sets, sequences and mappings are provided as standard types in Gypsy. Constructs are provided in the language to express values of these abstract types, and also to express changes in their values. Further, special operations are provided to manipulate the structures underlying these abstract objects directly. In other words, Gypsy provides (hidden) representations of types and standard implementations of their operations.

However, system specification techniques need notations for extending the mathematical vocabulary and encapsulating problem theories. Gypsy provides an Abstract Data Type mechanism that allows users to add their own abstract types by naming the new type, and specifying appropriate operations. A "concrete" representation is expressed in terms of the standard data types, and the implementations of these operations are specified in terms of that representation. The new data type name may then be referred to, and its operations used. Variables of abstract type may be assigned to, but the chosen representation and implementation remain hidden.

Before discussing the abstract data type mechanism further, consider the standard abstract types of sets, sequences and mappings. The use of these will be familiar to readers from chapter 2, and of course sets are implemented in Pascal. In Gypsy, set types can be introduced using the **set of** type constructor. For example, the unbounded set ss is declared to be a set of integers by

> **type** intset = **set of** integer;
>
> ...
>
> ss : intset

and a set sn that can contain at most n (n > 0) integers is declared:

> sn : **set** (n) **of** integer

Then ss can be assigned a set value, for example the set containing the numbers 1, 2, and 3 by the assignment

> ss := [**set**: 1, 2, 3]

The basic set relations of membership (in) and subset (sub), and set operators union, intersection, and difference, are provided, but there is no set comprehension term for describing sets using predicates.

Sequence types may also be introduced, for example:

> **type** intseq = **sequence of** integer;

with the variable s declared

> s : intseq;

and assigned the sequence of values 8 followed by 6 followed by 9, say:

> s := [**seq**: 8, 6, 9]

Mapping types are constructed from the **mapping** type constructor. For example, the mathematical abstraction of a multiset, or bag, could be represented as a mapping from elements of some set T, say, to the integers as follows:

> **type** bag = **mapping from** T **to** integer;

So the number of elements x in b: bag is found by applying the mapping bag to its argument x, written b(x). Of course, for a mapping b to truly represent a bag, b(x) must be non-negative for any x in the domain of b.

The bag b', with x inserted, is described by the expression:

> b' **with** ([x] := b'[x] + 1)

Commands are available for explicitly manipulating rather than assigning copies of fragments of objects. For example, the expression

> ss = ss' **omit** 2

describes the set ss as itself before an operation, with the integer 2 removed. This might be part of the specification of a procedure, but how can this specification be achieved imperatively? One way would be to assign ss′ omit 2 directly to ss, thus:

ss := ss **omit** 2

but operationally this would mean that two copies of the same structure would be generated in the machine. This is a problem generally with data structures that can change their "shape" during execution. These are so-called *dynamic types*. To overcome this inefficiency, Gypsy provides a special set manipulating command, called **remove**. So the above statement could have been written:

remove element 2 **from set** ss

Similar structure-manipulating commands are supplied for all of the standard dynamic types, to move components of structures between structures, and to add new elements to structures. For example, the number 2 could be removed from ss and added onto the back of the sequence s, as follows:

move element 2 **from set** ss **to behind seq** s

leaving

s = [**set**: 1, 3]
ss = [**seq**: 8, 6, 9, 2]

We now move on to introducing user-defined abstract data types. Recall the definition of the type bag above. The mapping representation has already been chosen, and the invariant property that elements are non-negative has been noted. Common operations on a bag are inserting a new, or duplicate element, and counting the number of occurrences of a given element. The bag definition can be declared as an abstract data type as follows:

type bag **initially** empty < empty, insert, count > =
begin
        b : **mapping from** T **to** integer;
        hold all x : T, x **in** domain(b) → b[x] ge 0;
end;

The essential empty bag and insert and count operations are named here to grant access to the concrete mapping type representation, needed in the definitions and proofs of these functions and procedures. All data types in Gypsy have a default initial value. For example, the default sequence of type intseq is the null sequence represented null(intseq). The default initial value for bag is stated to be empty.

Note that the data type invariant is introduced as the hold assertion. There are proof obligations for operations which have concrete access to abstract data types to show that the hold condition is preserved. Hold assertions are identical to state invariants in Z.

Each bag operation is specified in terms of the concrete representation by **centry** and **cexit** clauses. The abstract effects of the operation is specified by **entry** and **exit** clauses. For example, the empty bag has a zero count for any element of T, as the following declaration specifies:

> **function** empty : bag =
> **begin**
>   **exit all** y:T, count(result, y) = 0
> **end**;

Note that a concrete exit condition is not provided here, since empty is treated as an arbitrary constant of type bag. Now consider the insert operation, declared as follows:

> **procedure** insert (**var** b : bag; x : T) =
> **begin**
>   **cexit** b = b' **with** (into [x]:= b' [x] + 1);
>   **exit all** y : T, count(b, y) = **if** x = y
>   **then** count(b', y) + 1
>   **else** count(b', y) **fi**;
>   pending;
> **end**;

Bag insertion is represented in the concrete specification by incrementing the count value that the mapping associates with x. The same increment is expressed in the abstract exit clause purely in terms of the other operations, and it is this predicate that the VCG uses in a VC for a unit that does not have concrete access to bag. There is of course an obligation to prove that the exit and cexit clauses match up, that is

> cexit → exit

and in general to prove that

> centry → entry

and that the code (shown as **pending**) implements the concrete specification. Note that since equality on bags may be used in units that do not have concrete access, it is necessary to define an equality function that the VCG can use in that context. It is necessary to prove that such equality extensions are equivalence relations.

The Gypsy abstract data type mechanism allows the user to hide the underlying implementation of a type from other programs, and to present its own semantics only by properties and relationships between the operations on the data type. It is not possible to record multiple representations of a single data type in Gypsy. In other methods, such as the Vienna Development Method [Jones86] or HDM [Crowe86], the specifier is encouraged firstly to devise a formal representation of the system state which has the minimal properties required. This may be expressed in terms of sets of mapping structures or whatever is the most appropriate. Then, the development process is viewed as the production of a series of *refined* data types, with the rewriting of the system operations in terms of the newer data type at each stage. There are proof obligations to show that the refinement has been carried out correctly: that is, that the refined data type is furnished with at least the same objects as the original data type (called reification in VDM, and theory interpretation in HDM), and secondly that the re-specified operations model the original operations (operation modelling). This kind of technique is not possible in Gypsy because it does not support multiple representations for each data type.

It is clear that Gypsy can be used to specify systems by describing states, perhaps using abstract data types to hide implementation details, and specifying procedures that operate on parts of the state. The calling structure of procedures and functions determines the architecture of the subsequent program, as the procedure code lives in the same unit as its specification. This might seem to be a drawback, since program module structure rarely mirrors specification structure naturally. However, the enforced alignment of specification and program structure provides Gypsy with its *principle of independence*: that is, any program unit is proven with respect to its entry/exit specification in isolation from all other units.

So it seems that Gypsy is suitable for system specification at a single level of abstraction only, perhaps top-level specification, or security policy modelling. This application of Gypsy is quite distinct, however, from its primary function of code-level verification, and so broadens the scope of the method.

4.7 Future directions

It is difficult to predict how existing formal verification environments such as Gypsy will change in the future, because the technology is still relatively young, and not widely used.

The GVE is currently supported by Computational Logic Inc. of Austin Texas, but the original developers at the University of Austin, under the guidance of Don Good, have already embarked on the development of the next generation of Gypsy, called Rose. The major departure from the traditional line of research is the theme of integrating existing verification technology to achieve a highly reliable development system, at the cost of limiting the scope of application.

In the case of Rose, all the GVE tools, except the theorem prover, are being redeveloped for a Gypsy-like language called micro-Gypsy. This is a very restricted subset of Gypsy. The simplification afforded is allowing the development teams to put more focus on the design and implementation of the development environment itself. The ultimate goal is to provide absolute assurance in the end product by inheriting assurance from the development environment.

The Rose system will also make more use of modern MMI techniques, for example to allow subexpressions to be selected directly from the theorem prover screen, to reduce the amount of information that needs to be repeatedly typed.

The micro-Gypsy tools are to be integrated with the Boyer-Moore theorem prover to provide a powerful environment for solving problems in limited applications areas. The emphasis then is on achieving much higher levels of assurance for small systems.

However, it seems that more can still be done for Gypsy to make it applicable more widely and to system development projects of slightly greater complexity than have so far been attempted.

The infancy of verification techniques (indeed the apparent introspective nature of verification research) coupled with the lack of suitably qualified software engineers and auditors imposes a ceiling on the levels of trustworthiness which are currently realizable. But to put the apparent urgency of this problem in perspective, it would seem fair to point out that other technologies must also mature. For example, trusted database management systems must be developed, suitably structured for the emerging verification technology to be readily applied.

In the meantime it seems that software of only relatively small size can be proven correct. Such software is routinely embedded in safety-critical systems, where the (small) software component often represents the only software component. This contrasts with the size and complexity of distributed secure office automation systems. The technology already used to give A1 assurance in secure systems, and that which is being developed for higher assurance, must surely find a place in other types of projects; for example, providing confidence in the dependability of software which controls physical systems and which may put life at risk if it malfunctions. We view verification technology in this more general setting, that is the production of the high-integrity software needed for the development of safety-critical software.

Consider what might be done to the Gypsy language in order to make it more widely applicable, and how the GVE could be enhanced to reduce the often prohibitive costs of formal proof. As pointed out in section 4.2, variant records are not accommodated by the syntax of the language, which is consistent with the widely held view that these are not "type safe" in Pascal. However, the lack of any type union construct (such as that found in Z) is disappointing in Gypsy, as this precludes the prescription of abstract syntaxes of formal languages by mutually recursive rules. To put this in a more general problem solving context, Gypsy cannot describe tree structures.

So any attempt to develop tools (formally) for development systems—such as Gypsy itself—would be severely limited. Even descriptions of less-grand concepts, such as alternative message formats in communications protocols for instance, must resort to clumsy structures. The introduction of type safe unions into specification and programming languages is an area which needs attention if all the data modelling potential of mathematics is to be realized in mastering the complexity of software.

Mathematical abstractions, such as sets, sequences and mappings, are provided within Gypsy, both for specification purposes and for imperative programming. Once an abstraction is chosen for program specification purposes, then that abstraction must also be used as the basis of the implementation. This is why the above structure manipulating commands are provided. Essentially, the specifier is constraining the programmer to the chosen data types, because Gypsy provides no means for recording multiple representations of data types. This argument was expanded in section 4.6, but the point is that Gypsy is seen primarily as a program verification method, and not so much a system development method. The provision of mathematical set theoretic abstraction types therefore seems inappropriate, if the programmer is bound to rely upon standard implementations.

The purpose of designing a program is to exploit properties of the target machine/environment in delivering an efficient implementation of the required system, and this is not supported by Gypsy. Using the Gypsy mathematical types and their associated commands in imperative programs is really "rapid prototyping". This distinction could be made useful. It would seem appropriate, given the complexity of the proof process, to permit programmers to run programs on simple test data, before attempting proof. This might remove many trivial errors, before the cost of proof is met. Similarly, it would seem appropriate for the specifier to run (certain restricted) specifications, before coding and proof is begun, in order to gain confidence that the specification captures adequately the intended behaviour.

One could even conceive of running the specification and the code in parallel, and to have the respective results checked automatically. Moving a stage further, the techniques of structural/dynamic testing [see chapter 7] could be used to record not only code coverage metrics, but also specification coverage metrics (given a suitable notion of specification coverage). The presence of both sets of results for suitably equivalent test data sets might lead to further pre-proof information. For instance the knowledge that the test set "covers" 100% of the code, but only 10% of the specification, should reveal incompleteness in the function of the implementation. It is even plausible that such objective testing might be adequate in less critical projects.

Moving back to the current GVE, it is widely recognized that one key to increased productivity in software engineering is reusability. The GVE supports re-usability in a limited way by permitting pending definitions (especially of types). However, a type instantiation method is not supported, so theory re-use usually means editing source code.

A particular set of programs and their theorems/proofs is a theory, which might be useful in a number of contexts. It would therefore seem reasonable to include that theory in the current application theory, but without having to re-parse all of its text files, and re-prove all of the theorems. Even if this were possible, the GVE as currently arranged would merge this information in a single database, which could not be subsequently split back into the base theory and application theory databases. A feature of this kind is necessary if all users of a theory are to benefit from theory enhancements.

It seems that the process of formal verification requires a database of the level of sophistication that most current Relational Database Management Systems (RDBMS) already offer. The only extra feature not already provided by such products, of course, is storage for program units, VCs and proof logs.

The potential is then for a large project development environment, with many databases used concurrently by teams of developers, perhaps one per module. The RDBMS kernels provide the mechanism of "views" to filter out irrelevant parts of a system design from a particular developer's point of view. Beyond this even, the system administrator could deny all access privileges to all units needed by each user, only permitting access to certain views of the total verification environment. This project support automation is really a step towards facilitating formal verification in the large, and is certainly not implemented by the GVE. Indeed, the concept of different users, concurrent or otherwise, is not addressed by GVE. However, this discussion at least serves to put the current GVE's contribution into perspective, i.e. that of verifying small systems (less than 3000 lines of code).

The GVE is relatively advanced in its integration of verification tools, much more so than many other verification systems. However, the developers of Integrated Programming Support Environments (IPSEs) have already addressed many of the issues of management visibility and configuration control. The incorporation of these tools into IPSE products seems a natural next step: in other words, to refashion the Gypsy database and tools into a proprietary or open IPSE product. This advance would at least provide the infrastructure to support verification in the large, although the base technology may be too immature for this purpose.

One might question whether or not the underlying approach, i.e. of imperative programs, VCGs, first-order logic assertions, etc., is the real limiting factor. For example, constructing loop invariants from entry and exit specifications is a nontrivial task (consider nested loops). For this reason, it is often preferable to write recursive programs, which yield fewer verification conditions. Recursive procedures have the advantage of not requiring loop invariant predicates to be constructed by the user. The proofs of these verification conditions tend to be more natural too, in that their inductive structure closely resembles the recursive structure of the programs. In the production of safety-critical software, many practitioners argue that recursive programs are unsatisfactory, because of the possibility of runtime stack overflow. However, given the mathematical simplicity of proving recursive programs, quite apart from the elegance of a recursive solution, it seems more fruitful to encourage developers to write recursive software, and to have that systematically transformed to an equivalent non-recursive form for operational purposes. The onus here lies with the developers of verification methods to produce transformation techniques, with the requisite tool support.

There is then an added burden of providing assurance that these and other (e.g. compiler) transformation tools preserve the semantics of the original program. This raises the issue of verified development environments (beyond A1), but it seems more pressing that the few people already skilled in the application of verification techniques apply these to more publicly visible applications, partly to testify that the methods themselves are feasible, but also to raise awareness levels in the industry, and so grow a skill base of verification expertise. This clearly takes priority over introspective exercises in producing industrialized trusted verification systems. That is not to say that the concept of formally verifying verification systems (bootstrapping) should not be carried on an academic scale, perhaps to pre-empt foundational problems. But the industry is firstly concerned with achieving high assurance levels, and this requires not absolute confidence in the verification technology but abstract software facilities for managing software verification after specifying complex systems using powerful notations.

Finally, experience with the interactive theorem prover has led to concern over the lack of control the user has over the ordering of subgoals. Although the user may regress back up a proof, and may reorder conjuncts in hypotheses or conclusions, it is not possible to suspend the proof of one subgoal, and then attempt another subgoal of the same theorem. By concentrating (or perhaps struggling) too hard on details of one branch of the proof tree, the overall shape of the proof often becomes lost. The proof tree facilities are particularly useful in this situation, but the depth-first proof paradigm should be questioned. By analogy with structured programming, it is more satisfactory to first sketch a proof outline of the major steps involved and then to expand the details of each major step in isolation. The authors have encouraged this approach by writing proof outlines on paper before entering a proof session, but the tool provides no mechanism for moving across branches in the tree, to create a frontier of subgoals to be proven.

Many of our suggestions in this section have concentrated on broadening the position of Gypsy on the verification and validation spectrum. For instance, the use of structural testing techniques on specifications and code increases analytical power whilst decreasing cost, and our wish for more and better specification data types improves the expressive power of the notation, and makes Gypsy more applicable throughout the development life-cycle.

4.8 Conclusions

In this chapter we have introduced the Gypsy approach to formal verification, and illustrated how the Gypsy Verification Environment provides support for all aspects of the development of verified programs.

Gypsy should be viewed primarily as a source code verification system that provides a high degree of automated assistance to the developer of small chunks of simple but critical software. Although Gypsy has been enhanced for example with notation for data abstraction which is essential for system-level specification, the seemingly powerful linguistic additions are not yet sufficiently supported by the GVE to make Gypsy widely applicable to the entire formal development life-cycle.

Within these limitations, it is clear that Gypsy represents the most successful program verification system developed to date, and is a vital benchmark against which to measure the next generation of industrial specification and verification systems.

Acknowledgement
The authors are grateful to Matthew Arcus for putting the Search example through the Gypsy Verification Environment.

References

[Akers83] Akers, R. L., *A Gypsy-to-Ada Program Compiler*, Report No. 39, Institute for Computing Science, University of Texas at Austin (1983).

[CIP85] CIP Language Group, *The Munich Project Vol I: The Wide Spectrum Language CIP-L*, Springer Verlag, Lecture Notes in Computer Science 183 (1985).

[Crowe86] Crowe, J., et al, *SRI Specification and Verification System User's Guide*, SRI, Menlo Park (1986).

[Floyd67] Floyd, R., "Assigning meaning to programs", *Mathematical Aspects of Computer Science* (Ed. J. T. Schwartz), American Mathematical Society (1967).

[Good86] Good, D. I., et al, *Report of Gypsy 2.05*, Institute for Computing Science, University of Texas at Austin (1986).

[Hoare78] Hoare, C. A. R., "An axiomatic basis for computer programming", *CACM*, vol. 12, no. 10 (1978).

[Jensen75] Jensen, K. and Wirth, N., *Pascal User Manual and Report*, Springer Verlag (1975).

[Jones86]   Jones, C. B., *Systematic Software Development Using VDM*, Prentice Hall (1986).

[Lampson77]   Lampson, B. W., et al, *Report on the Programming Language Euclid*, ACM SIGPLAN Notices, vol. 12, no. 2 (1977).

[Martin-Lof82]   Martin-Lof, P., "Constructive mathematics and computer programming", in *Logic, Methodology and Philosophy of Science VI*, North Holland, Amsterdam (1982).

[Smith88]   Smith, L., *Using the Gypsy-to-Bliss Translator*, Note 123, Institute for Computing Science, University of Texas at Austin (1988).

[Warren77]   Warren, D. H. D. and Pereira, L. M., "PROLOG—the language and its implementation compared with LISP", *Proceedings of the Symposium on Artificial Intelligence and Programming Languages* ACM SIGPLAN Notices, vol. 12, no. 8 (1977).

[Woodcock88]   Woodcock, J. and Loomes, M., *Software Engineering Mathematics*, Pitman, London (1988) and Addison-Wesley, Reading, Ma., USA (1989).

5 Reliable programming in standard languages

Bernard Carré, Program Validation Limited

5.1 Introduction

The designers of programming languages are presented with many, often conflicting, requirements; support for high-integrity programming is only one of them. As an extreme example, in the case of C, aimed at convenience of use and efficiency for low-level systems programming, it is clear that formal verification was not a major preoccupation. The design of Ada was obviously more professional, but its expressive power and generality were only achieved at great cost in complexity; in consequence, it too suffers from many ambiguities and insecurities.

Our purpose here is to consider the extent to which it is nevertheless possible to use "standard" imperative languages such as Pascal and Ada in a reliable way—for at the moment the only alternative is to use assembly code, which is feasible only for very small systems. The ultimate aim of course, is to find ways of producing verifiable software. It will be assumed that programs are to be developed by professionals, supported by whatever tools are available, and that if necessary substantial resources will be expended in achieving high integrity of software prior to its application; but the problems involved in proving its fitness for purpose must be tractable, in practical terms.

Previous chapters have already discussed requirements capture and the formal specification of programs; this one is primarily concerned with their code implementation. But clearly, to assess the value of a programming language for high-integrity work we must consider much more than the possible abuses of goto statements and pointers: the programming activity must be viewed in the context of the entire software development process. Thus the ease with which a formal specification, in VDM or Z for instance, can be formally related to a program design, and its code implementation, is a very important consideration. We must also remember that our ultimate concern is with the fitness for purpose of the binary code which will actually be executed: this must be guaranteed, either through the use of a formally

verified translator (compiler or assembler), or by verifying the correspondence between source and binary.

The next section discusses our requirements of a programming language
from all these aspects. In fact the requirements are not met by any existing
programming language, taken in its entirety. The only immediate solution to
this problem is to select, from current "standard" languages, the ones best
suited to our purposes, and to ensure that they are employed in a dependable
way. This will be achieved by, for instance, forbidding the use of their
unsatisfactory features, adding annotations ("formal comments") to resolve
language ambiguities, and providing tools to help the validation of programs
in these restricted languages. Section 5.4 explains how this has been done for
Pascal and Ada, and the final section discusses the effectiveness of our
approach, in the light of practical experience.

5.2   Language requirements for high-integrity programming

5.2.1   Logical soundness

The first essential, for strict reasoning about a program to be possible, is that
the programming language be logically coherent and unambiguous, with
formally-defined semantics.

Already we are in difficulty, for although a few programming languages
have been formally designed (see for instance [Craigen1987]), all the
"standard" languages available to us were initially developed informally;
their early quite imprecise definitions suffered from severe imperfections.
The more important ones have undergone considerable refinement, the
discoveries of their deficiencies and of ways of rectifying these having come
partly through experience of using the languages, partly through attempts to
construct their formal definitions retrospectively. However, in all cases quite
serious problems remain. Our choice of standard languages and the extent to
which we "prune" them will largely be dictated by the need for language
kernels that are logically sound yet with formal definitions in consonance
with their usual informal interpretations, and in particular the interpretations of compiler authors!

5.2.2   Complexity of formal language definition

A formal definition of a programming language is essential to underpin the
informal language description which may be needed for everyday use. And
of course in high-integrity programming, the formal definition is the
necessary foundation for reasoning about programs, and the basis of all
tools for processing the language, such as compilers and formal verification
tools.

If the formal definition of a language is extremely large (as in the case of

Ada [CEC1987], for which it runs to eight volumes), the logical coherence of the language itself becomes very hard to establish; its complexity precludes the social processes essential to its justification and eventual refinement [De Millo1979]. Reasoning about programs will also become convoluted and uncertain, and formal tool development impractical. In the design of SPARK (the SPADE Ada Kernel), some Ada features such as derived types were discarded not because they were logically inconsistent in themselves, but in the belief that the complexities they introduced were not justified.

Features which substantially complicate a formal definition do require close scrutiny however. In their formal definition of Pascal, Andrews and Henhapl [1982] noted that "the problems caused by variant records, both in the formal definition and in the 'safe' implementation of Pascal, imply that they are not a good concept". In the initial formalization of Ada [Bundgaard/Schultz1980; Pederson1980] and the definition of ANNA (a language for annotating Ada programs [Luckham1987]), it again emerged that the language features which caused most difficulty were those which are the most problematic in practice and the hardest to implement in compilers. None of this is very surprising. Rather alarming though is the fact that an unsatisfactory language feature, asking to be removed from a formal definition, can often be described informally with beguiling simplicity. To the casual reader of a book on Pascal, variant records will seem rather nice.

As has already been mentioned, our ultimate concern is the fitness for purpose of binary code. No formally-verified compilers exist for standard languages (because they are too complex), and although we may be relatively confident of compilers which have passed validation tests, such tests are not stringent enough for safety-critical work. In any case, real-time control software invariably uses some implementation-dependent features, such as Ada address clauses. In some applications it is still desirable, therefore, to verify formally the consistency between source and object code. Correctness proofs have been constructed for modules of *manually*-produced assembly code [O'Neill1988], against the module specifications, and tentative experiments have confirmed that the proof of correspondence between source and compiled code is also possible. However, the correspondence between program variables and memory addresses must be known, and the code generators must employ quite simple mappings from source to object code. A requirement to perform such code verification imposes quite severe, but not intolerable, constraints on the high-level language design (precluding, for instance, any features whose implementation imposes the use of dynamic heap storage allocation). SPADE-Pascal and SPARK meet this requirement.

5.2.3 Expressive power

Historically, we have seen the gradual enrichment of programming languages, with the inclusion of structured statements, then strong typing and support for procedural or operational abstraction, and more recently, "modules" or "packages" supporting data abstraction, and "specification" parts of subprograms and packages distinct from their code bodies. The aim clearly has been " ... to transfer more and more of the work of producing a correct program, and verifying that it is consistent with its specification, from the programmer and verifier (human or mechanical) to the language and its compiler" [Lampson1977]. Indeed, as such features have been incorporated, progressively more of the information which previously would have been regarded as "specification" or "design documentation" has been captured in the "executable code". The task of showing that programs perform their intended functions, formerly requiring very extensive testing, has thereby been transformed to a significant extent into the checking that the programs obey the syntactic and "static" semantic rules of their languages, which can mostly be done mechanically.

Obviously, the ease with which a specification can be "refined" systematically towards an implementation depends very much on the expressive power of the programming language. (Indeed, it was the need of support for data abstraction in such refinement, which is not provided by Pascal, that originally led to the development of SPARK.) Expressive power is limited however, by considerations of complexity and by the essential requirement of language security, which is discussed in the next section.

5.2.4 Security

An *insecurity* is a feature of a programming language whose implementation makes it impossible, or even very difficult, to detect some violation of the language rules, by mechanical analysis of a program's text (rather than its execution).

It has always been considered important to detect and report language violations, but until recently such errors have been viewed very much in terms of the practical capabilities of compilers: language errors have been classified as "compilation errors" (covering syntactic and static semantic errors) and "run-time errors" (including for instance range violations of values of dynamically-evaluated expressions). Whilst attempts are made to detect as many errors as possible at compilation time, their detection at run-time has usually been regarded as a tolerable alternative. In a safety-critical real-time system however, even a well-signalled run-time error could have disastrous consequences; for our purposes *all* language violations must be detectable prior to program execution.

All standard programming languages suffer from insecurities [Welsh/ Sneeringer/Hoare1977; Wichmann1988b]. Some language errors can be almost impossible to detect even at run-time. For instance, in Ada it is possible to employ an illegal order of elaboration of compilation units, without an indication of this error being given. As another example, in the interests of efficiency the Ada language allows parameter passing of non-scalar values to be by copy or by reference, which can give different results if parameter passing by reference causes aliasing. The Ada language reference manual states that "The language does not define which of these mechanisms is to be adopted for parameter passing, nor whether different calls to the same subprogram are to use the same mechanism. The execution of a program is erroneous if its effect depends on which mechanism is selected by the implementation." In practice, detection of this dependence is almost impossible.

To make matters worse, in a number of respects the rules of standard languages are in any case not strict enough for high-integrity programming. As a simple example, if a function subprogram has side-effects then different "legal" orders of evaluation of an expression referring to the function may give different results, so the result actually obtained may depend on the choice of compiler. An ISO-Pascal program suffering from this phenomenon would not be erroneous, according to the language definition, though it would certainly be *ambiguous*, i.e. of uncertain meaning. In Safe Ada [Holzapfel/Winterstein1988], there is a rule stating that functions shall have no side-effects; but since it is not possible automatically to detect all violations of this rule in Safe Ada (or in any of the standard languages), the ambiguity is simply replaced by an insecurity. Ada does not ban side-effects of functions, but it prohibits their various unfortunate consequences, which leads to eleven different insecurities [Wichmann1988b]. Playing with words cannot solve the essential problem: that for reliable programming, the rules of the programming language must be strong enough to allow the detection of all side effects, prior to program execution. The ways in which this has been achieved, in SPADE-Pascal and SPARK, will be described below.

It would be impossible to catalogue here the many different kinds of language error that may go undetected, but the most common and dangerous of all, the use of an uninitialized variable, merits some comment. It is of particular concern because the validity of our program proofs, which are based on classical rather than three-valued logic, depends on all referenced values being defined. Again, the rules of standard languages are not strict enough for it to be possible to capture all such errors prior to program execution; their detection by run-time checks is also unreliable. A solution will be described to this problem also.

Some program errors, such as range violations of values of dynamically evaluated expressions, will inevitably be hard to detect prior to program execution. To overcome this kind of problem (and some of its other foibles), Ada has *exceptions*. For instance, when a computed array index is out of range, a CONSTRAINT_ERROR exception is raised: and if one anticipates that a particular kind of exception may occur in a part of a program one can write an "exception handler" there, defining a recovery action for it. Programmers may define and use their own exceptions. Unfortunately we have some objections to this concept. An exception is, after all, a run-time error. In our opinion it is easier and more satisfactory to write a program which is exception-free, and prove it to be so, than to prove that the corrective action taken by exception-handlers would be appropriate under all possible circumstances. If checks with recovery actions are required, these can still be introduced without resorting to exception handlers, and in general the embedded code will be easier to verify.

Quite the opposite approach to that of Ada is taken in NewSpeak [Currie1986], whose author describes it as "an unexceptional language". In his view, a language for high-integrity programming should be designed in such a way that it is secure, with all errors being detectable, automatically, in the course of compilation. For instance, uninitialized variables cannot cause any problems in NewSpeak, because they do not exist: all variables are initialized when they are declared.

As the reader will see in the following sections, our own position is quite close to that of Currie in many respects. Our language definitions are inevitably less restrictive, since they are based on standard languages. However SPARK is secure insofar as all violations of the language can be detected prior to run time, with the exception of range errors, by fast (polynomial-time) algorithms provided in SPADE tools. Range checking involves formal proof; the associated theorems will be generated automatically and proven using the SPADE proof-checker, in much the same way as verification conditions.

5.2.5   Verifiability

Chapter 2 introduced the notion of *refinement* of specifications, whereby correctness of a program is guaranteed through its rigorous construction from its specification, by repeated application of transformation rules. The chapter also discussed the important question of what form the implementation language should take, for refinement to be reliable, and also "natural".

The need to be able to demonstrate correctness of the process, by logical reasoning, is why we have made formal definition an essential requirement of a programming language. The simplicity of the definition determines whether verification will be feasible in practice. (Our experience, like that of Sennett, is that the scope for formal verification is restricted not by lack of expressive power, but by the complexity of the theorems to be proved.) Security helps ensure that the results of refinement have well-defined semantics.

In section 2.3 it was stated that "Refinement is concerned with reasoning about fragments of programs with respect to fragments of specification...". The major problem we have to face is that, in standard languages, it is almost impossible to reason about program fragments out of context. In the next section on SPADE-Pascal it will be explained how methods of "encapsulating" subprograms had to be found, making explicit the transaction between these and their environments, so that language violations would be easier to detect. The adopted form of subprogram encapsulation has also simplified verification considerably. This is not very surprising, since the search for language violations involves logical reasoning too (even when it can be mechanized), and the achievement of it required the "separation of concerns". SPADE-Pascal has been used to implement small systems from VDM specifications [Bromell/Sadler1987].

Whilst operation refinement to SPADE-Pascal may be feasible, it would be impossible to achieve data refinement satisfactorily in this language. SPARK was designed to support data abstraction, by means of Ada's package feature and private types (which can be used to hide concrete interpretations); an example will be given below. It was still not possible to isolate program fragments satisfactorily however; by far the most difficult part of the design of SPARK was the simplification and refinement of Ada's very complicated scope and visibility rules, to meet this requirement.

5.2.6   Bounded space and time requirements

In real-time control applications it is necessary to establish that the memory requirements of a program will not exceed that available. This is a strong argument for not employing language features whose implementation involves dynamic heap storage allocation. (We have already given other reasons for not employing these, in section 5.2.2.) All constraints should be statically determinable. It may be necessary also to bound the depth of procedure calls to calculate the space required for these, but this problem should be tractable.

To ensure that execution times are satisfactory, bounds on numbers of loop iterations should be obtained by proof methods, similar in nature to proofs of termination. If execution times are critical, uncertain behaviour of garbage-collection mechanisms may be another reason for not using features which require dynamic heap storage allocation.

5.3   The use of standard languages

5.3.1   Why use standard languages?

If standard languages suffer from so many ambiguities and insecurities, is there any point in trying to use them at all, for high-integrity programming? Would it not be better to start afresh, and formally design a new language specifically for this purpose? Quite a number of languages have been developed with this aim, of which the best-known are probably Gypsy [Ambler1977] and Euclid [Lampson1977]. Most recently, this approach has been followed in NewSpeak [Currie1986] and m-Verdi [Craigen1987]. None of the earlier languages were widely adopted. They were produced at a time when ideas on systematic program construction were still developing rapidly (as they still are!) and, indeed, they contributed substantially to these developments. But before these languages could mature they were overtaken by events, of which the most significant was probably DoD's adoption of Ada. The notion persists however, for good reason. Chapter 6 describes NewSpeak in some detail.

At the same time, there are strong pragmatic arguments for using standard languages where possible. High-integrity programming in any language requires powerful, reliable support tools. Compilers in particular, if they are not verified, should at least be subjected to extensive validation tests. A great deal of good documentation and pedagogical effort is also required. And since even logicians are fallible, we must have a large community of users, exploring all the features of the language and exercising its support tools in the most eccentric ways. With the science of programming still in full evolution, the political problems in thus "establishing" a new language seem very severe.

Finally, our motive here is not simply to create a language appropriate for achieving total correctness in a few restricted spheres of application. The need for better software engineering is reaching crisis proportions in most areas, civil and military: many programmers must be trained (and sometimes coaxed) into using new methods. Fortunately the additional rules imposed by our annotated subsets of standard languages can largely be regarded as rather strict design and documentation rules, and rules of "good style". New languages point the way; adaptations of standard languages persuade people to follow.

5.3.2   The choice of a "host" language

Some languages are more suitable for high-integrity programming than others obviously. (For informal but nevertheless very helpful comparative studied see [Cullyer/Goodenough1987], and [Wichmann1988a]). Appropriate high-level languages, for which annotated subsets have been defined to allow formal verification, include Pascal [Carré/Debney1985] and Ada [Carré/Jennings1988]. Modula-2 could become another candidate, when its formal definition is completed and its BSI validation service established, though commercial considerations may inhibit its adoption in favour of Ada. C is quite unsatisfactory for high-integrity programming [Feuer-/Gehani1982]. It is not well enough defined, it does not provide enough protection for the user, and it is insecure: if one removed its dangerous features, little would remain.

When a host has been chosen, the next problem is to extract a sublanguage meeting the requirements discussed in Section 5.2. The following sections explain how this was done for Pascal and Ada.

5.4 Programming in Pascal and Ada

5.4.1 SPADE-Pascal

The first "semi-official' definition of Pascal was the "User Manual and Report" by Jensen and Wirth [1974]. This was quite informal, and incomplete and defective in a number of ways. However, the formal basis of the language was studied by many people, particularly important contributions being the axiomatic description of Pascal by Hoare and Wirth [1973], and its definition by Tennent [1981]. This work clarified a number of doubtful points, and drew attention to ambiguities and insecurities in the original version [see Welsh/Sneeringer/Hoare1977].

Most of these problems were eliminated in producing the language specification for the British Standards Institution [BSI1982], which has been adopted as an ISO standard. A formal definition of Pascal, as described informally by the ISO standard, was written in VDM by Andrews and Henhapl [1982]. The standard is also supported by a "model compiler implementation", written in the style of a book, whose code is in ISO-Pascal [Welsh/Hay1986], and a Pascal compiler validation suite [Wichmann/Ciechanowicz1983].

The derivation of SPADE-Pascal from this standard began with the elimination, piecemeal, of some language features whose use was considered particularly "dangerous", or which could make formal verification extremely difficult. As has been mentioned already, variant records caused great difficulty in the formal definition of Pascal, and it was therefore not surprising to find that we could not model their use in SPADE's functional description language, FDL. (This language, used to model programs for analysis purposes, will be described in chapter 8.) In practice, misuses of Pascal's variant records are notoriously difficult to detect, and in fact they provide a popular way of defeating the language's strong typing rules; we had no hesitation in eliminating this feature. The use of functions and procedures as parameters was also excluded, because of verification problems. Pointer types were removed with some regret, but it was found impossible to provide adequate protection against the aliasing and other insecurities associated with them.

Whilst the removal of these language features seemed essential, we could not eliminate all Pascal's defects simply by removing constructs which could be abused: there were too many of them and, eventually, impoverishment of the language would also make its use unreliable. As an illustration of our dilemma, support for procedural abstraction was obviously essential, if programs were to be verifiable; the ability to use function subprograms, in the sure knowledge that these could not have side-effects,was also very desirable. However in ISO-Pascal programs, the data transactions between a subprogram and its calling environment may not be at all obvious: some uses

110

of undefined variables, aliasing through parameter passing and side effects of function subprograms are extremely difficult to detect.

This problem was solved by introducing annotations (or formal comments) to the language, for describing the information flow between each subprogram and its calling environment, and adding some language rules to impose consistency between these annotations and the executable code. SPADE-Pascal annotations are ISO-Pascal comments (begining with the symbol #, as in figure 5.1), so the declarative and executable statements of a SPADE-Pascal program have precisely the same meaning as in ISO-Pascal; a SPADE-Pascal program can be compiled by any conformant ISO-Pascal compiler. To describe the information flow through a procedure, its heading is immediately followed by annotations of the following kinds (illustrated in Figure 5.1). If any of the variables whose values are "imported"or "exported" by a procedure are global variables rather than formal parameters, these must be named in a *global definition* of the procedure. Every procedure also has a mandatory *dependency relation*: this specifies which variables are imported, which are exported, and which (initial values of) imported variables may be required to derive (the final value of) each exported variable.

To guarantee consistency between these annotations and the executable code, SPADE-Pascal has rules which prescribe how global variables and parameters can be used, depending on whether they are imported or exported. For instance one of these rules, needed to prevent side-effects, states that a variable which is imported but not exported by a subprogram cannot be modified by the subprogram. Another rule, designed to prevent one form of aliasing, states that an identifier cannot occur both as an actual variable parameter and as a global variable of a procedure, if either the corresponding formal parameter or the global variable is exported. Conformance to these rules is checked by the SPADE-Pascal to FDL translator (which is rather like a compiler, except that it produces FDL models of programs rather than object code). Finally, it is of course essential to check mechanically that, for each procedure, the dependency relation truly describes the information flow which results from execution of the procedure body (for otherwise we would simply be introducing a new kind of insecurity!). This is done by another SPADE tool, the *information-flow analyser,* which computes the dependencies of the final value of each variable on the initial values of all variables, in the manner described by Bergeretti and Carré [1985].

It is important to note here that, since consistency between the annotations and code of a procedure can be checked, these annotations can be employed, rather than the code, in determining the information flow in routines which call the procedure. (The details are given by Bergeretti and Carré [1985].) Thus all side-effects and instances of aliasing that could arise through procedure calls and function references can easily be detected, at all levels in a hierarchy of subprograms.

```pascal
const VectorLength = 100;
type  IndexRange   = 1 .. VectorLength;
      Vector       = array[IndexRange] of Real;

procedure Interchange(var A : Vector; M, N : IndexRange);
{ This procedure transfers the contents of A[1] ... A[M] into A[N+1] ... A[N+M] while
simultaneously transferring the contents of A[M+1] ... A[M+N] into A[1] ... A[N] without
using an appreciable amount of auxiliary memory.  It is a Pascal version of
Algorithm 284: Interchange of two blocks of data, by W. Fletcher, Comm. ACM, vol. 9
(1966), p. 326.  The ACM publication explains the basis of the algorithm.}
  {# derives A from A, M, N;}
  var D, I, J, K, R : Integer;  T : Real;

  function GCD(X, Y : Integer) : Integer;
     var C, D, R : Integer;
  begin {GCD}
     C := X; D := Y;
     while D <> 0 do
        begin
           R := C mod D;
           C := D; D := R
        end;
     GCD := C
  end {GCD};

  procedure Swap(var TempVal : Real;  Index : IndexRange);
  { This procedure interchanges the values of TempVal and A[Index]. }
     {# global A;
        derives A         from A, TempVal, Index &
                TempVal from A, Index;}
     {# hide }
     {Text here is ignored by the SPADE-Pascal translator, but the translator will report
     that this block is hidden.  The block could be as follows:}
     var T : Real;
     begin T := A[Index]; A[Index] := TempVal;  TempVal := T  end;
     {# seek }

begin {Interchange}
  D := GCD(M, N);
  R := (M + N) div D;
  for I := 1 to D do
     begin
        J := I;
        T := A[I];
        for K := 1 to R do
           begin
              if J <= M then J := J + N else J := J - M;
              Swap(T, J)
           end
     end
end {Interchange};
```

Fig. 5.1 An extract from a SPADE-Pascal program, illustrating the use of global definitions, dependency relations, and hide-and-seek

As well as improving the security of the programming language, these procedure annotations serve another important purpose. The dependency relation of a procedure is derived from the procedure's specification, or design document (which should obviously specify the procedure's inputs and outputs, and how they are related). Thus, in mechanically checking that the text of a procedure obeys the rules of SPADE-Pascal, one is also checking that its executable code is consistent with its specification or design documents, at least with respect to information flow. This is a useful prelude to the much more onerous task of formal verification, since experience indicates that a large proportion of program errors can be detected by mechanical flow analysis; finding these errors through unsuccessful proof attempts would be much more difficult and eventually rather depressing.

It will be noted furthermore that the use of dependency relations in place of code, to determine information flow resulting from procedure calls, makes it possible in principle to declare and specify a procedure, and analyse parts of the program which call it before "refining" the procedure itself. To support this kind of programming, which is appropriate in the systematic development of programs from specifications, a SPADE-Pascal text may contain "hide and seek" directives to conceal incomplete procedure bodies from the analysis tools. (Again, see figure 5.1) Obviously the tools will continually remind the programmer of the existence of hidden bodies, and the entire development process requires good configuration management.

The "weak specifications" described here go some way towards providing the kind of separability we need for verification, discussed in section 5.2.5. The idea can be taken further, by introducing subprogram pre- and post-conditions (and loop invariants) in the form of annotations. Using SPADE's verification-condition generator and its proof-checker, we can then prove correctness of a program, by proving separately the correctness of its constituent subprograms. This matter will be discussed in more detail in relation to SPARK (which, with its packages and private types, is better suited to formal proof).

SPADE-Pascal employs a few other annotations, to resolve ambiguities. For instance in SPADE-Pascal a set-constructor is always preceded by an annotation, giving the name of the type of set to be constructed. Some other rules are imposed simply to avoid unnecessary and potentially dangerous confusion (for example a rule prohibiting the redefinition of constant and type identifiers within their own scope).

5.4.2 SPARK — the SPADE Ada Kernel

Ada resulted from the efforts of the "Common High Order Language Program", set up by the United States Department of Defense in 1974. The requirements of the language were finalized in 1978, and the final language definition approved as an ANSI/MIL standard in 1983. Ada is a very large

113

language: development of a compiler is a major undertaking, and a draft formal definition, a very large set of documents, has only recently been completed [CEC1987]. Thus, in contrast with Pascal, the language was standardized before it could be widely implemented and used, or subjected to much formal analysis. Some of the defects which subsequently came to light have been rectified (by the issue of "binding interpretations" of the official language definition), but the resolution of all the uncertainties raised to date (and 550 of them have been catalogued) will take until 1990. The language is currently being extensively reviewed, with the object of producing a revised standard in the nineteen-nineties; it is our impression that the wording of the standard definition may be improved significantly by this process, but that otherwise the language will change very little. Of course, clarification of the language definition would in itself be a major step forward; apart from unintentional obscurities, the definition was deliberately made "flexible" in places, so that implementations could be efficient in different environments. Unfortunately, in our terms this "flexibility" introduced ambiguities and insecurities. (For a frightening catalogue of Ada insecurities see [Wichmann1988b].) To produce the draft formal definition various uncertainties had to be resolved by its authors; but this definition has no official status.

On a more positive note, Ada has some very desirable features, not possessed by any other language likely to have widespread use. The designers of Ada were greatly influenced by experience with Pascal and its derivatives, and had the advantage of hindsight. At the centre of Ada is the core of Pascal, with some minor but nevertheless valuable improvements (for example in the form of the **case** and iterative constructs). Around this Ada has features such as packages to allow data abstraction and facilitate systematic program design. Some of these we regard as essential extensions to Pascal, for the rigorous construction of large programs from their specifications.

The question which naturally arises is whether it is possible to extract from the complete language a well-defined and logically coherent "kernel", containing these essential elements and little more. In our opinion, the core of Ada is sound. The contentious issues, the complexity and impediments to formal definition stem from Ada's more advanced features such as tasks and exception-handling, to name the most problematic. As confirmation of this, by 1980 formal definitions had already been produced for subsets of Ada [Bundgaard/Schultz1980; Pederson1980], which contained all but its most troublesome features (principally, separate compilation, generics, tasks and exceptions). Even in this work, "... the main problem in defining the static semantics turned out to be the handling of derived subprograms and the arranging of a proper model of the scope of predefined operators". We see little merit in derived types (other than integer and real types), and consider that overloading should be avoided wherever possible. In the hope that the outcome would therefore be positive, the development of an Ada subset for high-integrity programming was undertaken, which eventually resulted in SPARK [Carré/Jennings1988].

From the outset, a major concern in the design of SPARK was that it should not suffer from any of the uncertainties of the official Ada definition: features whose meaning was disputed in any way, or susceptible to change, were inadmissible. Furthermore, since the formal verification of Ada compilers is impossible, and their validation by testing could not possibly meet our integrity requirements, it would ultimately be essential to verify compiled SPARK programs against their source. SPARK would have to be quite small!

As for the development strategy, the complexity of Ada and of its many ambiguities and insecurities made it necessary to adopt a "constructive" approach initially, sketching out a kernel of essential features and then refining it, rather than trying to identify and "fix" problems one by one. To meet our requirements set out in section 5.2, it was decided at an early stage that the chosen kernel should consist essentially of the "Pascal core" of Ada, supplemented by packages, private types, functions with structured values, and the library system (with some restrictions). It would certainly exclude tasks, exceptions, derived types (other than integer and real types) and generic units, which would all make SPARK's formal definition intolerably complicated. The exclusion of tasking will not come as a surprise (its definition is in any case inadequate), and we have already given other reasons for eliminating exceptions (in section 5.2.4). Generics were removed with more reluctance; but they do not provide code re-usability as easily as one might imagine, since one should prove the correctness of every instantiation of a generic object, and they cause overloading.

The next strategic decision was that to achieve the essential simplicity of mappings from SPARK source to binary, the kernel would not contain any Ada features whose implementation imposed the use of dynamic heap storage allocation. (This would also ensure that space requirements could be bounded.) The decision excluded the use of access types which in any case posed severe problems of security and verifiability. The decision also eliminated dynamically constrained arrays, discriminants and recursion. In SPARK all constraints are statically determinable. It was also felt necessary to eliminate overloading as far as possible: in SPARK, overloading of character literals and enumeration literals is not allowed, and a user-defined subprogram may not overload any other subprogram.

Some security issues (such as protection against aliasing through parameter-passing, the use of undefined values, and side-effects of function subprograms), and problems of "encapsulation" of subprograms to allow their verification, were very similar to those encountered with Pascal. They were treated in a similar way by providing SPARK procedures with global definitions and dependency relations (see Figures 5.2 and 5.3), and introducing rules relating these to the executable code. Ada's block statements and renaming declarations were banned.

```
package GCD_Example is

--# proof function gcd(NATURAL, NATURAL) : NATURAL;

--# rule gcd(A, B) may_be_replaced_by gcd(B, A);
--# rule gcd(A, 0) may_be_replaced_by A;
--# rule gcd(A, A) may_be_replaced_by A;
--# rule gcd(A mod B, B) may_be_replaced_by gcd(A, B) if B /= 0;

procedure ExtGCD(m, n : in POSITIVE; x, y, z : out INTEGER);
--# derives x from m, n &
--#         y from m, n &
--#         z from m, n;
--# pre  (m > 0) and (n > 0);
--# post (x = gcd(m, n)) and (x = y * m + z * n);

end GCD_Example;


package body GCD_Example is

procedure ExtGCD(m, n : in POSITIVE; x, y, z : out INTEGER) is
   a1, a2, b1, b2, c, d, q, r, t : INTEGER;
begin
   a1 := 0;  a2 := 1;  b1 := 1;  b2 := 0;
   c := m;  d := n;
   while  d /= 0
   --# assert (c > 0) and (d >= 0) and (gcd(c, d) = gcd(m, n)) and
   --#        (a1 * m + b1 * n = d) and (a2 * m + b2 * n = c);
   loop
      q := c / d;  r := c mod d;
      c := d;  d := r;
      a2 := a2 - q * a1;  b2 := b2 - q * b1;
      t := a1;  a1 := a2;  a2 := t;
      t := b1;  b1 := b2;  b2 := t;
   end loop;
   x := c;  y := a2;  z := b2;
end ExtGCD;

end GCD_Example;
```

In SPARK, a comment which begins with the symbols --# forms part of an annotation. The first annotations in the package declare the gcd (greatest common divisor) proof function, needed to specify the subprogram, and define its properties (by rewrite rules, in the notation employed by SPADE's proof-checker). In the procedure specification, the pre- and post-conditions are expressed in FDL

Fig. 5.2 A SPARK version of the extended Euclid algorithm

```
--# proof type Seq_of_Int is sequence of Integer;
. . . . . .

package IntegerStacks is

   type Stack is limited private;

   --# proof const MaxStackLength : Integer;
   --# proof function AtoC_Stack(Seq_of_Int) : Stack;
   --# proof function CtoA_Stack(Stack) : Seq_of_Int;

   --# rule AtoC_Stack(CtoA_Stack(S)) may_be_replaced_by S;
   --# rule CtoA_Stack(AtoC_Stack(S)) may_be_replaced_by S;
   --# rule EmptyStack(S) may_be_replaced_by CtoA_Stack(S) = Seq_of_Int[ ];
   --# rule FullStack(S) may_be_replaced_by
   --#                        Length(CtoA_Stack(S)) = MaxStackLength;

   function EmptyStack(S : Stack) return Boolean;
   --# pre  true;
   --# post EmptyStack(S) = (CtoA_Stack(S) = Seq_of_Int[ ]);

   function FullStack(S : Stack) return Boolean;
   --# pre  true;
   --# post FullStack(S) = (Length(CtoA_Stack(S)) = MaxStackLength);

   procedure ClearStack(S : in out Stack);
   --# derives S from ;
   --# pre  true;
   --# post S = AtoC_Stack(Seq_of_Int[ ]);

   procedure Push(S : in out Stack; X : in Integer);
   --# derives S from S, X;
   --# pre  Length(CtoA_Stack(S)) < MaxStackLength;
   --# post S = AtoC_Stack(Seq_of_Int[X] @ CtoA_Stack(S~));

   procedure Pop(S : in out Stack; X : out Integer);
   --# derives S from S &
   --#         X from S;
   --# pre  CtoA_Stack(S) <> Seq_of_Int[ ];
   --# post S = AtoC_Stack(Nonfirst(CtoA_Stack(S~))) and
   --#      X = First(CtoA_Stack(S~));

private

   StackSize : constant Integer := 100;
   subtype IndexRange is Integer range 1 .. StackSize;
   type Vector is array(IndexRange) of Integer;
   subtype PointerRange is Integer range 0 .. StackSize;
   type Stack is
     record
        StackVector : Vector;
        StackPointer : PointerRange;
     end record;

end IntegerStacks;
```

To verify subprograms which employ the package, it is convenient to represent stacks abstractly by sequences. The function CtoA_Stack maps a concrete stack (whose representation is invisible outside the package) to an abstract one, i.e. a sequence. The function AtoC_Stack is the inverse of this mapping. In FDL, @ represents sequence concatenation, and S~ denotes the initial value of an imported variable S.

Fig. 5.3 A SPARK package specification, for stacks of integers

Much effort went into the simplification of Ada's very complicated scope and visibility rules relating to packages, and the elimination of ambiguity and side effects associated with package variables. The problems were eventually solved through some language restrictions and the introduction of further annotations: an *inherit clause* in a package declaration (to restrict penetration of the package to items specifically imported from other packages), and an *own variable clause* which may be required in a package specification (to make package variables visible to SPADE, i.e. to give them the appearance of global variables, and at the same time to restrict the reading and updating of such variables).

To support formal verification, a SPARK program may contain *proof contexts*, annotations to provide formal specifications of program units, somewhat similar to those of ANNA [Luckham/1987] and Asphodel [Hill1987]. The logical consistency of proof contexts with executable SPARK code can be checked by means of the SPADE verification-condition generator and proof-checker (which will be described in Chapter 8). In Figure 5.2 for instance, the procedure ExtGCD is specified by its *precondition and post-condition*, which in turn are expressed in terms of a *proof function*, gcd, declared in the package specification, and defined by means of rewrite rules. Using also the loop invariant in the procedure body, the SPADE tools can be used to generate and prove the verification conditions for the procedure. The formal specification of ExtGCD, and the properties of gcd, needed to prove correctness of subprograms which call ExtGCD, are visible wherever the procedure itself is visible. A model-based (Z-like) specification of a stack package is shown in Figure 5.3. Again, the proof contexts are visible wherever the stack type and its operations are visible, so that they can be employed in proving correctness of uses of the stack package.

We believe that SPARK meets the requirements set out in section 5.2 quite well, and even that it is easier to use, in a reliable way, than SPADE-Pascal. To confirm this, its formal definition is now being constructed; this will be much simpler even than the 1980 Ada subset definitions. A software tool, the SPARK Examiner, is currently being developed to support the language. As it parses a text, this tool performs information-flow analysis, checking that the annotations are consistent with the executable code. The Examiner also produces FDL models of SPARK source, so that SPADE's verification-condition generator and proof-checker can be used to construct correctness proofs. The FDL models provide for the automatic generation of theorems whose validity implies freedom from range errors.

The Examiner allows the temporary "hiding" of subprogram and package bodies, prior to their implementations: it can analyse the remaining "visible" parts of a program, using only the specifications and descriptive annotations of hidden parts. Thus the Examiner provides real support for systematic program development, by refinement of specifications and designs. The SPARK Examiner is being formally specified, implemented entirely in

SPARK (to allow it to analyse itself, and to show that SPARK has enough expressive power to be useful), and formally verified.

5.5 Practical experiences

Tool support for SPADE-Pascal was first introduced in 1985, since when the language has been used in a substantial number of safety-critical applications. We have been agreeably surprised by the acceptance, even popularity, of its system of annotations. As well as eliminating insecurities it provides useful documentation, all the more valuable because the programmer must keep it up to date!

In Wirth's original definition of Pascal there was a suggestion—no more, though it has since been greatly amplified by textbook authors—that in the interests of safety, where possible one should pass parameters by value rather than by reference; he also pointed out that passing large objects in this way can be expensive. We think this advice has had unfortunate consequences: it makes a virtue of writing procedures that tinker with large global objects, not passing them as parameters at all. SPADE's procedure dependency relations are about parameter-passing without fear; there is never any danger of mistakenly altering an imported-but-not-exported variable, so one can pass by reference freely, so one might as well pass large objects. This leads to a more functional style of programming, better suited to specification refinement.

Encouraged by these experiences, in SPARK we have extended the annotations, and placed these in the specification parts of packages and subprograms (separable from their bodies) as provided by Ada, which suit our purposes admirably. The result, without doubt, is a framework for rather rigorous *program design*. Some readers will wince, but there is no other name for it. We believe that to be able to construct sizeable programs rigorously, the notion of design will have to be made respectable again. That is why we are keen to produce a formal definition of SPARK, *including its annotation system*. To us this notion of rigorous design seems entirely compatible with Sennett's view of refinement—reasoning about fragments of program with respect to fragments of specification. It caters for the development of specifications and implementations in tandem, which may sometimes be inevitable and, dare we say it, perhaps even desirable.

Acknowledgements
This work was performed at Southampton University under MoD Contract Number D/ER1/9/4/2040/446/RSRE. The SPARK language was largely designed by Trevor Jennings of Southampton University. Figure 5.1 is taken from the SPADE-Pascal manual of Program Validation Ltd.

References

[Ambler1977]   Ambler, A. L. et al., "Gypsy: a language for specification and implementation of verifiable programs," *ACM SIGPLAN Notices*, 12, No. 3, pp. 1–10 (1977).

[Andrews/Henhapl1982]   Andrews, D. and Henhapl, W., "Pascal," in *Formal Specification and Software Development* (Eds. Bjorner, D. and Jones, C.), pp. 175–251, Prentice Hall.

[Bergeretti/Carré1985]   Bergeretti, J. F. and Carré, B. A., "Information-flow and data-flow analysis of while-programs," *ACM Trans. on Prog. Lang. and Syst.*, 7, pp. 37–61 (1985).

[BSI1982]   British Standards Institution, *Specification for Computer Programming Language Pascal, BS 6192: 1982.*

[Bromell/Sadler1987]   Bromell, J. Y. and Sadler, S. J., "A strategy for the development of safety-critical systems," in *Achieving Safety and Reliability with Computer Systems* (Ed. B. K. Daniels), pp. 1–13, Elsevier (1987).

[Bundgaard/Schultz1980]   Bundgaard, J. and Schultz, L., "A denotational (static) semantics method for defining Ada context conditions," in *Towards a Formal Description of Ada*, LNCS-98 (Eds. Bjorner D. and Oest O. N.), pp. 21–212, Springer Verlag (1980).

[Carré/Debney1985]   Carré, B. A. and Debney, C. W., *SPADE-PASCAL Manual*, Program Validation Limited (1985).

[Carré/Jennings1988]   Carré, B. A. and Jennings, T. J., *SPARK—the SPADE Ada Kernel*, Dept. of Electronics and Comp. Sci., University of Southampton (1988).

[CEC1987]   Commission of the European Communities, *The Draft Formal Definition of Ada*, Dansk Datamatik Center (1987).

[Craigen1987]   Craigen, D., *A Description of m-Verdi*, I. P. Sharp Technical Report TR-87-5420-02 (1987).

[Cullyer/Goodenough1987]   Cullyer, W. J. and Goodenough, S. J., *The choice of computer languages for use in safety-critical systems*, RSRE Memorandum 3946 (1987).

[Currie1986]   Currie, I. F., "NewSpeak—an unexceptional language," *Software Engineering Journal*, 1, pp. 170–6, IEE/BCS (1986).

[De Millo1979]   De Millo, R. A., Lipton, R. J. and Perlis, A. J., "Social processes and proofs of theorems and programs", *Comm. ACM*, 22, pp. 271–280 (1979).

[Feuer/Gehani1982]   Feuer, A. R. and Gehani, N. H., "A comparison of the programming languages C and Pascal", *ACM Computing Surveys*, 14, pp. 73–92 (1982).

[Hill1987]   Hill, A., *The formal specification and verification of reusable software components using Ada with Asphodel*, CEGB Report (1987).

[Hoare/Wirth1973]   Hoare, C. A. R. and Wirth, N., "An axiomatic description of the programming language Pascal", *Acta Informatica*, 2, pp. 335–355 (1973).

[Holzapfel/Winterstein1988]   Holzapfel, R. and Winterstein, G., "Ada in safety-critical applications," Ada-Europe Conference, Munich 1988.

[Jensen/Wirth1974]   Jensen, K. and Wirth, N., *Pascal User Manual and Report*, Springer Verlag (1974).

[Lampson 1977]   Lampson, B. W., Horning, J. J., London, R. L., Mitchell, J. G.

and Popek, G. L., "Report on the programming language Euclid", *ACM SIGPLAN Notices*, 12, No. 2 (1977).

[Luckham1987]   Luckham D. C., von Henke F. W., Krieg-Brueckner B. and Owe O., *ANNA—a Language for Annotating Ada Programs*, LNCS-260, Springer Verlag (1987).

[O'Neill1988]   O'Neill, I. M., Clutterbuck, D. L., Farrow, P. F., Summers, P. G. and Dolman W. G., "The formal verification of safety-critical assembly code," *Proceedings of SAFECOMP 88*, IFAC/IFIP International Symposium on Safety-Related Computers, (Fulda, November 1988).

[Pederson1980]   Pederson, J. S., "A formal semantics definition of sequential Ada," in *Towards a Formal Description of Ada*, LNCS-98 (Eds. Bjorner D. and Oest O. N.), Springer-Verlag, pp. 213–308 (1980).

[Tennent1981]   Tennent, R. D., *Principles of Programming Languages*, Prentice-Hall (1981).

[Welsh/Hay1986]   Welsh, J. and Hay, A., *A Model Implementation of Standard Pascal*, Prentice Hall (1986).

[Welsh/Sneeringer/Hoare1977]   Welsh, J., Sneeringer, W. J. and Hoare, C. A. R., "Ambiguities and insecurities in Pascal," *Software: Practice and Experience*, 7, pp. 685–696 (1977).

[Wichmann1988a]   Wichmann, B. A., "Notes on the security of programming languages," in *10th Advances in Reliability Technology Symposium* (Ed. Libberton G. P.), pp. 223–235, Elsevier (1988).

[Wichmann1988b]   Wichmann, B. A., *Insecurities in the Ada programming language: an interim report*, NPL Report DITC 122/88 (1988).

[Wichmann/Ciechanowicz1983]   Wichmann, B. A. and Ciechanowicz, Z. J. (Eds.), *Pascal Compiler Validation*, John Wiley (1983).

6 NewSpeak: a reliable programming language

I. F. Currie, Royal Signals and Radar Establishment

6.1 Introduction

Consider the following fragment of Pascal program for evaluating factorials:

i:=0; x:=1;

while i<n

begin i:=i+1;

x:=i*x

end

One could prove that this program does indeed implement $n!$ by the following reasoning. A useful invariant of the while-statement is $\{x = i!\}$. This is trivially proved by observing that $\{x = 1 = 0!\}$ initially and applying induction on i. Provided n is a positive integer, the loop will terminate with $i = n$ and hence the final value of x is $n!$. This proof could be formalized and even produced automatically by any one of a variety of program-proving systems.

Given this proof, one could be forgiven for assuming that this program is operationally correct. However, when I compile and run it, I find that $x = -25216$ at the end of the loop with $n = 8$. The reason for this patently wrong answer is not difficult to find. The machine running the program has a 16-bit word length and the Pascal compiler compiles integers as single words with all of the arithmetic as single-word 2's-complement operations and overflow has occurred. The mapping from Pascal to machine-code performed by the compiler has invalidated some of the assumptions made about the properties of integers in the proof. Note that getting an overflow trap does not improve the situation—I still have an unexpected result. To be satisfactory, the proof must take account of limitations imposed by both the

122

target machine and its compiler—the proof is *not* transportable between either different object machines or different compilers.

This disparity between the mathematical properties of numbers and their computer analogues can lead to quite amusing results. For example, since the sum of reciprocals of the natural numbers diverges, one would expect the following program to terminate:

i:=0; x:=0.0;

while *x < 16.0*

begin *i:=i+1;*

      x:=x+1/i

end

Once again, expectations are dashed by actually running the program on a machine using 32-bit floating point numbers as its representation of real numbers. The value of x stabilises at about 15.4 for positive i and so the program loops indefinitely. In fact, the count of i overflows, making it negative (in the absence of an overflow trap) and later positive again, without materially affecting the result. An unsophisticated user might assume that the value of (Σn^{-1}) actually converges to 15.4.

The finiteness of the computer can invalidate proofs in other ways, notably by exceeding limits imposed on space or time. For example, a recursive implementation of Ackerman's function will generally run out of storage space long before any numeric overflow occurs for quite small parameters. Also many apparently terminating algorithms are quite useless simply because they take too long for some input data. The timing problem is further exacerbated by the fact that most programming languages make it very difficult to estimate an upper bound of time required to evaluate a piece of program. If the specification of a program requires that a particular action must be performed within a given time, the programmer has little option but to test and analyse the program exhaustively and hope that all possible data dependencies have been covered. Even given this, unexpected events like interrupts or page faults might alter timings in the operational environment in a way which could not have been anticipated in the test environment.

For many applications, errors arising from the physical limitations of the computer are of little consequence; the interjection of a little human intelligence solves the problem. Indeed, even problems which are formally uncomputable in general can become tractable in particular cases where the programmer can modify the data or the algorithm when some time or space constraints are being exceeded. However, in situations where high reliability is required remote from effective human intervention, consideration of these limits becomes as important as the algorithm in the validation process. The rules for determining whether a program lies within the bounds of these three dimensions of space, time and numerical limits are just as vital as the general proof rules of the language used.

These extra rules defining the finite constraints of the computer (and compiler) used could be included in the proof rules of the language used to verify the program under consideration. However, these are just the rules where hand provers are extremely likely to mislead themselves; if the proof is done automatically then it further overloads already over-stretched theorem provers. Further, the proof rules would be, in general, different for each implementation of the language. I would prefer to "factor" out these implementation dependencies by imposing restrictions on the language so that we know that a correctly formed program already obeys the rules. The application of the constraints are then localized to the place where implementation differences are critical in any case—in the compiler for the machine in question. This is already done to a certain extent in most program proving systems; for example, the languages involved are usually restricted to subsets which only allow static storage allocation, effectively solving the difficult parts of the problem of the space constraints.

In the language NewSpeak, the enforcement of the rules for finite computation is achieved principally by defining a system of very strong types for all the values manipulated in the language. These types effectively define *finite* sets; a value of a given type is a member of the finite set given by that type. Any operation in the language produces a value of a type which is determined at compile-time from the properties of operation, using a simple worst-case analysis on the types of its operands. If the type can contain a value which is outside the constraints imposed by the object machine (e.g. word length) then the compiler refuses to consider the program as valid or runnable. However, if the constraints are satisfied, then the laws governing the manipulations of program and values are the same as if one were in the world of infinite sets and numbers. Thus, in proving a correctly compiled NewSpeak program, one can use familiar laws like the associativity of addition or the distributive law of multiplication of integers without further ado. This would not be so if there were the possibility of exceptional results due to arithmetic overflow for example; one would also have to show that the results of all the operations lie within the machine bounds. This property of "unexceptionality" of operations is extended over all the NewSpeak language so that there are no undefined results and normal mathematical laws apply throughout.

The elimination of other kinds of exceptions arising from space and time constraints are eliminated by restrictions in the control structure of NewSpeak, together with its type system. Since the types of all values are finite sets and recursion is forbidden, the compiler can compute exactly the storage requirements of a given program. There are no labels or gotos in NewSpeak and the number of iterations of each loop construction is bounded by the type of its control variable. Thus the compiler can trivially place an upper bound on the time required for each construction in the program. Of course, this upper bound might be unduly pessimistic. However, it would draw attention to those parts of the program which might fail time constraints and which require more sophisticated proving techniques than those provided rather crudely by the compiler. A similar situation occurs in the restriction of the type of an expression to a smaller set determined by the worst-case rules of the compiler because of some distant data-dependencies (see assertions below).

A preoccupation with the finite nature of the object machine is not the only design criterion for NewSpeak. The issue of the correctness of the compiler also looms large. There is little point in proving a high-level language program unless one is reasonably sure that its mapping to the object machine is also correct. I must confess that I find it difficult to foresee the time when one can formally prove a compiler for anything other than the most trivial of languages, for example a machine code assembler. The best that I can envisage is some demonstration that the mapping of a particular program is correct. Even here, the difficulties in doing a formal proof of the correctness of the mapping are formidable. Not the least of these difficulties is finding a formal definition of the target machine in question; they are few and far between , the RSRE Viper [Cullyer1987] being a notable exception.

NewSpeak tries to aid the process of validating particular mappings by ensuring that all the constructions in the language are compilable in a reasonably transparent way. This property of "transparency" is to some extent subjective and highly dependent on the compiler writer, but there are languages which force extremely opaque mapping methods; one looks at a piece of machine code and wonders why on earth it implements the corresponding high-level language construct. One illustration of the transparency of NewSpeak mappings is given by its static storage allocation. Each variable in the program can be mapped to a fixed store location; since there is no aliasing of variables we can be sure that each variable declared in the program text must correspond to a unique and distinct location in store. Note that the application of this transparency principle should not be equated blindly with restricting constructs in the language to very primitive ones, close to the machine representation. After all, the most transparent transformation would consist of writing the native instructions of the target machine; unfortunately, this loses all the large-scale structure of the program. Rather, I would prefer that commonly used compound operations are expressed as high-level constructs in the language and that the compiler writer produces code for these stereotypes in a uniformly recognizable manner, without too much clever optimization.

A prime consideration in any safety critical program is the environment in which it operates. The operating system should be as simple as possible to the point of non-existence. One cannot afford the luxury of unanticipated interrupts or page faults in time-critical applications even if they did not alter the program in any other way—this itself is often a very difficult thing to be sure of. The ideal would be that the program is its own operating system, polling its peripheral transfers at the most primitive level allowed by the hardware of the machine. Peripheral transfers are just operations involving another part of the environment, namely the outside world. In NewSpeak, such operations (which must perforce he implementation-dependent) are treated with the same worst-case scepticism as other operations in the language. For example, the type of the result of an input operation from an 8-bit port is a set that includes all the numbers from 0 to 255, regardless of any *a priori* knowledge, including protestations from the system designers that a particular pin is wired to zero.

A more subtle way that the outside world intrudes into the language design arises from the units of the values in the program. If one comes across the number 981 in a program, one can reasonably guess that it is g, the acceleration due to gravity; however, the same applies to 9.81 and maybe even 32 with a change of units. One cannot be certain that the internal working of a program is using the same system of units as the outside world; however, it is possible to ensure that the units used are consistent throughout the workings of the program. To this end, NewSpeak introduces a system of "flavours" within its type system and defines the operations involving these flavoured values to allow complete dimensional checking of the units used. This would prevent, for example, directly adding feet to metres, or, as has happened in one notable instance, confusing metres with nautical miles.

In the following description of NewSpeak, I have used a wide range of conventions for various lexical and syntactic constructions to aid legibility. Bold face is used to indicate **reserved words**, words starting with an upper-case letter are **Flavours**, and words totally in upper-case are TYPE-NAMES. Indexing is indicated by subscripting and exponentiation by superscripting in preference to [ ] and ** mentioned in the concrete syntax. One could regard these conventions as part of a "publication" standard. However, I see no reason why a compiler should not use them directly. A computer is quite indifferent to the legibility of its input to the human reader; for example, making a language insensitive to upper- or lower-case both complicates the compiler and confuses the reader. Similar considerations hold for the layout of the text of a program; I would prefer a compiler to take notice of layout insofar as any block of program which appears to the eye to belong to the same syntactic unit does, indeed, belong to it. The concrete syntax used is given in appendix 1 (section 6.11), expressed in fairly standard BNF, with two abbreviations to express optional and list constructs. These are, for any A:

A-List ::= A | A, A-List

A-Opt ::= A | <empty>

6.2 Types and values

The basic primitive types in NewSpeak are subsets of the integers and floating point numbers and a **Void** type corresponding to a unique value. All other types in NewSpeak (structures, vectors and unions) are composable from these primitive types in conjunction with flavouring (see below). Since NewSpeak is intended as a direct bridge to the target machine, it must concern itself to some degree with reasonably transparent representations of values in the object machine. Thus, the type of a number is given in two parts, one which gives a guide to its representation (e.g. bit, byte, word, two words, etc.) and the other which defines the subset of numbers possible together with, in the case of floating point numbers, accuracy constraints. Syntactically:

> <PrimitiveType> ::= **Void** |
>
> **Bit** <Set> |
>
> **Byte** <Set> |
>
> **Word**-Opt <Set> |
>
> **Float** <Set> <Errors>
>
> <other longer word and float types>

The subsets of numbers possible is constrained by both the representation guide and by the particular implementation. Bit values are restricted to 0 or 1 and byte values are between 0 and 255 while the word values are restricted to those integers representable by words in the object machine. Types can be given names, e.g.

> **Type** BOOL = **Bit**{0..1}
>
> **Type** CHAR = **Byte**{0..255}
>
> **Type** INT = **Word**{$-2^{31}..2^{31}-1$}

A constant in NewSpeak is a value whose type is just a singleton set; thus for these primitive values we have constants like *true* which has type **Bit**{1}, *a* in ASCII representation which has type **Byte**{97}, and *13* which has type **Word**{13}, usually abbreviated to {13}. The result of any expression whose type is a singleton set of whatever representation is obviously deducible at compile-time from the type and can be included as a constant in the run-time program.

The normal arithmetic operations are defined between integers so that the result of the operation is an integer whose type-set is the smallest range which can contain all possible answers. For example, if *x* has type {0..10} then (*x* + *13*) has type {13..23} and (*x*∗*x*) has type {0..100} while (*13*∗*13*) has constant type {169}. Note that, in keeping with NewSpeak's unexceptionality, division by a value whose type includes zero is not an operation in

127

the language. Also if the set defined by the type of an expression is outside the word length of the object machine an error is flagged at compile time.

Real numbers are intended to be approximated by floating point numbers in an implementation of NewSpeak. These floating point numbers clearly arise from finite sets, just like the integers; however the properties of these sets are a good deal more difficult to characterize usefully. The model used for the approximation uses two numbers, R and A, to give upper bounds to the possible error; if f is some floating point number then it represents some real number x, where:

$$x = (1 + r)*f + a \qquad \text{with } |r| \leqslant R \quad \text{and} \quad |a| \leqslant A$$

Thus, the maximum error associated with f in its approximation to x is $(A + R*M)$ where M is the maximum absolute value that f can attain. Both the absolute error A and relative error R are included since errors in some algorithms are more conveniently expressed in one form rather than the other; various constructions in the language allow one to trade off one against the other by limiting ranges to make this useable.

The type of a floating point value includes these relative and absolute error bounds, together with the set of the possible floating point values; thus f above could have type:

Float $\{L..U\} \pm \{A$ **Rel** $R\}$

where L and U are the limits of the possible values of f. Worst case rules also apply here for the evaluation of expressions. Thus, the type of $fs = (fa + fb)$ is defined to be

Float $\{Ls..Us\} \pm \{As$ **Rel** $Rs\}$
where $Ls = La + Lb, \quad Us = Ua + Ub,$
$\qquad As = Aa + Ab + Ra*\text{max}|\{La..Ua\}| + Rb*\text{max}|\{Lb..Ub\}|$
$\qquad\qquad + e_t* \text{ max } (|\{La..Ua\}| \cup |\{Lb..Ub\}|)$
$\qquad Rs = e_r$

The components of the expressions above involving e_t and e_r reflect the approximate nature of floating point addition, while the others are just the errors inherited from errors in the operands fa and fb. The particular values of e_t and e_r depend on the truncation and rounding performed by the target machine; for 32-bit 2's complement floating numbers they will be in the order of 2^{-24}. Similarly, the expression for As above may have to be modified if the range $\{Ls.As\}$ includes zero to cope with different methods in treating underflow. The types of other primitive floating operations, such as difference, product and exponentiation by a constant integer, are defined similarly. Once again, as with integers, division by a floating number which could be zero is uncompilable. However the constraint is stronger here; if the real number which the floating number approximates could be zero then the division is illegal.

The arithmetic used by the compiler to evaluate the error bounds, such as *As* and *Bs* above, just has to be sufficiently accurate and have sufficient dynamic range; most floating point implementations would be good enough. However, it is important that the arithmetic used to evaluate the limits of the type set ({*Ls..Us*} above) is identical to the target machine's arithmetic. A trivial obvious example of this is the evaluation of a constant literal real number in the text; the value of π, say, used both by the running program and the analysis of limits in the compiler must be the object machine's representation. Even given this, the limit evaluation given above relies on the target machine obeying certain rules. The most important of these, given that $+$, $*$ and $\geqslant$ are the machine operations, are

$$(x \geqslant a) \cap (y \geqslant b) \to (x + y) \geqslant (a + b)$$
$$\text{and} \quad (x \geqslant a \geqslant 0) \cap (y \geqslant b \geqslant 0) \to (x*y) \geqslant (a*b)$$

These may seem trivially obvious, but it should be noted that a possible related rule:

$$(x > 0) \cap (y > 0) \to (x*y) > 0$$

is seldom, if ever, true for floating point work and it is possible that, with badly chosen truncation, rounding and normalization algorithms, a floating point implementation could break the less stringent rules. If this were so, I would doubt whether the implementation is fit to be used in a safety-critical application in any case.

Floating point arithmetic is littered with traps for the unwary. None of the floating point operations are associative; NewSpeak insists that the binding required for any non-associative operator is made explicit by bracketing. Also, tests of equality between floats must be regarded with suspicion. In some floating point implementations, for example, there are representations for underflowed numbers, distinct from the representation for zero; these representations behave in most other respects in the same way as zero, with all the same potential for exceptional behaviour. In general, tests for inclusion in ranges are more reliable. NewSpeak provides some target-specific constants which can help here; for example, *minposfloat* is defined to be the smallest non-zero number in the standard representation.

Flavouring is a means of creating distinct types for values with the same representation. It is used to perform dimensional checking and also gives the selection and injection mechanisms for structures and unions. Flavours are defined by expressions in a dimensional algebra involving flavour-tags (such as Feet, Metres, Red, Green, etc.) chosen by the programmer. Thus one can have flavours like Feet Sec^{-1} or Grams Metres Sec^{-2}. Any type can be flavoured by modifying by a flavour, thus **Void** Metres, {6}Feet and CHAR Asci are valid NewSpeak types with flavours Metres, Feet and Asci respectively. The usual way of creating new flavoured values is using expressions involving flavoured void values, represented textually using the tags themselves. One can "multiply" and "divide" any value by a flavoured void to flavour the type of the result. For example,

$$983 * Cm / Sec / Sec$$

is an expression whose value has type $\{981\}Cm\ Sec^{-2}$, a more satisfactory way of representing g. The arithmetic operations between flavoured numbers are defined to preserve dimensional integrity so that addition is only defined between types with equal flavours resulting in a type with the same flavour, and multiplication results in a type with the obvious product flavour and so on. For example, if t is a value of type $\{0..2\}Sec$ then $(g^*t^2)/2$ is a value of type $\{0..1962\}Cm$. Note that unflavoured numbers (like the 2 in the expression) can be regarded as being flavoured by the unit of the dimensional algebra.

The types in NewSpeak form a semi-lattice, where types with the same representation and flavouring are related by the the normal set inclusion operation, while types with different representations or flavourings are unrelated (see appendix 2). This applies both to the primitive types and the compound ones described below. The lattice relationship forms the basis of the coercion (or automatic type changing) rules for NewSpeak; the set underlying the type of a value can be widened by being in a given context. Thus, the type of the value of a conditional expression is the least upper bound of the types of the two values given by the possible evaluation of the arms of the conditional, so that

If b Then 1 **Else** 2 **Fi**

has type $\{1..2\}$. Of course, if the least upper bound does not exist in the semi-lattice, the construction is illegal. This implicit type-changing can always be done by an explicit widening operation which mentions the type itself:

<Widening> ::= <Expression> :: <Type>

In addition, this widening operation can also perform some changes of representation which can not happen implicitly, including changing integers to reals and providing the injection operator for unions (see appendix 2, section 6.12).

A structure value in NewSpeak is a Cartesian product of a number of other values, with a type and representation which is effectively the Cartesian product of its component types and representations. For example, using flavours X and Y and t as defined above:

(1, 2)	has (constant) type	$(\{1\}, \{2\})$
*(1*X, 2*Y)*	has (constant) type	$(\{1\}X, \{2\}Y)$
(t, t)	has type	$(\{0..2\}Sec, \{0..2\}Sec)$

The individual components of the second example can be selected using the flavour-tags X and Y using the familiar dot-notation. For example if b is its name, then $b.X$ is the value $1*X$. Another form of selection allows one to strip off the flavour, so that $b./Y$ is the value 2. Structured declarations and assignments (see below) allow one to split a structured value into its components without explicit selection; this would allow access to the fields of the first and third examples above which do not have uniquely flavoured fields.

Vectors in NewSpeak are rather like structure values with all the elements of the same type. However they can be indexed dynamically, but only by values of some fixed integer type whose set has the same cardinality as the number of elements of the vector, which must perforce be compile-time known. A vector of three booleans, v say, might have type

Vec 0..2 **Of** BOOL.

Indexing this vector, by saying v_i for example, would only be legal if i was a word value whose type set was included in {0..2}. Thus the size of all vectors is known at compile time and all the indexing operations are unexceptional. There are more complicated ways of indexing, by trimming a vector for example, but in all of them the validity of the indices are fully checked at compile time. There are several ways of creating vector values, e.g.

[10, 11, 12, 13]

is a value of type

Vec 1..4 **Of** {10..13}.

Note that the element type is the least upper bound of the component types.

The only other method of constructing values in NewSpeak is by means of a discriminated union of other values of different flavours. These flavours provide the means of defining the injectors and selectors of the components of the union. For example, given

Type LENGTH = **Union**(INT Feet, INT Metres)

values of type LENGTH could be created using the explicit widening operation:

(15 * Feet)::LENGTH

or m::LENGTH

where m is some integer value flavoured by *Metres*. This gives the injection mechanism for unions. Selection of the current component of a union is done using a guarded declaration or a case construction (see sections 6.4 and 6.5); once again, these are unexceptional, unlike their exception-riddled equivalents (variant records) in Pascal and Ada. Note that unions can also be used to represent finite unordered sets using flavoured void values, e.g.

Type LIGHTS = **Union**(Red, Green, Amber, Red Amber)

It is intended that the representation of a union contains a unique number, chosen by the compiler, identifying the characteristic flavour of its current component together with the value of this component padded out if necessary to the maximum possible size. Thus, value of type LENGTH would probably be represented as two words, one for the flavour Feet or Metres and the other for the integer value; LIGHTS would just be one word.

To summarize the possible types in NewSpeak can be represented textually by

> <Type> ::= <PrimitiveType> |
>
> (<Type>-List) |
>
> **Vec** <Range> **Of** <Type> |
>
> **Union** (<Type>-List) |
>
> <Type>-Opt <Flavouring>
>
> <typename>

6.3 Declarations and variables

Declarations in NewSpeak give names to values, variables, procedures or types. Each declaration forms part of a scope where

> <Scope> ::= <Declaration> <Scope> |
>
>   <Declaration> **In** <Expression> **Ni**
>
> <Declaration> ::= **Let** <Identifiers> = <Expression> |
>
>   **Give** <GiveId> = <Expression> |
>
>   **Var** <Identifiers> := <Expression> |
>
>   **Package** <identifier>-List **From** <Scope> |
>
>   **Type** <typename> = <Type> |
>
>   <ProcDec>
>
> <Identifiers> ::= <identifier> |
>
>   (<identifier>-Opt-List)
>
> <GiveId> ::= <identifier>

The **Let** declaration is the simplest form of declaration in NewSpeak. It gives a name (different from any other in scope) to a value resulting from the evaluation of an arbitrary expression; this value is then substituted for the name throughout its scope, for example:

> **Let** x = *SomeExpression*
> **In** *AnExpression involving x*
> **Ni**

Here, *x* is not a variable in the sense that it can be assigned to; it retains the same value and type given by its initialization over its entire scope. Variants of this naming construction allow one to name components of a structure value, so that it is not always necessary to select these components explicitly. Another form gives one a more general way to initialize a similar "write-once" value by using the **Give** instead of **Let** in the declaration. Here one can terminate the evaluation of the initialization expression prematurely using the **Is**-construction which defines the value to be named; this is discussed in conjunction with loops in section 6.6 where it can be employed most usefully.

Variables are declared similarly (with rather more complicated substitution rules):

> **Var** v := *SomeExpression*
> **In** *AnExpression involving v*
> **Ni**

Every variable must be initialized; unset variables are a rich source of exceptions. The type of the initializing value limits the widest type that can be assigned to the variable; this means that most variable initializations in practice include an explicit widening operation. This is one of the few places in NewSpeak where one is obliged to express a type in full. In most other constructions, the type information is inherited from the evaluation of expressions; this is perhaps just as well, since the evaluation of types is quite tedious (though trivial) and better left to a computer.

An assignment allows one to alter the current value of some variable or variable of any type. The general form of assignment is

> <Assignment> ::= <Destination> := <Expression>
> <Destination> ::= <NamedValue> <Multiple>-Opt |
>   (<NamedValue>-Opt-List)

Using the structured form of a destination, a single assignment can split the fields of a structure into different variables. The multiple form allows one to assign a dynamically chosen part of a vector variable; this could be expressed as a loop. In all cases, the type of the source value must be capable of being widened to the initial type of the variable in question.

Assignments to variables are, in general, a distressingly efficient way of blurring type information; the type of a variable must be the widest type which can be assigned to it. Since the ideal would be to get the sharpest possible type information, the emphasis in NewSpeak is towards expression evaluation rather than state-changing assignments (which are regarded as void expressions in NewSpeak). To eliminate variables altogether is usually impracticable, but it is almost always a good idea not to invent unnecessary variables. The operations and constructions of NewSpeak try to keep the declaring of "house-keeping" variables to a minimum. As a trivial example of this, the sum of the elements of a vector is a defined operator, rather than relying on some loop construct with a variable to accumulate the sum. Others include expressions which can deliver multiple values like vectors and value-delivering loops.

6.4 Guarded declarations

A consequence of worst-case rules for the types involved in operations and assignments leads to some restrictions which at first sight seem severe. For example, the assignment

v:=v+1

is always illegal in NewSpeak, regardless of the type of v, since the type of the expression on the right-hand side of an assignment must always be included in the type of the variable on the left and types must always be finite sets. There has to be some safe way of countering the propensity of types to expand indefinitely. The basic method of doing this is provided using guarded scopes:

<GuardedScope> ::= <GuardedDeclaration> <GuardedScope> |

<GuardedDeclaration> **In** <Sequence>

Out <Sequence> **Ni**

<GuardedDeclaration> ::= <Declaration> |

Where <identifier>-Opt : <SkeletonType>

= <Expression>

Here the **Where** construction is equivalent to a **Let** declaration, provided that the value of the expression satisfies the tests implicit in the skeleton type; if not the **Out** sequence is obeyed. The type of the result of the guarded scope is the least upper bound of the types of the **In** and **Out** sequences. The skeleton type gives a framework which is fleshed out by the type of the expression to give the type of the identifier, provided that the tests are satisfied. For example, given that v above is an integer variable in the range

{0..9}, a safe way to increment v might be

Where s:{ ..8} = v
In v:= s+1
Out *Do something else*
Ni

The name s is identified with the value of v (not the variable itself!) provided that it is less than or equal to 8, defining its type to be {0..8}, permitting the safe evaluation of the assignment; if not, the **Out** sequence is obeyed. In fact, the type given to s is the intersection of the type of v and the skeleton type, so that if v has type {4..7} then s also has this type [however, the assignment would have failed to compile!]. In this case the **Out** part appears to be redundant. However, the type of v could depend on the type of a formal parameter of a procedure; given the procedure call mechanism (see below), different calls of the procedure could result in different types for v, not all of which would make the **Out** part redundant. Where we do have a redundant part (the **In** part could also be redundant), its type is taken to be the bottom of the type lattice so that the type of the entire expression depends only on the non-redundant parts.

A **Where** declaration can be regarded as an inverse to the explicit widening operation. It can be used to provide a safe means for the selection of a component of a discriminated union, using a flavour alternative of the skeleton type. For example, given l as a value of type LENGTH as above:

Where m:Metres = l
In *Work with m in Metric units*
Out .....
Ni

Sub-unions can also be extracted using a skeleton which describes the sub-union.

A **Where** declaration merely extracts a value with a sub-type of the expression; it can be applied to structures and vectors as well as ranges and unions. The dynamic test given by the skeleton type is a combination of either simple numeric comparisons or equality tests on flavours. Tests for accuracies of floating numbers cannot be done dynamically; they have to be resolved at compile-time. However trade-offs between relative and absolute errors by limiting ranges are possible, just as in the widening operation. In the context of

$x:$ **Float** {0..100} $\pm$ {**Rel** 10^{-8}}

135

the following is a legal fragment of program:

Where y:**Float** {0..0.1}±{10^{-9}} = x

In ...*uses y with abserror = 10^{-9}* ...

Out ....

Ni

If, on the other hand, the relative error in x were greater than 10^{-8}, then the program would fail to compile.

6.5   Cases and conditionals

All of the other conditional constructions can be expressed operationally in terms of guarded scopes. For example,

If B **Then** *Exp1* **Else** *Exp2* **Fi**

is identical to

Where :**Bit**{1} = B **In** *Exp1* **Out** *Exp2* **Ni**

The use of the **Andth** operator in conditionals can be treated similarly, e.g.

If *B1* **Andth** *B2* **Then** *Exp1* **Else** *Exp2* **Fi**

is the same as

Where :**Bit**{1} = *B1*

Where :**Bit**{1} = *B2*

In *Exp1* **Out** *Exp2* **Ni**

The operation of a case expression is also expressible as nested guarded scopes. All the different tests in guarded scopes are available but a case expression tests the same value in order in several different ways. Syntactically

<Case> ::= **Case** <Expression> <CaseLimbs> <OutLimb>-Opt **Esac**

<CaseLimbs> ::= <CaseLimb> I <CaseLimb> <CaseLimbs>

<CaseLimb> ::= **Of** <Tester> **Then** <Sequence>

<OutLimb> ::= **Out** <Sequence>

<Tester> ::= <SkeletonType> I

        <identifier> : <Tester>-Opt I

        (<Tester>-Opt-List) I

        <Tester>-Opt <Flavouring>

As an example of the use of a case expression using a structured control value, suppose that *hours*, *mins*, *secs* are integer values in the appropriate ranges; then an expression which delivers these values incremented by a second could be

Case (hours,mins,secs)

Of (, , s:{0..58}) **Then** (hours,mins,s+1)

Of (, m:{0..58},) **Then** (hours,m+1,0)

Of (h:{0..22}, ,) **Then** (h+1,0,0)

Out (0,0,0)

Esac

The type of the result of this case expression is the least upper bound of the types of its limbs, namely ({0..23}, {0..59}, {0..59}).

The above case can be transformed (automatically if need be) into nested guarded scopes:

Where s:{0..58} = secs

In (hours, mins, s+1)

Out Where m:{0..58} = mins

　　In (hours, m+1, 0)

　　Out Where h:{0..22} = hours

　　　　In (h+1, 0, 0)

　　　　Out (0, 0, 0)

　　　　Ni

　　Ni

Ni

Here the case expression is exhaustive over all the possibilities of the control value; this is guaranteed by the **Out** limb of the case. When the **Out** limb is absent, the compiler must still be sure that all possible elements of the control value are covered by at least one limb; we cannot have an exception if none of the tests are satisfied. For example,

Case (x,y)

In (sx:{0..5},) **Then** .....

In (bx:{5..9}, {1..10}) **Then** .....

Esac

would only be legal if the type of *x* was included in {0..9}. If the type of *x* was in {0..5} then the type of *y* could be in any range; otherwise it must be included in $\{1 .. 10\}$. In the former case, the second limb could not be obeyed for this x and y. Here the same rule about redundant limbs applies as in guarded scopes, so that the type of the case clause depends only on its first limb.

The type of a case clause depends on the type of the control value apart from this type dependence on active limbs. The type of any value named in the tester is the intersection of the type indicated and the type of the corresponding control value. Thus, if x in the example above had type $\{4 .. 8\}$, the type of sx in the first limb is $\{4 .. 5\}$. Also since the tests are ordered, the type of bx is $\{6 .. 8\}$. The redundant limb dependence can just be regarded as a special case where the intersection of the tester and type of the control value is empty.

6.6   Loops

In most programming languages, loops work by side-effect; if the body of the loop cannot do some kind of an assignment, it might as well not be there. In NewSpeak, loops can be value-delivering constructs; this often avoids the use of "housekeeping" variables which confuse the issue, particularly when describing invariants of the loop. They come in two forms, outer-loops and inner-loops (cf. outer and inner products):

<OuterLoop> ::= **Rep** <OverRange> **Giving** <Sequence> **Per** |

   Repall <OverVectors> **Giving** <Sequence> **Per**

<InnerLoop> ::= **For** <Control> **Do** <Sequence> **Rof** |

   Forall <OverVectors> **Do** <Sequence> **Rof** |

   ForTime <TimeInterval> **Do** <Sequence> **Rof**

In an outer-loop, the value delivered is a vector, each iteration of loop delivering an element of the vector; this evaluation is defined to be side-effect free, making the order of evaluation irrelevant. An inner-loop is more like the traditional form of a for-statement; however, in conjunction with the **Give** form of declarations, its iterations can be terminated prematurely, giving, if desired, the effect of a while-construct as part of the loop, at the same time delivering a value to be named. In both forms, the number of iterations is bounded at compile-time; this number is usually derived from the type of whatever control variable is used for the loop.

An outer-loop which constructs a vector of the squares of its indices could be

   Rep i:$\{1..10\}$ **Giving** i^2 **Per**

The result of this expression is a vector of the first ten squares and has type **Vec** $\{1 .. 10\}$ **Of** $\{1 .. 100\}$; the control variable i is scoped by the loop and has type $\{1 .. 10\}$, giving the type of the indices of the resulting vector.

138

An outer-loop looks quite conventional in NewSpeak. It is a void expression; one of its forms is

For i:{1..10} **Do**
    Some side_effects using i
Rof

However, inner-loops can be sensibly used without side-effects as part of a "write-once" declaration, where the iterations of the loop are stopped by an **Is**-construction supplying the initializing value for the declaration. For example, to find the index of the first non-space character in a vector of characters, *vc*:

Give ind =
  Seq
   For i:{1..80} **Do**
    If vc_i ≠ ' ' **Then** ind **Is** i **Fi**
   Rof;
   0
  Qes

The value given to *ind* is just *i* in the range {1..80} if the condition is satisfied and 0 if the loop terminates normally with only space characters in the vector; its type is the least upper bound of these, namely {0..80}.

Other forms of inner-loop include variations on how the control variable is introduced, for example using a familiar from-to construction. Also, it is often convenient to proceed with the next iteration of a loop prematurely, just as one might want to prematurely terminate it; **Next** applied to the control variable has this effect. Both inner- and outer-loops have variants to allow control variables to step through vectors; this could be expressed using the simpler versions but these variants are likely to be much more efficient. Another example, with a similar theme to the one above, finds the first vector containing all zeros in a vector of vectors, *vv*:

Give ans =
  Seq
   Forall i : vi **In** vv **Do**
    Forall vij **In** vi **Do**
     If vij ≠ 0 **Then Next** i **Fi**
    Rof;
    ans **Is** i
   Rof;
   0
  Qes

This example can be expressed more elegantly (and probably more efficiently) by observing that the compound condition is really one which tests to see if a vector has a particular (constant) type and hence can be expressed using a guarded scope:

Give ans =
  Seq
    Forall i : vi **In** vv **Do**
      Where : **Vec Of** {0} = vi
      In ans **Is** i
      Out **Skip**
      Ni
    Rof;
    0
  Qes

6.7 Procedures

Procedures in NewSpeak present a special problem. Usually, a procedure is regarded as total encapsulation of some algorithm operating on its parameters; the applicability of the procedure to some parameters depends only on their type and the type of the result is defined at its declaration. In NewSpeak, the type of the result of a procedure call may depend on the types of its actual, rather than formal, parameters. This is a restricted form of polymorphism which reflects the limits and accuracies of numbers of the actual parameters in the limits and accuracies of the result of a call. There is very little point in asserting, for example, that a sin routine is accurate to ten figures if one does not know the relationship between the errors in some computed value x and an evaluation of $\sin(x)$. Of course, this particular relationship is well known, but this would not be true for an arbitrary procedure and it is only too easy to deceive oneself about accuracies in this area.

If the body of a procedure were expanded at its call with the appropriate substitution of its actual parameters, then the normal type evaluation of expressions would give the sharpest limit and accuracy information that could be expected. This is the model on which NewSpeak procedures is based. The parameters of a NewSpeak procedure are all passed by value; there are no variable or reference parameters in any guise. Thus the substitution mechanism for a procedure call, $f(act)$, could be represented as

Let for = act

In *Body of f using formal parameter for*

Ni

There are some important caveats on this simplistic approach. For a start, following the rule of transparency of representations, one must insist that there is only one copy of the code for the procedure body. This, for example, would rule out the possibility of having an identity function applicable to any parameter as a procedure; its body would have to be different for actual parameters with different representations. One implication of this is that the declaration of the procedure must specify (at least) the representation required for its actual parameters for the correct evaluation of its body. For example, the declaration of a square-root routine might be

Proc sqrt = (x:**Float**) $\rightarrow$ *Expression evaluating root x*

In *Scope of sqrt ....*

Ni

Note that the type of neither the parameter nor the result is fully explicit here. Only the representation of the parameter is given; from this the representation of the body, including its result, can be deduced. It is only when *sqrt* is called that the compiler can deduce the full type of the result of this particular call by substituting the type of the actual parameter.

The example of square-root is interesting in various respects. It is not applicable to all numbers and any attempt to apply it to a range which includes negative numbers must be forbidden by the unexceptionality of NewSpeak. The body of *sqrt* could include something like

Case x

Of pos:{0.0.. } **Then** *evaluate root pos*

Esac

and the rule which enforces the exhaustion of all possibilities in the control variable x would eliminate any application of an actual parameter which could include negative numbers; the call simply would not compile. However, this would mean that there was an unnecessary test in the body of *sqrt* and it would be better to restrict its domain of applicability explicitly:

Proc sqrt = (x:**Float**{0.0.. }) ->

  Case x

  Of pos:{minposfloat.. } **Then**

     ... *evaluate root pos by Newton's method* ...

  Out 0.0

  Esac

This version of *sqrt* would apply only to unflavoured numbers; its use would lose any dimensional information. One would like to use routines like this so that they preserve the correct dimensionality for any given actual parameter. Hence, a formal flavouring can be introduced which will define local flavour-names; these local flavours will be replaced consistently by the flavours in the actual parameter supplied in the call. A better definition for *sqrt* might be

$$\textbf{Proc } sqrt = (pos:\textbf{Float}\{0.0.. \} \textbf{ Flavoured } Dummy^2)$$

A body for this *sqrt* could start with an approximate square-root flavoured by *Dummy*; better approximations, using Newton's method, would automatically also be flavoured *Dummy*. A call of *sqrt* with a parameter of dimension *Metres*, say, would give a result flavoured $Metres^{1/2}$. Formal flavours cannot be used to form unions in the body of the procedure; their representation would depend on the actual parameters. Where more than one formal flavour is involved with more than one parameter, the matching of formal to actual flavours must be unambiguous; this can be determined from the formal flavours alone.

Unlike the square-root example, it is not always possible to ensure the correct application of a procedure by making a simple restriction on the sets of the parameters like this, particularly where more than one parameter is involved. Consider the following rather contrived example of finding the digit value corresponding to a character in either decimal or hex:

$$\textbf{Proc } digit = (char:\textbf{Byte}, hex:\text{BOOL})$$

    -> **Case** (char,hex)

        Of (d:{'0'..'9'},) **Then** d - '0'

        Of (h:{'a'..'f'}, {true}) **Then** (h - 'a') + 10

        Esac

Given *b* as a BOOL value, *oct* as a **Byte** {'0' .. '7'}, the following situations obtain:

digit(oct, b)	has type **Byte**{0..7}
digit('a', true)	has (constant) type **Byte**{10}
digit('a', b)	is illegal and fails to compile
digit('*', b)	is illegal and fails to compile

Two points arise from this example. First, it is clear that the "type" of a procedure is not just a simple transliteration of the heading of its declaration; the type of the result (and indeed the legality) of the call of a procedure may depend on the conditional structure of the body of its call. Second, as illustrated by the call *digit* (*'a'*, *true*), the type of the answer can define its value; the compiler could have replaced this call by the constant byte value

10. The type analyser of NewSpeak expressions is a generalization of an interpreter for the language; if the set implicit in the type of an expression without side-effects is a singleton, then the singleton value is the value of the expression.

All parameters to NewSpeak procedures are transferred by value; one could regard the entire parameter package as a single structure value. Similarly, the result of a procedure is a single value; if more than one value is required to be delivered, then they must be put together as a single structure value. The structured declarations and assignments allow these multiple results to be split into their components without explicit selection.

A NewSpeak compiler must be able to determine whether the evaluation of an expression is side-effect free. For example, a binary operation is only defined if the evaluation of its operands has no detectable side-effects. This means, among other things, that the compiler has to notice whether a procedure assigns to any of its non-local variables. It is probably a good idea if a human reader can also see immediately which identifiers used in the body of a procedure are non-local. Thus a NewSpeak procedure which uses non-locals must introduce them explicitly at its declaration, as though they were fixed parameters to the procedure. The same introduction is used to allow declarations giving the effect of own-variables. The following example illustrates this, along with some of the properties of loops and unions. In the context of

Type CRES = **Union**(CHAR Asci, Eol)

and **Var** line := **Rep** {1..80} **Giving** (' '::CHAR)* Asci **Per**

and **Proc** readline = () -> *(next line of 80 chars from somewhere)*

consider the definition of the procedure *readchar* given as the top item on page 144.

The parameterless procedure *readchar* reads lines of characters from some source given by *readline* into a non-local vector, *line*, and delivers a union of type CRES containing the successive characters of the line (so long as there are any) and the *Eol* alternative of the union at the end of lines. It ignores leading spaces and collapses contiguous spaces into one. It uses two own-variables *lastind* and *last* declared in the **Use** introduction, to remember the position in the line and last character read.

This use of own-variables is just a particular method of hiding names. A more general method is the use of a package declaration to hide some of the names in a given scope, allowing others to be visible outside.

Use line, readline

    Var lastind := 80::{0..80},

    Var last := (' '::CHAR)*Asci

In

 Proc readchar = ()

  $\rightarrow$ **Give** res =

    Seq

      For i **From** lastind+1 **Upto** 80 **Do**

        Case (line_i , last)

        Of ({' '}, {' '}) **Then** **Next** i

        Of (c: ,) **Then** lastind:=i; last:=c;

                    res **Is** c::CRES

      Esac

    Rof;

    line := readline;

    lastind:=0;   last:= ' '*Asci;

    Eol::CRES

   Qes

   In res

   Ni

To summarize, the syntax of a procedure declaration is

<ProcDec> ::= <NonLocals>-Opt <ProcHeading> $\rightarrow$ <Expression>

<NonLocals> ::= **Use** <identifier>-List-Opt

                    <Declaration>-List-Opt **In**

<ProcHeading> ::= **Proc** <ProcId> = (<Formal>-List-Opt)

<Formal> ::= <identifier> : <Representation> <FormalFlavour>-Opt

---

6.8 Assertions

The worst-case rules for the evaluation of the type of an expression often give quite crude limits on the sets involved. The type of the result of an arithmetic operation depends only on the types of its operands. This means that, if one wrote $x^2 - 2*x + 1$ instead of $(x-1)^2$, the compiler would not deduce that the answer was positive, which might be vital for unexceptional behaviour. One is often forced to appeal to some higher level of justification than the compiler provides to demonstrate that the program behaves unexceptionally. NewSpeak allows for this by permitting the programmer to assert that a value has a smaller type than that indicated by the normal rules, provided that the programmer gives some justification and an identification. Thus, the value of the expression:

Assert x^2-2*x+1 :{0..16}

Because x^2 - 2x +1 = (x-1)^2 and x:{0..5}

Signed I F Currie.

has the value $x^2 - 2*x + 1$ with type $\{0..16\}$ instead of $\{-9..25\}$, as evaluated by the worst-case rules. Just as with the testers in case expressions, only a skeleton of the type of the assertion need be given; the full type will be deduced in conjunction with the control expression.

The form of the justification of an assertion is not specified; however it must be understandable to anybody attempting to validate the program. It could contain hints and expressions to aid formal verification, but this is certainly not mandatory. I have no doubt that any theorem prover worth its salt could prove the assertion given above. However, many assertions are likely to be far beyond the scope of any automatic theorem prover, particularly those dealing with mathematical functions, where references to textbooks are likely to be the order of the day. For example, the polynomial expression:

Let sqz = z^2

Let a0 = 0.7853881608

Let a1 = 0.8074543252 E-1

Let a2 = 0.2490001007 E-2

Let a3 = 0.35950439 E-4

In z*(a0-sqz*(a1-sqz*(a2-sqz*a3)))

Ni

is an approximation to $\sin(\pi z/4)$, correct to 8 decimal places for $z: \{-1.0..1.0\}$, according to a well-known textbook on numerical methods. This bald statement on its own is quite difficult to prove, requiring considerable knowledge about series expansions and numerical approximations. In addition, it ignores the influence of possible errors in z in the accuracy of the answer. Coarse bounds on the true errors involved could be found by taking the errors derived from the worst-case rules in the evaluation of the polynomial and adding $5*10^{-9}$ to its relative error. This would be the safest estimate to take but, provided that the floating representation is sufficiently long, more precise bounds can be found by applying a little mathematical knowledge. Given that *poly* is the result of the polynomial and that the error in z is entirely expressed by a maximum absolute error *abs*, the following could be an appropriate assertion:

Assert poly: **Float** $\pm\{(\text{pi}*\text{abs})/4$ **Rel** $((\text{pi}*\text{abs})^2/32) + 5\,\text{E-}9\}$

Because

poly is $\sin(\pi z/4)$ to 8 decimal places with exact z, giving the

$5\,\text{E-}9$ term in relative error; see:

Routine 3040, Computer Approximations, Hart et al, Wiley & Son.

Since $\sin(\pi(z+e)/4) = \sin(\pi z/4)\cos(\pi e/4) + \cos(\pi z/4)\sin(\pi e/4)$

errors due to propagation of errors in z are:

absolute error $\leq |\sin(\pi e/4)| \leq \pi\,\text{abs}/4$

relative error $\leq 1-|\cos(\pi e/4)| \leq (\pi\,\text{abs}/4)^2/2$

Signed I F Currie.

Here it is convenient to use the absolute error of z to assert the accuracy of the sin routine. In other cases, it is more convenient to use relative errors only. For example, a similar assertion to the one above could say that the relative error in a square-root arising from a relative error, r in the parameter, is $r/2$.

Obviously, quite complicated expressions can be required for error and limit computations. They must all be evaluated at compile-time and clearly there must be operations in the language to extract and manipulate these errors and limits from numerical results so that the expressions can be written conveniently. The operations, **Relonly** and **Absonly**, change the type of a floating number so that its error is expressed entirely in either relative form or absolute form, while **Relerr** and **Abserr** deliver the relative and absolute errors, respectively, of a floating value, with similar operations to extract the upper and lower limits of the set involved. Thus, the value *abs*, above, could have been derived from z by

Let abs = **Abserr Absonly** z

It is important to ensure that a value derived like this from errors or limits within a procedure does not "leak" out from compile-time to run-time evaluation. It cannot affect the value delivered by the procedure in any way other than in its type; otherwise, different calls of a procedure could require different bodies, depending on the types of their actual parameters. The method chosen to enforce this is another use of flavouring. The result of operations like **Abserr** are flavoured by an anonymous flavour, Φ say. Numbers flavoured by Φ cannot be assigned or delivered as part of the result of a procedure and Φ remains as a flavouring to the result of any operation involving them. The only places where the Φ-flavouring is removed is the limit and error parts of a type involved in an assertion or an explicit widening operation.

In an assertion on the accuracy of a real number, like *poly* above, it is unlikely that one would be able to check dynamically that the assertion is satisfied; certainly, not without some very exotic floating point implementation. However, the limit assertions could easily be checked at run-time, e.g. the previous assertion could check that the expression is in the range $\{0..16\}$. I would expect that any NewSpeak implementation would do dynamic checks like this for all assertions for which it was possible, such as testing fixed limits or flavours. If the dynamic check fails, either the justification is wrong or the machine is faulty. In either case, no further reliance can be placed on outputs from the program and some emergency mode of operation, independent of the machine, would have to be activated to recover the situation. In a Viper microprocessor, for example, the STOP flag would be raised. This halts processing immediately and signals to the outside world that an error has occurred to allow some external agency to proceed. Any safety-critical application is bound to have more than one processor involved with some comparison of their outputs. Where each processor was running the same program, simultaneous STOP signals would be highly indicative of a software rather than a hardware error.

6.9   Timing

In many applications, the time taken by a portion of program can be highly critical; often this would form an important part of the specification of the program. A NewSpeak compiler can compute maximum and minimum times required for any program fragment, at least in terms of cycles in the target machine. A programmer can delimit the time taken by the evaluation of an expression using the **Takes** construction:

   Some expression **Takes** $\{l..u\}$ Millisecs

where the units of time, here Millisecs, are known and defined by the compiler; they are just denoted by some flavour and could be Secs, Microsecs or even Cycles. If the time taken to evaluate the expression could be outside the prescribed range, then the program fails to compile. It will sometimes happen that the programmer can deduce better limits for the evaluation time because of some hidden data dependencies and can assert that these limits apply using an **AssertTime** construction; just as with type assertions justification and identification are required. The compiler will then take these narrower limits in computing times for enclosing parts of the program, provided, of course, that they intersect with the ones that it computed normally.

Often, particularly when dealing with peripheral transfers, it is necessary to perform timed waits or time-outs. NewSpeak provides an inner-loop to do this whose control variable is expressed in terms of the times computed by the compiler. A dynamic wait of approximately one millisec might be

ForTime {1000..1010} Microsecs **Do Skip Rof**

Note that a real-time clock is not involved here; the compiler computes the number of times the loop is obeyed from its knowledge of the timing of the body of the loop. It must, of course, find a number which satisfies the time-range constraint for both the minimum and maximum duration of the body.

A real-time clock could be part of a system using NewSpeak. If it is external to the processor accessible by some kind of peripheral transfer, then it should be subject to the same degree of scepticism as any other external data transfer. In general, any peripheral transfer in NewSpeak is done by a monadic operation defined by the compiler, specific to the target machine. These operations should be designed to be unexceptional; in particular, they must avoid unlimited waits for external channels. A millisecond clock, for example, could be read using an operation, **Timenow**, which can be applied at any time, delivering the most recent value of the external clock. Of course, the clock could go wrong; one possible malfunction is that it sticks. This could be disastrous if the program wanted to wait for a tick of the clock; a possible way of not getting too badly out of step might be

Let clockok =
Seq
  ForTime {1000..1050} Microsecs **Do**
    Let time = **Timenow** ()
    In
      If time > lasttime **Then** lasttime := time; clockok **Is** true **Fi**
    Ni
  Rof;
  false
Qes

This declaration gives a boolean saying whether or not the clock actually ticked. Similar techniques would have to be applied to give time-outs when polling for other kinds of transfers.

6.10 Conclusion

It is possible to write wrong programs in any language; no language or methodology can be guaranteed to eliminate errors in the end product completely. However, NewSpeak will eliminate many potential errors, including the possibility of the programmer overlooking the finite nature of the underlying hardware or mixing incompatible units, while still having a flexible, well structured language capable of efficient mapping into standard hardware.

6.11 Appendix 1: summary of syntax

In the following concrete syntax for NewSpeak, various binding considerations are ignored, notably in operations. Alternative expansions of a syntactic class are denoted by the | symbol. Class names starting with an upper case letter are further expanded in the syntax; others are distinguished lexically. There are two abreviations: -Opt and -List, which, for any A, are expanded to

A-List ::= A | A , A-List

A-Opt :: = A | <empty>

<Program> ::= <Expression>

<Expression> ::= <Operation> | <OuterLoop> | <Assignment> |
               <Assertion> | <TimedExpression> |
               <SeqChange>

<Operation> ::= <MonOperation> |
               <MonOperation> <BinOp> <MonOperation>

<MonOperation> ::= <MonOp> <MonOperation> |
                 <Multiple>-Opt <VectorOp> <MonOperation> |
                 <Value>

<BinOp> ::= + | - | * | ** | **Max** | **Min** |
          / | % | **Mod** | **Divmod**
          Concat |
          > | < | $\geq$ | $\leq$ | = | $\neq$ |
          And | **Or** | **Andth** | **Orel**

<MonOp> ::= - | **Abs** | **Discard** | **Not** | **Odd** | **Entier** | **Round** | **Float** |
          Mantissa | **Exponent** |
          <CompileTimeOp> |
          <compiler-specific operation>

<CompileTimeOp> ::= **Inf** | **Sup** | **Relonly** | **Absonly** | **Relerr** | **Abserr**

<Multiple> ::= **From** <Operation> <ToPart>

<ToPart> ::= **Upto** <Operation> | **Downto** <Operation>

<VectorOp>::= **Sum** I **Product** I **All** I **Some** I **Parity** I
                Vecmax I **Vecmin** I **Flatten**

<Value> ::=   <Widening> I
           <NamedValue> I
           <ConstantValue> I
           < Call > I
           <Scope> I
           <GuardedScope>
           <Conditional> I
           <InnerLoop> I
           Seq <Sequence> **Qes** I
           (<Operation>-List) I

           [<Operation>-List] I

<NamedValue> ::= <identifier>
                <NamedValue> . <Flavouring>
                <NamedValue> ./ <Flavouring>
                <NamedValue> [<Operation>]
                <NamedValue> <VecTrimming>

<Flavouring> ::= <flavour-name> <rational-power-denotation>-Opt I
              <Flavouring> <Flavouring> I

<VecTrimming> ::= [$\geq$ <CompileTimeValue>] I
              [$\leq$ <CompileTimeValue>] I
              [@ <CompileTimeValue>]

<CompileTimeValue> ::= <Operation>

```
<ConstantValue> ::= <integer-denotation> |
                    <floating-denotation> |
                    true | false |
                    '<asci-character>' |
                    "<asci-string>"  |
                    <Flavouring> |
                    Skip
                    <compiler-specific constant>


<Call> ::=  <ProcId> ( <Operation>-List-Opt )
<ProcId> ::= <identifier>


<Sequence> ::= <Expression> | <Sequence>; <Expression>


<Widening> ::=  <Expression> :: <Type>


<Type> ::= <PrimitiveType> |
           ( <Type>-List ) |
           Vec <Range> Of <Type> |
           Union (<Type>-List) |

           <Type>-Opt <Flavouring>
           <typename>


<PrimitiveType> ::= Void |
                    Bit  <Set> |
                    Byte <Set> |
                    Word-Opt  <Set> |
                    Float <Set> <Errors>
                    <other longer word and float types>
<Set> ::= { <Range>-List }
<Range> ::= <CompileTimeValue>-Opt .. <CompileTimeValue>-Opt
<Errors> ::= ± {<CompileTimeValue>-Opt  <RelErr>-Opt }
<RelErr> ::= Rel <CompileTimeValue>
```

```
<Scope>  ::=  <Declaration> <Scope> |
              <Declaration> In  <Expression> Ni


<Declaration> ::= Let <Identifiers>  = <Expression> |
                  Give <GiveId>  = <Expression> |
                  Var <Identifiers> := <Expression> |
                  Package <identifier>-List From <Scope> |
                  Type <typename> = <Type>  |
                  <ProcDec>


<Identifiers> ::= <identifier> |
                  ( <identifier>-Opt-List )
<GiveId> ::= <identifier>


<ProcDec>  ::=  <NonLocals>-Opt  <ProcHeading> → <Expression>


<NonLocals> ::= Use <identifier>-List-Opt
                <Declaration>-List-Opt In


<ProcHeading> ::= Proc <ProcId> = (<Formal>-List-Opt)

<Formal> ::= <identifier> : <Representation>  <FormalFlavour>-Opt


<Representation> ::= <PrimitiveRep> |
                     ( <Representation>-List ) |
                     Vec <Range> Of <Representation> |
                     Union(<Representation>-List) |
                     <Representation>-Opt <Flavouring> |
                     <Type>
<PrimitiveRep> ::= Byte <Set>-Opt |
                   Bit <Set>-Opt |
                   Word-Opt <Set>-Opt
                   Float <Set>-Opt <Errors>-Opt
                   <longer reps for words or floats>
```

153

<FormalFlavour> ::= **Flavoured** <Flavouring>

<GuardedScope> ::= <GuardedDeclaration> <GuardedScope> |
                       <GuardedDeclaration> **In** <Sequence>
                                    Out <Sequence>   **Ni**

<GuardedDeclaration> ::= <Declaration> |
                     Where <identifier>-Opt : <SkeletonType>
                          = <Expression>

<Conditional> ::= **If** <Expression> **Then** <Sequence> **Fi** |
               If <Expression> **Then** <Sequence>
                           Else <Sequence> **Fi** |
            Case <Expression>
                   <CaseLimbs> <OutLimb>-Opt **Esac**
<CaseLimbs> ::= <CaseLimb> | <CaseLimb> <CaseLimbs>
<CaseLimb> ::= **Of** <Tester> **Then** <Sequence>
<Tester> ::= <SkeletonType> |
           <identifier> : <Tester>-Opt |
           (<Tester>-Opt-List) |
           <Tester>-Opt <flavouring>
<SkeletonType> ::= <Type>
               <Set>-Opt <Errors>-Opt |
               (<SkeletonType>-Opt-List) |
               <SkeletonType> <Flavouring> |
               Vec Of <SkeletonType> |
               Union (<SkeletonType>-List)
<OutLimb> ::= **Out** <Sequence>

<OuterLoop> ::= **Rep** <OverRange> **Giving** <Sequence> **Per** |
               Repall <OverVectors> **Giving** <Sequence> **Per**

<OverRange> ::= <Count>-Opt { <Range> }

<Count> ::= <LoopId> :

<LoopId> ::= <identifier>

<OverVectors> ::= <Count>-Opt <OverVector>-List

<OverVector> ::= <identifier> **In** <Operation>

<InnerLoop> ::= **For** <InnerControl> **Do** <Sequence> **Rof** |
      Forall <OverVectors> **Do** <Sequence> **Rof** |
      ForTime <TimeInterval> **Do** <Sequence> **Rof**

<InnerControl> ::= <OverRange> |
       <LoopId> **From** <Operation>
         <Bypart>-Opt <ToPart>

<Bypart> ::= **By** <Operation>

<TimeInterval> ::= { <Range> } <TimeUnit>

<TimeUnit> ::= <flavour-name for compiler's time units>

<Assignment> ::= <Destination> := <Expression>

<Destination> ::= <NamedValue> <Multiple>-Opt |
      (<NamedValue>-Opt-List)

<Assertion> ::= **Assert** <Expression> : <SkeletonType>
      Because <justification>
      Signed <signature>.

<TimedExpression> ::= <Expression> **Takes** <TimeInterval> |
       <TimedAssertion>

$$\langle\text{TimedAssertion}\rangle ::= \langle\text{Expression}\rangle \textbf{ AssertTime } \langle\text{TimeInterval}\rangle$$
$$\textbf{Because } \langle\text{justification}\rangle$$
$$\textbf{Signed } \langle\text{signature}\rangle.$$

$$\langle\text{SeqChange}\rangle ::= \langle\text{StepLoop}\rangle \mid \langle\text{GiveAnswer}\rangle$$
$$\langle\text{StepLoop}\rangle ::= \textbf{Next } \langle\text{LoopId}\rangle$$
$$\langle\text{GiveAnswer}\rangle ::= \langle\text{GiveId}\rangle \textbf{ Is } \langle\text{Operation}\rangle$$

6.12 Appendix 2: type lattice and widening

For type T_1 to be coercible to T_2 , then $(T_1 \cup T_2) = T_2$ where $\cup$ is the lattice least upper bound given by:

for sets X and Y :
$$\textbf{Word } \{X\} \cup \textbf{Word } \{Y\} = \textbf{Word } \{X \cup Y\}$$
$$\textbf{Byte } \{X\} \cup \textbf{Byte } \{Y\} = \textbf{Byte } \{X \cup Y\}$$
$$\textbf{Bit } \{X\} \cup \textbf{Bit } \{Y\} = \textbf{Bit } \{X \cup Y\}$$
$$\textbf{Float } \{X\}\pm\{a_1 \textbf{ Rel } r_1\} \cup \textbf{Float } \{Y\}\pm\{a_2 \textbf{ Rel } r_2\}$$
$$= \textbf{Float } \{X \cup Y\}\pm\{\max(a_1, a_2) \textbf{ Rel } \max(r_1, r_2)\}$$

for flavour F and types T_1 and T_2:
$$(T_1 \text{ F}) \cup (T_2 \text{ F}) = (T_1 \cup T_2) \text{ F}$$

for types $T_1, T_1,... T_n$ and $S_1, S_2,...S_n$
$$(T_1, T_2,... T_n) \cup (S_1, S_2,... S_n) = (T_1 \cup S_1, T_2 \cup S_2,... T_n \cup S_n)$$
$$\textbf{Union}(T_1, T_2,... T_n) \cup \textbf{Union}(S_1, S_2,... S_n)$$
$$= \textbf{Union}(T_1 \cup S_1, T_2 \cup S_2,... T_n \cup S_n)$$

for range R:
$$\textbf{Vec R Of } T_1 \cup \textbf{Vec R Of } T_2 = \textbf{Vec R Of } (T_1 \cup T_2)$$

for all T
$$\perp \cup T = T$$

($\perp$ is type of **Next** or **Is** constructions or redundant limb) for any other T_1 and T_2:

$$T_1 \cup T_2 = \ \mathcal{T}$$

   ($\mathcal{T}$ is illegal top of lattice)

Any value whose type is changed according to the above rule does not change its representation. The type of any legal construction having several alternative results is the least upper bound of the types of these results, provided it is not $\mathcal{T}$. In any sequence, (... A;... B) say, the type of A must be **Void** and the value of the sequence is the value of B.

For types T_1 and T_2 and $x:T_2$, then the application of the widening operation $x::T_1$ is only legal if $T_1 \geq T_2$ where $\geq$ is a partial ordering defined on types not including $\mathcal{T}$ or $\perp$, given by $((T_1 \cup T_2) = T_1)$ or some example of the following:

For sets X, Y, W, Z with $X \supseteq Y \supseteq W \supseteq Z$

   Float$\{X\} \pm \{$**Rel** r$\} \geq$ **Word**$\{Y\} \geq$ **Byte**$\{W\} \geq$ **Bit**$\{Z\}$

      where r is related to integer and floating lengths

   Float$\{X\} \pm \{a_1$ **Rel** $r_1\} \geq$ **Float**$\{Y\} \pm \{a_2$ **Rel** $r_2\}$

      where $(a_1 + r_1 * \max|Y|) \geq (a_2 + r_2 * \max|Y|)$

For types $T_1, T_1, ... T_n$ and $S_1, S_2, ... S_n$

   Union$(T_1, T_2, ... T_n) \geq S \ = (\exists \ i: T_i \geq S))$

   Union$(T_1, T_2, ... T_n) \geq$ **Union**$(S_1, S_2, ... S_m)$

         $= (n \geq m) \cap (\forall \ i:(\exists \ j: (T_j \cup S_i) = T_j))$

For flavour F:

   $(T_1 \ F) \geq (T_2 \ F) = \ (T_1 \geq T_2)$

For any other T_1 and T_2:

   $(T_1 \geq T_2) \ =$ false

An assignment, $x:=y$, is legal if and only if $(T_x \geq T_y)$.

In a procedure call, $g(x)$, let T_f be a type formed from the representation of the formal parameter of g by filling in any unspecified ranges and accuracies or formal flavours from the corresponding fields and flavours of T_x, the type of the actual parameter x. Then for the call to be legal we must have $(T_f \geq T_x)$.

Reference

[Cullyer 1987]   Cullyer J., "Implementing safety-critical systems: the Viper micro-processor", *Proc. Hardware Verification Workshop*, University of Calgary (Jan. 1987).

7 Program analysis and systematic testing

M. A. Hennell, University of Liverpool
D. Hedley and I. J. Riddell, Liverpool Data Research Associates Ltd

7.1 Introduction

The authors of this chapter have had considerable experience with the use of automated testing tools, both in the real world of industry and commerce, as well as in a research environment. The automated testing tools referred to are various derivatives of the LDRA Testbeds [1]. These tools in various languages, namely Ada, C, Cobol, Coral 66, Fortran, Pascal, PL/1, and PL/M86 have been used in industry since 1975 and have been the subject of extensive experimentation at the University of Liverpool since 1970.

The experimental work at Liverpool University has been directed to the development of testing and quality control tools primarily for use in the development of software within the Department of Statistics and Computational Mathematics. This department has produced a considerable amount of software which is marketed by various software houses. The experimental work has been extensively supported by the UK Science and Engineering Research Council, the UK Alvey Directorate, the EEC and a number of industrial corporations.

The use of the tools in industry was initially the result of the enthusiasm and need of a number of concerned individuals who, having heard of the presence of the tools in the University, used persuasive powers firstly to extract copies of the tools and secondly to persuade the originators to incorporate "improvements". Later the tools were marketed throughout the world.

The current mode of working is as follows. In the University new tools are hacked together and experiments performed to see if there is any merit in the new tool. If there is merit then the tools are rebuilt by LDRA to yield variants of marketable quality.

7.2 The basic requirement

It seems to the authors that the main requirement of a validation software tool for use by a software producer is that the tool will guarantee that the producer's software is wholly correct, is of appropriate quality, and will satisfy the users. This requirement is akin to the search for the holy grail or elixir of life. Fortunately for such software producers a variety of suitable tools are available in the market place. They range from structured X techniques (for all X), through 4 GLs, to formal methods. The literature contains many conference papers which show that each tool leads to greater productivity and higher quality.

Most software producers will have tried at least one such tool. Whether or not a given tool improves the producers software depends very largely on how bad things were before the use of the tool. It is probably true to say that for most producers any methodical tool or technique would bring about immediate benefits. This effect makes judgments about the merits of particular techniques and tools extremely difficult. It also serves to explain the rise and fall of chief programmer teams, structured programming, structured design, clean rooms, constructive proving and so on.

In addition to guaranteeing the quality of the software, the use of the tool must not incur additional costs in manpower or time. Preferably it should reduce these costs substantially. Of all the techniques and tools available, those which are least attractive involve the testing of the software. This is widely recognized, so that many non-testing technique vendors explicitly reassure their customers on the point by stating that their technique is so good that there is no need to test the software, it is already correct!

This chapter is addressed to those who have already produced "correct", "structured", "data flowed", "formally specified", etc., software and still search for the grail. All that is offered is "blood, sweat and tears" and worse!

The "Problem Software" in general must satisfy a large number of often conflicting, changing and poorly understood requirements. It must be cheap, of high quality (whatever that means), highly efficient, usable, reliable, etc., and delivered on time. It must be maintainable, expandable, simple and not pirateable. All this must be accomplished despite human frailty. The fact that most other industries have much the same problems is usually considered irrelevant, the answer must be technical.

The disabusement of the users normally starts from the testing phase onwards and hence the tester is usually present at this happy time. Naturally the more thoroughly the software is tested the more likely it is to fail and hence the more unpopular the tester becomes. The abandonment of the testing phase is therefore highly attractive to all including the users. The users would prefer to abandon the phase because then they could take delivery of the software much earlier and hence look good in their own environment. It is only subsequent unreliability (bad luck) which spoils this happy situation.

7.3 The Liverpool experience

In the late 1960s and early 1970s two of the authors together with other colleagues were attempting to build high-quality numerical software using formal specifications, very-high-level languages, structured methods and very-high-quality personnel. In the event, much of the software was found to suffer from serious deficiencies. A careful examination of both the problems and software generally showed that almost every possible error had been made. Somehow software engineers of the highest calibre had convinced themselves and frequently their colleagues that the software contained no faults (the zero-defect syndrome).

Following this experience we instituted the best possible managerial and automated procedures and tools which were then obtainable anywhere in the world [2]. Tools such as BRNANL [3], PFORT [4] and DAVE [5] were gathered in and experimentation performed to evaluate their effectiveness. Most tools were for Fortran which was not our implementation language so the lessons learned had to be applied by the construction of new tools. Over the years, every testing technique described in the literature has been applied to examples of software and evaluated. These range from the backwards and forwards data flow analyses of Balzer [6], the assertion checking of Stucki [7], the symbolic execution of Howden [8], King [9] and Clarke [10], and the mutation techniques of de Millo, Budd et al [11] [12]. The authors benefited from many discussions with Fosdick and Osterweil at the University of Colorado, John Brown and his colleagues at TRW, and C. S. E. Phillips at RSRE Malvern.

Not only have most techniques been implemented and evaluated but so also have most software metrics. The literature abounds with metrics of all types. Some purport to measure control flow characteristics, others concern data flow, and a large class involves fault detection.

The principal criterion applied by the authors to a metric is that it must impart information and this information should be clear, unambiguous and useful. In addition if the metric is the bearer of bad news then this news must be explicit and more importantly it must be obvious what steps must be taken to ensure that in the future the value of the metric will be in an acceptable range.

There are two major constraints which we impose on any tools. First, they must be capable of analysing (the code, design, requirements, etc.) without imposing additional unwanted constraints. Thus code analysers must be capable of handling operating system calls, interrupts, ON-conditions, arbitrary control and data flow structures, and so on. In other words, real code. The imposition of arbitrary constraints introduced solely to simplify the tasks of a tool would be intolerable.

The second constraint is that, regardless of theoretical purity and technical difficulty, all messages should be simple and straightforward and preferably in terms of the line numbers of the offending code or text. There are times when this requirement cannot be fulfilled but these occasions are surprisingly few.

7.4 The Liverpool experiments

There have been two aspects investigated at Liverpool. Firstly, can the technique assist with the types of problem which we encounter in-house with our own software projects? Secondly, are the techniques any good for a wider class of software?

The structure of the experiments has been as follows. Firstly we carefully analysed all our errors and tried to establish how these errors had been made, how they had evaded detection, and how they had been made manifest. The last of these was often unknown because users had filled in standard error report forms which had not asked for adequate information. Indeed it was never clear what questions should be asked.

Having gained some insight into the faults of our working methods we then sought to introduce techniques which would detect these errors if they were made again [2]. The belief existed that if it were known amongst project members that such errors would definitely be trapped then the project members would have a vested interest in the development of management processes to minimise the occurrence of errors in the first place. The practice has shown this belief to be fulfilled.

It is worth noting that we failed to find techniques for exposing errors due to misunderstood requirements, an area which plagues us to this day.

Clearly it is easy to experiment with our own code. The code is easily available and runs on our in-house machines. Software from the world at large is harder to use for experimentation. Many companies have graciously sent us tapes of software. Most of this software is, however, machine or compiler dependent and, of course, not for the ones which we possess. Other software requires libraries and utilities which are only available at the user's site. Consequently the sample of runnable software available is smaller than we would have wished. Nevertheless there are still hundreds of thousands of lines of code. The majority of this code has been analysed many times.

The second class of experiments which we performed involved this code sent to us by third parties. We found that much the same problems which we had encountered in our own code were present in this other code. In addition there were examples of errors which we knew were not present in ours, through the use of better compilers, languages, or tools. In many cases the owner of the code already had mechanisms to detect these errors. The classic examples were two banks who used PL/1 but only ever with the optimizing compiler. The PL/1 checkout compiler which they already possessed would have found these errors.

In widening the analysis to this arbitrary class of programs it was found that extensions to the analysis algorithms were necessary in order to cope with PL/1 ON blocks, Ada exceptions, Fortran I/O, recursion, procedural parameters, label parameters, arbitrary language extensions and other goodies.

The principal conclusion which we have reached is that very few errors are directly detectable by Static Analysis techniques. This is in direct contradiction to the claims made by vendors of such tools. It is possible to detect many quality-reducing characteristics and thousands of anomalies, but very few certain errors. However for the cost of the analysis these few are very worthwhile detecting provided that human effort is minimal.

Dynamic Analysis has, however, shown itself very effective in detecting errors or, more accurately, forcing situations where the errors become manifest. This is in line with experiments performed by other researchers [19, 20, 23].

In comparing the efficiency of Static and Dynamic Analysis two points must be borne in mind. For our own software we use a large number of tools which prevent the occurrence of a wide class of errors so that, when the code is analysed at the testing stage, the number of errors is smaller than occurs in other environments. Secondly when we analyse external code we usually cannot tell whether an anomaly is an error or not. One needs to know a great deal about the code in order to decide. With Dynamic Analysis it is very often easier to decide whether an error has occurred because the program either crashes or the outputs are very obviously wrong. Subtle errors may, however, be undetected even though they have been provoked. Sometimes considerable expertise is required to detect the presence of an error.

7.5 The LDRA Testbeds

These toolsets are derived from the experience gained at the University of Liverpool and elsewhere. They represent the techniques which were judged to be the most effective and universally applicable.

The tools consist of two conceptually distinct parts which in practice are closely linked. They are the Static and Dynamic Analysis components. The roles of these will be described separately but it should be understood that the Dynamic Analysis depends very heavily on the Static Analysis.

The Static Analysis scans the code submitted for testing (the source code text). The scan constructs internal tables and a number of user visible displays. The user visible displays are also of two types: those which are needed in order to understand the subsequent analysis (informational displays) and those which report defects.

Display 1 This is a reformatted (pretty printed) listing of the source code text. All messages and analyses refer to this listing and not to the source code text file itself. The reformatting strategy is carefully designed to expose the control flow structure so that all future messages can be referenced unambiguously by line numbers. Originally it was felt that the user's code should be left untouched. It took many years before we reluctantly faced up to this bad decision.

Display 2 This is a management report file which contains a complete breakdown of all the violations of a large set of programming standards. These standards have been culled from standards manuals obtained from industry [13]. A complete synopsis of the application of all the complexity and testing metrics to the source text is also provided. The purpose of the display is to give an overview of the current state of the testing activity and overall software quality. It is targeted in the main towards the manager's view of the software process. Indeed the display even includes a penalty function which is incremented for each deficiency found in the software. Then a busy, or not technically minded, manager can use the value of this penalty function to help with acceptance decisions. At least such managers can feel that they have a measure of control.

Display 3 This is a listing of the source code text annotated with details of path fragments called LCSAJs which later will form the highest level of testing [1]. This is an information display. This display also indicates the presence of unreachable code. The origins of LCSAJs lie in the observation that the execution paths share common sequences of code. Ideally it would be desirable to test all the paths but the number of paths is usually unmanageable, and worst still most of them are infeasible (see [14]). The set of LCSAJs has the property that the size of the set increases on average linearly with the length of the programs and hence always stays manageable. Then, because the LCSAJs are themselves paths (or fragments of paths), they have the characteristic of being feasible or infeasible. Studies [14] have shown that reducing the number of infeasible LCSAJs will significantly reduce the number of infeasible paths, improve code readability, reduce the size of the code, and decrease run-time. Since the benefits are so great the effort seems worthwhile. The LCSAJ display is primarily targeted towards those programmers who want to remove the infeasible LCSAJs and who require a display which shows how the LCSAJs arise.

Display 4 This is both an information and report display. It contains a source code listing annotated to show the numbered basic blocks, a basic block being essentially a piece of straight line code. The way in which these basic blocks connect together is then presented in terms of a list of each node (basic block) together with a list of its successor nodes. From this information it is straightforward to display the directed control flow graph of the program by manual or automated means.

The next analysis component is the interval analysis [15] which seeks to show the natural looping structure of the program. This information is particularly useful if it is required to optimize the source code text. The analysis explores the full extent of nesting. All the nodes which contribute to each interval are listed together with the entrance (or header node).

Then follows a structured programming analysis. The users are permitted to define structures such as "if then else", "do while", etc. which they deem to be desirable programming features. The Testbed then reports on the structure of any code which is not written in terms of these structures. The users make the decision as to whether this unstructured code is desirable or not. Note that this unstructured code may arise, for instance, from the use of explicit error mechanisms in the code, interrupt handlers or similar devices. The role of the Testbed is simply to report these constructs, not to criticise them. The authors do not subscribe to the view that these structures necessarily cause any significant problems.

Finally the complexity of the code is measured in terms of McCabe's and the knot measures (see [16]) both before and after the structured programming verification. The latter are known as essential complexity metrics. The essential complexity metrics are indicators of unnecessary complexity.

Display 5 A data flow graph is an enhanced representation of the control flow graph to which knowledge of the uses of each variable is added. This data flow graph is examined both for items of information and also items of report. The information consists of the procedure-calling hierarchy and the roles of the parameters of these procedures. These roles comprise variables whose value becomes changed, those where values are never changed, those which receive a value, and those which are never used. This analysis is carried over all levels of the calling hierarchy. It is up to the user to check that these results conform with design requirements.

Data flow anomalies are reported. These are: variables used before being initialized (UR anomaly); variables reassigned a value when the previous value has never been used (DD anomaly); and variables receiving a value which is never used (DU anomaly).

This analysis is performed for the whole source code program even in the presence of recursion. Technically, it works for acyclic non-planar disconnected graphs. This includes interrupt handlers, ON-conditions, unstructured programs and so on.

Display 6 The Testbeds can produce a complete program cross-reference including all the uses of global variables. This option is for those users (including the authors) who have rotten compilers which do not produce this useful information. The cross-reference informs the user not only in which routines a particular variable is used but also what those uses are in terms of definitions and references.

The Testbed Dynamic Analysis is obtained by instrumenting the source code text with various types of software probes (inserted code). Typically this instrumentation records the control flow paths as the source text is executed. Users are able to perform other analyses if they wish. Examples are variable tracing, variable range analysis, assertion checking and other diagnostic activities.

Instrumentation is a complex technique and a wide variety of strategies are possible. Most languages do not permit probes to be placed at optimal points without changing the semantics of the program. Usually the probes require additional brackets and other constructs to be instrumented in order to preserve the original program's meaning. The actual nature of the probe depends very strongly on the type of information which is required. Thus for control flow analysis a probe which records the entry into a basic block is adequate. The temporal sequence of such entries is kept in an execution history. If the values of specific variables are required then probes must be inserted immediately after or during the assignment of values to the variable. The current test tool instruments probes which record LCSAJs. This is for reasons of efficiency.

The main objective of the control flow analysis is to measure the success of the testing activity. To this end three metrics are provided: TER1, the proportion of the statements which have been executed by the cumulative tests to date; TER2, the proportion of the branches executed; and TER3, the proportion of the LCSAJ path fragments which have been executed.

The experiments at Liverpool have shown that this third level of testing removes essentially all of the errors of commission. In general it causes many software faults to be discovered. Experiments have shown that in the course of the search for the necessary high-quality test data to achieve this level many errors of omission will also be discovered in the source text. However, there is no certainty that errors of omission will be found.

The Dynamic Analysis can be performed over the whole program, over a range defined by a pair of line numbers or over specific subroutines. It leads to a number of displays:

Display 7 This is an information display. It presents (for smallish segments of code) a detailed control flow trace. This is for small segments (say 500 lines of code) because in general the trace can be extremely extensive which makes it too big for comprehension. The trace is highly useful for checking exactly which paths are taken since it provides a line-by-line execution sequence. This has proved useful in two distinct situations: firstly when it is suspected that a program has obtained the right answers for the wrong reasons, and secondly when a program crashes and a visual representation of the execution sequence will give inspiration.

The trace is followed by a source text listing. Each such line of text is annotated with the number of times that line of code is executed, for the current set of test data, the cumulative total for all previous test data sets, and the cumulative total for all test data sets to date. The user can increase these totals by rerunning the instrumented program with new test data. This display is the most useful component of the Testbed. At a glance the user can discover the code which has not been executed. Such code is highlighted by putting a number of asterisks next to the lines with zero coverage. The user still has the most difficult part ahead. It is to generate new test data which will actually execute the offending code. The only clues which a standard Testbed offers lie in the directed graph representation of the programs and the Basic Block and LCSAJ displays. Automated techniques to perform this particular job have been developed, but in general these are not necessary for most types of software. This aspect will not be discussed further in this chapter.

A summary of the percentage of all the executable lines of code executed (TER1) is then presented. This is the first of the test effectiveness metrics.

The annotated source code listing is followed by a similarly annotated list of the control flow branches. Again unexecuted branches are highlighted. A summary table leading to the second test effectiveness metric TER2 is then presented.

Finally an annotated list of all the LCSAJs is presented which also leads to the third summary table and the TER3 metric.

Display 8   This is a Dynamic Data Flow Analysis which is a Testbed option. The user is informed variable by variable which uses of that variable are executed and which are not.

The display therefore consists of a list of each use of each variable annotated as in display 7 with the number of executions from the present test data set, the total from all previous executions, and finally the total from all executions to date.

The features described previously are those which the experiments at Liverpool have shown yield the most benefits for a given amount of effort. Some other features have been implemented but their use is limited by major technical problems which arise in the analysis of real programs. In addition there are also some severe limitations to the data flow analysis. The features subject to these problems are as follows:

a) *Data Flow Analysis*

The principal technical problem with Data Flow Analysis arises from two programming constructs: indexed variables (such as arrays) and pointer variables. The values taken by these variables are frequently determined dynamically and hence a static method such as Data Flow Analysis cannot determine precisely what happens. The consequence is that a reference to a specific element such as A[i] cannot in general be resolved because the value of i is not known precisely. The Analyser must therefore treat an indexed variable as though it were a simple variable. This reduces the power of the analysis considerably. A further practical problem is that of calls to utilities, such as operating system functions, or calls to procedures (subprograms, etc.) which are linked from libraries. When a data flow analyser encounters such an entity it knows nothing about the actions on the parameters or returned values. It therefore must assume the worst, e.g. that all parameters obtain new values in the call. This weakens the analysis and worse still leads to erroneous anomaly messages. The solution is to build a library containing the necessary information and in turn this introduces management problems for updating, deletion and insertion. The LDRA Testbed maintains a simple library of such calls. It is the user's responsibility to ensure that the information contained within is up-to-date. However, if a variable is referenced on only some of the paths in a procedure it is not obvious how this should be represented.

The principal practical problem is the huge set of anomaly messages which such a tool produces. This large number of messages problem is common to all Static Analysis techniques. In general it is not uncommon for as many messages to be generated as there are lines of code. Most of the messages are not due to errors, indeed usually only a few percent are actually errors. Worse still the messages are very difficult to verify. That is, the message informs the user of the existence of an anomaly between two occurrences of a given variable. The anomalous path is not given because the very essence of the analysis is that path information is never generated. Unfortunately the bemused user cannot see the offending path perhaps because the path is subtle or because it is too long. Either way the cost in hours and user irritation is high.

b) *Symbolic Execution*

This technique is part way between Static and Dynamic Analysis but still cannot handle dynamically determined values adequately. It essentially works by taking a path and replacing all occurrences of computed variables by an expression consisting of input values only. Thus all predicates (i.e. conditions which determine control flow) and output values are expressed in terms of expressions over the input values (variables). In principle it is possible to solve these predicates and determine either the feasibility of the path, or explicit test data which will exercise the path. In practice most such paths are infeasible and the complexity of the predicate makes solution impossible with current technology [14].

Deficiencies in symbolic execution arise as follows:

Firstly, the choice of paths is difficult in the presence of loops. This is because it is hard to decide which loop cycles to use. These cycles are usually determined by computed values. The symbolic execution merely generates expressions for the loop indices which in general can have a wide range of values for which bounds may not be available.

Secondly, subprogram (operating system or utility) calls introduce a huge class of problems. Strictly such a call ought to introduce a decision table of constraints and corresponding actions. In general such a table would be huge and hence unmanageable. The normal solution is to treat such a call like an input (i.e. read) statement, with all parameters treated as input variables. A library of information on such calls, as used in data flow analysis, can of course help.

Finite arithmetic problems are not handled. Thus rounding and truncation effects can distort the output results.

It is worth noting that there is very little difference between a so-called formal verification system and a symbolic executor. Thus the problems of the latter will all hold for the former.

c) *Automated Test Data Generation*

This option takes a path and its corresponding symbolically executed predicates and solves them to obtain a test data set which will cause execution of the given path. This optional module was implemented to help construct test data to increase coverage in cases where this is difficult to perform manually. In practice, infeasible paths and non-linear predicates reduce its value considerably. Infeasible paths essentially cause noise in the sense that any arbitrary path is highly likely to be infeasible. The symbolic execution will almost certainly discover this fact but only after considerable analysis. Non-linear predicates cannot be handled by the analytic predicate solving routines but such predicates can sometimes be solved by a random test data generator approach.

Only users with special needs are encouraged to use these extra modules. Considerable research is needed before any of these techniques can be widely applied to real programs.

7.6 Interpretation

Users of the Testbed are usually interested in improving the quality of their software. They are therefore interested not only in the extent (or goodness) of the testing activity but in other more long-term issues such as maintainability and efficiency. In this section these issues will be addressed.

1 *Efficiency*

The Testbeds offer a number of routes for those interested in the efficiency of their code. Firstly, from the Dynamic Analysis displays a user can immediately see where effort can usefully be employed. This is in the region of the hot-spots, i.e. regions of code which are executed a very large number of times. There is therefore no thought or insight required to isolate the points since the appropriate places are clearly indicated.

The first step is to examine the code within each Basic Block in the hot regions. Due to the nature of a Basic Block it is completely safe to compute common sub-expressions (if any) and store them in temporary variables which are then used in place of these common sub-expressions. The next step is to look at the lowest-level intervals containing the hot-spots. Again common sub-expressions appearing in any of the Basic Blocks contained within the interval can be computed and stored in the header node of the interval and safely reused anywhere within the interval. This process is precisely that used by optimizing compilers. It is however safer because humans can detect the sort of programming constructs which lead to problems with optimizing compilers and thus avoid the corresponding pitfalls.

2 *Unnecessary complexity*
Many software qualities are greatly improved if unnecessary complexity is eliminated. The Testbed not only indicates many different types of unnecessary complexity but also explicitly measures others. Some of the sources of unnecessary complexity are as follows:

a) Unused variables, labels, procedures and unreachable code. These are all indicated by the Testbed and hence can be removed.

b) Infeasible code is not explicitly indicated unless extensive use is made of the symbolic executor. However its presence can be inferred in the following way. Suppose that a number of test data sets have been constructed and the test coverage has reached at least 80% of the branches; i.e. TER2 = 0.80. Then an inspection of the LCSAJ coverage tables will show that a considerable number of these, i.e. 20% or greater, will not have been executed. Close inspection of these unexecuted LCSAJs will probably reveal that many are actually infeasible. A detailed investigation into this problem can be found in [14]. Whenever these infeasible LCSAJs occur it will always be found that they can be eliminated by rewriting the code more carefully.

The benefit of removing infeasible code is felt in many areas. The code will be more compact, it will execute faster, and it will be easier to read. Thus testability, maintainability and efficiency will improve.

Note, however, that the presence of infeasible code need not necessarily be bad. It may happen that the design allows for code which is believed to be infeasible when the compilers and hardware are correct but might be feasible in the presence of errors. Naturally testing such code is very difficult.

c) Poor code organization. Most program designs are graphical in nature and can be represented in terms of directed graphs. The graphs are two-dimensional and hence must be linearized when converted to code. This linearization can be accomplished in many different ways, some of which are better than others. The criteria which separates the good from the bad is usually that of readability, i.e. do components which relate to each other logically actually occur close together physically in a recognizable construction. The Testbed is able to measure the departure from the optimum by means of the essential knot metric. Reordering the Basic Blocks so that the knot metrics are minimized has the benefit of increasing readability and hence maintainability and testability.

3 Testedness

The primary purpose of the Testbeds is to provide unambiguous measures of software testedness. This they accomplish by means of structural test effectiveness measures. Thus $TER1 = n$ means that $n*100\%$ of the statements have been executed. In this context a statement can be taken to mean a line of executable code. A more rigorous measure to fulfill is that of TER2 which reflects the percentage of the branches which have been executed. It is well known that test data which satisfies $TER2 = 1$ can detect significantly more errors than test data which satisfies $TER1 = 1$. The Testbed goes further and provides the capability of ensuring that every LCSAJ is executed ($TER3 = 1$). This is again a significant improvement over TER2 in the number of errors which can be detected. Experiments have shown that achieving $TER3 = 1$ leaves very little potential for residual errors. Errors can remain undetected but they will be very rare since they must satisfy obscure relationships [1].

7.7 Applicability and benefits

The recommended techniques described previously and which are essentially encompassed in the LDRA Testbeds are of a very wide applicability. It has been reported that similar tools have been used by TRW to analyse up to 2 million lines of code.

In practice there are conflicting constraints. Both the Static Analysis and Dynamic Analysis increase in power as the amount of code analysed increases. Thus data flow anomalies involving variables in widely separated modules will be detected, and all calls and returns to subroutines will be executed. However, the human effort involved in analysing all the resultant messages will increase more than linearly and probably with the square of the amount of code analysed. From a human standpoint experience has shown that analysing between 5000 and 20 000 lines of code provides an adequate "head-full".

In general the techniques are suitable for any type of code in any programming language. The only major area where problems can be encountered is that of real-time and real-time embedded systems. Recently considerable progress has been made even in this area. All the static analysis techniques can be applied and the dynamic analysis is only impractical for very unusual temporally bound systems and even for these it is only small components which can elude analysis.

Any user of a particular tool is entitled to ask what benefits accrue from the use of the tool. In addition they may also be interested in costs. The Testbeds are structure-based analysers. The underlying philosophy is that the basic structure of the program is essentially correct and that testing should consist of exploring this structure. Therefore it is clear that the

Testbed cannot directly indicate missing code or functionality. Misunderstood functionality can however usually be detected.

The Testbed therefore largely but not exclusively detects errors of commission, i.e. features which were thought of but which for various reasons were incorrectly implemented. The ability to detect errors of omission depends on whether some parts of these features have been implemented in error, a not-so-infrequent possibility. Naturally forcing the tester to generate data to explore these areas can open the mind to wider possibilities and hence there is a chance of detecting errors of omission.

With the errors of commission the Testbeds perform remarkably well. Given only fairly restrictive conditions on the complexity of expressions and control flow structure it is possible for all the errors to be detected. The restrictions on the expressions are that they should be low-ordered polynomials and the limits on the structure are that the directed graph should not consist of splitter, node-collector, node-splitter, node sequences, i.e. the procedures should be tree-like. Detailed analyses of program structure have shown [17, 18] that on the whole the first condition is frequently met. Not enough is known about the second area for a judgement to be made.

The authors have conducted extensive experiments to try and determine the error-detecting capacity of the Testbeds. Since the basis of successful experimentation is a methodical approach, the mutation testing method was used to systematically generate all cases of particular classes of error over a class of software. The ability of the Testbeds to detect these errors was then examined. It was found that a very high proportion (high nineties) of the errors were detected. Of the undetected seeded errors most were of the equivalent program type; i.e. if there is a $<$ operator in a comparison on a path where previous constraints ensure that the data cannot satisfy the equality possibility, then replacing the $<$ operator by $<\,=$ cannot generate an error. The reason why we cannot be sure that all undetected errors are of this type is that it is often very hard to demonstrate that the mutated program is indeed equivalent to the original.

The mutation experiments have shown that the error-detecting capability of the Testbeds is very high. However there is still the possibility that errors which cannot be easily expressed in terms of mutants could escape detection. The authors have addressed this problem by means of generalized models. For example, it is possible to show that loop errors which satisfy recurrence relationships of order less than or equal to 3 must be detected when testing all the LCSAJs.

Costs There are a number of perspectives for the costs of using a Testbed. They are primarily short-term, long-term and introductory costs.

Introductory costs These are the costs incurred in training and start-up procedures. Actual training seems to be a minimal problem because the vast majority of LDRA customers do not require training programs even though they are offered. They feel that once a specific technician has mastered the art (which takes one day) this person can easily teach the rest. The procedures to use the Testbed usually come in two flavours. The first is to put the Testbed on general access and the second is to confine its use to a quality assurance group. In the former case the set-up costs are minimal but in the second there can be considerable costs if such a group does not already exist.

Short-term costs   When any tool of this type is introduced it enforces a considerable amount of rework of existing code. This is because the existing code is unlikely to satisfy the wide range of standards. The rework process will inevitably prolong the time before the software can be delivered. Much of this time or more can be recovered from the reduced need for maintenance and long term rework.

Long-term costs   Once a Testbed has been in use for some time the programmers and analysts will adapt to the additional constraints. For example, in transforming from a design construct to an equivalent coding construct, programmers will select one which does not introduce infeasible code. The result is that the overhead in testing to the higher standard is significantly reduced as time goes by.

In the context of delivered systems these costs must be balanced with regard to the cost of subsequent software failure and consequent rework. In the experience of the authors, the cost of using the tools in their own environment is not high.

7.8   Safety-critical systems

The significance of the Testbeds in relation to safety-critical software is complex. A safety-critical system must have many software characteristics such as freedom from errors, fault tolerance, error detection and control, and so on. Yet other factors such as high quality are relevant. The major contribution of the Testbed is in quality control, where quality is an assessment of the "fitness-for-purpose" over a range of viewpoints, such as maintainability, reliability, enhanceability and so on. Many of these issues are not confined to safety-critical systems but are of general concern. The use of a Testbed and a concerned response to its output messages result in a more readable, more maintainable, more efficient software system. Its reliability is also substantially improved because of the high error-detecting capability.

Nevertheless a Testbed cannot protect a user from errors of omission or misunderstanding. Indeed no technique of any sort can provide such protection because all techniques must rely on underlying structure, whether it be of the application area or of the information-capturing notation.

It is not possible to make any direct inference about in-use reliability from the output of a Testbed (or any other validation tool for that matter).

Preliminary results of investigations in this area can be found in [21]. Neither is it possible to infer that, because no errors have been found either in the Static Analysis or in the process of achieving TER3 = 1, there are no errors in the software, or that they are likely to occur infrequently [22].

The authors regard the achievement of adequate levels of testing for safety-critical software to be beyond current technology.

For safety-critical systems it is necessary to show that all the significant (critical) patterns of use are successfully tested by the actual test patterns. This link between use and testing is completely missing in the technology. Currently the authors are participating in an ESPRIT project which is attempting to provide this link [21].

Conclusion This chapter is a summary of the experience of one group of software validators. It attempts to explain what has been found to be usable and what has not. It gives a glimpse of the advantages and disadvantages of the particular tools. The authors know that the tools referred to are not the solution to all software problems but believe that they are the best methods currently available for thorough systematic testing of software.

References

[1]   M. A. Hennell, D. Hedley and I. J. Riddell, "Assessing a Class of Software Tools", *Proc. 7th. IEEE Int. Conf. on Software Engineering*, Orlando, 1984.

[2]   M. A. Hennell and D. F. Yates, "A Configuration Management System for Software Implementation", *Proc. Hawaii Int. Conf. on Systems Sciences*, pp. 84–89, January 1981.

[3]   L. D. Fosdick, *BRNANL, A Fortran Program to Identify Basic Blocks in Fortran Programs*, Report CU-CS-040-74, Computer Science Dept., University of Colorado, 1974.

[4]   B. Ryder, "The PFORT Verifier", *Software Practice and Experience*, Vol. 4, pp. 359–377, 1974.

[5]   L. J. Osterweil and L. D. Fosdick, "DAVE-Validation Error Detection and Documentation System for Fortran Programs", *Software Practice and Experience*, Vol. 6, No. 4, pp. 473–486, September 1976.

[6]   R. M. Balzer, "Exdams: Extendible Debugging and Monitoring Systems", *AFIPS*, Vol. 34, p. 567, 1969.

[7]   L. G. Stucki and G. L. Foshee, "New Assertion Concepts for Self-Metric Software Validation," *Proc. 1975, Int. Conf. Reliable Software*, Los Angeles, pp. 59–71, April 1975.

[8]   W. E. Howden, "Methodology for the Generation of Program Test Data", *IEEE Transactions on Computing*, Vol. 24, No. 5, pp. 554–559, May 1975.

[9]   S. L. Hantler and J. C. King, "An Introduction to Proving the Correctness of Programs", *ACM Computing Surveys*, Vol. 8, No. 3, pp. 331–353, September 1976.

[10]   L. A. Clarke, "A System to Generate Test Data and Symbolically Execute

Programs", *IEEE Trans. Soft. Eng.*, Vol. 2, No. 3, pp. 215–222, September 1976.

[11]   R. A. De Millo, R. J. Lipton and F. G. Sayward, "Hints on Test Data Selection: Help for the Practicing Programmer", *Computer*, Vol. 11, No. 4, pp. 34–41, April 1978.

[12]   T. A. Budd, R. J. Lipton and F. G. Sayward, "The Design of a Prototype Mutation System for Program Testing", *AFIPS*, NCC, 1978, Vol. 47, pp. 623–627.

[13]   D. F. Yates and M. A. Hennell, "An Examination of Standards and Practices for Software Production", *Computers and Standards* 1, pp. 119–132, 1982.

[14]   D. Hedley and M. A. Hennell, "The Causes and Effects of Infeasible Paths in Computer Programs", *Proc. 8th. Int. Conf. on Software Engineering*, London, August 1985.

[15]   F. E. Allen and J. Cocke, "A Program Data Flow Analysis Procedure", *Communications of the ACM*, Vol. 19, No. 3, pp. 137–147, March 1976.

[16]   M. Woodward, M. A. Hennell and D. Hedley, "A Measure of Control Flow Complexity in Program Text", *IEEE Transactions on Software Engineering*, Vol. 5, No. 1, pp. 45–50, January 1979.

[17]   M. A. Hennell and J. A. Prudom, "A Static Analysis of the NAG Library", *IEEE Transactions on Software Engineering*, Vol. SE-6, No. 4, pp. 329–333, July 1980.

[18]   D. E. Knuth, "An Empirical Study of Fortran Programs", *Software Practice and Experience*, Vol. 1, pp. 105–13, 1971.

[19]   W. Howden, "An Evaluation of the Effectiveness of Symbolic Testing", *Software Practice and Experience*, Vol. 8, pp. 381–397, 1978.

[20]   L. Lauterbach, preliminary paper presented at CSR Certification Workshop, Gatwick, September 1988. Research Triangle Institute, PO Box 12194, Research Triangle Park, NC 27709 USA.

[21]   E. Fergus, A. C. Marshall, A. Veevers, D. Hedley and M. A. Hennell, "The Quantification of Software Reliability", *Proc. 2nd IEE/BCS Conf. on Software Engineering*, Liverpool, pp. 43–49, May 1988.

[22]   M. A. Hennell, M. Woodward and D. Hedley, "The Testing of a Software Tool", *Proc. International Symposium on Applications and Software Engineering*, Montreal, September 1979, pp. 16–20 (ACTA press, ed. M. H. Hamza, 1980).

[23]   Holthouse and Hatch, *Proc. Workshop on Testing*, Fort Lauderdale, Florida, December 1978.

8 Program analysis and verification

Bernard Carré, Program Validation Limited

8.1 Introduction

Chapter 5 drew attention to the dangers in using "standard" programming languages and explained how, for a few of them at least, programming could be made more reliable by confining it to a sublanguage, and employing annotations (formal comments) to provide information not directly expressible in the standard language. The necessary connection between the annotations and the executable code was made by additional language rules, and conformance to those rules was checked at the same time as syntax and static semantics, by a tool similar to the "front end" of a compiler.

Our principal aims were to make the language employed logically coherent and as secure as possible (in the sense of section 5.2.4), and to allow us to reason about a program relatively easily. Reasoning is needed firstly to prove that language rules relating to "dynamic semantics" (and concerning principally the range restrictions on values of dynamically evaluated expressions) are not violated, in any of a program's possible executions; and secondly to prove that program code is in consonance with its specification. These proofs are tractable only if program "fragments" can be studied in isolation.

This chapter describes analysis and verification methods, applicable to programs in well-defined languages such as SPADE-Pascal and SPARK, after performing the language conformance checks indicated above. The same techniques and tools can also be used to verify programs written in appropriate annotated subsets of assembly codes [Clutterbuck/Carré1988; O'Neill1988]. For illustrative purposes our examples here will be in SPARK.

SPARK with its support tools also facilitates the rigorous development of a program in fragments. At each stage the fragment under consideration may be the main program, a complete library unit, or a constituent package or subprogram. In creating such a program fragment one first writes its specification (as in Figure 8.1 for instance). With its SPARK annotations, this specification describes the relationship between the fragment and its environment sufficiently well to allow implementation, analysis and

```
      --# proof type Seq_of_Int is sequence of Integer;
      . . . . . .

package IntegerQueues is

   type Queue is limited private;

      --# proof const MaxQueueLength : Integer;
      --# proof function AtoC_Queue(Seq_of_Int) : Queue;
      --# proof function CtoA_Queue(Queue) : Seq_of_Int;

      --# rule AtoC_Queue(CtoA_Queue(Q)) may_be_replaced_by Q;
      --# rule CtoA_Queue(AtoC_Queue(Q)) may_be_replaced_by Q;
      --# rule EmptyQueue(Q) may_be_replaced_by CtoA_Queue(Q) = Seq_of_Int[ ];
      --# rule FullQueue(Q) may_be_replaced_by Length(CtoA_Queue(Q)) = MaxQueueLength;

   function EmptyQueue(Q : Queue) return Boolean;
      --# pre   true;
      --# post EmptyQueue(Q) = (CtoA_Queue(Q) = Seq_of_Int[ ]);

   function FullQueue(Q : Queue) return Boolean;
      --# pre   true;
      --# post FullQueue(Q) = (Length(CtoA_Queue(Q)) = MaxQueueLength);

   procedure ClearQueue(Q : in out Queue);
      --# derives Q from ;
      --# pre   true;
      --# post Q = AtoC_Queue(Seq_of_Int[ ]);

   procedure EnQueue(Q : in out Queue; X : in Integer);
      --# derives Q from Q, X;
      --# pre   Length(CtoA_Queue(Q)) < MaxQueueLength;
      --# post Q = AtoC_Queue(CtoA_Queue(Q~) @ Seq_of_Int[X]);

   procedure DeQueue(Q : in out Queue; X : out Integer);
      --# derives Q from Q &
      --#          X from Q;
      --# pre   CtoA_Queue(Q) <> Seq_of_Int[ ];
      --# post Q = AtoC_Queue(Nonfirst(CtoA_Queue(Q~))) and
      --#        X = First(CtoA_Queue(Q~));

private

   QueueSize : constant Integer := 100;
   subtype IndexRange is Integer range 0 .. QueueSize;
   type Vector is array(IndexRange) of Integer;
   subtype PointerRange is Integer range 0 .. QueueSize + 1;
   type Queue is
      record
         QueueVector : Vector;
         FrontPointer,
         BackPointer : PointerRange;
      end record;

end IntegerQueues;
```

Fig. 8.1 A SPARK package specification for queues of integers

verification of the fragment in isolation. The specification of a fragment can also be precise enough to allow tool-supported analysis and verification of other fragments that employ it, without prior refinement and implementation of its body. (The implementation may be deferred by means of the SPARK "hide" directive described in chapter 5.) Thus one can progressively flesh out a design towards its final implementation, concentrating development in whatever area one chooses, with the ability to check the logical coherence of the work produced at every stage.

8.2 Program modelling

The analysis of a program must be based on the mathematical meaning or semantics of its programming language. Using this, the program must be described at a level of abstraction and in a form suitable for analysis. Our method is based on an operational definition of the programming language. To analyse and verify a fragment of code we construct a mathematical model of it, very like a "flowchart program" as defined by Manna [1974, chapter 3]. This section describes our modelling technique.

8.2.1 Flowchart programs

The model of a main program or a subprogram is constructed as follows.

We distinguish three types of variables, grouped as three vectors: (1) an import vector $W = [w_1, w_2, ..., w_a]$, whose component values are initially specified and do not change during computation; (2) a program state vector $X = [x_1, x_2, ..., x_b]$ whose components at a given time have the values currently assigned to the program variables; and (3) an export vector $Y = [y_1, y_2, ..., y_c]$, whose components are assigned values when computation terminates. Correspondingly we have (1) an import domain D_w, (2) a program state domain D_x, and (3) an export domain D_y.

Our model consists of a directed graph (often described as a control flow graph) $G = (N, U)$, where N is a set of nodes (or "statements"), and $U \subseteq N \times N$ is a set of arcs, defining the possible successors of each node (statement) in a program execution. The arcs of the graph are labelled with functions, to capture the semantics of the program code, in the following way. We distinguish four kinds of statements on G:

1   The (unique) program *start* statement. This has exactly one successor, and the arc from the start statement to its successor is labelled with a total function

$$f: D_w \to D_x$$

2   A *mapping* (or multiple assignment) statement. This has exactly one successor, and the arc from a mapping statement to its successor is

178

labelled with a partial function

$$g : D_x \to D_x$$

(Such mappings are used to describe all state changes, resulting from the execution of an assignment statement for instance, or the calling of a procedure, including possibly "input" or "output" procedures.)

3 A *switch* (or test) statement. This has at least two successors. Each arc incident from a switch statement is labelled with a partial predicate

$$h : D_x \to \{false, \ true\}$$

4 The (unique) program *finish* statement. This has exactly one predecessor. The arc incident to the finish statement is labelled with a total function

$$k : D_x \to D_y$$

Given a value of the import vector W, a flowchart program can be executed (provided that it satisfies certain rules of "well-formation" which will be discussed below). Execution begins at the start statement, traversal of the arc incident from this statement "initializing" X to $f(W)$. This may represent for instance the passing of parameters if the program fragment being modelled is a subprogram, and the definition of the initial status of all other objects external to the flowchart program (such as input or output files) which it may inspect or modify. Execution then proceeds by following a path through the flowchart program, from statement to statement. Whenever a mapping statement is reached, the current value of X is replaced by $g(X)$. When a switch statement is reached, execution follows that arc incident from it whose "traversal condition" $h(X)$ holds for the current value of X (and by the method of construction of the flowchart program, this condition will apply to at most one arc incident from the switch statement). If execution terminates, traversal of the final arc causes Y to be assigned the current value of $k(X)$. This represents the returning of parameter values and of the final status of other external objects.

Such a model of a program fragment will only be logically coherent if every node on the graph G lies on a path from the start to the finish and if, for every possible execution, the arguments and values of all the applied functions and predicates on the execution path are well-defined, at the points where these functions are evaluated. The static semantic checks performed on the source text and flow analyses performed on the flowchart program (as described in section 8.3) provide some safeguards in this respect. However, these preliminary checks do not ensure that the values of dynamically-evaluated expressions always lie within their permissible ranges. Neither can we be sure, in modelling the call of a procedure or function subprogram, that its pre-condition is always met. Thus construction of the flowchart model gives rise to proof obligations, which we express in the following way.

In addition to the vectors W, X and Y defined above, we associate with our flowchart model a proof vector $Z = [z_1, z_2, ..., z_d]$ whose components, called "proof variables" or "ghost variables", are used for storage of values of program variables at particular nodes of a flowchart. The domain of Z is denoted by D_z. Then, in addition to the kinds of statements described above, the following kinds of proof statements may be employed. (These each have a single successor.)

5 A *save* statement. The arc incident from it is labelled with a function mapping D_x into D_z. Save statements are employed to record values of program variables at particular points of a computation, allowing reference to them in other proof statements.

6 An *assert* statement, labelled with a predicate over $D_x \times D_z$. Assert statements allow the inclusion of inductive assertions, such as loop invariants, required for correctness proofs.

7 A *check* statement, labelled with a predicate over $D_x \times D_z$. Check statements express proof obligations, such as checks of ranges of dynamically-evaluated expressions or checks of pre-conditions of subprograms at their points of call.

8 An *assume* statement. The arc incident from such a statement is labelled with a predicate over $D_x \times D_z$. Assume statements serve to introduce facts, such as post-conditions of procedures after they have been called.

Finally, the start statement may be labelled with a pre-condition (a predicate over D_w) and the finish statement may be labelled with a post-condition (a predicate over $D_w \times D_y$). The uses of all of these kinds of proof statements will be demonstrated below.

The logic employed in SPADE is classical first-order predicate calculus, with quantification, this being supported by a natural deduction Proof-Checker which will be described in section 8.4.2. With regard to the domains of variables, SPADE supports boolean, integer and enumerated types and their subrange types, and polymorphic array, record, set and sequence types; the SPADE Proof-Checker's knowledge base contains proof rules for the more common operations on all of these. Abstract data types can also be employed.

As was mentioned in chapter 5, the SPADE tools that perform the syntax and static-semantic analysis of SPADE-Pascal and SPARK texts also produce their flowchart models, describing them in a Functional Description Language (FDL). The textual description of the models is quite direct, with only as much syntactic sugar as is necessary to make texts reasonably easy to comprehend. Its use will be illustrated in the next section.

8.2.2 An illustration of program modelling

A SPARK procedure ReverseQueue, which reverses a queue of integers by pushing its successive members into a stack and then enqueuing them again as they are popped, is shown in Figure 8.2. This procedure employs the stack and queue packages whose specifications are given in Figure 5.3 and Figure 8.1 respectively. It will be noted that these packages introduce the stack and queue types as abstract data types; within the procedure ReverseQueue the specified functions and operations on stacks and queues can be applied, but only their specifications (in terms of sequences) are visible there, not their concrete implementations. The procedure ReverseQueue is also specified in terms of sequences.

The FDL model of ReverseQueue is shown in Figure 8.3. Its declarative part in Figure 8.3(a) lists the types, constants, functions and variables

```
with IntegerStacks;  use IntegerStacks;
with IntegerQueues;  use IntegerQueues;

. . . . . .

procedure ReverseQueue(Q : in out Queue);
--# derives Q from Q;

--# proof function Reverse(Seq_of_Int) : Seq_of_Int;
--# rule Reverse(Seq_of_Int[ ]) may_be_replaced_by Seq_of_Int[ ];
--# rule Reverse(Seq_of_Int[X]) may_be_replaced_by Seq_of_Int[X];
--# rule Reverse(X @ Y) & Reverse(Y) @ Reverse(X) are_interchangeable;
--# rule Length(Reverse(X)) & Length(X) are_interchangeable;

--# invariant (Length(CtoA_Queue(Q)) <= MaxQueueLength) and
--#          (Length(CtoA_Queue(Q)) <= MaxStackLength);
--# pre   true;
--# post  Q = AtoC_Queue(Reverse(CtoA_Queue(Q~)));

procedure ReverseQueue(Q : in out Queue)
is
   S: Stack;
   X: Integer;
begin
   ClearStack(S);
   while not EmptyQueue(Q)
   --# assert (Reverse(CtoA_Queue(Q)) @ CtoA_Stack(S) = Reverse(CtoA_Queue(Q~)));
   loop
      DeQueue(Q, X);
      Push(S, X);
   end loop;
   while not EmptyStack(S)
   --# assert (CtoA_Queue(Q) @ CtoA_Stack(S) = Reverse(CtoA_Queue(Q~)));
   loop
      Pop(S, X);
      EnQueue(Q, X);
   end loop;
end ReverseQueue;
```

Fig. 8.2 A SPARK procedure for reversing a queue of integers

title procedure ReverseQueue;

proof type Seq_of_Int = **sequence of** Integer;

type Stack = **pending**;

function EmptyStack(Stack) : Boolean;
function FullStack(Stack) : Boolean;
const ClearStack : Stack = **pending**;
function Push(Stack, Integer) : Stack;
function Pop_1(Stack) : Stack;
function Pop_2(Stack) : Integer;

proof const MaxStackLength : Integer = **pending**;
proof function AtoC_Stack(Seq_of_Int) : Stack;
proof function CtoA_Stack(Stack) : Seq_of_Int;

type Queue = **pending**;

function EmptyQueue(Queue) : Boolean;
function FullQueue(Queue) : Boolean;
const ClearQueue : Queue = **pending**;
function EnQueue(Queue, Integer) : Queue;
function DeQueue_1(Queue) : Queue;
function DeQueue_2(Queue) : Integer;

proof const MaxQueueLength : Integer = **pending**;
proof function AtoC_Queue(Seq_of_Int) : Queue;
proof function CtoA_Queue(Queue) : Seq_of_Int;

proof function Reverse(Seq_of_Int) : Seq_of_Int;

var Q : Queue;
var S : Stack;
var X : Integer;

proof var Saved_S : Stack;
proof var Saved_Q : Queue;

Fig. 8.3(a)   Declarative part of the FDL model of ReverseQueue

required to construct the model, beginning with those associated with the stack and queue packages. Most of the functions here correspond directly to functions declared in the packages, but some are introduced to describe the effects of procedure calls (since the notion of a procedure is foreign to our abstract model). For instance, the stack package specification of Figure 5.3 contains the procedure specification

```
procedure Pop(S : in out Stack; X : out Integer);
--# derives S from S &
--#          X from S;
--# pre  CtoA_Stack(S) <> Seq_of_Int[ ];
--# post S = AtoC_Stack(Nonfirst(CtoA_Stack(S~))) and
--#      X = First(CtoA_Stack(S~));
```

derives Q **from** Q;

invariant (Length(CtoA_Queue(Q)) <= MaxQueueLength) and
    (Length(CtoA_Queue(Q)) <= MaxStackLength);
pre true;
post Q = AtoC_Queue(Reverse(CtoA_Queue(Q~)));

```
 1       start
 2       S := Clear_Stack;
 3       assume S = AtoC_Stack(Seq_of_Int[ ]);
 4     1: assert (Reverse(CtoA_Queue(Q)) @ CtoA_Stack(S) = Reverse(CtoA_Queue(Q~)));
 5       case not EmptyQueue(Q) of
             false : goto 2;
             true  : skip
         end;
 6       check CtoA_Queue(Q) <> Seq_of_Int[ ];
 7       save Q as Saved_Q;
 8       Q := DeQueue_1(Q) &
         X := DeQueue_2(Q);
 9       assume Q = AtoC_Queue(Nonfirst(CtoA_Queue(Saved_Q))) and
                 X = First(CtoA_Queue(Saved_Q));
10       check Length(CtoA_Stack(S)) < MaxStackLength;
11       save S as Saved_S;
12       S := Push(S, X);
13       assume S = AtoC_Stack(Seq_of_Int[X] @ CtoA_Stack(Saved_S));
14       goto 1;
15     2: assert (CtoA_Queue(Q) @ CtoA_Stack(S) = Reverse(CtoA_Queue(Q~)));
16       case not EmptyStack(S) of
             false : goto 3;
             true  : skip
         end;
17       check CtoA_Stack(S) <> Seq_of_Int[ ];
18       save S as Saved_S;
19       S := Pop_1(S) &
         X := Pop_2(S);
20       assume S = AtoC_Stack(Nonfirst(CtoA_Stack(Saved_S))) and
                 X = First(CtoA_Stack(Saved_S));
21       check Length(CtoA_Queue(Q)) < MaxQueueLength;
22       save Q as Saved_Q;
23       Q := EnQueue(Q, X);
24       assume Q = AtoC_Queue(CtoA_Queue(Saved_Q) @ Seq_of_Int[X]);
25       goto 2;
26     3: skip
27       finish
```

Fig. 8.3(b)   Specification and statement parts of the FDL model of ReverseQueue

and it follows from its parameter list and dependency relation that the effect
of executing this procedure can be described by the simultaneous application
of two functions:

    function Pop_1(Stack) : Stack;
    function Pop_2(Stack) : Integer;

deriving S from S and X from S respectively. The complete FDL translation of the procedure call Pop(S, X) in ReverseQueue is (cf. Figure 8.3(b), statements 17 to 20)

```
check CtoA_Stack(S) <> Seq_of_Int[ ];
save S as Saved_S;
S := Pop_1(S) &
X := Pop_2(S);
assume S = AtoC_Stack(Nonfirst(CtoA_Stack(Saved_S))) and
       X = First(CtoA_Stack(Saved_S));
```

in which $<>$ denotes inequality and Seq_of_Int[ ] represents an empty sequence of integers.

The translation begins with a check statement, in which the predicate is the pre-condition of the procedure (with formal parameters replaced by actual ones). The initial value of the stack S is then saved (because S is modified by the procedure, and its post-condition relates initial to final values of S). The save statement is followed by a mapping statement, representing the change of state by two simultaneous assignments (whose descriptions are separated by a & symbol). It will be noted that the functions Pop_1 and Pop_2 are not defined explicitly, only the types of their arguments and results have been declared. This information suffices to model an execution of the procedure with respect to control-, data- and information-flow. The semantics of the procedure are captured by the final assume statement, whose predicate is the procedure's post-condition, with occurrences of formal parameters again replaced by the corresponding actual ones.

The declarative part of an FDL text is followed by a specification (cf. Figure 8.3(b)), consisting of a dependency relation and (optional) pre- and post-conditions, replicas of those in the SPARK text. Recall that the dependency relation names the variables whose initial values are imported and those whose final values are exported; hence it defines the import and export vectors W and Y of section 8.2.1, and the functions f and k applied respectively by the start and finish statements of the flowchart program.

The specification part is followed by a statement part (cf. Figure 8.3(b)). The correspondence between flowchart program statements as defined in section 8.2.1 and FDL statements is fairly obvious, except perhaps for the representation of switch statements: in FDL, a switch statement is expressed as a case statement, in which every case-list-element simply specifies a successor statement, by means of a skip statement or a goto statement.

8.3 Flow analysis

The soundness of reasoning about a program in terms of such a simple flowchart model rests on a number of assumptions about the program code, whose validity cannot be checked entirely by syntactic and static-semantic analysis of the usual kind. For instance to reason using classical logic, we must be sure that program variables are value-defined before they are referenced. Again, the absence of aliasing and of side-effects of function subprograms, assumed in the construction of the flowchart models, is only guaranteed if the annotations of a program text are consistent with its code; in particular, the dependency relations of subprograms must correctly specify their imports and exports (in the manner explained in chapter 5). To ensure that all such assumptions apply, flow analysis is always performed, on the flowchart models, before the study of their semantics.

The performance of such analyses before attempting program proof is important for another reason. However carefully a program is implemented, it is very likely that some mistakes will be made. Even if there are no serious misconceptions in the design, false assumptions about initial conditions and slips such as transpositions of variable names in parameter lists are very common. Flow analysis methods, as well as justifying our assumptions, can be made to reveal a substantial proportion of the program errors; since they employ fast (polynomial-time) algorithms and require no interaction, their preliminary application lightens the verification task appreciably.

8.3.1 Control flow analysis

The syntax rules of some languages (such as Gypsy and SPARK) ensure that the control-flow graph of a program is satisfactory for our purposes, and with such languages control-flow analysis is unnecessary: all the information concerning control structure required for other kinds of analyses is easily obtained from the syntax tree formed when the program is parsed. However, with languages having goto statements (such as SPADE-Pascal and assembly codes), control-flow analysis is always performed, to detect errors, discourage convoluted programming, and also to extract information about control structure that can be employed by other analysis tools.

The SPADE control-flow analyser first establishes whether the essential requirements are met, that a program fragment to be analysed has a single entry point (corresponding to the start node on its control-flow graph G) and a single exit (represented by the finish node), and that on G all statements lie on paths from the start to the finish. If so, the graph is decomposed into its sections (the single-entry single-exit subgraphs of G whose entry nodes are the dominators [Carré1979] of the finish node on G), and analysis proceeds section by section.

For each section, the control-flow analyser parses the graph, employing a graph grammar very similar to the *semi-structured flow graph* (SSFG) grammar of Farrow [1975]. A graph grammar consists of a set of production rules, each defining the production of one partial graph from another. As simple examples we may have (1) a sequence rule, for replacing a node which has exactly one predecessor and exactly one successor by a pair of nodes, joined by an arc, and (2) an if-then-else rule, replacing a node with unique predecessor s and unique successor t by a node with predecessor s and two successors, which both have the unique successor t. Graph parsing is performed by reverse application of production rules, which progressively collapses a graph to a single node.

The family of graphs generated by SPADE's graph grammar is precisely the family of control-flow graphs of sequences of statements that can be generated from the SPARK grammar. (This has Ada's if-statement, case-statement, loop-statement and exit-statement, but no goto-statement or exceptions, and minor restrictions on the positioning of exit-statements and return statements.) When a graph is parsed, each of its nodes has associated with it a trace, an extended regular-algebraic expression which defines the subgraph represented by the node (or more precisely, the set of all paths through this subgraph). On applying a production rule (in reverse), the trace of the resulting node is formed by combining the traces of its constituents. The trace of the final node, describing the complete flowchart program, is used in the construction of the flow relations, described below. If required, it also makes it easy to construct a pictorial representation of the control flow. (Many older programmers secretly draw a little flowchart from time to time; for assembly code in particular, it can be helpful.)

In cases where a control-flow graph does not obey the rules of the graph grammar, the control-flow analyser establishes whether the graph is reducible [Hecht1977], that is whether it is free from cycles with multiple entry points. If not it indicates the offending subgraphs. (If a graph is not reducible, the notions of a "program loop" and of "loop nesting" break down, and verification or testing become virtually impossible.) For a reducible graph, the analyser gives the direct dominators of all nodes and a description of the loops and their nesting.

8.3.2 Data flow analysis

At the start of execution of a flowchart program, variables whose initial values are not imported are in an undefined state. Even after values have been assigned to them, they may become undefined; for instance, on termination of a Pascal for-statement its control variable becomes undefined. The primary purpose of data-flow analysis is to ensure that undefined values are never employed in evaluating expressions.

In SPADE, data-flow analysis is based on the concept of *reaching definitions* as presented by Hecht [1977]. To outline the basic method, let d be (a statement with) a definition or an undefinition of a variable v. (If v is an import we regard the start statement as a definition of v, otherwise we treat it as an undefinition of this variable.) For any statement s on G we say that *d reaches s* if there exists a path from d to s which does not traverse any definitions or undefinitions of v. Now let s be a statement containing an expression in which v occurs. If any undefinitions of v reach s we say that a data-flow error occurs at s. If at least one definition of v also reaches s the error is conditional, otherwise it is unconditional.

The sets of nodes that definitions and undefinitions may reach are easily found, using an algorithm for finding accessible sets on a graph [Carré1979] or by algebraic methods [Hecht1977]. If a data-flow error at a node s is conditional, it may be necessary to determine whether any of the paths by which undefinitions can reach s are executable; this can be done using SPADE's *symbolic interpreter* (which reports data-flow errors as they occur in the course of a symbolic execution).

Following a similar approach, the data-flow analyser also detects conditional and unconditional data-flow anomalies, that is definitions of variables that are never employed. These are not serious in themselves, but they are often symptomatic of serious errors, such as the omission of statements or misnaming of variables. Using the notion of constant propagation employed in compilers, the data-flow analyser also detects ineffective tests (whose expressions always have the same value), and with the description of loop structure provided by the control-flow analyser it can indicate invariant definitions within loops.

8.3.3 Information flow analysis

Our method of information-flow analysis will be described in terms of the very simple language of Figure 8.4. It is not necessary to specify the grammar or semantics of expressions, but it will be assumed that the evaluation of an expression does not have side-effects.

We denote by V the set of variables in a program, and by E the set of all instances of expressions in it; also, for each expression e in E we let $\Gamma(e)$ stand for the set of all variables which appear in e. For any statement S we denote by D_s the set of variables that may be assigned values by S; formulae for D_s are given in Figure 8.5.

Our method of analysis is based on the construction of a binary "input-output" relation ρ_s on V for each statement S of a program in turn. For any two (not necessarily distinct) variables v and v' in V, the condition $v \, \rho_s \, v'$ can be interpreted (loosely) as "the value of v on entry to S may affect the value of v' on exit from S". A precise description of the relation for each

```
program = compound statement.
statement = assignment statement | compound statement |
            conditional statement | repetitive statement.
assignment statement = variable ":=" expression.
compound statement = "begin" statement {";" statement } "end".
conditional statement = "if" expression "then" statement "else" statement |
            "if" expression "then" statement.
repetitive statement = "while" expression "do" statement.
```

Fig. 8.4 Syntax of a simple programming language

Assignment Statements. For an assignment statement S, which assigns a value to v and whose expression part is e,

$$D_S = \{v\} \qquad \text{[1a]}$$

$$\rho_S = (\Gamma(e) \times \{v\}) \cup (\iota - \{(v, v)\}) \quad \text{[1b]} \qquad\qquad \mu_S = \{(e, v)\} \quad \text{[1c]}$$

Sequences of Statements. For a sequence S of two statements $(A; B)$,

$$D_S = D_A \cup D_B \quad \text{[2a]}$$

$$\rho_S = \rho_A \rho_B \qquad \text{[2b]} \qquad\qquad \mu_S = \mu_A \rho_B \cup \mu_B \quad \text{[2c]}$$

Conditional Statements. For a statement S of the form: **if** e **then** A **else** B

$$D_S = D_A \cup D_B \qquad \text{[3a]}$$

$$\rho_S = (\Gamma(e) \times (D_A \cup D_B)) \cup \rho_A \cup \rho_B \quad \text{[3b]} \qquad\qquad \mu_S = (\{e\} \times (D_A \cup D_B)) \cup \mu_A \cup \mu_B \quad \text{[3c]}$$

For a statement S of the form: **if** e **then** A

$$D_S = D_A \qquad \text{[4a]}$$

$$\rho_S = (\Gamma(e) \times D_A) \cup \rho_A \cup \iota \quad \text{[4b]} \qquad\qquad \mu_S = (\{e\} \times D_A) \cup \mu_A \quad \text{[4c]}$$

Repetitive Statements. For a statement S of the form: **while** e **do** A

$$D_S = D_A \qquad \text{[5a]}$$

$$\rho_S = \rho_A^*((\Gamma(e) \times D_A) \cup \iota) \quad \text{[5b]} \qquad\qquad \mu_S = (\{e\} \times D_A) \cup \mu_A \rho_A^*((\Gamma(e) \times D_A) \cup \iota) \quad \text{[5c]}$$

Fig. 8.5 Definitions of information-flow relations

kind of statement is given in Figure 8.5, in which ι denotes the identity relation on V and ρ^* denotes the transitive closure of a relation ρ.

For an assignment statement which assigns the value of an expression e to a variable v, the variables whose initial values may affect the final value of v are precisely the members of $\Gamma(e)$, and the value of every variable other than v is unchanged; thus we have the ρ-relation (1b). As an illustration, for a program with $V = \{x, y, z\}$ the statement

$$x := y + z$$

has the ρ-relation $\{(y, x), (y, y), (z, x), (z, z)\}$.

For a composite statement, the ρ-relation is expressed in terms of the ρ-relations of its constituents. For a sequence S of two statements $(A; B)$, ρ_s is the composition of ρ_A and ρ_B (relation (2b)). In the formula (3b) defining ρ

for a conditional statement, inclusion of the Cartesian product $\Gamma(e) \times (D_A \cup D_B)$ captures the fact that initial values of members of $\Gamma(e)$ may determine whether A or B is executed, and in this way may affect the final value of every variable in D_A or D_B. The formula (4b) is obtained by similar reasoning. As an illustration, the compound statement

> **begin if** x > 0 **then** y := 1; z := 2 * y **end**

has the ρ-relation $\{(x, x), (x, y), (x, z), (y, y), (y, z)\}$.

A repetitive statement **while** e **do** A is equivalent to

> **if** e **then begin** A; **while** e **do** A **end**

from which it follows by (4b) and (2b) that for this statement,

$$\rho_s = (\Gamma(e) \times D_A) \cup \rho_A \rho_s \cup \iota$$

The expression (5b) is the least solution of this equation.

Given a syntax tree of a program, it is easy to construct its ρ-relation by forming the ρ-relations of all its statements in turn, as the tree is traversed in post-order. (This ordering ensures that when the ρ-relation of a composite statement is to be constructed, the relations for its constituents have already been obtained.) The techniques employed in SPADE's information-flow analyser are very similar, except of course that since it analyses flowchart programs, it constructs the ρ-relations of non-terminals of its graph grammar rather than of language statements. The form and order of evaluation of the ρ-relations is defined by a trace, of the kind described in section 8.3.1.

For a flowchart program, the ρ-relation states which imported values may affect each exported value: these relationships should be the same as the dependency relations specified by the programmer in the form of annotations, and the information-flow analyser indicates any discrepancies. The tool also checks that initial values which are not imported cannot affect any exported values (which would indicate the use of uninitialized variables). Of course the flow analysis does not take account of the semantics of expressions, it being assumed that for every expression e, all variables in $\Gamma(e)$ may affect the value of e. (This would not be the case for instance for an expression "min (0, y)" if y were a natural number.) However, the analysis is "conservative" in this respect: at worst it could indicate information flows precluded by the program semantics.

Another flow relation of interest is the μ-relation from E to V, also defined in Figure 8.5. For a statement S the condition $e \, \mu_s \, v$ signifies that "the value of e in S may affect the value of v on exit from S". As an illustration, the compound statement

> **begin if** x > 0 **then** y := 1; z := 2 * y **end**

contains three expressions, e1 = "x > 0", e2 = "1" and e3 = "2 * y", and has the μ-relation $\{(e1, y), (e1, z), (e2, y), (e2, z), (e3, z)\}$. This relation is important because each expression of a program is associated with a particular statement: μ tells us which *statements* of a program fragment may affect a particular exported value. If, for a given exported variable v, we replace statements which cannot affect its final value by empty statements, then we obtain a new program, possibly much simpler than the original but equivalent to it in that it returns the same value of v. SPADE has a *partial program extractor* to perform this task, embedded in both its verification-condition generator and its symbolic interpreter. Some other useful relations, extensions and applications of the methods described here are discussed by Bergeretti and Carré [1985].

8.4 Formal verification

8.4.1 The generation of verification conditions

The method used to prove partial correctness of a program fragment (i.e. to prove that if its pre-condition holds initially, and its execution terminates, then its post-condition holds on termination) is essentially the inductive assertion method, as presented for instance by Manna [1974, 1980]. This involves firstly choosing on the flowchart model a finite set of nodes, called *cutpoints*, in such a way that every loop traverses at least one of them. (For instance, in the example of Figure 8.3(b) we may choose as cutpoints the entry points of the two loops.) Now let us define a *basic path* as a path whose initial endpoint is the start node or a cutpoint, whose terminal endpoint is a cutpoint or the finish node, and which does not contain any cutpoints other than possibly its endpoints. Clearly a basic path does not contain any cycles. The selection of the cutpoints effectively "decomposes" a flowchart program into a collection of basic paths; every execution path, from the start node to the finish node, consists of a sequence of basic paths (in which some basic paths may be repeated).

For a basic path p, from node i to node j say, we shall denote by $t(X)$ the condition for this path to be traversed (in terms of the value of the state vector X at node i), and by $a(X)$ the transformation of the values of X performed when this path is traversed. Thus $t(X)$ is a partial predicate over D_x and $a(X)$ is a partial function mapping D_x to itself.

Next we label the start and finish nodes of the flowchart model with its pre- and post-conditions respectively, and we label each cutpoint with an inductive assertion, i.e. a predicate over X which purports to characterize the relation among the program variables at this point.

Now for a basic path p from node i to node j, let Q and R be the predicates labelling i and j respectively. The *weakest pre-condition of p with respect to R*, which we denote by $wp(p, R)$, is the weakest predicate which must hold at node i in order that, if the path p is traversed, R shall hold at node j. For any state vector X at node i such that $t(X)$ is true (so that p is traversed), the corresponding state vector when execution reaches node j is $a(X)$. Hence

$$wp(p, R) = (t(X) \rightarrow R(a(X)))$$

The *verification condition for p with respect to Q and R* is

$$Q(X) \rightarrow wp(p, R)$$

or

$$(Q(X) \wedge t(X)) \rightarrow R(a(X))$$

If the verification conditions associated with all basic paths are true, then the program is partially correct (with respect to its pre- and post-conditions), as is shown by Manna [1974].

SPADE's verification-condition generator (VCG) computes the path traversal condition $t(X)$ and the transformation $a(X)$ of program variables for each basic path on a flowchart, and from these, the corresponding verification conditions. If other proof obligations are to be met (as specified by check statements for instance), it also constructs the corresponding theorems. As an illustration, in the FDL model of Figure 8.3(b), loop invariants have been planted at the loop entry points (statements 4 and 15); check statements have also been included (statements 6, 10, 17 and 21), to introduce the pre-conditions of the procedures DeQueue, Push, Pop and EnQueue respectively. The theorems produced by SPADE's VCG from this text are shown in Figure 8.6, each theorem being given in the form of a list of hypotheses H1, H2, ... and a list of conclusions C1, C2, ... inferred from the hypotheses. There are nine theorems altogether, five of these being verification conditions (one for each basic path) and the other four being associated with procedure pre-conditions.

The path traversal conditions $t(X)$ and program variable transformations $a(X)$ are derived from the functions $g(X)$ and predicates $h(X)$ which label the individual arcs incident from mapping and switch statements (as described in section 8.2.1). The "backward substitution technique" described by Manna [1974] or symbolic execution methods [King1976] are often recommended for this purpose. In the method employed in SPADE, which is more efficient, the functions and predicates on the arcs are used to construct a set of fixpoint equations representing the flowchart program (of a similar form to those of Blikle and Mazurkiewicz [1972]). Partial reduction of these equations (by a variant of Gauss elimination in which the operations of addition and multiplication of reals are replaced by union and composition of partial functions) yields an equivalent flowchart program, whose nodes are the start, cutpoints and finish node of the original and whose arcs correspond to the original basic paths. The functions labelling the new arcs give the required path functions directly.

An important reason for computing the path traversal conditions and variable transformations explicitly is that unfortunately, the specifications

RESULTS OF SPADE SEMANTIC ANALYSIS
PVL SPADE TOOL VERSION : 4.3
Program Validation Limited, Southampton, England

procedure ReverseQueue

DATE : 13-NOV-1988 TIME : 16:35:24.87

VERIFICATION CONDITIONS
(not simplified)

For path(s) from start statement to (assertion) statement 4 :

procedure_ReverseQueue_1.
H1:   Length(CtoA_Queue(Q)) <= MaxQueueLength.
H2:   Length(CtoA_Queue(Q)) <= MaxStackLength.
H3:   ClearStack = AtoC_Stack(Seq_of_Int[ ]).
    ->
C1:   Length(CtoA_Queue(Q)) <= MaxQueueLength.
C2:   Length(CtoA_Queue(Q)) <= MaxStackLength.
C3:   Reverse(CtoA_Queue(Q)) @ CtoA_Stack(ClearStack) = Reverse(CtoA_Queue(Q)).

For path(s) from statement 4 to (assertion) statement 4 :

procedure_ReverseQueue_2.
H1:   Length(CtoA_Queue(Q~)) <= MaxQueueLength.
H2:   Length(CtoA_Queue(Q~)) <= MaxStackLength.
H3:   Reverse(CtoA_Queue(Q)) @ CtoA_Stack(S) = Reverse(CtoA_Queue(Q~)).
H4:   not (EmptyQueue(Q)).
H5:   DeQueue_1(Q) = AtoC_Queue(Nonfirst(CtoA_Queue(Q))).
H6:   DeQueue_2(Q) = First(CtoA_Queue(Q)).
H7:   Push(S,DeQueue_2(Q)) = AtoC_Stack(Seq_of_Int[DeQueue_2(Q)] @ CtoA_Stack(S)).
    ->
C1:   Length(CtoA_Queue(Q~)) <= MaxQueueLength.
C2:   Length(CtoA_Queue(Q~)) <= MaxStackLength.
C3:   Reverse(CtoA_Queue(DeQueue_1(Q))) @ CtoA_Stack(Push(S,DeQueue_2(Q))) =
      Reverse(CtoA_Queue(Q~)).

For path(s) from statement 4 to (check) statement 6 :

procedure_ReverseQueue_3.
H1:   Length(CtoA_Queue(Q~)) <= MaxQueueLength.
H2:   Length(CtoA_Queue(Q~)) <= MaxStackLength.
H3:   Reverse(CtoA_Queue(Q)) @ CtoA_Stack(S) = Reverse(CtoA_Queue(Q~)).
H4:   not (EmptyQueue(Q)).
    ->
C1:   CtoA_Queue(Q) <> Seq_of_Int[ ].

For path(s) from statement 4 to (check) statement 10 :

procedure_ReverseQueue_4.
H1:   Length(CtoA_Queue(Q~)) <= MaxQueueLength.
H2:   Length(CtoA_Queue(Q~)) <= MaxStackLength.
H3:   Reverse(CtoA_Queue(Q)) @ CtoA_Stack(S) = Reverse(CtoA_Queue(Q~)).
H4:   not (EmptyQueue(Q)).
H5:   DeQueue_1(Q) = AtoC_Queue(Nonfirst(CtoA_Queue(Q))).
H6:   DeQueue_2(Q) = First(CtoA_Queue(Q)).
    ->
C1:   Length(CtoA_Stack(S)) < MaxStackLength.

For path(s) from statement 4 to (assertion) statement 15 :

procedure_ReverseQueue_5.
H1:   Length(CtoA_Queue(Q~)) <= MaxQueueLength.
H2:   Length(CtoA_Queue(Q~)) <= MaxStackLength.
H3:   Reverse(CtoA_Queue(Q)) @ CtoA_Stack(S) = Reverse(CtoA_Queue(Q~)).
H4:   not (not (EmptyQueue(Q))).
      ->
C1:   Length(CtoA_Queue(Q~)) <= MaxQueueLength.
C2:   CtoA_Queue(Q) @ CtoA_Stack(S) = Reverse(CtoA_Queue(Q~)).

For path(s) from statement 15 to (assertion) statement 15 :

procedure_ReverseQueue_6.
H1:   Length(CtoA_Queue(Q~)) <= MaxQueueLength.
H2:   CtoA_Queue(Q) @ CtoA_Stack(S) = Reverse(CtoA_Queue(Q~)).
H3:   not (EmptyStack(S)).
H4:   Pop_1(S) = AtoC_Stack(Nonfirst(CtoA_Stack(S))).
H5:   Pop_2(S) = First(CtoA_Stack(S)).
H6:   EnQueue(Q,Pop_2(S)) = AtoC_Queue(CtoA_Queue(Q) @ Seq_of_Int[Pop_2(S)]).
      ->
C1:   Length(CtoA_Queue(Q~)) <= MaxQueueLength.
C2:   CtoA_Queue(EnQueue(Q,Pop_2(S))) @ CtoA_Stack(Pop_1(S)) = Reverse(CtoA_Queue(Q~)).

For path(s) from statement 15 to (check) statement 17 :

procedure_ReverseQueue_7.
H1:   Length(CtoA_Queue(Q~)) <= MaxQueueLength.
H2:   CtoA_Queue(Q) @ CtoA_Stack(S) = Reverse(CtoA_Queue(Q~)).
H3:   not (EmptyStack(S)).
      ->
C1:   CtoA_Stack(S) <> Seq_of_Int[ ].

For path(s) from statement 15 to (check) statement 21 :

procedure_ReverseQueue_8.
H1:   Length(CtoA_Queue(Q~)) <= MaxQueueLength.
H2:   CtoA_Queue(Q) @ CtoA_Stack(S) = Reverse(CtoA_Queue(Q~)).
H3:   not (EmptyStack(S)).
H4:   Pop_1(S) = AtoC_Stack(Nonfirst(CtoA_Stack(S))).
H5:   Pop_2(S) = First(CtoA_Stack(S)).
      ->
C1:   Length(CtoA_Queue(Q)) < MaxQueueLength.

For path(s) from statement 15 to finish statement :

procedure_ReverseQueue_9.
H1:   Length(CtoA_Queue(Q~)) <= MaxQueueLength.
H2:   CtoA_Queue(Q) @ CtoA_Stack(S) = Reverse(CtoA_Queue(Q~)).
H3:   not (not (EmptyStack(S))).
      ->
C1:   Q = AtoC_Queue(Reverse(CtoA_Queue(Q~))).

Fig. 8.6 Verification conditions for ReverseQueue

and designs of safety-critical programs are not always precise enough to support formal verification of their code implementations. Under such circumstances, manual inspection of path functions can be helpful; indeed, many serious errors have been found in this way.

8.4.2 The SPADE Proof Checker

The SPADE Proof Checker is an interactive proof assistant, fully integrated with the SPADE VCG and other tools. It inherits the type discipline of FDL, and supports this with built-in expression simplification and standardization tools and a library of standard proof rules about the FDL data types and type constructors. The Proof Checker is a first-order predicate calculus tool, so that all verification conditions which can be generated with SPADE can also be manipulated with the Checker. It uses a natural deduction system, so that interactive proof sessions can be conducted in a very straightforward way and the proof logs created by the Proof Checker can be read and checked without difficulty.

The Proof Checker is written entirely in Prolog and significant proofs of soundness of its components have been carried out (both as part of the research during its early development at the University of Southampton and subsequently at Program Validation Limited). Although it is written in Prolog, the mechanisms of Prolog logic, e.g. negation by failure, are not directly employed within proofs, so these limitations of Prolog's logic are not reflected in the Proof Checker. The tool has already been used on significant proofs of avionics software [O'Neill1988] and is now in use in industry.

The use of this tool to construct formal proofs of verification conditions has the following advantages:

1) The proof attempt is policed, so that the "slips" associated with pencil-and-paper proofs are avoided.
2) In proving non-trivial pieces of software, the associated formulae can often be quite large and (seemingly) complex; proofs of such formulae would be virtually impossible without tools to support formula manipulation.
3) A large body of knowledge is available, in the form of the built-in proof rule libraries.
4) Complicated goals can be broken down into more manageable sub-goals, with the Checker keeping track of what has been proved and what remains to be proved, at all levels.
5) By the use of "wildcards", the Checker can be used to search the available proof rules for useful matches, with the user exercising control of how wide or narrow the search.
6) Facilities are provided to ease the burden of manipulating large

formulae and to help control, save and resume proof sessions over disjointed periods of time.

7) The Proof Checker generates a proof log which, as well as recording the detailed proof steps carried out, also records which proof rules (both built-in and user-supplied domain-specific proof rules) were used in the proof of each verification condition, providing valuable documentation of the proof session.

Thus, use of such a proof tool means that significant proofs of programs can be undertaken, and without the limitations of purely manual methods. The advantage of this approach over the use of an automatic, non-interactive proof tool, however, is that the user (who is generally much more mathematically sophisticated than any proof tool in existence at present) can guide the proofs and arrive at comprehensible and traceable proof logs.

8.5 Conclusions

As the expressive power of programming languages has increased, so has that of mathematical formalisms for defining them, to the point that a denotational definition even of Ada has been produced [CEC 1987]. There is some prospect of applying such definitions directly to the construction of compilers, and one might contemplate the use of quite rich models of dynamic semantics in verification tools.

In comparison our objectives will seem very modest. We believe that reasoning about programs can only be in terms of fragments, freed from their contexts, that the programmer can mentally encompass. To make this possible for standard languages, in chapter 5 we imposed some language restrictions and annotations for "encapsulating" fragments, making their relationships with their environments explicit. With additional static semantic checks, of the consistency of annotations with code, it becomes possible to verify a program fragment in isolation, without the encumbrance of scope and visibility rules, or aliasing or side-effects. By protecting ourselves from undesirable phenomena of this kind, we eliminate the need for formalisms rich enough to describe them. This is our justification of the very simple model of a program fragment, with direct binding of identifiers to values and no concept of environment. To be sure, we would like to be able to deal with pointers, but we have been quite surprised by the general reluctance (for good reason) of those people engaged in safety-critical programming to employ any language features requiring dynamic heap storage allocation: it means that the subsets of standard languages presented in chapter 5 (and similarly designed subsets of assembly codes), supported by the tools described here, are of much wider applicability than one might imagine. And of course where they are applicable, their simplicity is their strength.

The need to subject the models to different kinds of "well-formation" tests and to carry with them a variety of proof obligations makes modelling and verification rather untidy, conceptually, but this seems inevitable in using "standard" languages and assembly codes not designed for verification. The use of SPARK allows simplifications since it does not require control-flow analysis, data-flow analysis can be formulated in terms of binary relations similar to those used in information-flow analysis, and all these relations can be constructed in the course of parsing; the SPARK Examiner exploits these facts. The separation of the checks of well-formation performed by flow analysers from the proving process does bring important benefits however. Proving program correctness may become easier but it will always be laborious, and a very expensive way of finding coding slips and lacunae. Fortunately, flow analysis can eliminate many of them, and the mechanical checking of the "weak specification" provided by a dependency relation is a valuable preliminary to an attempt at complete proof.

References

[Bergeretti/Carré1985]   Bergeretti, J. F. and Carré, B. A., "Information-flow and data-flow analysis of while-programs", *ACM Trans. on Prog. Lang. and Syst.*, 7, pp. 37–61 (1985).

[Blikle/Mazurkiewicz1972]   Blikle, A. and Mazurkiewicz, A., "An algebraic approach to the theory of programs, algorithms, languages and recursiveness", in *Mathematical Foundations of Computer Science*, Warsaw (1972).

[Carré1979]   Carré, B. A., *Graphs and Networks*, Oxford University Press (1979).

[Clutterbuck/Carré1988]   Clutterbuck, D. L. and Carré, B. A., "The verification of low-level code", *Software Engineering Journal*, 3, pp. 97–111, IEE/BCS (1988).

[CEC1987]   Commission of the European Communities, *The Draft Formal Definition of Ada*, Dansk Datamatik Center (1987).

[Farrow1975]   Farrow, R., Kennedy, K. and Zucconi, L., "Graph grammars and global program flow analysis", *Proc. 17th Annual IEEE Symp. on Foundations of Computer Science* (1975).

[Hecht1977]   Hecht, M. S., *Flow Analysis of Computer Programs*, North-Holland (1977).

[Kennedy1981]   Kennedy, K., "A survey of data flow analysis techniques", in *Program Flow Analysis* (Eds. Muchnick S. S. and Jones N. D.), Prentice Hall (1981).

[King1976]   King, J., "Symbolic execution and program testing", *Comm. ACM.*, 19, pp. 385–394 (1976).

[Manna1974]   Manna, Z., *Mathematical Theory of Computation*, McGraw Hill (1974).

[Manna1980]   Manna, Z., *Lectures on the Logic of Computer Programming*, CBMS-NSF Regional Conference Series in Applied Maths. vol. 31, Society for Industrial and Applied Maths (1980).

[O'Neill1988]   O'Neill, I. M., Clutterbuck, D. L., Farrow, P. F., Summers, P. G. and Dolman W. C., "The formal verification of safety-critical assembly code", in *Safety of Computer Control Systems 1988* (Ed. Ehrenberger, W. D.), IFAC Proceedings Series no. 16, pp. 115–120.

9 The algebraic specification of a target machine: Ten15

J. M. Foster, Royal Signals and Radar Establishment

9.1 Introduction

Ten15 is a formally defined abstract machine and a target for high-level language compilers. It provides a basis for formal methods over the whole area of programming, from operating systems to users' programs, from assembler-like constructions to high-level languages, and from simple text construction of programs to elaborate transformation systems. It also provides a practical basis for creating programs and for program manipulation. So it is something on which to found a programming environment. Meeting these requirements together is not easy, but there have been enough advances in recent years for this to be a timely moment to make the attempt. Experience and practical use of Ten15 have demonstrated the possibilities. This chapter considers the requirements and describes in outline how Ten15 has met them.

It is not to be expected that one class of formal methods will satisfy all needs. At present there are groups of methods with various foundations, particularly in predicate calculus and algebra, and within these groups there are competing techniques. All of these techniques are needed in our armoury. Ten15 is intended as a groundwork for as many of them as possible, so that tools using different methods have at least some common factors. This will be of advantage to avoid the duplication of work and to enable tools to cooperate with each other. Ten15 does not make a break with current practice and start afresh; green field solutions to old problems face almost insurmountable difficulty in becoming accepted, and it is unwise to discard systems which have shown themselves to have at least some of the needed characteristics. It is aimed at current methods of producing practical programs, current operating systems and current problems, while avoiding constraining the introduction of new methods. Practical usefulness is paramount. Ten15 is something out of which people build a variety of systems, not a single Procrustean system, to which users have to fit their problems.

In outline, the requirements are these. Ten15 needs to be expressive enough to account for all the necessary kinds of programming and data. It needs to be well matched to the way people want to think about programs, because at times it will have to serve as an interface between tools and users. It needs to cover a wide spectrum, from high- to low-level constructs, if it is to serve as a basis for transformations. It must be possible to translate it into efficient code for conventional machines, since it is to be used. It needs to be in the intersection of predicate calculus and algebra, since it is to serve as a basis for tools based on each of them.

9.1.1 Expressive range

Programming languages started with assemblers, autocodes and Fortran, and have proliferated wildly. Only a few established themselves generally; each of these has serious shortcomings, and there is no universal language available, nor is there likely to be. The very heat and passion of the debate between languages and its eternal fruitlessness is evidence of the need to retain a choice. The best language depends on the problem. There are problems for which Ada is better than Lisp, and problems for which Lisp is better than Ada. Problems which cut across such categories are in difficulty. A programming environment needs to have a number of languages available, and to have the languages capable of working together, in the sense that systems can be made out of components written in different languages and such systems can be analysed.

Operating systems developed on different lines from application programs. Early operating systems were introduced in order to make the best use of the computer, and to provide standard ways of driving peripherals and allocating resources. They evolved by adding features to make this more convenient for users, particularly by introducing job control languages. These languages were developed *ad hoc*, and were interpreted, not compiled. It has often been remarked that they were programming languages and should be considered as such, and that considered as languages they were crude. But progress along this line has been disappointing.

The programming of the operating system itself has usually been done in a mixture of assembly code and high-level language, the high-level language wherever possible and the machine code for the parts which could not be expressed in the language or which would be too slow if they were. Operating systems and the corresponding programs in operational computers are among the most important programs to be analysed, since on them the correctness of all other programs depends. No matter how well a program is validated in itself, if the operating system wrongly allocates store to it or to other programs then that validation is destroyed, and the errors that can be introduced may be very difficult to diagnose.

Ten15 is intended not only to provide a basis for conventional users' programming but also for the programming of operating systems and for the equivalent of job control language, so that analysis and manipulation can be carried out on all these classes of program.

The need to support operating systems as well as user programming forces Ten15 to include types and operations which are adequate to express the extra features. For example, types to handle database and network values are essential. The kinds of value which conventional systems handle on backing stores and in databases are curiously rudimentary. It is common that the only method of communicating between programs is through files, the structures of which are closely related to the physical properties of disc drives. In some cases sequences of lines of characters are the only data structure supported and dictionaries provide the only way of accessing them. Even in more sophisticated databases the data structures are closely tied to the specific view of data which that particular system uses, and are usually provided in order to implement individual and elaborate mechanisms. Ten15 provides types and operations which can be composed to make such systems, while retaining the advantages of type checking. The data structures on backing store need not differ very greatly from those used in main store. Certainly the relative speeds of operations are different in the two cases, but the needs are much the same. In terms of an appropriate set of types for backing store all the conventional types of data management system may be programmed and more besides.

Similar remarks apply to networks. The growing use of remote procedure calls [Xerox1981, Foster/Currie1986, Spector1982] suggests that for loosely coupled networks many of the kinds of data familiar from main store can be used. A number of important problems arise here, outside the scope of this chapter [Currie/Foster1987].

Operating systems have to handle users' programs as data, since they have to be able both to allow for their creation and to supervise their running. Procedures and processes are the basic ideas here, and this implies that true procedure values are needed. Operating systems also have to provide debugging facilities; this is an interesting area to treat formally.

A characteristic of operating systems and of the control programs for operational computers is that they contain deliberately non-terminating programs. A command line interpreter is an example; it interprets every line as it is presented and goes on doing this indefinitely. The formalism has to deal with this situation.

Concurrency is another topic which must be included. Unfortunately, pseudo-parallel processing on one computer, loosely coupled networks of computers and tightly coupled networks each seem to require different primitives [Hoare1978, Milner1980]. At present Ten15 does not include methods of treating tightly coupled networks and research in this area is continuing. The problem is not to provide the primitives for tightly coupled networks, but to unify the treatment of all types of concurrency.

9.1.2 Structured for people to use

In spite of the deficiencies of current languages, it would be generally agreed that there has been progress in their design. One important area of improvement has been in the use of types. Types were originally introduced because compilers needed to know the size of objects and the meaning of operations on them in order to produce the appropriate code. But other advantages soon became clear. The types introduced in Algol60 provided checks that found many errors in programs at compile time. The code that was produced did not have to check for these errors at run time and so could be more compact and faster. There were only a fixed number of types in Algol60—ignoring the dimensionality of arrays—but later languages, for example Pascal, introduced the generation of indefinitely many types. Neither Pascal nor Algol had a system of types which made it easy to be sure at compile time that there were no type errors, since parameter types were not fully specified. The importance of strong type checking was realized later.

Strong type checking guarantees that, on any path through a program, operations expecting arguments of a particular type are applied only to values of that type, which provides a powerful check at compile time against certain errors. But this fact can be considered in a different way. Type checking guarantees that only operations expecting type X values can be applied to a type X value, but it also ensures that a value of type X must have been generated by one of the operations which produces type X values and by no other operation. This means that it is relevant to integrity and to information hiding. For example, suppose that a reference is passed from one program regime, P, to another, Q. Consider a type system in which there are values of type *reference*, which can be written and read, and values of type *read-only reference*, which can only be read. Let there also be an operation which converts references into read-only references, without otherwise modifying them, but no operation to perform the reverse transformation. Then if P applies this operation to one of its references and passes the result to Q, it can be sure that Q can at any time read the contents of the read-only reference, but cannot ever alter it, because of the absence of operations to do so. This particular access control is similar to that which can easily be provided on capability machines or in file stores, where the operations are interpreted. But the type mechanism is potentially a much more refined method of access control, and it operates at compile time, so avoiding the interpretive overhead.

The concept of types is so important and useful that it must be considered as a requirement of Ten15. This presents a difficulty, since the type systems of the various languages in use have been developed in isolation from each other, and are in any case each inadequate for the total job. Furthermore, work on possible systems of types has advanced considerably beyond the systems used in well known languages [Reynolds1985, MacQueen/Plotkin/ Sethi1986]. So Ten15 must have a global system of types into which the types in existing languages can be mapped, which is capable of describing all the necessary constructions efficiently, and which may be extended as new needs arise.

Another tendency in the development of programming languages has been the invention of constructions which allow programmers to separate decisions. Perhaps the first example of this was the use of labels in assembly code, so that one did not have to give the absolute address of the instruction which was to be the destination of a jump, but could delay filling in that address until the program was assembled. Such constructions usually permit decisions to be delayed, but it would be better to speak of controlling the time of taking decisions, since it is often separating the decisions, rather than delaying them, which is important. The skill of programming may be regarded as the choice of the right moment to take decisions. Examples of this abound. The identification of variables, the introduction of procedures, arrays of dynamically chosen size, heap storage and separate compilation are all instances of this development. It is of the greatest importance that Ten15 should facilitate such separation.

Among the most important features of operating systems is the use of interactive working, both on multi-user systems and on single-user work-stations and personal computers. Here is another case of the delaying of decisions, in this case the decision of what to do. The characteristic of interactive working is that at the start of a session the user does not know exactly what to do, which procedures will be applied to which values, and in what order. Constraints which prevent programs from working together, or which funnel interactions through a narrow data channel, such as converting the output of one program into a text file and then recreating a similar data structure from it in the next program, are quite against the style of interactive work. Data must pass directly between programs, the combination of which was not anticipated, and this without compromising the integrity of the programs or the system. Clearly, common store is needed, so the question of integrity is raised. Strong type checking is exactly the mechanism needed to permit and control such access.

9.1.3 Wide spectrum

In the past, programs were created by writing a text version and then compiling this into machine code. Separate compilation complicated this picture only slightly; the running program was still produced by the compiler from texts, and it was only the compiler that produced programs. Indeed one acted as if the text was the program. More recently, it has become common to produce programs by other means. For example, in the Flex system [Foster/Currie/Edwards1982], many programs exist to which it is not natural to attribute a text version, since they were not created by compiling text, but by applying other program-creating programs to non-text data.

An example of this tendency is the creation of programs by program transformation, which has been a research topic for many years. One might want to write a program in a clear way which can be seen to be correct, and transform it, by methods which are known to produce programs of equivalent effect, into a version which will run with adequate efficiency. If this is to be done, all the various versions of the program must be in a formalism which can be manipulated by the transforming program. This needs to move continuously from high-level constructs down to constructs which correspond sufficiently closely with conventional machines to be fully efficient. Ten15 must have a wide spectrum of constructions.

9.1.4   Efficiently translatable

Program analysis needs to be tied as directly as possible to the program which actually runs. If an Ada program is translated into Ten15 and analysed and then taken away to another system to be translated with an independent Ada compiler, some confidence in the original analysis has been lost. The Ada program or the operating system of the distant computer may not exactly correspond to the way Ada was translated into Ten15. If instead Ada is translated into Ten15 and then that same Ten15 into machine code, this particular discrepancy does not exist. Neither Ada nor any other language is sufficiently well specified for anyone to be confident that there are no such differing interpretations. The same point arises even more strongly for mixed language working or the production of programs by transformation. In that case Ten15 may be the only available expression of the program from which code is to be produced. So the Ten15 constructions must be directly translated into machine code. If this is to produce real operating systems the resulting code on conventional computers must be efficient. Certainly it is permissible to pay a small price in speed and space for the extra facilities and confidence provided by Ten15, but only a small one. The amount is arguable; perhaps 25% is tolerable.

9.1.5   Formal aspects

One result of the textual bias of compiling systems has been too great an emphasis on syntax. The syntax of a language is only there to provide a representation for programs for an underlying machine. The bones of a language are the operations of that underlying machine; the syntax is cosmetic. Too often gross complexity is introduced in the syntax and explained in terms of it, but only an elementary machine lies behind the facade. Though the syntaxes of languages vary greatly, in many cases the algorithmic constructions behind them are very similar. Procedures, conditional statements, loops, subscripted arrays and variables are common to most languages. If one is manipulating or proving properties of programs it is these essential constructions with which one is concerned, rather than the details of the text representing them. Of course, the manipulation has to be in terms of some representation, but the linear text string of letters is unlikely to be the appropriate one. A representation which reveals the structure is appropriate. For many years the term "abstract syntax" has been used for something like this concept, but it has not been well defined and it tends to be associated with specific languages, in the sense that one might speak of the abstract syntax of Pascal or the abstract syntax of Ada.

A curious byproduct of the textual bias has been the use of macros. Macros were introduced early into programming languages as a method of doing textual substitution before compiling. However, they did not have to respect the syntactic structure of the program so long as the final output of the macro stage was syntactically correct. This led to some very rebarbative and impenetrable programming techniques. It is often useful to carry out systematic substitutions in programs before they are compiled, but these should form a part of the process of generating programs by transformation and should respect the structure of programs.

Whether tools are based on predicate calculus or on algebra, they need some way of describing programs which corresponds to the essential structure of the program. Consider, as an example, conditional expressions. Any particular conditional expression has a number of sub-expressions, and the meaning of the whole is related to the meanings of the parts in a particular way which is characteristic of this construction. In predicate calculus this relation will be described by means of predicates and in algebra by algebraic means.

For the definition of an abstract machine, the atomic program constructions and the ways of combining them to produce more elaborate pieces of program have to be specified. Giving a definition of these structures is the same as giving a semantics of the machine.

The commonest methods of defining the semantics of machines have been to give definitions by means of denotational semantics, weakest pre-conditions or operational semantics [Scott1970, Dijkstra1976]. These methods all study the meaning of the evaluation of a program. Each becomes more complex when applied to non-terminating programs and procedure values. Instead of using one of these methods, the definition of Ten15 is given by developing the whole of a program, as an infinite object, and defining which programs are equal. This method uses laws as in Hoare et al [Hoare1987] but in this case to give a formal and complete definition. The intended significance of equality is that programs are equal if and only if they behave identically in all possible circumstances. This, however, is only the intuitive meaning; the definition of equality is given purely formally. In order to do this some constructions have to be introduced into Ten15 especially for the purpose. The determination of the equality of Ten15 programs is not a computable problem, nor is this desirable, for if it were computable Ten15 would not be sufficiently expressive. But it is possible to isolate parts of Ten15 where equality is computable, and indeed this is part of the process of showing that Ten15 is adequately defined.

Later sections will show how the Ten15 algebra is defined inductively. The basic algebra is rather like a word algebra with extra constructions. A congruence is then given on this algebra and Ten15 is identified with the quotient of this algebra by the congruence relation. Many properties may be evaluated by means of homomorphisms on the algebra, and by other algebraic means. This definition lies easily within a predicate calculus formulation and so allows predicate calculus based tools to be used. Whether the form of the definitions will prove intuitively easy to use remains to be seen.

9.1.6   Present state

Ten15 is an abstract machine, formally defined as an algebra. It is the target of a number of compilers which are in various stages, including compilers for Ada, Pascal and Algol68, and more are planned. It can also be produced by transformations and other non-compiler tools. It can be translated into machine code for conventional computers, at present Vax and the Flex computer. Programs for Ten15 can be the object of manipulation, by both algebraic and predicate calculus methods. It supports the range of programming discussed above.

Some of the manipulations of Ten15 that are needed have been discussed, in particular compilation into machine code and the transformation and combination of programs to yield new ones. Many other kinds of tools will be needed and, though it would be against the spirit of this chapter to think that an exhaustive list could be given, it would be useful to skim through some of the possibilities. Possible tools, in no particular order, are: proof of correctness, proof of properties, examination for deadlock, symbolic evaluation, showing that a program lies in a particular class such as time-bounded programs, showing that particular stylistic programming rules have been met, producing a concordance, producing other program annotations to help in understanding it, showing that overflow cannot occur, showing that there can be no error in indexing arrays, finding the places in a program that would be affected by a proposed change, producing an abstract program that can be specialized to particular uses in a systematic way, and making systematic changes to a program that can only be done if its structure is known.

The rest of the chapter discusses the type system, the Ten15 machine and its formal definition.

9.2 Types and operation

Strong typing has been used in many programming languages, but not in a completely uniform way. Different languages have had different ideas of what types mean.

Ten15 regards types as sets of values. Types are used for a number of different purposes: to give control over access, to guard against programming errors of certain kinds, and to allow the translator to deduce constraints on the program that allow it to produce better code. The types of conventional programming languages must be mapped into the Ten15 types, in the sense that values belonging to the Ten15 types serve to represent values operated on by the programming languages. The needs are not antagonistic, but the conclusions to which they lead have to be merged together into a coherent system.

The types are related to the operations in an obvious way. If an operation is said to take a parameter of type X it must be applicable to all values of that type. If an operation is said to deliver a type, then all values that it can deliver must belong to that type. These rules do not determine which sets can be chosen as types. The choice is a pragmatic one.

Consider some simple examples. Suppose that there is a conditional expression, yielding an integer answer

if $a<10$ **then** $2*a$ **else** $a/2$ **fi**

The type of the result depends on the original value of a. Suppose that *min-evenint* is twice the integer part of *minint/2*. If the original value of a lay between *minint* and 10, then the values less than half *minint* will cause an overflow and so will not appear here. The remaining ones will produce all the even values between *min-evenint* and 18. If the original value of a lay between 10 and *maxint*, the result will be all the integers between 5 and the integer part of *maxint/2*. Thus the result values considered as a function of the value of a are given by the following expressions:

$$a \in minint, minint+1, \dots 9$$
$$\rightarrow min\text{-}evenint, minevenint+2, \dots 18$$

$$a \in 10, 11, \dots maxint \rightarrow 5, 6, \dots entier(maxint/2)$$

What can be said about the type of the conditional expression? The type could be a function from the state of the machine to possible sets of values, which is approximately what is written above. The disadvantage of this approach is that it discards no information: the type theory is no different from the semantics of the machine. Indeed, if general loop constructions are introduced the type is not in general computable. But the types must be deduced at compile time from the program, and the above sense of type will not allow this.

The input state information could be discarded, giving a type like

min-evenint, min-evenint+2, ... 5, 6, ... maxint/2

but even this formulation is too difficult to handle. It is quite a complex set description in itself, and for arbitrary expressions the complexity increases very rapidly. A much cruder viewpoint says that the sub-set is determined just by its smallest and greatest members. In this case the type would be

min-evenint .. maxint/2

and this is the type chosen for Ten15. This is an arbitrary notion of type, but it has the advantage that it can be computed and that it is useful for all the purposes outlined above. All type systems in use are arbitrary in some such way. For the purposes of Ten15 a type system must of necessity discard information, and there is no uniquely satisfactory way of discarding it, nor need there be.

The Ten15 notion of type, then, is an arbitrary but carefully chosen collection of sets which is such that the type of the result of each of the machine operations can be calculated if the types of its parameters are known.

An area where programming languages have differed is in type declaration. There appear to be three different ideas involved. First, a new type could be defined to be equal to some composite type purely as a shorthand way of referring to that type. Second, a new type could be defined as being a different kind of thing from any present type, and represented by some existing composite type. This is really part of the notion of abstract data type. Third, a type could be defined as being equal to a type expression as part of the definition of a circular type, that is, the intention is to solve the type equations. Pascal mixed up the functions of the first two reasons, and made similar type declarations in different places in the text produce different types. The intention was probably to achieve the effect of abstract data types, but this was not made explicit. The effect in fact was to tie these type declarations to the text in a way which made it difficult to make them global. Algol68 used type declarations for the first and third purpose. This meant that it was necessary to recognise what was going on if one wanted to see which were the circular types. Ten15 provides abstract data types and circularity as separate essential constructions; renaming is available, but merely a convenience.

The type system is built up from basic types, from type constructors which form types from given types, and in more complex ways such as polymorphism and abstract data types. In various places in the basic types, pragmatic choices have to be made. This is especially true about floating point numbers, since, even with the advent of the IEEE standard, there is a great variety in floating point implementations on machines. A choice which made great difficulty for some common machine would be unfortunate, so compromise forces a less-than-ideal solution. Similar remarks apply, though less strongly, to integers, where different word lengths and conventions about signed and unsigned arithmetic apply. Apart from these two major areas, it has been possible to make satisfactory decisions, without much constraint arising from the nature of existing machines.

9.2.1 Basic types

Ten15 has a large but finite set of basic types. This is not a necessity, as similar arguments could have led to an infinite but countable set of basic types.

The simplest basic type is *Void*, a type which has exactly one value. This being so, no bits are needed to represent it. The name *Void* for the set is a clear misnomer, but it has been traditional since the days of Algol68 and has been retained in Ten15. In effect, this is the value delivered by an operation which has no genuine value to deliver, because it is an operation performed for its side-effects. Thus assignment delivers a *Void* value.

Other simple types are *Bottom* and *Top*. *Bottom* is the empty set, which can only be the result of an operation if control cannot reach that point, and *Top* is the set of all values, which is not delivered by any operation, but can arise in error situations. The names are chosen because of the position of these sets in a lattice of types.

Integer types force the consideration of the word lengths of practical machines. If arbitrary integer ranges were allowed, some constructions might be excessively slow. These considerations dictate a compromise, which may be uncomfortable to the purist, but which has worked without much awkwardness in practice, no doubt because of the similarity of many current machines. Ten15 has chosen a number of preferred lengths, corresponding to one bit, eight bits, 32 bits and 64 bits, and permits contiguous subsets of the corresponding numbers as integer types. Normal arithmetic operations are defined on these types. With this scheme a type might be (64 bits, $-5..63$) or (8 bits, $10..10$). The latter type contains only the one value and is the type of a suitable constant value in a piece of Ten15. The subset information is used to guarantee that operations are permissible without run-time checks; for example indexing a vector by means of a subscript known to lie within its domain need not be checked. This means that overflow must always produce an exception, since an unchecked overflowed value might not lie in the correct range.

For *Real* types, again something of a misnomer, floating point would be better, Ten15 works in terms of numbers of bits, in this case significant bits in the mantissa and exponent. A *Real* type is specified just by these two parameters, and questions of accuracy and range are not dealt with in the type system. The usual arithmetic is defined.

There are a small number of cases where run-time checks have to be performed because, in some cases, they cannot be made at compile time from the particular types given. The important ones are conventional:

overflow, division by zero, and index check. These checks can usually be implemented directly in terms of hardware constructions. The mechanism is described later, but it involves a type, *Exception*, which gives information about such errors back to controlling procedures. Though this control is provided in Ten15, it is not intended for use as a control mechanism by normal users since it seems to be bad practice, though it is required by Ada. Other safer mechanisms are provided in Ten15.

There are other minor basic types which are not discussed here, including the type of type values itself. The only other major basic type is *Typed*, which is described later.

9.2.2 Type constructors

Given any type, X, a type of vectors of such values can be created. On this type the main operations are the creation of the vector, indexing and obtaining the number of elements. So *Vec* is a way of making a new type from a given type and there are many such type constructors.

The type constructors are not confined to having only type parameters: *Vec*, for example, takes a type parameter, and also a boolean parameter which says whether values of the type are read-only. It also takes a further type parameter, the type of the size of the vector, so the full vector type has the form

Vec(type of item, read only, type of size)

Vectors are indexed by positive integers. A compiler, say for Pascal, wishing to translate an index which is an enumerated type, will use the representation of that enumerated type. If the type of the size of a vector is given as (32 bits, 5..5), for example, then the vector will have exactly 5 elements. This will enable the translator to omit index checking if the type of the index is appropriate. Indexing the vector gives a reference to a *type of item*, and this reference is read-only if the vector is read-only.

It is frequently necessary to consider whether one set of values is a subset ($\subseteq$) of another. This is affected by the type constructor. For example, if $A \subseteq B$, the relation between *Vec A* and *Vec B* can be considered. It is possible to put values into the vector by assignment to a reference obtained by indexing, and get values out by de-referencing. If *Vec A* were a subset of *Vec B*, then every operation which can be done to a *Vec B* would be possible on a *Vec A*. However, a value of type B can be put into a *Vec B* but cannot necessarily be put into a *Vec A*, since some B's may not be A's. So *Vec A* is not a subset of *Vec B*. Conversely, if *Vec B* were a subset of *Vec A*, the values obtained by applying an operation to a *Vec B* would be a subset of the values obtained by applying the same operation to a *Vec A*. But the values that can be extracted from a *Vec B* belong to B, and those from a *Vec A* to A, and B is not necessarily a subset of A. So even though $A \subseteq B$ neither *Vec A* nor *Vec B* is a subset of the other.

This holds because the vector types could be both assigned to and de-referenced, which is true if neither is read-only. But suppose that both vector types are read-only. In this case it is true that $Vec\,A$ is a subset of $Vec\,B$.

Values of type $Ref\,X$, are references to values of type X. Again there is a read-only property. De-referencing is defined on all references, and assignment is defined if the reference is not read-only.

Values of type $Ptr\,X$ have de-reference and assignment defined, but are not able to point inside other structures. They can be implemented by packing the value of type X into a new block and giving the address of that. Whereas references might be to parts of such a block, pointers have to be to the whole of it. Pointers are only provided because they can be implemented in less data space than references; efficiency rather than necessity is the rationale.

The type $Struct(A, B \ldots N)$, where $A, B \ldots N$ are any number of types, is the Cartesian product of its parameters. The operations are tupling, which creates a structure, and selection, which selects a field from a structure. Here $P \subseteq Q$ implies that $Struct(P, B \ldots N) \subseteq Struct(Q, B \ldots N)$ and similarly for all fields.

There are also union types, $Union(A, B \ldots N)$. This is disjoint union, not set union. It can be implemented as sets of pairs of numbers and values.

$$(1, a_1), (1, a_2), (1, a_3) \ldots (2, b_1), \ldots (n, n_1) \ldots$$

$P \subseteq Q$ implies $Union(P, B \ldots N) \subseteq Union(Q, B \ldots N)$.

Values belonging to $Proc(X, Y)$ are procedures, expecting a parameter in X and delivering a result in Y. A $Proc(1 \ldots 10, Y)$ can be used everywhere where a $Proc(2 \ldots 5, Y)$ is needed, since the first proc is applicable to all $2 \ldots 5$ values. So if $A \subseteq B$, then $Proc(B, Y) \subseteq Proc(A, Y)$. This is an illustration of the usual Galois relation between sets of values and sets of procedures. In Ten15, a procedure has just one parameter, so the $Struct$ construction is used to group them if more are needed.

A special type construct, $Unique\,X$, is discussed in a separate section. There are other minor type constructors for main-store values, but the major type constructors which remain are concerned with backing store and with network values. $Remote\,X$ is the type of any value of type X in another computer on the network. Full details are beyond the scope of this chapter, but are discussed in [Foster/Currie1986].

In Ten15, backing store information is organized into data stores, which are identified by values of basic type $DataStore$. A computer may have access to any number of data stores. In Ten15 operations are provided to manipulate these explicitly, though of course the data store operations can be made invisible to users by software built on top of these primitives. The types involved are $Persistent\,X$ and $Persistent\text{-}Variable\,X$ [Currie/Foster/Core1987, Atkinson/Morrison1985]. Any type of value can be written to data stores and the result of writing a value of type X is a $Persistent\,X$. The

210

operation to read this value back produces a copy of the original value, of exactly the same structure: that is, common pointers and references remain common. Writing a value in this way puts it in a new area in the data store as an atomic operation. In order to be able to change information in a data store a persistent variable has to be used. The operations on this are assignment and de-referencing, just as in main store. Ten15 provides facilities for the atomic update of a number of persistent variables within one data store. The more difficult problem of atomic update of data distributed between different computers on the network can be solved, but the primitives for this are still under development.

9.2.3 Circular types

Consider the type of conventional linear lists of values of type A. Such a list might be either null or a pointer to a structure containing an A and also another list:

$$List = Union(Void, Ptr\ Struct(A, List))$$

This equation is not just a renaming for convenience but has in some sense to be solved in order to obtain the actual type. Exactly the same techniques used elsewhere in this chapter to explain loop constructs in programming can be used here to give a meaning to the solution of this equation. An equation-solving operator, Y, is introduced, so that $List$ can be defined in a way which is a renaming:

$$List = Y\ \lambda t.\ Union(Void, Ptr\ Struct(A, t))$$

The Y operator, least fixed point or equation solution, can be extended to multiple equations in a direct manner. It can be shown that the equations can be solved, one at a time, in any order, giving the same result. This interchange theorem also applies to program semantics.

9.2.4 Polymorphism

Ten15 supports both conventional kinds of polymorphism [Reynolds1985]. If lists are as defined above, a procedure, *map*, could be defined with two parameters, one a *List* and the other a *Proc(A, Void)*—taking an A parameter and delivering nothing—which applies the procedure to each member of the list:

$$map \in Proc(Struct(List, Proc(A, Void)), Void)$$

The body of the procedure *map* would be the same no matter what the type A was. It is quite practical to implement *map* so that the same code will suffice for all A. The implication is that the value *map* is a member of all the types obtained by putting a particular type in for A. Hence it is in the intersection of all such types. This type will be written as

$$\cap \; \lambda u. \; Proc(Struct(Y \; \lambda t. \; Union(\; Void,$$
$$Ptr \; Struct(u, t)),$$
$$Proc(u, \; Void)),$$
$$Void)$$

meaning the intersection of all types arising by substitution of any type for u in the lambda expression.

The procedure *map* is polymorphic in the sense sometimes referred to as ∀-polymorphism, since the value lies in *all* the types of the given form.

It is important to be clear about the difference between the type of *map* looked at from the outside, where it lies in all suitable types, and the type of the parameters of *map* looked at from the inside, that is how the parameters appear in the body of *map*. When the body is being compiled the parameters are known to lie in a particular instance of their form. During the whole of the body it is known that the same u is involved, although it is not known what actual type u is. This is a dual kind of polymorphism, often called ∃-polymorphism. The value lies in a type which is some instance of the given form.

As another example, consider the operation de-reference and the set of values to which it is applicable. Can this set be described as a type? It consists of all values of types of the form *Ref X* for some X. That is to say they are in the set union of all these types. By analogy this type is $\cup \lambda u. \; Ref \; u$. When de-reference is applied to a value of this type it is known to be a reference, but the type of the contained value does not have to be known in order to see that the application is permitted. This kind of polymorphism has been described as being what is involved in abstract data types [Mitchell/ Plotkin1985], but in Ten15 it is used much more widely.

A further very important use is discussed in the section on the type *Unique X*.

9.2.5 Abstract data types

Abstract data types have been included in Ten15, though it would be possible to argue that they were more properly constructions of the languages that might be translated into Ten15 than of Ten15 itself. On balance it seemed better to provide a standard mechanism, following the argument that Ten15 must be a wide-spectrum machine in order to permit transformations.

It is possible to define both new basic abstract types and new abstract type constructors. In all cases the mechanism is to specify the representing type and the defining operators. The change from abstract type to its representation is itself protected from unauthorized access by the type checking, in the same way as other forms of access control.

9.2.6 The type *Typed*

Ten15 itself is strongly typed, but so far in this chapter no mechanism has been described by which programs can be written which themselves check types, at least not in a way which makes sure that they cannot err. Nor has a way been given of writing programs which handle values of types not known at compile time. Such programs are needed; for example, a command line interpreter will have to handle values of types determined by the user, and these must not be limited to a fixed finite set of types by using the Union construction, which is the only mechanism so far described which is at all helpful. Furthermore, the command interpreter must check types before it applies procedures to their parameters, and this check must be guaranteed by the type system.

Ten15 provides the single basic type *Typed*. This can be thought of as a value and its type wrapped up together. There is an operation to extract the type from a *Typed*, but this cannot be used to do guaranteed type checking, since the association between this type and the original value is lost. The typed value is something like the union of an infinite number of types, and so it would be possible to consider a *case* construction to decompose the values, one level at a time, without loss of strong typing. After experimenting with this approach it became clear that it was too difficult to implement effectively. Ten15 in fact implements operations on typed values which are derived from the corresponding ordinary operations.

For example, there is an operation, *Call*, which has two parameters, a procedure, f, of type $Proc(A, B)$ and a value, v, of type A. *Call* applies the procedure to the other parameter and delivers a value, $f(v)$, of type B. From this an operation is derived which takes two *Typed* values, checks that the actual types correspond, applies the procedure, and delivers the resulting values as a *Typed*. This is just like interpreting the *Call* operation, the data being everywhere typed. It is a heavyweight operation, so other methods should be used whenever possible.

A typical use of *Call* is in a command line interpreter. A *Typed* value has been obtained by looking up a name in a dictionary; the user thinks it is a procedure and has also provided what seem to be suitable parameters; again these are *Typed* values. Now the user asks for the procedure to be applied to the parameters. The command line interpreter is an ordinary program which has been produced by translating Ten15 into machine code. In order to make sure that the procedure can only be applied to parameters of the correct type the command line interpreter uses the typed version of the *Call* operation. The translation of this operation into machine code contains instructions which check that the actual typed values supplied to it do indeed match in the correct way. There is no way of applying the procedure to its arguments without performing this check. Clearly in this case the check has to be dynamic, since it was not known what procedure value might be fetched.

9.2.7 The type *Unique X*

Every designer of PSEs has found that many uses can be made of a way of constructing tags such that each new tag created is guaranteed to be different from every other tag on the current machine and every other machine. In effect this can be implemented as a combination of the identity of the current machine and the date and time. In Ten15 it has been found that this idea is especially useful if these tags have a type associated with them, so *Unique X* is a type constructor with one type parameter.

As an illustration of this Ten15 use, consider a structure of the following type:

$$\cup \; \lambda t. \; Struct(Unique \; t, \; Ptr \; t)$$

Suppose there is a tag which is a *Unique Real*. This can be compared with the *Unique* value in the structure, since equality can be tested between *Unique* values of whatever type. If they are equal, that in the structure must be a *Unique Real*, and so the associated pointer must be a pointer to a *Real*. Ten15 provides an operation (of the kind called assertion in Ten15 and described later) with two arguments, a *Unique* value and a pair of this sort, which performs this test and delivers the associated pointer value, now with known type. Given a vector of such pairs, in which each pair contained in the vector can be a different instance of the form, and given a *Unique*, the vector can be scanned, using this operation, to look for an associated value and to obtain it with known, guaranteed type. This is much more efficient than using a *Typed* value for the same purpose.

This is an operation of wide utility and an interesting use of the ∃-polymorphic types. The pair is something like a Union, but the decision about which types to unite has been delayed. It has proved particularly useful in writing a loader, which would otherwise have had to use the much slower interpreted *Typed* operations in a place where speed is very important.

9.3 Features of the Ten15 machine

In many respects Ten15 is conventional, as indeed it must be to act as an easy target for conventional languages. It provides such constructs as case expressions, conditionals, loops of various sorts, integer and real arithmetic, boolean operations, string handling, vectors and arrays. This section will take these for granted and concentrate on the less usual features.

Ten15 is defined algebraically; complex pieces of program are built out of less-complex ones by means of composition constructs. It is essentially tree-like. As an example a conditional expression is built out of an expression which delivers a boolean and two expressions which deliver values of types which have a least upper bound (not *Top*). Each of the expressions below, and the whole, are pieces of Ten15 program:

if(boolean expression, expression1, expression2)

The expressions just considered are called *Loads* in Ten15, since a technical term is needed. The name is chosen because *Loads* produce values when evaluated in some state of the Ten15 machine. They may also produce a change in the state, that is a side-effect. Note that these are items in the Ten15 algebra, that is fragments of program for a Ten15 machine.

A unary operator is a piece of Ten15 which takes in a value and from it produces a value, whereas a *Load* produces its result value from nothing. A conventional basic unary operator, such as *Not*, can be applied to a *Load*, using the construct *operate1*.

operate1(Not, expression)

The result of this is itself a *Load*.

The standard unary operators are examples of *Unary-Operator*, but operators do not need to be basic and can also be built up by means of Ten15 constructs. One construct in particular, *make-op*, builds a *Unary-Operator* from a *Load*, *exp1*, and an *Identifier*, *id*. Operating with such an operator on a *Load*, *exp2*, identifies the value produced by *exp2* with the given *id* and evaluates *exp1*, using that value wherever *exp1* contains *id*.

9.3.1 Assertions and solve

Ten15 has to have both high-level and low-level features. Among the low-level features are some which correspond roughly to labels. This is an inevitable consequence of the aim of providing a wide-spectrum machine and being able to transform programs sufficiently close to conventional machines to achieve efficiency. But unrestricted labels and *gotos* lead to programs which can be difficult to analyse. The Ten15 mechanisms for achieving these effects are assertions and the *solve* expression.

Ten15 takes the viewpoint that a collection of labelled expressions is in fact a set of simultaneous equations, in which the labels play the role of the variables being solved for, and may occur in the expressions. Solution is interpreted with a least fixed point meaning. This being so, the labels would be formal *Loads*, for which the equations could be solved to produce a collection of actual *Loads*. The *goto labels* would correspond to the uses of the formals in the equations. In practice, real machines jump with values and unary operators expect values so the labels are formal *Unary-Operators* rather than *Loads*. The solution of the simultaneous equations produces a collection of actual *Unary-Operators*. This, among other advantages, gives a much better loop construction. The construct *solve* takes number of pairs of formal operators, the labels, and actual operators, and solves the equations.

Within the context of a *solve* construction a straightforward jump is represented by a construct which takes a label and builds a *Unary-Operator*, *g*. When *g* is applied to a value it will jump with that value to the label. Control never reaches the point immediately after the jump, so the value there is of type *Bottom*.

High-level constructions, such as *case union*, are expressible in terms of lower-level constructions. Clearly *case union* works by examining the union value to see which of the possible members is actually present and jumping to the appropriate place. Note how, in this construction, jumping with a value is right. The branch of the *case union* must be arrived at with the component value present and ready to be identified.

Conventional programming languages, because they use boolean values to control conditionals and loops, make it difficult to retain type information which should be available. Consider as an example the conditional

IF x < 0 THEN -x ELSE x

It is clear that if *x* is in *-10..10* then the result will be in *0..10*. Not many compilers would notice this fact. Going through the boolean value has made it difficult to obtain the type information about *x* in the two branches. Ten15 uses *Assertions* to generalize the notion of conditionals while simultaneously making type information more explicit.

The *case union* shows how it can be done. In place of the conditional, control must split into the two possibilities, carrying into each branch a value of the appropriate type which can be identified in the branch. Making up some syntax by way of illustration:

IS x < 0 ?
IF SO t: -t
IF NOT u: u

If *x < 0* then take the first branch, identifying *x*, now known to be negative as *t*; if not take the second branch identifying *x*, now known to be non-negative, as *u*. If *x* is in *-10..10* then *t* is known to be in *-10..-1* and the result of the first branch is in *1..10*. In the other branch *u* is known to be in *0..10* and so is the result of that branch. Hence the result of the whole construction is the least upper bound of *1..10* and *0..10*, which is *0..10*.

The two branches are unary operators, created by *make-op*. The test is an *Assertion*, and when combined with the two *Unary-Operators* and the two argument *Loads*—for *x* and zero—it yields a *Load*.

It is interesting to contrast this approach with that of "continuations". In Ten15 the program, which might be unbounded but countable, is created by solving the program equations before any question of evaluation arises.

9.3.2 Procedures and ions

Ten15 supports true procedure values with an unbounded number of binding times for non-locals [Landin1964]. These partly bound values have been called *ions*.

The Ten15 procedure values are just the conventional closures of Landin, except that instead of having only one bind time for non-locals, many bind times have been allowed for. Though one bind time is logically sufficient, having many allows for much greater efficiency in some important cases. Ten15 calls the partly bound objects ions.

Consider a procedure created inside another one and treated as a true value, so that the "display" implementation will not work. It is normal that the internal procedure will have some non-locals which are non-locals of the external procedure. Conventionally this would cause us to bind these values as non-locals of the external procedure, and then copy them into the non-locals of the internal procedure. Very often this will be the only use of these values in the external procedure. In this case it is clearly better to bind them as the first of two sets of non-locals of a constant ion, and to give this partly bound ion as a non-local to the external procedure. This then just copies out those of its locals which form the second set of non-locals to the ion to give the required internal procedure.

9.3.3 Exceptions

When an operation fails a run-time check, as for example if an arithmetic operation produces an overflow, an exception is produced. This exception is treated as a value, and every operation but one which has an exception value as a parameter is deemed to give an exception result. This would fail all the *Call* operations which had called procedures leading to this situation. If this were all, control would rapidly fall out of the program, and since the operating system itself is also in Ten15, the whole machine would stop. However there is an assertion, called *trapply*, which can be used to prevent this. This assertion takes *Unary-Operators*, the second of which expects a value of type *Exception*. From these is built a binary operator which takes a procedure and an appropriate parameter for that procedure. The effect of the assertion is to apply that procedure to its parameter in just the same way that the ordinary *Call* operator does. If the procedure when run produces an exception, then the assertion uses the second operator, giving it the value of type *Exception* produced. This value contains information sufficient to produce diagnostics if necessary. If the procedure terminates normally, the first operator is used, so it must expect a value of the type delivered by the procedure. The whole delivers a value of type given by the least upper bound of the types produced by the operators.

Normally when an exception value is delivered, action will be taken to clean up the state of the machine, stuck semaphores will be cleared and so on. It is not expected that this mechanism should be used in ordinary users programs, but since users can write programs which are like operating systems, these facilities have to be available.

9.4 The formal method

Ten15 is defined entirely by means of intrinsic equations which say which programs are equivalent. There is space here only for a brief exposition and discussion of the method.

A system will be defined which is closely related to a conventional many-sorted algebra [Goguen 1976]. The definition starts with a finite number of "sorts" of which *Load*, *Operator* and *Assertion* are examples, and then introduces a finite number of constructs, each of which takes a number of parameters from particular sort and produces a result in a given sort. For example,

$$operate1 : Unary\text{-}Operator, Load \rightarrow Load$$

Some of these have no parameters, in which case they denote constants in the result sort. For example,

$$load\text{-}void : () \rightarrow Load$$

which will be written as

$$load\text{-}void : Load.$$

The sorts and the constructs together form a "signature".

Some of the sorts are designated as semi-lattices, in which case they contain the constructs, least upper bound, written $\cup$, and bottom, written $\perp$. Least upper bound is associative, commutative and idempotent, and has bottom as its identity. If the sort is L, then

$$\cup : L, L \rightarrow L$$
$$\perp : L$$

Given these definitions a partial order, $\leq$, can be defined by saying that $a \leq b$ is equivalent to $a \cup b = b$.

Let there be, for each of the sorts, a countable set of variables. Now define inductively a set of terms. With each term will be defined its sort, and its set of free variables. For each sort, S, S_0 consists of all the constructs with no parameters which have S as result, and also all the variables of sort S. The constructs have no free variables; the variables have themselves as their only free variable.

For each n, S_n contains the following constituents and no others. First, it contains all the expressions, $f(t_1, t_2, \ldots t_k)$, where the terms t_i have the sorts required as parameters by the construct f. The t_i lie in sets indexed by $m < n$, and at least one of them lies in a set indexed by $n - 1$. The result sort of f is S. The free variables of this term are the union of the free variables of the t_i. Second, if S is a semi-lattice sort, S_n contains all the terms $Y\lambda x . t$, where x is a variable in S and t is a term in S_{n-1}. The part of this term after

218

the Y is called the controlled λ-expression. The free variables of this term are the free variables of t less x. Y is to provide a method of solving equations.

Now the set of terms in S is defined to be the union of all the S_n. The terms in S which have no free variable are called the ground terms. The carrier set of the algebra for each sort consists of the ground terms belonging to that sort. This construction is very like a conventional word algebra, differing only in the introduction of the Y terms, and it will be called a word algebra in this chapter. The word algebra is determined entirely by the signature and by which sorts are semi-lattices, for example one can speak of the Ten15 word algebra.

Congruences are defined in the usual way to be equivalence relations, one for each sort, which have the property that if in $f(t_1, \ldots t_n)$ and $f(u_1 \ldots u_n)$ the parameters are pairwise equivalent, then so are the terms. The quotient of the carrier set by a congruence is also defined conventionally.

A word algebra and its quotients form a class of algebras. It is a class of algebras of this nature which will be used to define and study Ten15. A major topic, therefore, is how to specify congruences.

One common technique for specifying a congruence is to give a set of "laws" which specify which pairs of values are to be equal. If the laws are of an appropriate kind there will always be a smallest congruence which satisfies them. The signature, the semi-lattices and the laws then define an algebra.

The Ten15 word algebra defines the set of Ten15 programs which are well-formed, but nothing is known about their meaning. One could perhaps call this the abstract syntax of Ten15. As more laws are specified, the quotient by the smallest congruence approaches more closely to the required semantics of Ten15, which could be called the semantic congruence. This is not to indicate that this process is intended to be a limiting one; all of the necessary laws will be given, though not in this chapter. But it is valuable to look at particular programs in more or less detail, that is with more or less laws, in order to analyse them.

As an illustration of this, consider the simple but useful task of examining a piece of Ten15 and listing the identifiers which it uses. Clearly, making a systematic change to the identifiers would not affect the meaning of a Ten15 program; this would yield an equal program in the semantic congruence. Therefore programs which are the same except for the identifiers used must lie in the same congruence class of the semantic congruence. So one cannot ask about this congruence class "what identifiers does it use?". This question cannot be asked or answered in the full algebra. But in the word algebra, it is a possible question.

It is possible to define the usual idea of homomorphism mappings between quotients of the word algebra. The only extension consists of defining the mapping of the Y terms, to give the corresponding terms in the image. Many analytic properties of programs may be obtained by evaluating homomorphisms, including for example the task of the previous paragraph.

9.4.1 Particular laws and Y

The form of laws needs to be chosen, especially the treatment of the Y terms. The simplest way of specifying laws is to give a number of pairs of terms of the same sort, $t_1 = t_2$. The interpretation of such a law is that equality is to hold for all systematic substitutions of the free variables contained in the terms by ground terms of the same sort as the variables.

Such a set of laws is not adequate to carry out the definition. The form of the laws can be extended by allowing conditional laws of the form

$$t_1 = t_2 \wedge t_3 = t_4 \ldots \rightarrow t_n = t_{n+1}$$

with the understanding that for every substitution for all the free variables by ground terms, if the terms on the left of the implication sign are equal as specified, then so is the term on the right. Even so, a finite number of such laws is not enough. A countable infinity is needed, with a finite way of expressing them.

In fact enough generality can be achieved by using special sets of variables to stand for the lambda expressions of each sort in laws of the above conditional form. These laws are first instantiated by lambda expressions for the special variables and then by ground substitutions for the ordinary variables. This can easily be shown to define a smallest congruence.

Of course, Y is intended as a least fixed point operator in the semi-lattice sorts, thus providing solutions for the equations which define loops and recursion [Landin1964]. Ten15 does not in fact use *least* fixed point as the basic definition. Let the variables for lambda expressions be Greek letters. The laws are

$$Y\alpha = \alpha(Y\alpha)$$
$$\alpha(z) \leq z \rightarrow Y\alpha \leq z$$

The first says that Y is a fixed point, the second that it is a lower bound to all values which are decreased by α (less than or equal). From these it is a consequence that Y gives the least fixed point of α and the least upper bound of the approximants, $\alpha^n(\perp)$. It is not the case that substituting the second law by a least upper bound law would be equivalent.

These laws have been chosen for Y because it is possible to prove an important interchange theorem which says that multiple equations can be solved one at a time in any order, rather in the fashion of Gaussian elimination for simultaneous equations, and the results will be equal no matter what order is chosen. Furthermore, the second law is a natural, finite way of expressing what is required.

9.5 Formal definition of Ten15

The purpose of this section is to illustrate the laws of Ten15 and to convince the reader that intrinsic equations are sufficient to define its semantics. It is easy to see that more complex constructions such as *for* statements and *case union* can be defined by equations in terms of simpler ones. This section will be confined to showing that the same is true of declarations. It will omit many important areas, such as the definition of assignment and procedure values.

Some more of the constructs for building Ten15 and some more sorts will be needed. *Value* is the sort of the values which Ten15 programs manipulate. It is defined algebraically, just like all the other sorts.

The discussion will be confined to these constructs.

$$load\text{-}name : Identifier \rightarrow Load$$
$$load\text{-}value : Value \rightarrow Load$$
$$seq : Load, Load \rightarrow Load$$
$$operate2 : Operator, Load, Load \rightarrow Load$$
$$identity : Identifier, Load, Load \rightarrow Load$$

The intuitive interpretations are as follows. The construct *load-name* produces as its result the value associated with the identifier by some governing declaration, and does not change the machine state. Likewise *load-value* is a piece of program which delivers the value parameter. This is therefore a denotation for a constant, and it is an important part of our equational definition mechanism, since it can be applied to any kind of value, reference, procedure or persistent value as well as integer.

A sequence is constructed from two *Loads*: it discards the value produced by the first parameter, and produces that given by the second. The sequence construction will only become important when assignment is introduced, and the first parameter might change the state of the machine, but the laws for sequences will be described. For example the associative law for sequences is

$$seq(x, seq(y, z)) = seq(seq(x, y), z)$$

For binary operators, *operate2* applies the binary operator to the two arguments.

The *identity*, a declaration, associates the value delivered by its first *Load* parameter with the *Identifier* while it processes the second *Load*. During this processing, wherever a *load-name* for the *Identifier* is used, the value produced from the first *Load* is intended. In order to be able to use identifiers, one must be able to determine whether or not they are equal. Notice that the method of definition enables us to state that two things are equal, but inequality is quite another matter. If inequality is to be used, then what is effectively an algorithm for determining it must be given. To be able to do this another sort, *Bool*, is needed. This contains two values, *true* and *false*, and no laws relating them. So they will be different in the smallest congruence. Let

$$zero: () \rightarrow Identifier$$
$$succ: Identifier \rightarrow Identifier$$

and let there be no more laws for *Identifier*. Then the smallest congruence provides the other three of Peano's axioms and makes *Identifier* just the natural numbers. This is more convenient than defining *Identifier* as a string of characters.

The auxiliary construct *eqid* is introduced in order to define equality and inequality of *Identifiers*. The sorts and laws for *eqid* are

$$eqid : Identifier, Identifier \rightarrow Bool$$
$$eqid(zero, zero) = true$$
$$eqid(succ(x), zero) = false$$
$$eqid(zero, succ(x)) = false$$
$$eqid(succ(x), succ(y)) = eqid(x, y)$$

Clearly, because *Identifiers* are just the natural numbers, *eqid* is completely defined by these laws for any pair of arguments.

Some of the laws for the constructs will be discussed, with comments on them to clarify their purpose. The aim is to show that declarations can be defined with equations alone. A piece of Ten15 which uses only identifiers, which are declared within it, will be said to have no free identifiers. The laws discussed in this section, when applied to a piece of Ten15 with no free identifiers, which only uses the constructs introduced above, will show that it is equal to *load-value*(v) and determine the value, v. The proof of this result is not difficult and is left to the reader. A proof can be based on showing that every expression except a *load-value* can be simplified by the equations, and that this process will terminate. In the following laws simplification is achieved by using the equalities to replace the left-hand side by the right-hand side.

The first law shows the obvious basic meaning of declaration:

$$identity(i, x, load\text{-}name(i)) = x$$

In the next law the inequality of identifiers is used:

$$eqid(i\ j) = false \rightarrow$$
$$\quad identity(i, load\text{-}value(v), load\text{-}name(j)) =$$
$$\qquad load\text{-}name(j)$$

The following law moves a sequence out of the definition part of a declaration:

$$identity(i, seq(x, y), z) = seq(x, identity(i, y, z))$$

The computation of x, which is being discarded since it is the first parameter of a *seq*, is only being performed for the sake of its side-effects. Accordingly, provided that it is carried out before the computation of y, it can be inside or outside the declaration.

The strategy is to reduce the definition part of an *identity* to a *load-value*, so that it can have no side-effects. Then other laws are used to move that definition into the constructions in the controlled part of the identity. For example, the following law moves a definition part, which has been reduced to a *load-value*, into a sequence:

$$identity(i, load\text{-}value(v), seq(x, y)) =$$
$$seq(identity(i, load\text{-}value(v), x),$$
$$identity(i, load\text{-}value(v), y))$$

If the definition part were not a *load-value* but an *operate2*, it would have to be reduced to use the above law. So not only declarations but also *operate* have to be removed while still making the term "simpler". For each basic binary operator there is a function, f, such that a law of the following form holds:

$$operate2(b, load\text{-}value(x), load\text{-}value(y))$$
$$= load\text{-}value(f(x, y))$$

In fact, this is not really adequate, since operators can change the state of the machine, and the laws which are relevant to state change have not been introduced.

Two laws enable sequences to be moved out of *operate*:

$$operate2(b, seq(x, y), z) = seq(x, operate2(b, y, z))$$
$$operate2(b, load\text{-}value(v), seq(x, y))$$
$$= seq(x, operate2(b, load\text{-}value(v), y))$$

These two laws are not symmetric, because x might have side-effects. Whether or not this is so, the first law holds, but in the second law the operand must be in the form of a *load-value* so that the move can be made. Clearly this pair of laws defines the order in which the arguments of operators are evaluated. A different form could have been used if the order of evaluation were to be undefined.

By the next law a declaration is moved into an *operate2*:

$$identity(i, load\text{-}value(v), operate2(bin, x, y)) =$$
$$operate2(bin, identity(i, load\text{-}value(v), x),$$
$$identity(i, load\text{-}value(v), y))$$

and by the following law into another declaration:

$$identity(i,$$
$$load\text{-}value(v),$$
$$identity(j, x, y))$$

$$= identity(i,$$
$$load\text{-}value(v),$$
$$identity(j,$$
$$identity(i, load\text{-}value(v), x),$$
$$y))$$

The above laws are sufficient to remove declarations and *operate2* from a piece of Ten15 with no free identifiers, which uses only the given constructs. Since operators affecting the state of the machine were not included, sequences played a rather irrelevant role.

This can be taken as a complete definition of the meaning of pieces of Ten15 which use the constructs discussed, even though this has been shown only for those with no free identifiers. For consider a piece of Ten15 which does use some free identifiers, and so does not necessarily reduce to a *load-value*. It could be incorporated in a set of declarations which define the spare identifiers as *load-values*. For each way of doing this, the resulting program can be completely reduced since the result now has no free identifiers. Clearly this can be interpreted as a definition of the piece of Ten15, since we know its effect in any environment.

Of course there are many complications when the amount of Ten15 that is described by laws is extended, especially when the effect of the Y operator is included. No such simple way exists for seeing that the whole definition is adequate.

9.6 Conclusions

Enough experience has been gained to see that many of the aims of Ten15 have been met. Compilers have been written producing Ten15, as have translators from Ten15 to Flex and to Vax. Programs translated in this way run with conventional efficiency. Programs written directly for the Ten15 machine and translated run in some cases with substantially greater efficiency, because constructions are available which cannot be utilized by the conventional languages. Various homomorphisms have been tried. The translator which produces Vax code was written as a homomorphism on the Ten15 word algebra.

Other aspects of Ten15 need more examination. In particular, the question whether the definition of Ten15 is sufficiently convenient to admit useful proofs being carried out is still to be decided.

In some respects Ten15 is still incomplete. The most important area in which this is so is that of close-coupled parallelism.

References

[Atkinson/Morrison1985] M. P. Atkinson and R. Morrison, "Types, binding and parameters in a persistent environment", *Workshop on Persistence and Data Types*, Appin (1985).

[Currie/Foster1987] I. F. Currie and J. M. Foster, *The Varieties of Capability in Flex*, RSRE Memorandum 4042 (1987).

[Currie/Foster/Core1987] I. F. Currie, J. M. Foster and P. W. Core, "Ten 15: an abstract machine for portable environments", *Proc. 1st European Software Engineering Conference*, Strasbourg, pp. 149–159 (1987).

[Foster/Currie1986] J. M. Foster and I. F. Currie, *Remote Capabilities in Computer Networks*, RSRE Memorandum 3947 (1986).

[Foster/Currie/Edwards1982] J. M. Foster, I. F. Currie and P. W. Edwards, "Flex: a working computer with an architecture based on procedure values", *Proc. International Workshop on High-level-language Computer Architecture*, Fort Lauderdale (1982).

[Goguen1976] J. A. Goguen, J. W. Thatcher, E. G. Wagner and J. B. Wright, "An initial approach to the specification, correctness and implementation of abstract data types", *Current Trends in Programming Methodology* (1976).

[Hoare1978] C. A. R. Hoare, "Communicating sequential processes" *Comm. ACM*, Vol. 17, No. 8 (1978).

[Hoare1987] C. A. R. Hoare, I. J. Hayes, He Jifeng, C. C. Morgan, A. W. Roscoe, J. W. Sanders, I. H. Sorensen, J. M. Spivey, B. A. Sufrin, "Laws of programming" *Comm. ACM*, Vol. 30, No. 8, pp. 672–686 (1987).

[Dijkstra1976] E. Dijkstra, *A Discipline of Programming*, Prentice Hall (1976).

[Landin1964] P. J. Landin, "The mechanical evaluation of expressions", *Computer Journal*, Vol. 6, No. 4, pp. 308–320 (1964).

[MacQueen/Plotkin/Sethi1986] D. MacQueen, G. Plotkin and R. Sethi, "An ideal model for recursive polymorphic types", *Information and Control*, Vol. 71, pp. 95–130 (1986).

[Milner1980] R. Milner, *A Calculus of Communicating Systems*, Springer (1980).

[Mitchell/Plotkin1985] J. C. Mitchell and G. Plotkin, "Abstract types have existential type", *12th ACM Symposium on Principles of Programming Languages*, New Orleans (1985).

[Reynolds1985] J. C. Reynolds, "Three approaches to type structure", *Proc. TAPSOFT*, Springer (1985).

[Scott1970] D. Scott, *Outline of a Mathematical Theory of Computation*, Tech. Monograph PRG-2, Programming Research Group, Oxford University (1970).

[Spector1982] A. Z. Spector, "Performing remote operations efficiently on a local computer network", *Comm. ACM*, Vol. 25, No. 1, pp. 39–59 (1982).

[Xerox1981] Xerox Corporation, *Courier: the Remote Procedure Call Protocol*, Xerox Report XSIS 038112 (1981).

10 Assurance in high-integrity software

John McDermid, University of York

10.1 Introduction

This book is concerned with the production and assessment of software for high-integrity systems. Many of these systems, for example nuclear reactor and flight control systems, are subject to public enquiries or certification before they can be deployed. In general it is necessary to provide assurance to non-technical personnel of the safety or security of a system containing computers and software, and possibly involving sophisticated human-computer interaction. Thus we require techniques and measures which can be used to achieve and to demonstrate the security, integrity or safety of such systems; the measures must be accessible and convincing to laymen including the systems' operators.

To paraphrase a number of dictionaries we can define assurance as:

"subjective certainty, confidence, feeling of subjective certainty"

Consequently we should not expect to be able to produce objective, quantitative, measures of assurance. This may seem to make the discussion of assurance inappropriate to a technical treatise on high-integrity systems. However it is appropriate, indeed it is a key issue, as we need to be able to provide convincing evidence or arguments that the technical processes which we have employed make a software system trustworthy. It is not a vacuous study as we can provide a comparative, qualitative, assessment of the contribution to assurance of different approaches to software development and evaluation. Further we can use this assessment as a basis for deciding whether or not to deploy a system, even though we cannot eliminate all the subjectivity in assessing different software development technologies.

Thus the issues addressed by this chapter are

- What is the nature of assurance?
- How can we measure or assess assurance in the technical domain?
- How can we translate from assurance in the technical domain to assurance in the lay domain?

These topics are considered in an application-independent manner. However, as far as is possible, the discussion is illustrated with examples from the domains of commercial security, military security, and safety-critical systems.

Much of the material presented in this chapter has been used as the basis of a proposed set of "Assurance Metrics" in the domain of military computer security [McDermid1987a, McDermid1987b]. Since this work was performed under contract to HMG these reports are not generally available.

We confine our discussion here to principles, and do not try to define a general set of assurance metrics for high-integrity systems. Indeed we concentrate on the technical issues which underly assurance. However there is some discussion of metrics primarily because a number of the important aspects of assurance can best be drawn out by discussing it from this point of view.

The remainder of this introduction is concerned with the meaning and use of assurance measures. The second section discusses the requirements for assurance measures, the nature of assurance and outlines the technical issues pertinent to assessing assurance. Thesse technical issues are discussed in more detail in sections 10.3–10.11. The chapter concludes by considering the problem of providing assurance to laymen, and discussing some of the issues in providing assurance in complete hardware/software systems.

10.1.1 What is assured?

A characteristic of high-integrity systems is that a system failure can be catastrophic in a number of ways. For a given system these catastrophes might include loss of human life, destruction of valuable equipment or resources, or disclosure of sensitive information. In general we require assurance that these catastrophes cannot occur or, at least, that they are very improbable.

There is a significant distinction between high-integrity and "ordinary" systems. For this latter class all failures are treated uniformly. With high-integrity systems this is not the case. For example the mis-spelling of an error message: "*inlett valve stuck open*" is unlikely to be of any consequence. However failure to produce the message in a timely manner if the valve did stick open could be catastrophic.

Failures in systems can occur in essentially one of three ways:

● as a result of mechanical or physical faults, for example metal fatigue, or the effect of radiation on an electronic component;
● due to logical or design flaws in software or hardware;
● due to failure of the system to protect itself against external threats or "attacks".

We would like to have assurance about all of these failure modes for a complete system; however not all the failure modes can occur in software.

Hence we require assurance, for the software in a system, of

- its freedom from design flaws which could lead to catastrophic failure;
- its ability to protect itself against failure of other components of the system, and from external threats or attacks which could cause catastrophic failure.

We shall expand on these concepts later in the chapter, but they represent the essence of what is to be assured.

10.1.2 The meaning of high assurance

It might be thought that assurance is a simple binary concept: either a system is trustworthy, or it is not. Alternatively it might be thought of simply as a probability—such as a reliability figure. At present there are no widely accepted objective reliability measures for software (see section 10.2.1). Even if we did have such measures we could not use them directly for assurance as they do not address the issue of "self-protection" introduced above nor do they differentiate between catastrophic and "acceptable" failures.

As indicated above we can produce a set of qualitative measures of assurance but, of course, these do not have the precise meaning of, say, a hardware reliability figure. Thus it is appropriate to ask "what does the term high assurance mean?" It is easiest to answer this question by illustration from a number of different application domains for high-integrity software. In the case of military security it means that

- for a given level of threat we will allow high-assurance systems to handle more highly classified information, or a greater range of classifications, than low assurance systems;
- for a given level, or range, of classified information handled by a system the requisite assurance level will rise as the perceived threat rises.

Similarly for a safety-critical system:

- the greater the consequence of a particular failure the greater is the level of assurance required that that particular failure cannot occur.

This illustrates the meaning of "high assurance" in terms of our willingness to deploy a system. We give a technical interpretation of the term in sections 10.3–10.11. The identification of a particular level of assurance as being appropriate for some facility or system is a function of risk analysis and is outside the scope of this chapter.

10.1.3 The use of assurance measures or metrics

In order to be truly useful, a set of assurance metrics or measures would have to be applicable throughout the complete software procurement process. This means they have to be usable in five different scenarios.

First, procurement of a high-integrity system will start with a definition of requirements and a risk or threat assessment for the system. It should be possible to specify the requisite assurance level for each facet of the system software, based on the risk assessment. In other words the assurance measures need to be meaningful in terms of the threat scenario.

Second, the measures must be applicable during software development in order that the development process can be geared to produce an engineered level of assurance for the software. In practice this means that the measures must help in selecting between the different available approaches to software development.

Third, for critical systems it is usual to carry out independent assessment or evaluation of the system. The measures should be capable of use by an evaluation team, specifically they should form the basis of the assurance judgements made in evaluation.

Fourth, if a system or component is to be used in a number of applications it is necessary to have a "certificate" indicating the assurance level of the component independent of its application. It must then be possible to interpret that level for a given application. Again we would expect the assurance measures to be usable in certification.

Finally, the measures must help in making the decision whether or not to deploy a given system in a particular environment. Thus we must be able to compare the achieved assurance levels with the required assurance levels and determine whether or not the implemented system meets or exceeds its requirements.

In this chapter we discuss assurance primarily from the point of view of the technical development and evaluation activities, although we do touch on the other aspects of the procurement process. Therefore this chapter will primarily benefit the technical manager or software engineer wishing to understand the comparative strengths of different approaches to producing high integrity software. One aim of the chapter is to provide the basic information necessary to enable technical specialists to start definition of a set of assurance metrics for some given application domain.

10.2 Requirements and technical basis for assurance measures

Since we are going to be discussing technical factors which contribute to assurance, and requirements for assurance measures, it is instructive to discuss possible bases for a set of measures.

10.2.1 Possible bases for assurance measures

Ideally we should like to base measures on well-understood scientific principles underlying software and software development. There have been a number of attempts to define a scientific basis for software, perhaps the most well known of which is Halstead's Software Science [Halstead1977]. However all these theories have been discredited or are, at best, regarded as being suspect. In fact there is no general agreement on a scientific basis for measuring software, and we cannot rely on finding such a basis in the near future (as there are no promising models emerging).

One might also view a software reliability measure as being a scientific model of software. We alluded to some of the limitations of software reliability models above. However since they seem so attractive as a basis for assurance, and because reliability levels are often specified by certification authorities, it seems necessary to amplify the point. A recent paper by Abdel-Ghaly, et al [Abdel-Ghaly1986] makes a telling point in a comprehensive survey of reliability models:

> "There are certain predictions for which our techniques are not directly useful. One important example is the prediction of the time necessary to achieve a particular level of reliability...before a product can be shipped. Problems of this kind require further study."

Thus reliability models cannot be used to achieve an "engineered assurance level" in the sense outlined above.

Perhaps more significantly, with high-integrity systems one is looking for very low failure rates, perhaps of the order of 1 in 10^9 hours of operation. Most reliability prediction models work by predicting future failures based on failure data from software testing. At this sort of reliability level, and within a practical testing time, there will not be any significant test results from which to extrapolate.

There are no other pre-existing candidate scientific bases for assurance measures, so we have to develop a suitable basis. We have chosen a basis which is essentially a comparative analysis of the capabilities of different approaches to software development, and which identifies a range of factors which contribute to assurance. There is a good pragmatic reason for this—it helps project managers and technical staff to decide how to select between available development methods. There are also some deeper reasons for adopting this approach as we shall see below when we consider requirements for measures in more detail.

10.2.2 Objectives in designing measures

Fundamentally we require a set of measures which are sound, that is fewer failures occur in systems judged to have high assurance than those judged to have low assurance. The direct method of assessing measures, therefore, is via the normal scientific process, that is we treat the soundness of the measures as a hypothesis to be proven, then we seek evidence which can be used to increase our confidence in, or refute, the hypothesis. In practice this means that we need to employ the measures in "real world" situations in order to provide evidence of how they work in practice.

However, prior to real world use of any measures, we must subject them to peer review so that we are reasonably confident that they are sound. We now present a set of requirements for measures which should be helpful in any peer review process and which drive the selection of technical factors which we believe contribute to assurance. For completeness we repeat some of the requirements identified above:

- *Scale* The measures should be applicable across the spectrum from small-scale, special-purpose systems through to large, multi-user, general-purpose distributed computer systems.
- *Assurance Levels* These should span the range from that gained in well tried commercial software to the highest level achievable with current (and to some extent future) software engineering techniques.
- *Uses* The measures need to be applicable in specifying requirements, to assist in performing evaluation, to be usable as guidelines in development, and to form a basis for certification.
- *Users of the Measures* The measures need to be meaningful both to technical staff developing and assessing systems, and to "laymen" who may not have a deep technical understanding of software engineering.
- *Consistency in Application* The metrics must ensure that consistent results are produced by different evaluation teams; this means, *inter alia*, that if two different teams evaluate the same system they will produce the same assessment of assurance.
- *Profiles* It must be possible to derive an assurance profile for a system, that is to assess the assurance in individual functions and properties of a system, rather than giving a blanket assurance level for the whole system.

It is assumed that the reasons for stating the first five objectives are self-evident. The final point is less obvious. There will be situations where different facets of a system are expected to be subject to different levels of threat. It is expensive to achieve high assurance levels so it may not be cost effective to develop a complete system to a uniformly high assurance level. Instead it may be better to have an assurance profile where there are high assurance defences against the most serious threats, but where the rest of the system is developed to a lower level of assurance.

Further it is undesirable to have to give a low assurance level to a complete system if a single flaw is found which only affects one minor function. Thus it is desirable both to specify an assurance profile in requirements, and to produce a profile in evaluation.

10.2.3 Fundamental principles of assurance

We will follow the current fashion and use the term "dependability" from now on to encompass safety, commercial security, military security, etc. In other words we are adopting it as a synonym for high integrity. This simplifies the presentation and voids some potential ambiguity where we wish to use the term "integrity" with a more precise meaning.

We observed earlier that assurance is a subjective concept. Thus the question we have to address is what factors contribute to our subjective feelings of certainty, and how can we quantify and measure a subjective concept?

The fundamental tenet which we have adopted is that assurance arises from *comprehension*. Simplistically we can say that the greater our comprehension of some artefact, the greater our confidence about the dependability of the artefact. There is nothing remarkable about this statement—it simply reflects the fact that confidence increases with understanding.

More practically we recognise that in developing or evaluating a putatively dependable system we may discover a flaw, or flaws. Clearly discovery of a flaw reduces our confidence in the dependability of the system. Thus we can define assurance in the following way:

> "Assurance that we have correctly assessed the dependability of an artefact increases as our comprehension of the artefact increases."

Thus, from the software engineering point of view, we need to base our discussion of assurance on an assessment of which methods and techniques yield the greatest understanding of the system under development. This begins to address the question of how we quantify and measure assurance despite the fact that it is a subjective concept.

There is a corollary to the above definition of assurance. At any given level of comprehension there will usually be a number of facets of a given artefact which we do not understand. We refer to these facets as *residual doubts*. We may also have residual doubts reflecting uncertainty in the risk or threat analysis. Since we are concerned with high levels of assurance we would expect to have relatively small numbers of residual doubts, and the greater the number of residual doubts the lower the assurance. Practically this means that residual doubts would form an important facet of any measure of assurance. Indeed we shall see that they form a basis for the presentation of assurance information to a layman. Sections 10.3–10.11 are based on a "direct" approach to assurance, but we return to the concepts of residual doubt in section 10.12.

It is helpful to consider the concept of assurance arising from comprehension in more detail. In conventional quality assurance a distinction is drawn between assurance in the product, and assurance in the process, and these can be thought of as alternative ways of carrying out QA. A similar distinction is appropriate here: we are concerned with assurance that some artefact is dependable, i.e. that it conforms to its dependability requirements. For a simple artefact we may be able to gain sufficient comprehension of the artefact itself that we can directly assess its conformance to the requirements. For a more complex artefact we may find it more cost-effective to gain assurance in the process, especially if the process is to be used in the development of more than one system. In practice it is helpful to address assurance from both points of view so we include factors relating to both the process and the product.

There is an important subsidiary point. Software tools, that is programs designed to assist in the development and analysis of other programs, are extensively used in developing dependable systems. The use of the tools is nugatory unless we can trust them. Consequently we require assurance in the tools themselves! There are two consequences of this. First, assurance in tools is one of the factors in assurance of a "target" system. Second, for very simple artefacts greater assurance may arise without the use of tools as the benefits of using the tools may be outweighed by the need to comprehend them.

This discussion enables us to clarify the fundamental principle behind our discussion of assurance.

> "Assurance arises from comprehension of the complete procurement process, including the artefact which is developed, and the methods and tools used in development and evaluation."

This principle should be evident in the ensuing discussion.

10.2.4 The technical basis for assurance

We pointed out above that there is no agreed objective measure of relevant aspects of software, such as reliability and complexity, on which to base assurance measures. Consequently we identify below the factors which we believe contribute to assurance and, in sections 10.3–10.11, discuss what would lead to high assurance in each of these factors.

As stated earlier we are concerned with assurance throughout the whole procurement process. An associated requirement is that assurance relates to the installed system, not simply what is produced in development or checked in evaluation. This means that our assurance factors have to include facets of the procurement process from initial elicitation of requirements through to the procedures for installing and updating the software in the operational environment.

We have identified nine factors which contribute to assurance:

- Development
- Requirements
- Architecture
- Evaluation
- Configuration Control
- Complexity
- Human Computer Interaction
- Staff Issues
- Tools

Many of these factors are multi-faceted. We discuss each factor briefly here, then given a more detailed analysis in the sections 10.3–10.11.

Development Development is concerned with the technology deployed in the production of the trusted components. It is generally agreed that the use of mathematically based software development techniques yields high assurance that the software meets its requirements. This factor is therefore largely concerned with our confidence in the process used for developing the high assurance parts of the system. It could be argued that requirements and architecture are simply facets of this development factor. However, there are aspects of requirements and architecture which are not simply reflections of the development technology employed, and both of them are critical in the sense that flaws in either are likely to manifest themselves as flaws in the installed system. Consequently it is desirable to maintain the distinction between these three factors.

Requirements Requirements are critical in any development as errors here will manifest themselves as flaws in the system developed. For dependable systems we are also concerned that the requirements correctly reflect the critical properties of the environment in which software is to work. In security this means that the requirements must correctly reflect the security policy. In a process control or avionics system the requirements must correctly reflect the control laws for the enclosing system, together with an identification of critical situations, for example the limits of the aircraft flight envelope. Thus assurance in requirements reflects confidence in the accuracy of the model of the operational environment for the software, and the normal software engineering issues of confidence that the requirements elicitation process has correctly identified the specific requirements for the system.

Architecture It has long been recognized that it is impractical to develop large-scale dependable systems where a uniformly high level of trust is placed in all the software. It is now the accepted wisdom that systems should be structured into trusted and untrusted components. The architecture is a high-level design description which identifies the trusted and untrusted components and the interdependencies between the components. The architecture is a critical aspect of the system as flaws in the architecture could prevent the system from being dependable, regardless of the level of assurance we have in the trusted components. High assurance in the architecture primarily reflects our confidence that it is adequate for meeting the requirements.

Evaluation There are two primary facets to evaluation: checking that the development process has been carried out properly, and analysing and testing the product to look for flaws. The latter activity includes testing for vulnerabilities to external threats or attacks, and internal failures. Thus, evaluation is concerned with confirming the validity of the work carried out in development, and assessing the resistance of the system to attack. Thus it is both looking for design flaws and assessing the ability of the system to protect itself, as indicated in section 10.1.1. Consequently, in practice, much of the assurance arises out of the work carried out in evaluation. Further it may be possible to do a small amount of remedial development work in evaluation to overcome weaknesses in the development process.

Configuration control   Configuration control is concerned with the ability to identify all the components of the system, through all stages of development and evaluation, and to control how they are changed. Thus, if a system is claimed to have been developed to some particular level of assurance, we need to be able to identify unambiguously all the relevant evidence in evaluation. We include in this factor the mechanisms for transferring the software from the development and evaluation environment into the operational environment. Clearly this is a critical factor as we cannot have high confidence in a system if we are not sure that we have all the parts of the system under strict control, nor that the executable software has been delivered unmodified to its operational environment.

Complexity   Complexity clearly impacts comprehensibility, so we would expect assurance to go down as complexity goes up. There are a number of technical difficulties in assessing complexity, including the lack of objective complexity measures alluded to above, and the problems of correctly assessing the complexity of systems with repetitive structures. Complexity is not clearly orthogonal to the other factors as high assurance development techniques can be applied effectively only to simple systems. Given the importance of the complexity in safety-critical systems, however, it seems essential to include it in the set of factors.

Human computer interaction   Many critical systems interact with one or more human operator thus making human computer interaction (HCI) an important issue. For example, during the nuclear reactor incident at Three Mile Island [Kemeny1979] some of the failures were attributable to the inability of operators to cope with the volume of information given to them during safety-critical "events". Other accidents occur when operators override safety mechanisms because they have an inappropriate "cognitive model" of the system they are controlling. High assurance in this factor would reflect our confidence that the operators would be able to comprehend the information from the computer system even during a safety-critical event. This factor seems to be less relevant for secure systems.

Staff issues   Staff issues relate to the skills of the staff employed in development and evaluation. Skills are a major issue as we can have little confidence in the results of applying particular methods and tools if the staff carrying out the work do not have the requisite skills to use the tools properly. In the case of secure systems, staff clearances (or their level of trust in a commercial environment) are also an issue because the software itself, or its test data, may be sensitive. More significantly it is possible for development of evaluation staff to plant deliberate flaws in a system. Assurance will increase with the level of trust it is possible to place in each individual.

Tools   As outlined above we need to have assurance in the tools which are used in support of development and evaluation. We use the same metrics for assurance in the tools as we do for assurance in the system, although certain of the factors do not apply in their entirety. The degree of assurance required depends on the nature of the tool. In essence the level of assurance required will depend on the damage which a given tool can cause.

10.2.5   Completeness

It is hard to be certain that one has identified all of the factors relevant to assurance. In fact it is clear that there are other factors which have some impact on assurance. What we have aimed to do is to select those which we believe have the most significant impact. It is impractical to discuss all the factors which we have considered and rejected; however it does seem worthwhile discussing two omissions from the above list: project management and quality assurance.

It could be argued that we should have greater assurance in projects which are well managed than in projects which are poorly managed, so the project management methods used in development should be included in the list of assurance factors. In general it is true that good management increases confidence, but we believe that good management has significant impact on productivity and timely completion of the project, but little direct impact on the quality of the end product. The technical process is the dominant factor in this latter area. Further we are dealing with a special case where the results of development are independently assessed, so the impact of the management practices ought to be picked up in the judgement made in evaluation and we can safely eliminate project management from our set of factors.

In general we will have greater confidence in systems judged to be of high quality, rather than those judged to be of low quality. Quality assurance is usually concerned with general facets of quality, rather than issues specific to dependability. In fact quality is a multi-faceted concept [Kitchenham1986] covering many of the factors identified above and other issues such as maintainability. However it is possible to have a system which is of low quality in some respects (for example it may be very expensive to maintain), but which is perfectly suitable for deployment in its intended role (being expensive to maintain does not prevent a system from being dependable). Clearly we need to identify the dependability-relevant quality issues—and this is exactly what the factors are. Thus we believe that our factors represent a detailed view of the quality issues which relate to dependability, and that inclusion of quality assurance as a separate factor would be superfluous.

The following sections present a brief discussion of what leads to high assurance in each of the nine factors identified above, and outlines some of the issues in developing measures of assurance. Part of the discussion on architecture also considers combination of assurance measures. This acts as a precursor to consideration of the production of measures for laymen in section 10.12.

10.3 Development

Development covers the technology applied in producing, verifying or validating any of the system representations. Thus development applies to requirements and design as well as to the lower-level design and implementation activities. Although we have made requirements and architecture separate factors we will refer to them here in describing development, as this simplifies the presentation.

The assurance model we derive for development is very complex and it would not be practical to include it directly in a set of assurance measures. We elaborate the model here in order to make clear the principles relating to this factor, and to make clear what simplifications would have to be made in order to produce a workable measure.

10.3.1 Introduction

We believe that there are two primary factors governing assurance which relate to development:

- The development technology used in the sense of formal, structured or informal methods;
- The number of stages of the life cycle for which the methods are used.

This leads to two principles for the assurance metric:

- For a given development technology, assurance increases the further it is applied through the life cycle towards the executable code;
- For a given set of life cycle stages, assurance increases with the formality of the representations and of the verification and validation techniques.

We now apply these principles to analyse the relative assurances gained from application of the different types of development technology at the different stages in the life cycle. We start by considering the levels of assurance which apply to the representations and the verification and validation techniques.

10.3.2 The levels

One of the basic principles behind our treatment of assurance is that assurance increases with understanding of the artefact being developed or evaluated. Therefore we need to consider the understanding arising from the use of each of the classes of development method.

Informal "methods" typically make use of natural language prose and diagrams with no fixed syntax or semantics. Confidence in the accuracy, consistency and completeness of informal specifications is low due to the ambiguity in the medium used for the representation.

Structured methods often use well-defined graphical notations and they permit precise description of system structure. This allows some analysis of consistency and completeness to be undertaken and hence they yield greater understanding than the use of informal representations.

The use of mathematically based, formal techniques enables both system structure and functionality to be described precisely. This enables a thorough analysis of the system behaviour to be carried out and thus gives the greatest confidence in the veracity of the representations.

In summary, understanding increases with the degree of formality, as the formal techniques give more information about the artefact being specified, and the information given is more precise. Hence, we regard formal methods as superior to structured methods, which are, in turn, superior to informal "methods".

In order to carry out verification we need mappings between the representations. For example we need to know which components in the architecture implement the functions identified in the requirements. There is a constraint on these mappings that they cannot exceed the level of formality of the representations between which they apply. It may seem that the mapping need only ever convey structural information; however this is not the case. For example if we have two formal representations which use different data structures to represent the same information, then we have to state how to convert the data from one form to the other in order that we can carry out verification. This equates to a formal mapping as, in general, we have to specify a function for carrying out the conversion.

We now need to discuss the levels for verification and validation (V&V). For both verification and validation the term formal is used to mean that the evidence presented is based on the concepts of mathematical proof. More strictly it means proofs where all the detail of the mathematical argument is presented. We can have very great confidence in the correctness (with respect to the specification) of a formally verified system, but the cost of gaining this confidence is very high.

An alternative style of verification known as the rigorous approach [Jones1986] is entering use in industry. With the rigorous approach it is acceptable to present much less detailed proofs, or arguments, and

238

"obvious" truths will be accepted without any requirement to present an explicit argument. With the rigorous approach much of the benefit of formal proofs is gained at a much lower cost. Thus assurance levels for verification and validation include "rigorous", which is intermediate between formal and structured, and "none", that is no verification or validation evidence is provided.

It could be argued, with some justification, that rigorous proofs are more intelligible than formal proofs and hence they should be regarded as giving higher assurance. In the abstract this argument is probably valid.

In practice formal proofs are extremely difficult to carry out correctly, hence tools have been developed which, to varying degrees, automate the proof process. We might perhaps view an ideal prover as one which carried out the very detailed steps and left the "user" with the equivalent of a rigorous proof. This ought to yield very high assurance, given suitable confidence in the prover (see section 10.11 below). The counter to this argument is that, for very small systems, the extra complexity of the prover outweighs the extra confidence gained by having the proofs automated. However, in general, we believe that the formal approach gives greater assurance as there is less scope for undetected error.

The level of the validation is limited by the level of the representation as it is impractical (and probably meaningless) to produce, for example, formal proofs based on informal descriptions. Similarly the level of the verification is limited by the mapping. However, it is possible to produce verification and validation evidence at a lower level than the mapping or representation respectively.

For example, one could produce an informal validation of a formal requirement by producing a narrative description of how the formal representation represented the "real world" and the artefact that was to be produced. By way of contrast, formal validation would involve proving theorems about the requirement, e.g. showing that it corresponded to its environment model.

At a more prosaic level, V&V includes testing and program analysis, and we would expect to use well founded techniques for systematic testing such as those described by Woodward [Woodward1980], and tools such as Malpas [Bramson1984] (see also chapters 7 and 8). These techniques have to be judged on their contribution to understanding of the artefact or process by comparison with formal (and other) techniques. In effect a complete formal proof shows that some specified property holds for any possible inputs and any possible sequences of inputs. The effectiveness of the testing or program analysis techniques has to be judged against this stringent yardstick. Nonetheless it is clear that high levels of assurance can be achieved by systematic "white box" testing techniques, and these approaches have to be included in our levels of assurance for V&V.

There are some other salient aspects of V&V which we can best draw out when we discuss tools in section 10.11.

10.3.3 The model

It is now possible to combine the degrees of formality of representations, mappings and V&V to give an ordering of levels of assurance. We have to do this in terms of the stages in the life cycle, and we use requirements, design, source code and implementation (executable code) by way of example. By their very nature, implementations are formal objects.

The greatest level of assurance arises from the use of formal techniques throughout, including the V&V activities. The lowest level uses informal techniques except for implementation. Intermediate levels include, for example, the use of formal representations but rigorous V&V. Thus the levels are ordered; however they are only partially ordered because some possible approaches to development are incomparable. For example formal requirements and structured design cannot be said to be inferior to structured requirements and formal design. This simply implies that we cannot say *comparatively* to what extent precision at each stage of development contributes to our overall understanding of the procurement process. The partial ordering limits the advice we can give to developers, and the judgements that can be made in evaluation.

More importantly this model of assurance levels is unhelpfully complex. For example it represents a number of possibilities which, whilst technically feasible, are implausible, so that there is no good reason why software should be developed that way. Consequently a practical metric would be much simpler, and would possibly be reduced to a total order, by making value judgements on the merits of different approaches. However the full description of the levels is important as it sets out the principles underlying several of the factors. Similarly the fact that the levels of assurance are partially ordered is important as it indicates one of the fundamental difficulties in producing measures of assurance.

10.3.4 Conclusions

There may be some confusion over the interpretation of the levels. They are used here simply to represent orderings and not inclusion in any sense. There is no implication that the techniques used to gain one level of assurance are a subset of those used to gain a superior level. In practice some techniques will be used at most, if not all, levels. For example, we would expect systematic testing techniques to be applied at all levels. In contrast, some techniques, e.g. use of structured techniques, will be completely supplanted at higher levels, e.g. by the use of formal techniques.

There are a number of limitations to the above model. For example, the capabilities of formal techniques are not all the same, nor are all structured techniques equivalent. In the formal case the use of a particular method may give better analysis of some important property, for example information flow, than any of the other methods. We have already commented on the complexity of the model as it stands. The further analysis of the capabilities of particular methods would serve to make the model more complex, most likely by introducing sub-classes of methods. It is anticipated that a comparatively small number of techniques will be recommended for use in developing dependable systems. Consequently a general analysis of the comparative capabilities of different methods would be nugatory.

At a more practical level it is instructive to consider what methods and tools, if any, are available at the different levels of assurance. It is instructive first to consider functionality, then timing.

To the author's knowledge there are no tools and techniques which give formal support down to the level of executable code (in general formal development systems assume that the compiler is trustworthy). In practice it may be possible to use tools such as Malpas to compare the input to and output from a compiler to achieve formal assurance to the level of an implementation.

There are a number of systems which give formal support down to the level of source code, for example Gypsy [Good1984]. These systems have been, or are intended to be, used in the domain of military computer security.

In safety-critical systems timing is more of an issue, and some formal techniques have been developed to deal with timing in the design domain, for example Real-Time Logic [Jahanian 1986]. It is not clear that timing has been addressed in a formal sense at the level of an implementation, but Leveson has done work on applying hardware fault tree analysis techniques to software which might lead to this level of capability [Leveson1983].

Thus the highest levels of assurance which we have identified in the development dimension are beyond current technology, but there is evidence that current research programmes provide some of the necessary technology for achieving these high assurance levels.

In summary we have based our analysis of assurance in the development dimension on the contribution of different development techniques to comprehension of the artefact and of the procurement process. An outline model of assurance has been presented and this model enables different approaches to development to be ranked (in a partial order). A more detailed model is given in [McDermid1987a]. This treatment of assurance in development underpins many of the other assurance factors. It is used directly in considering assurance in requirements and architecture. It is also used implicitly in other factors as the effect of say, configuration control, is best thought of in terms of the impact it has on our understanding of the development process.

This model is complex, and it is unlikely that it could be used directly in practice. It is certainly inappropriate for presentation to a layman. We address the issues of simplifying the model in section 10.12.

10.4 Requirements

We consider requirements analysis from a software engineering point of view and also discuss the specific issues associated with dependable computer systems. One important facet of a dependable system is the modelling of the properties of the environment in which the system will operate. Thus the requirements for a dependable system will have two important components:

- a model of the properties of the environment;
- system-specific requirements, e.g. auditing, authentication, behaviour in the event of hardware failure.

We first discuss the software engineering aspects of establishing the system-specific requirements, then consider issues in modelling properties of the environment.

10.4.1   Software engineering issues

Requirements Analysis is the first stage of the development process concerned with documenting the user's or customer's perceived needs by "transformation" from the initial concepts of what the system should do. The distinguishing characteristic of requirements analysis is that it is primarily an information-gathering exercise which can only be validated, not verified.

The results of requirements analysis should describe both the *system* and the *environment* in which it operates. This is the case for two reasons:

- the environment may change, impacting the functionality required of the system;
- the boundary of the system is not known *a priori*.

It is hard to bound precisely that part of the environment which should be considered in requirements analysis, but it should cover at least those systems, individuals, etc. which interact directly with the system to be developed. In the case of secure systems it will probably be appropriate to include agencies which represent threats to a system. In the case of safety-critical software it will probably be necessary to represent the controlled systems, and possible sources of threats.

The results of requirements analysis are the primary basis for communication between the user or customer and the development team. For this reason it is desirable that the representation should be as precise as possible, e.g. formal. However it is rare for users to be educated to understand the necessary formalisms. Consequently it seems that formal techniques either cannot be used at this stage, or if they are used some interpretation of the formalism is required for communication with the customer. For example it would be possible to use techniques of animation in validation of requirements, i.e. the specifications can be interpreted to provide a "simulation" of the specified behaviour.

Requirements analysis methods needs to deal with causality, e.g. "when this event occurs in the environment the system must perform the following actions", and other properties such as behaviour of the system under hardware failure conditions and timeliness of response. Currently most requirements are specified informally. Structured methods such as CORE [Mullery1979] do address some of the technical problems alluded to above and are used in requirements analysis. There are few formal methods oriented towards requirements although the work described in [Maibaum1986] and [Potts1986] is noteworthy as it deals with issues such as formally representing causality and giving guidelines for requirements capture.

There are a number of research problems which have to be overcome before formal techniques can be used widely for requirements analysis. The most crucial of these is the development of notations which are rich enough to specify functional, causal, and non-functional requirements but which can be presented to a user in an acceptable manner without substantial loss of precision. Despite these limitations it seems appropriate to use formal techniques for the highest levels of assurance; however stress must also be laid on the information-gathering and validation techniques.

10.4.2 Modelling properties of the environment

The production of models of properties of the environment is important for all classes of dependable systems as it gives the opportunity for carrying out more thorough validation than is possible by simply reviewing requirements. In the domain of military computer security there is considerable homogeneity between systems as these properties are essentially those of the paper world. This means that it is possible to produce generally applicable models in this domain.

There is less uniformity in commercial security because of the diversity of applications and the absence of a central security authority. Nonetheless some work is now being put in to finding general principles of security for commercial systems which might form the basis of a generic commercial security model.

The situation is more extreme for safety-critical systems as the environment is essentially the physical process being controlled. These systems are as diverse as nuclear reactors, military and civil aircraft, cars, chemical plant, and automated factories. It seems improbable that there can be general models for safety-critical systems given this diversity, and the author knows of no work to produce such a model.

In the military domain the term "security model" is used to cover a number of related concepts concerned with the security requirements for systems. We use the term security model in a generic sense to refer to the framework for expressing particular security requirements or policies. This is not an entirely precise division, but one which we believe is helpful. For example we would regard the non-interference work of Goguen and Meseguer [Goguen1982] as being concerned with models, and that of Bell and La Padula [Bell1976] as being concerned with policies. In the context of assurance we can expect to validate the model which we use independently of any particular system, but we will need to validate policies for particular systems.

Security models may be thought of as theories which we wish to validate. Consequently assurance arises via the normal scientific process discussed above. In practical terms this means that we will expect to use some particular model and reject or revise the model if circumstances are found which are incompatible with the model.

Recently Clark and Wilson [Clark1987] have analysed the differences between military and commercial security and proposed a "commercial security policy" which is similar in character to the Bell and La Padula model alluded to above. Similarly, in the UK, there have been studies [Brewer1987] of commercial systems which have attempted to identify a set of general principles, referred to as "prerequisites", which encapsulate the essence of security for such systems. Again this work is subject to validation by means of the scientific process including practical use of systems built according to these principles.

The situation is rather different where safety-critical systems are concerned. Here the environment model will typically be in the domain of some other, well understood, engineering discipline, such as control or chemical engineering. In general it is to be expected that the model will be well understood and accepted in that discipline and that assurance relates primarily to the accuracy of the formulation of that model in a notation suitable for use in the software development process. Thus we are, once more, looking at informal validation by technical experts.

Dobson has carried out work on modelling threats in the environment of a critical system and, more generally, the work of Checkland [Checkland1981] deals with the general relationships between computer systems and the organizations which they serve (see chapter 11). Work of this nature may lead to the ability to gain high assurance that the requirements correctly reflect the possible impact of external agencies on a dependable computer system.

For all domains, assurance is derived essentially from the scientific process including the fact that the models have not yet been found wanting in practice. However this appears to indicate that we will only have high assurance in the latest model, but the situation is slightly more subtle. We do not necessarily have low assurance in a system just because the environment model used is outmoded. The system requirements may be such that it is satisfactory to base systems on old theories. This is best seen by analogy: Newtonian mechanics is inaccurate, but it is perfectly adequate so long as we are dealing with non-relativistic speeds. Assurance in the model depends, to some extent, on the specific system requirements and this may be an area where the factors are inevitably somewhat subjective.

10.4.3 Summary and general issues

Assurance in the requirements is both critical and global. That is, errors here will affect all elements of the system equally, and they are likely to reduce the assurance in the overall system to a very low level. Thus it is essential to pay close attention to assurance in requirements.

In conclusion, high assurance in requirements will derive from use of the best available formal methods for both the environment model and the system-specific requirements, and use of techniques such as specification animation for validation. Further we obtain high assurance in the environment model in the domain of security by employing a particular approved style, or styles, of policy model. There is no clear analogous "approved model" for safety-critical systems and reliance will have to be placed on forms of validation based on application domain expertise.

Testing a system and using it after installation provide continuing validation of the requirements. Testing is certainly part of the validation process, and we would expect considerable effort to be expended on testing during development and evaluation. However there is an implicit requirement that systems must be dependable as soon as they are installed so we have to base assurance on the process used to produce the requirement. In other words we cannot afford to use the system live in order to find flaws so we cannot include use of the system as part of the assurance factor for requirements.

10.5 Architecture

The architecture is the highest-level design description of the system. It defines the major components of the system and in particular identifies which system components are trusted, and which do not need to be trusted. More specifically the architecture must identify the dependencies between the components and the target assurance levels for the components.

From a software engineering standpoint the architecture must demonstrably *satisfy* the system requirements. There are two facets to demonstrating the satisfaction of requirements. First we need to know that the architecture is sound, that is that if the system components are implemented correctly then the security requirements will be met. Second we need to know what assurance we have in the individual functions and properties in the requirements, given the assurance in the components.

We amplify on the concept of satisfaction of requirements below, then discuss the combination of the assurances in the individual components. In order to put the discussion on satisfaction of requirements and combination of assurances into context we first outline the architectural principles on which we expect dependable computer systems to be built.

10.5.1 Architectural principles

A general principle in the design of dependable systems has been the separation of trusted functionality from untrusted functionality. That is, functions which are critical to the achievement of high integrity are protected from those which are not and from each other, so that we only have to consider the trusted functions in assessing the dependability of the system as a whole.

In a safety-critical system this principle has usually manifested itself by having independent safety sub-systems which are physically isolated from the primary functionality of the system. Often redundant designs are used, for example a mechanical governor on a software-controlled generator. In more modern systems, such as fly-by-wire aircraft, it has become less easy to achieve this physical separation, and it is becoming necessary to consider logical separation within the software.

This has long been the case in military computer security. Historically there have been a number of approaches to the production of secure systems, such as the reference monitor approach of the UCLA secure UNIX project [Kampe1976], and Rushby's ideas of using separation techniques in distributed secure systems (DSS) [Rushby1983]. All the approaches have been based on the idea of minimizing the amount of trusted mechanisms and, in the case of Rushby's DSS, using a mixture of physical, logical, temporal and cryptographic separation techniques.

In the domain of commercial security it has been common to use a security product which mediates access by the users to the underlying operating systems facilities. Although the details of this approach are different to those described above, the principle employed is again that the trusted mechanisms (in this case a complete program) are separate from the other untrusted programs, and are self-protecting.

From the point of view of making our treatment of assurance general we do not want to assume any particular approach to system architecture. However we can adopt separation as the basis for system architecture without loss of generality. If separation is not used then we can treat the system as having one component, and assurance in the separation mechanisms does not apply. In practice it is unlikely that this assumption will be ill-founded and we assume an architectural approach based on separation for the rest of this chapter.

From the assurance point of view the mechanisms enforcing separation are critical because a weakness allowing uncontrolled communication between different components could render the whole system ineffective. If we regard the separation mechanisms, *per se*, and the mechanisms for mediating interdomain communication as simply facets of a *separation kernel* then we can say that the assurance in the system as a whole is contingent on the assurance in the separation kernel. More precisely the assurance in each component is contingent on the assurance in the separation kernel.

It is not only the separation kernel which is trusted. Particular system components will be trusted (to different degrees) to carry out particular functions, whilst others will be completely untrusted. The assurance in the system as a whole depends on the way that these trusted and untrusted components interact.

10.5.2 Satisfaction of requirements

As explained above we need to know that the architecture is sound, that is that if the system components are implemented correctly then the requirements will be met. This is primarily a software engineering issue and assurance comes largely from the verification that the architecture satisfies the requirements. We would expect assurance in the architecture as a whole to be of the same type as that for the individual components, and we would measure it in the same way as for development.

The architecture is only an abstraction so it would be possible to have a perfect architecture but an unsatisfactory system, for example because separation was not achieved in the executable code. We deal with this issue below but note that it implies that assurance in (the software component) of separation mechanisms is a key factor in assessing assurance in the system as a whole.

10.5.3 Combination of assurances

We explained above the necessity for having an assurance profile, so in practice we need to be able to calculate assurance in the individual functions and properties in the requirements, given the assurance in particular system components. This involves considering which component properties are involved in the provision of particular properties or functions as specified in the requirements and how their individual assurance levels can be combined.

Where there is only a single component in the architecture, or there is a one-to-one correspondence between properties in the architecture and functions or properties in the requirements, then the situation is straightforward. That is, the assurance in a particular aspect of the requirement is that in the implementing property, taking into account the effect of the assurance in the separation mechanisms and the architecture itself. Where more than one property is involved we need to derive a composite assurance from the assurances for the individual properties or components. For the sake of simplicity we base our discussion on dependencies between components.

Components can depend on one another in a number of different ways.

First, and most commonly, there is *mutual dependence*. That is, the level of assurance in each of two, or more, components has to be high in order that the assurance in the properties which they support is high. The obvious example here is that all components depend on the separation kernel for protection from over-writing by rogue processes, etc. so assurance in them is contingent on having high assurance in the separation mechanisms. If we had suitable assurance measures we would expect the rule for combining the measures to be multiplicative.

It is possible for components to be *alternatives* as in the case of protective redundancy, where the assurance in the combination would be the greatest of the assurances in the individual components. It is worth pointing out that approaches such as software design diversity, see for example [Bishop1986], would manifest themselves at this architectural level, rather than in development, and the assurance in each diverse program would depend on the technology used in its development. We return to this issue of diversity below.

It is possible for a component to *mask*, or mediate, the behaviour or failures of another. Here the resultant assurance would be that of the masking component. A physical, rather than a software, example is the use of a mechanical governor to overcome failures in a generator control system. Software examples include the use of message authentication codes, sequence numbers, etc., to achieve reliable transmission over an inherently unreliable communication network.

It is also possible to combine components in such a way that the overall assurance is greater than the assurance in any one particular component. We refer to this as *reinforcement*. An example of this would be the use of a series of fairly low assurance authentication checks instead of one high assurance check. High assurance is derived from the low probability of common-mode failure and the low probability of bypass.

There is no architectural approach which is fully satisfactory for specifying and manipulating these assurance measures. Existing work, e.g. the ideas of Trust Domains used by Neely and Freeman [Neely1985], is relevant, and [McDermid1987a] outlines a possible set of combination rules based on these ideas. This document contains both an example of how the inter-component dependencies might be specified, and presents a formal specification of a proposed set of combination rules. Whilst we have not discussed details it should be clear that it is possible to take into account the dependencies between different system components, and to derive assurance profile in terms of the required properties.

There are three observations that it is worth making. First, it is not entirely clear how to treat fault tolerant approaches within this sort of scheme. For example in a Triple Modular Redundant (TMR) system, or in the use of diverse programming, there is clearly a mutual dependency between the voter and the combination of the redundant components. The redundant components are intended to reinforce each other, but it is not obvious how to quantify the effect. If common-mode failures are likely then this scheme is equivalent to an alternative, but if they are not likely then the assurance reflects confidence that majority voting will mask individual component failures. Further study of this issue is required, but it is interesting to note that various proposed models of reliability of diverse programs proved unsound [Scott1984] so it is clear that there is not an easy solution to this problem.

Second, the approach which we advocate gives a basis for dealing with assurance against particular classes of threat. For example we can imagine an editor with a Trojan Horse which tries to access data above the relevant clearance. However we know that the protection mechanisms (separation, etc.) will counteract this threat in the same way as for "positive" properties of the system.

Third, the approach to evaluating assurance described above is slightly at variance with traditional wisdom about how to structure systems. The traditional wisdom is to look at a system as a set of "onion-rings" and to say that the properties of the outer rings depend on those of the inner rings. The above model says that the properties of the inner rings can also depend on those of the outer rings, for example a separation kernel will rely on some of the properties of the authentication mechanisms.

Ignoring, for the moment, the fact that machine-to-user communication uses low-level primitives in the inner rings we can see that we must trust outer layer functions if we are to establish trustworthy communication between the low-level facilities and the user. Nonetheless, by implementing a judiciously chosen set of functions in the kernel it should be feasible to make it completely self-protecting, although this may lead to a counter-intuitive system structure. Whilst this may be possible it does not necessarily lead to efficient system design, and it may be much better to have mutual trust between components. It certainly is not desirable to rule out this approach, so we believe that a model of assurance should retain this flexibility.

10.5.4 Summary

We have identified some facets of architecture which we believe are critical to the achievement of high-assurance systems. We have addressed the ways in which the assurances in individual components can be combined to derive assurance levels for requisite system properties. While the approach has not been described in complete detail it should be clear how it may be applied in practice, and with components of widely varying assurance level. It is now appropriate to discuss evaluation which is assumed to be largely responsible for the assignment of assurance levels to the individual components.

10.6 Evaluation

Conceptually the requirements and environment models should state all that a dependable system is intended to do, from the dependability point of view, and all those things which the system would not do. In principle therefore, evaluation "simply" involves checking that a putatively dependable system does conform with its model and requirements.

In practice this is not the case as the requirements will not be fully detailed. For example, in the domain of computer security, although there may be a general statement regarding covert channels they will not identify, and hence ban, all possible covert channels because the requirements will not go down to the level of machine resources which are exploited in such channels. Similarly, requirements for safety-critical systems will include general statements about behaviour in the event of hardware failure, but will not identify the details of the expected failures. The essence of the point is that these aspects of the requirements are not, and probably cannot be, defined in such a way that they are directly testable.

Thus evaluation consists of two parts:

- establishing conformance to the requirements and environment model;
- establishing that there are no undesirable properties of the system which contravene the "spirit" of the requirements.

In practice the first problem is bounded but the second one is not.

The above observation may seem surprising, as it goes counter to the basic software engineering wisdom that we gain confidence in a system by demonstrating that it satisfies its requirements. The observation may also seem alarming as it implies that we can never carry out a complete evaluation. We discuss this general issue in some detail before considering the technical aspects of evaluation.

10.6.1 The limits of specification

One of the major problems of developing large-scale systems is the management of complexity, and development methods have evolved to overcome this problem. In general the solution has been to provide *abstraction* mechanisms: techniques for producing a complete and consistent description of a system without giving all the details of the implementation.

Abstraction is an essential weapon in developing complex systems but with dependable systems it is a two-edged sword. Imagine a system which is formally specified and verified to be secure down to the level of the source code programs. The specifications and proofs will, for example, demonstrate that there is no information flow in the system. However none of the specifications will refer to machine registers, so it is possible for the system to be verified against its specification, but for there to be insecure flow at the register level. This is not a contradiction: all that we have said is that we have verified a system against its specification and that we do not know anything about those things outwith the specification.

In practice this means that we have to place trust in a number of facets of the development, for example that the compiler preserves the program semantics and that the implicit model of the hardware in the specifications is accurate. This is consistent with the earlier principle that our confidence in the system depends on how far through the development process verification is carried out. There are a number of observations to make.

First, we have identified what might be called an *abstraction failure*; when one has worked down to a particular level of abstraction one of the residual doubts is that the abstraction may be flawed and may have caused important details to be omitted. This is not a widely accepted concept. However it seems clear that many breaches in supposedly secure systems arise through abstraction failures. For example a covert channel can arise because the abstraction of infinite store offered by the virtual machine is inaccurate and information is passed when real memory is exhausted. From the point of view of safety-critical systems abstraction failures can occur in respect of the hardware. For example one failure mode of semiconductor memories leads to non-independence of store locations including write-through from one location to another, which may lead to unpredictable software behaviour and catastrophic failure.

Second, it seems plausible that covert channels would vanish as a concept if the specifications were taken down to a low enough level, presumably down to the lowest level, at which a computer can be regarded as a discrete system, or state machine. Again, so far as we are aware, this is not a widely held view. However it is clear that covert channels are properties of computer systems and if we could produce "complete" descriptions of computer systems these descriptions must, by definition, encompass covert channels. Similarly hardware failures could, in principle, be modelled if we incorporated enough semiconductor physics, etc. in our specifications. Thus undesirable properties of systems seem to be distinct from violations of the specifications only because of our inability, or unwillingness, to produce completely detailed specifications.

Third, it seems impractical, or at least not cost-effective, to produce completely detailed specifications which include possible hardware failure modes and all possible attacks against a system. If nothing else it is likely that the effort expended in producing such a specification would be better spent in developing and testing the system.

10.6.2 Checking activities

Checking consists primarily of independent verification that the activities which were claimed to have been carried out in development were actually carried out, and were carried out correctly. This activity also involves assessment that the software and specification are under proper configuration control (see below) and that the specification of inter-component dependencies in the architecture is correct.

There is no new technical information to discuss. This aspect of evaluation is primarily a technical review activity, establishing assurance judgements in terms of the metrics defined for requirements, architecture, development, and configuration control.

10.6.3 Search for undesirable properties

As explained above, this aspect of evaluation encompasses normal testing activities and searches for undesirable properties. This means that evaluation will apply techniques such as covert channel analysis, and penetration testing for secure systems. Similarly it will carry out failure modes effects analysis on the software, perhaps adapting hardware techniques [Leveson1983]. In general the aim will be to try to find flaws, but it will be particularly important to assess the separation mechanisms by trying to find loopholes in them, given their fundamental role in ensuring system integrity.

There are standard techniques for penetration testing which will be employed in evaluation. Evaluation of dependable systems will also involve the use of program analysers such as Malpas [Bramson1984] to establish the information flow through critical software components. It is also anticipated that systematic testing techniques, e.g. the use of coverage analysis [Woodward1980], will be employed in dynamic analysis of the software behaviour.

It would be possible to survey a range of techniques for analysing software with a view to using the capabilities of the techniques as a basis for a measure for this aspect of assurance. However there are some practical problems associated with this aspect of evaluation which make production of such a measure unhelpful. We discuss the problems of searching for undesirable properties and derive an alternative way of defining assurance in this aspect of evaluation.

We stated earlier that this aspect of evaluation is unbounded. We now need to justify this statement. The basic aim of the search for undesirable properties is to test all possible uses of the software, including those that violate the assumptions which are implicit in the software design. The impracticality of exhaustive testing is well understood [Shooman1983] and it was at least partially the realization of the impracticality of exhaustive testing that led to the introduction of formal specification and proof techniques as an alternative approach to developing high-integrity software systems.

This formal view of software may be exploited in some situations using existing tools, such as the Malpas semantic analysers, to give similar results to, but better performance than, testing. For example savings come from eliminating the need to test all possible state values, by recognizing those sets of states which yield the same output values from the system.

However there remain analysis problems due to combinatorial state explosion when we come to consider the possible interleavings of concurrent processes. Loosely coupled processes will not give very much difficulty and the number of control flow paths through the system may be little more than the sum of the number of paths through each process. For closely coupled systems, and those dominated by interrupts, the situation will be very different as even a small system may have many millions of possible paths.

Further problems include the need to test for

- timing as well as functional problems;
- software behaviour in the presence of hardware faults;
- the operator's ability to cope with the workload under critical conditions and so on. There are many other technical issues which make this aspect of evaluation difficult, but it seems unnecessary to labour the point.

However there is an important non-technical point. As well as the computational cost there is the human cost of looking at potential flaws and determining whether or not they are real flaws. Tools such as Malpas tend to give "false alarms", i.e. point out potential flaws which are not real flaws. However understanding of the purpose of the program is required to determine whether or not the potential flaws are actual flaws. This seems to be a problem which is inherent in this type of analysis as the tools must take a "conservative" approach in order not to miss potential flaws. This greatly elongates the analysis time.

Consequently, whilst there may be theoretical bounds on the time taken to look for undesirable effects, the length of time required will be much longer than the useful lifetime of the system so, from the practical point of view, we can regard this problem as unbounded. This means that a theoretical analysis of the relative capabilities of the tools is useless as they will rarely, if ever, be used to their theoretical capabilities. Hence we need to find a different basis for any possible measure.

In essence we can finesse the problem by allowing the search for undesirable properties to result in the assignment of the development assurance level "untrustworthy" to a component. This would occur if the analyses had detected flaws in particular components, although it might be acceptable to permit the use of flawed components if suitable "work-arounds" can be found, e.g. manual procedures can be instituted to overcome an operational deficiency of a system. If there are no flaws then the level deduced from the checking activities will be allowed to stand.

We do, of course, still need to specify how these properties will be sought. This is resolved by prescribing the allowable techniques, and the length of time for which they should be applied. Time is important as, in general, the likelihood of there being undetected flaws goes down as the analysis time goes up. In section 10.12 we return to the idea of adopting a prescriptive approach to measures in order to make them workable.

10.6.4 Summary

Evaluation is critical for two reasons. First it provides independent assessment of the development activities. Second it is the only part of the procurement cycle involved in seeking flaws which are outwith the specification for the system and which might lead to security breaches or unsafe behaviour of a system. We have discussed some of the problems of evaluation and, implicitly, the problems of producing a measure for evaluation. Our recommendation is to avoid the problem by prescribing the use of particular methods and tools in evaluation.

It is perhaps worth noting that there is a correlation between our characterisation of evaluation and normal quality assurance (QA) practice. The checking activities in evaluation correspond roughly to quality assurance in the process, and the search for undesirable property corresponds to quality assurance in the product. The distinction is not exactly the same as in normal QA practice as the evaluation of the process is particular to one system, and will involve study of the representations of the system under investigation. However this observation supports the assertion made earlier that the relevant facets of QA are included in our metrics.

10.7 Configuration control

Configuration control is concerned with identifying the components of the system and their related representations, and with controlling the ability to modify any of these items or relationships.

10.7.1 Configuration control issues

Configuration control *per se* is a complex issue, see for example [McDermid1984]; however the requirements for configuration control are fairly straightforward in the present context.

The fundamental requirement for configuration control is that all the items which are used in making assurance judgements are uniquely and unambiguously identifiable, and that they are immutable once they have been delivered for evaluation (clearly it must be possible to change items in development). Thus the scope of configuration control is all the representations produced during the procurement process, and the verification and validation evidence. Configuration control must also apply all the way from initial specification of requirements through to installation of the system in its operational environment.

There are some circumstances where the same support environment (an IPSE) can be used for the whole procurement process, namely requirements analysis, design, development, evaluation and delivery to the execution environment. This is possible with environments which support "down-line loading" from a host computer into a target (execution) computer. However it will be rare to be able to procure dependable systems in this unified way, which makes configuration control more difficult to achieve. In practical terms it is helpful to consider the main development and evaluation processes and the final system delivery independently.

10.7.2 Configuration control in development and evaluation

As stated above we need to be able to uniquely and unambiguously identify all the end products of development in evaluation. In essence therefore the measure we require is binary, i.e. all the evidence necessary to judge a component to be at its claimed assurance level is present, or it is not. In practice the situation is more complex.

It is possible that a component which is claimed to have been formally validated has associated with it both formal proofs and a textual validation argument. If the proofs are not properly under configuration control, but the informal validation evidence is, then we should take "informal" as being the putative validation level. Thus the configuration control measure identifies those development levels for each component which are available for the checking phase of evaluation. Configuration control also identifies the appropriate evidence to do with requirements, architecture, etc. Thus configuration control may be regarded as a "filter" on the evidence which goes forward for checking in evaluation.

In principle we would expect evaluation to be prevented from modifying any of the evidence which it receives, otherwise we are potentially faced with configuration control problems as identified above. Worse it might be possible for someone to introduce malicious mechanisms into a system prior to delivery. However there may be circumstances where it is legitimate to want to modify items under configuration control in evaluation. For example it may be possible, and desirable, to correct a flaw in some particular component and re-verify and validate it.

Consequently it is desirable to be able to make changes under controlled situations. In general we will have a set of integrity requirements for the development environment. The study of such requirements is still a research issue but there have been some suggestions concerning possible integrity controls for an IPSE [Sennett1987].

Configuration control can be enforced in a number of ways from manual procedures, through to fully automated facilities in an IPSE. Assurance in the configuration control mechanisms (as opposed to the effects of configuration control) will impact overall assurance judgements. We view this as being an issue of assurance in tools, and we treat configuration control facilities as part of the infrastructure (see section 10.11).

10.7.3 Trusted delivery

We use the term "Trusted Delivery" to refer to the mechanisms for getting the operational system from the evaluation environment to the operational environment. Since the operational environments are potentially very diverse, e.g. on a battlefield, in a submarine, in a satellite, in a factory, in a bank, it is very hard to make general statements about trusted delivery mechanisms.

We assume that the same individual is responsible for defining the delivery mechanisms and that the measure we require therefore is binary— conformance to the defined standards. In practice we might expect that there will be a set of standard mechanisms and that it will normally be possible to choose a standard mechanisms in a given situation.

10.8 Complexity

Complexity clearly impacts comprehensibility, so we would expect assurance to go down as complexity goes up. The difficulty comes in providing a suitable basis for assessing complexity. As indicated in the introduction there are a number of theories which purport to model important properties of software including complexity, for example Software Science [Halstead1977]. In general these models appear to give good estimates of software properties, such as development time, in some circumstances, and very poor ones in other circumstances. There does not seem to be a systematic reason for this variability in results, so there is no obvious way of improving these models to give more uniform estimating performance.

There are crude measures, such as lines of code, which are easy to understand but clearly limited as, for example, a line of code in assembler and one in a high-level language are not equivalent in complexity. Other approaches such as cyclomatic complexity [McCabe1976] are intuitively more appealing as they are based on measurable properties of program control flow graphs and are largely independent of the level of programming language used. However, since we are concerned with comprehensibility as a basis for assurance we should really be looking for psychological measures for the cognitive complexity of programs.

Work by Green, et al [Green1984b] indicates that there is a considerable divergence between psychological perception of complexity and the graph theoretical measures. For example, multiple exit loops can be quite clear to a programmer, yet very difficult to analyse, and hence complex, in terms of the control flow graph. Some studies have addressed the comparative complexity of programming language constructs, and other aspects such as layout. For example Sheil [Sheil1981] presents the results of some experiments investigating error rates in comprehension of particular program structures. Whilst these techniques do give statistically significant comparisons between different programs at a microscopic level they do not appear to give an adequate basis for assessing complexity at macroscopic level.

There are also some difficulties associated with assessing software systems, as distinct from individual programs. For example we can imagine two distributed systems, both designed using the same principles and components, but where one has twice as many workstations as the other. A simplistic assessment of complexity would say that the larger system was more complex, whereas we would expect to have the same assurance in each system. Thus we need to be able to take into account "unique complexity" and to discount the contribution to complexity of the repetition of components.

This argument is perhaps a little suspect. For some algorithms, e.g. interactive consistency [Pease1980], the behaviour does vary with the number of components (nodes in a network) in the system. Indeed the correctness of the above algorithm depends on having a minimum number of nodes in the network. However it seems that this is essentially a second-order effect, and certainly one which is insignificant given the accuracy of existing complexity measures. Consequently we believe it is an issue which we can safely ignore.

Perhaps unsurprisingly we must conclude that there is no satisfactory technique for assessment of complexity in the context of assurance. Clearly, however, complexity is a vital factor and some assessment must be made. Perhaps the much-maligned "lines of code" adapted to discount repeated code is the best we can achieve given current knowledge. In the long run we must hope that satisfactory psychological measures will be developed.

10.9 Human computer interaction

High assurance in Human Computer Interaction (HCI) reflects confidence that the users will be able to operate the system correctly. More technically this means that they should have an appropriate and accurate cognitive model of the system and the way that it operates. From an operational point of view it means that users should make few errors in interacting with the system. There are a number of ways of addressing this issue, and we will discuss three.

10.9.1 Principles in the design of interactive systems

First we consider analysis of the interaction, and the use of principles in the design of interactive systems. Many researchers including Norman [Norman1984] have divided interaction in to four "stages":

- Intention—deciding what needs to be done;
- Selection—finding the right commands and data to implement the intention;
- Execution—invoking the appropriate command or commands;
- Evaluation—checking that the desired effect has been achieved.

These can be sequential stages but often they will be interleaved, for example, evaluation after each command invocation during execution. Intention and selection are essentially intellectual tasks, but they are often machine aided, e.g. in finding information on which to base decisions about intentions.

This analysis is important as it has been observed (see for example [Norman1984]) that different styles of interface are more effective (produce lower error rates) in each stage. Further, many safety-critical events occur because of errors in intention rather than execution, so it is helpful to consider these stages separately to try to minimize the possibility of errors in each. Experience with evaluation of interfaces for each stage of interaction can be used to guide the design of the different stages of interaction.

Some current work in HCI is concerned with the establishment of principles for HCI, and the formalization of principles so that they can be used in generating or, more probably, validating designs of interactive systems. While this work tends to be general it should be possible to extend it so that we become able to identify principles which are appropriate at each stage of the interaction.

The principles are geared towards ease of user understanding and interaction, and they therefore reflect implicit psychological concepts to do with human cognition. Principles being investigated [Dix1987] include:

- Predictability—it should be possible to determine unambiguously the effect of a command from knowledge of the command and from the data displayed at the time of invoking the command;
- Commutativity—the order in which multiple parameters are supplied should not affect the sense of the operation.

These principles are intuitively appealing, and have been validated by means of experiments on modest scaled systems. The formalization of these principles makes them compatible with the technology for achievement of high assurance in the domain of software development.

10.9.2 Analysis of errors

Another approach to the development of high assurance interactive systems is to study the nature of errors made when using interactive systems, and to use this information to reduce the likelihood of common classes of error arising in a dependable system. It is common to use the terminology *mistake* to refer to errors in intention, and *slip* to refer to errors in selection or execution [Reason1979]. We will focus on slips, although mistakes may be more important in dependable systems. It is probable that a system will be able to detect and correct, or at least point out, user slips but it is less obvious that mistakes can be detected and corrected. This perhaps implies that control systems should have an explicit model of the control process in order to validate intentions.

Experimental evidence shows that users often make the same kind of errors when using particular systems. For example Green et al [Green1984a] cite frequent command errors in certain types of editor, and use a model of interaction to analyse the causes of errors. One class of error which they identify is the omission of trailing "end" symbol in nested commands which they attribute to the difficulty of dealing with nested syntactic constructions.

An oft-cited form of error is known as "mode error" [Monk1986]. Mode errors correspond to the user carrying out an action other than that indicated because the system is operating in a different mode from that in which the user thought it was. The simplest example of this is the distinction between "overwriting" and "insertion" modes in a text editor. Clearly confusion of these two modes will lead to erroneous changes to text.

It is valuable simply to have knowledge of common forms of error. However this information can be used positively in deriving principles for the design of interactive systems, and there have been a number of suggestions about ways of overcoming common slips, such as mode errors. These include developing mode-free systems, and the use of visual or auditory cues to identify different modes.

The results of analyses of sources of error and the derived design principles can be used to reduce the likelihood that systems encourage common classes of slip, and therefore to increase assurance that the system can be used without error.

10.9.3 Explicit user modelling

Another possible approach is to model explicitly the user's understanding of the system, and to use the model as part of the process of validating the system design or implementation. Some work has been carried out on the development of "user programs", based on standard psychological models [Runciman1986]. In principle the complexity of the user programs reflects the difficulty which the user will have in interacting with the system.

Clearly the veracity of the user programs depends on the adequacy of the psychological models of cognition. If these models can be demonstrated to be adequate (via experimentation) then the user programs could be used as a basis for analysing the complexity of the design from the point of view of user understanding, and thus could be used in validation of the system design.

10.9.4 Conclusions

There is considerable difficulty in assessing assurance in the interactive aspects of a dependable system. The problems include the variance in the ability of operators, and the weakness of the existing psychological models relevant to the analysis of interaction. Nonetheless there are approaches which enable us to make some judgements on the level of assurance that we have in the ability of a user to interact correctly with a system, and there are techniques we can use to raise this level of assurance.

At least one author [Rouse1981] claims that there is already adequate understanding of user interaction in the control of complex dynamic systems that we can make qualitative comparisons between different systems, or designs for the same system.

10.10   Staff issues

The skills of the staff employed in development and evaluation can impact the assurance we have in a system quite considerably. The greater the staff skills the less likely it is that flaws will be introduced accidentally in development, or overlooked accidentally in evaluation.

For systems involving the processing of classified information, staff clearances are also relevant. The higher the clearances the less likely it is that flaws will be introduced deliberately in development, or overlooked deliberately in evaluation. For the purposes of this chapter it is appropriate to focus on staff skills and we will not discuss clearances in more detail.

It is quite clear that the skill of software development staff greatly influences their productivity and their ability to produce reliable or correct programs. Some studies have reported differences of 10:1 in productivity even amongst professionals employed in industry. The production of high-assurance systems involves the use of the most sophisticated software engineering tools so this ratio is probably even greater.

Intuitively therefore the skill of the staff employed on a development or evaluation project should be a dominant factor in our assessment of assurance, particularly at the highest levels of assurance. There is a counter argument, however. At the higher levels of assurance the development technology leaves less scope for subjective judgements, and provides more objective evidence for future review and analysis. This implies that the impact of staff skill will be greater on performance, e.g. completion of a project to schedule, than it is on assurance.

It is instructive to consider the issues of providing measures for staff skills. In the context of military computer security the "Orange Book" [DoD1983] defines skill levels for security testing (the search for undesirable properties in our terminology). The Orange Book defines skills in terms of academic level attained, specifically Bachelor's or Master's degrees, and familiarity with particular evaluation techniques. This is specific but it does not really get to the heart of the matter as there are highly skilled software engineers who do not have the relevant qualifications, and vice versa.

Work oriented towards estimating software development productivity has also tried to quantify skill levels. Boehm in his *Software Engineering Economics* [Boehm1981] defines skill levels as one of the "cost drivers" in his COCOMO cost estimation model. Similarly Walston and Felix

[Walston1977] classify experience with the relevant development technology (hardware, programming languages, etc.) as a basis for cost estimation. Walston and Felix state that there are only three meaningful levels of experience from the point of view of cost estimation: minimal, average and extensive. Again this classification seems crude, although it is clearly better than ignoring skills altogether.

It does not seem possible to produce a good measure for staff skills, yet it is clearly an important facet of our model of assurance. This is perhaps the strongest psychological underpinning for assurance: we simply have more confidence in systems produced by people whom we believe to be highly skilled. We believe that the only semi-objective measure available to us is the Walston and Felix approach of experience with the relevant technology. This is not an entirely satisfactory basis for assessing assurance arising from staff skills, but we believe that it is the best solution available to us given the state of knowledge regarding assessment of this factor.

10.11   Tools

As identified above, assurance in the tools used in development and evaluation has a significant impact on the assurance we have in the system being procured. Assurance in the tools is a second-order effect but none-theless it is important. If a theorem prover in a program verification environment is unsound and it can prove false theorems, then systems produced using that environment might contain hidden flaws.

For the sake of our discussion we divide tools into four classes:

- Clerical tools
- Verification and validation (V&V) tools
- Transformation tools
- Infrastructure

The distinction between the classes is made largely on the basis of the type of work which the tools do. However we will need to assess the level of assurance required in each class of tool, which is directly related to the scope they have for introducing potentially catastrophic flaws.

We clarify the distinction between these classes of tool below, and discuss the scope which each class has for the introduction of flaws, and hence assess the level of assurance required in each class of tool. For safety-critical systems we can probably discount maliciously introduced flaws, although there can be no guarantee that a safety-critical system would not be attacked in this way. For secure systems it is necessary to assume that modifications to tools could be seen as an effective means of compromising a system whilst it is under development.

We also make some general observations about the choice of tools for development and evaluation.

10.11.1 Clerical tools

Clerical tools are involved in the production, modification, display and printing of the system representations and the verification and validation evidence produced in development and evaluation. Typically these tools will include editors, printer drivers, print spoolers, terminal drivers and window management software. These tools have considerable opportunity for modifying representations and other vital information. However the output from these tools will be subject to frequent and thorough human scrutiny and it is fairly unlikely that accidental or malicious modification would go unnoticed.

It is more likely that a modification to an item would go unnoticed if it were introduced the last time the item were modified as it would undergo much less human scrutiny. However it is very improbable that a malicious tool could detect its last use (the "final edit"). An accidental fault would have to be a data-sensitive bug which did not affect any version of an item except the last one, and this seems very improbable, though not impossible.

One can imagine more subtle flaws, e.g. a tool which displayed one form of an item but held another one internally and passed on this internal form to other tools for further processing. Again it is very likely that this form of flaw would be detected, for example a programmer would get error messages from a compiler which did not correspond to the source text which was displayed.

Finally it is difficult to see how clerical tools could maliciously produce potentially catastrophic flaws. These tools do not have much semantic information about either the system under construction or the representation (or whatever) being processed. Consequently it is difficult to see how clerical tools could produce such flaws. Perhaps more importantly, it seems unlikely that anyone would choose to attack a system by modifying the clerical tools because of the difficulty of achieving a worthwhile effect.

In conclusion, clerical tools can have a much lower level of assurance than the system being developed or evaluated. It is unlikely that clerical tools will contain maliciously introduced flaws; however some assurance is required that there are no accidentally introduced flaws which will not be manifest to their users. The higher the risk associated with system failure the greater the damage that could be done by an accidental flaw. Consequently the assurance required in the clerical tools will rise with the assurance required for the system, but the level of assurance can be much lower.

10.11.2 Infrastructure

The infrastructure is the software which "supports" the other three classes of tools. Thus it includes file systems, the database facilities in an IPSE, the operating system and other forms of utility. It is distinguished from the clerical tools primarily by the fact that it is responsible for storing the information relating to the different aspects of the procurement process, and should not be involved in modifying the information.

The infrastructure has very similar opportunities for malfeasance as the clerical tools, and similar arguments apply concerning the levels of assurance required in the two classes of tool. Indeed, in our proposed metrics [McDermid1987a] we require largely identical assurance levels for clerical tools and the infrastructure.

It is worth noting that there will be "security" or "safety" requirements on the support environment (infrastructure) which are different to those pertaining to the system under development. Sennett has investigated these issues and has proposed an approach to IPSE infrastructure design based on the concept of integrity [Sennett1987].

10.11.3 Verification and validation tools

These are tools which are used to analyse any of the system representations, and to produce evidence that different representations bear the correct correspondence to one another. They will normally include testing facilities, program analysis tools such as Malpas, and for particularly high assurance systems they will probably also incorporate theorem provers or checkers in support of formal verification. It is also possible that tools for specification animation or execution may be used in validation of the earlier representations.

Verification and validation tools have to be of comparatively high assurance as we tend to rely on them to detect flaws in the system being developed or evaluated. They will also provide some protection against faults in clerical tools or the infrastructure. In some circumstances they will be able to detect flaws in the transformation tools.

V&V tools should be prevented from modifying the representations relating to the system being developed or evaluated (this is one of the facets of integrity discussed by Sennett). Consequently their main opportunity for damage is to fail to report flaws or, to put it another way, to claim that something is fault-free when it is not. Most of the work of V&V tools will be subject to independent assessment either by human scrutiny or by other tools, and we would expect to test a system even though we had formally verified that it satisfied its requirements.

We can generalize this idea to consider cross-checking between the V&V tools. If we think of the V&V tools as each having a domain of applicability, i.e. there is a set of properties which the tools can be used to investigate, then we can reduce the risk of flaws in the tools causing problems by ensuring that these domains overlap. More specifically we would like to have each property checked by at least two tools.

Clearly there can be flaws in V&V tools which have been accidentally introduced. However it seems unlikely that there would be maliciously introduced flaws in V&V tools. Consider the following scenario. A V&V tool analyses some piece of program text and discovers a flaw. In order to determine whether or not this is serious, or exploitable, the tool has to assess it against the intended function of the system, knowledge of the operational environment, etc. If it decided that the flaw was exploitable it has to report the flaw to someone who wishes to use it, but not to the evaluators or developers.

The above behaviour seems too far-fetched to be credible, especially the ability to determine whether or not the flaw is exploitable—the tools simply would not have the necessary information available. Yet this analysis is essential otherwise the tool would have to treat every flaw as potentially exploitable, and failure to report any flaws to the development of evaluation staff would be highly suspicious. A "statistical approach" might be feasible but we have to conclude that it is unlikely that there will be malicious flaws in the V&V tools.

On the other hand the V&V tools are the last line of defence before a system is certified and approved for use. Further it is possible that human scrutiny will fail to find flaws in verification or validation evidence. This is perhaps most probable with high assurance techniques such as theorem provers and the more sophisticated Malpas analysers. Consequently we believe that V&V tools need to be of higher assurance then clerical tools or infrastructure especially for very high assurance systems. However these tools can still be at a significantly lower assurance level than the system itself.

10.11.4 Transformation tools

Transformation tools can be involved in automating the transformation from any one representation to another. In practice, however, there are very few transformation tools in existence apart from compilers. We include utilities such as linkers and loaders in the general class of transformation tools as they are included in the chain which derives executable code from source code.

Transformation tools, especially compilers, have considerable opportunities to introduce flaws. For example, a compiler might plant a Trojan Horse in a supposedly secure system, or a code generation fault could lead to some undesirable effects, e.g. incorrect representations of control words for an effector could lead to the wrong action occurring at some time. Testing and other evaluation activities may detect these flaws but, as we outlined above, it is very difficult to analyse programs to find *all* serious flaws and it is quite possible that flaws introduced by a transformation tool, especially a compiler, will find their way into the operational software.

All dynamic testing is carried out on executable code, so some judgement is required as to when enough V&V is done at the object level to reduce the possibility of undetected compiler errors to an acceptable level, without having high assurance in the compiler. If substantial V&V is carried out directly in terms of the object code, then we probably require highest assurance in the V&V tools. However if the lowest level at which V&V is applied is the source then we require transformation tools to have the highest assurance of any of the classes of tools. The assurance level still does not need to be as high as in the system itself (see below).

10.11.5 General issues and tool procurement

We believe that it is appropriate to use a similar measure for assurance in the tools, as in the system under development, although particular issues, e.g. the environment model, are not applicable. There are some further general observations.

First, the assurance in the tools is a second-order effect. In other words it is harder to introduce faults into the system *via* the tool than it is to do it directly. Thus the tools can be of lower assurance than the system itself.

Second, in principle, we have to consider the tools used to make the tools, and so on. As we require lower levels of assurance in the tools than those which they are used to build, this recursion terminates. It is a moot point whether or not it is worthwhile considering tools beyond those used directly in building the application as the possibility for inflicting damage is much lower. However there is at least one case quoted of a flaw introduced maliciously via several levels of tools. This involved flaws introduced into the compilation system for a linker for a Unix system so that the linker made insecure modifications to code as it was constructing the executable code for loading.

Third, it is hard to introduce malicious flaws into a tool if you don't know what the tool will be used to do. Thus a policy of buying tools prior to announcement, or even definition, of the development project must reduce the risk of malicious flaws. However it does not eliminate the risk of accidental flaws.

Fourth, the use of different tools in development and evaluation gives some further level of assurance (it is a form of protective redundancy). For example it would be possible to use two different vendors' Ada compilers, or, more radically, different methods and hence completely different tools could be used for development and evaluation.

The most important pragmatic point to recognize is that assurance in tools impacts assurance in the application, and that consideration should be given to this fact when procuring tools for the development and evaluation of a particular high integrity system.

10.12 Towards assurance measures

We have discussed nine factors which we believe contribute to assurance in the software for a high-integrity system. In some cases there is a basis for at least a qualitative measure of assurance, if not a quantitative measure.

However it is clear that any set of measures generated directly from the descriptions above would be complex, and certainly would not be accessible to a layman. We first discuss the production of simple assurance measures for the individual factors, then consider ways in which the measures could be combined to produce a unified assurance judgement. Finally we consider translation into laymens' terms.

10.12.1 Individual measures

First of all we note that our discourse has been *descriptive* rather than *prescriptive*. That is, we have tried to describe the range of possibilities in, say, software development rather than to prescribe an approach for achieving a particular level of assurance. We can produce fairly simple measures by taking a prescriptive approach, and we have the benefit of being able to judge their adequacy in terms of the analysis, or description, presented above. This prescriptive approach has been adopted for practical assurance measures, as in the Orange Book [DoD1983] so there is a historical precedent for adopting this tactic.

It is perhaps easiest to see how this principle would work by considering a number of examples, so we discuss four of the factors below.

In the case of development technology we could specify a number of possible approaches, and then rank them in terms of assurance. For example we could produce a simple hierarchy:

1 Formal development down to object code
2 Formal development down to source code
3 Rigorous development down to source code
4 Structured approach to requirements analysis, then rigorous development down to source code
5 Structured development down to source code
6 Ad hoc techniques down to source code

with the obvious interpretation that lower numbers represent higher levels of assurance. Although this is couched in the terms of formal methods any development approach which yielded the same amount of information about the system as the identified approach would be regarded as being at that level. Thus, for example, appropriate use of the Malpas conformance analysers [Bramson1984] or SPADE [Carré1986] could be assessed as being at level 2 in the above hierarchy.

Any development approach not represented would be mapped onto the highest level which required a strict subset of the techniques used in the actual approach, e.g. rigorous development down to object code would map onto level 3 in our levels above. In our proposed metrics for computer security [McDermid1987b] we have adopted this approach although we have a rather more complex set of assurance levels.

In the case of tools we could apply the same set of levels, but simply require that, say, the assurance level in the tools had to be no more than two levels below that in the application. We could be more discriminating, following the discussion in section 10.11, and identify (relative) levels of assurance for each class of tool. It would be possible to take this further and to specify the use of particular approved tools to achieve each level of assurance. The value of such an approach would depend on a number of factors including the stress which a certification agency placed on uniformity of approach across a number of applications.

In the domain of HCI we could adopt a quantitative approach and base measures on operator error rates in use of the system under specified test conditions. It is perhaps more likely that it will prove effective to be prescriptive in the extreme, that is to specify what principles (in the sense described in section 10.9.1) should be used in the development of the interactive aspects of the system.

The case of models of the environment is somewhat less clear. In the military security domain it may be possible to choose a favoured security model to apply across all applications. This, again, represents an extreme form of prescription. In other application areas for high-integrity system it will probably be necessary to rely on the expertise of domain experts in validation of presented models, but the measure for this factor is still likely to be binary, i.e. the model will be deemed acceptable, or deemed to be flawed and hence unacceptable.

We have not explicitly considered all the factors, but it should be clear that we can adopt a prescriptive approach to all the factors identified above. Most of the measures for the factors became binary, representing adherence to a prescribed standard, or comprise a set of qualitatively distinct "levels" which provide a ranking in assurance. In the case of our security metrics [McDermid1987b] most of the metrics are binary, but those based on development are a fairly complex partial order, recognizing the fact that we cannot directly compare all approaches to software development from an assurance point of view.

In many cases, the measures have to be profiles representing the degree of assurance in each component or property of the system, rather than in the system as a whole. We discuss manipulation of these profiles to produce overall assurance judgements for a system in the next section.

10.12.2 Combination of measures

There are two aspects of combination. First, we need to be able to combine the measures in each of the factors to be able to produce a "unified" assurance measure for each component. Second, we need to be able to combine the assurance levels in individual components or properties identified in the architecture to obtain an assurance profile for the properties identified in the requirements. Section 10.5 outlined the way in which we can carry out this latter operation, but we need to consider the former aspect of combination in more detail.

There is an inherent problem in producing a unified measure: we have to combine measures which are qualitatively different. The approach we adopted for the security metrics mentioned above was to identify one measure as the key and to represent combination with other factors in terms of the way in which they modified the assurance in the key factor.

For the security metrics we adopted development as the key measure, and most of the other factors could easily be related to this. For example, if the information relating to formal verification was not properly under configuration control, but informal arguments of correctness were, then we would say that the configuration control defects reduced the assurance in the verification aspects of development from formal to informal.

This approach was satisfactory for the security metrics, but, for various reasons, we did not include complexity and HCI amongst the factors (see below). It is less clear how to unify these two factors with the other seven. Even if one unified measure cannot be produced, reducing the number of factors to two or three will greatly simplify presentation and interpretation of assurance measures.

10.12.3   Translation into laymen's terms

Having produced a unified measure, or at least a small number of measures, we still have the issue of translation into laymen's terms. Clearly, in the example cited above, definition of assurance in terms of types of development method would not be clear to a layman. However we can provide a suitable translation by returning to the idea of residual doubts.

In the example given above we used development as the "unifying" measure, and identified six levels of assurance. At the highest level the residual doubts are:

- there may be flaws in the mathematical theory underlying the verification approach;
- the environment model and requirements may be flawed, although they are adequate given the current state of knowledge in the application domain;
- there may be flaws introduced via the tools despite their high level of assurance;
- the user may misunderstand the system specification and hence misuse it;
- undesirable properties may exist which are undetectable with current techniques;
- system behaviour in the event of hardware failures is not known.

This may seem a fairly horrendous list of doubts, but with the exception of the last point they are all inescapable. At the next level there is an additional doubt that the compilation system may be flawed, and that the validation at the level of executable code has not detected the error.

These concepts can be adequately explained to the intelligent layman. If this turns out not to be the case then it would be possible to simplify the presentation of the measures still further, by saying that level 1 above represents the best that can be achieved given current scientific understanding. This is not a very satisfactory resolution of the problem as it begs the question: how good is our scientific understanding?

We believe that an approach of explaining the measures in terms of residual doubts is both satisfactory and practical.

10.12.4   Practical development of assurance measures

It has not been our intention in this chapter to describe specific metrics or measures; however there are a few further issues associated with the development of specific measures which are worthy of consideration. We discuss them in the order in which they would apply in the practical development of a set of measures or metrics.

First, for a given application area, not all of the factors may apply. Again it is easiest to use the example of metrics in the domain of security.

The factors for complexity and HCI were omitted from these metrics. The omission of complexity was not entirely satisfactory, but the essence of the argument was that the development technology got harder, and more expensive, as the assurance level rose. Hence it was only possible to achieve high assurance for small systems, and we could view development technology as implicitly incorporating complexity.

If an ordinary user has difficulties with the HCI then this cannot compromise security. The only problem is that there might be a high rate of false alarms from auditing accidental or malicious attempts to violate security. The HCI for the security officer seems more critical, as the officer will have to set up the security controls. However there is considerable opportunity to validate the security officer's work so this should, at worst, impact productivity, not security.

In general it should be possible to analyse the assurance factors and decide which ones are important in a particular application domain. The irrelevant ones can be eliminated, and not considered when we come to consider the production of unified metrics.

Second, we can use the principle of prescription to define measures for each of the factors deemed to be relevant. These factors can then be used to generate the unified metric using the ideas of combination described above.

Third, we gave a set of criteria in the introduction. In producing a set of measures for some application domain these criteria can be used to validate the individual measures, and the unified measure. Again, in the case of our security metrics, we were able to produce arguments that the bulk of the criteria were satisfied, and that the other criteria could only be checked by use of the metrics.

This outline indicates the way in which metrics might be developed in practice, based on the analysis of the factors which we presented above.

10.13 Conclusions

We have discussed the requirements for assurance measures, and considered in detail nine factors which we believe contribute to assurance. We have also considered some of the differences between military and commercial security, and between secure and safety-critical systems.

There clearly are differences between these classes of system but the high degree of commonality between the technical approaches required to achieve high assurance in each application area is quite striking. Thus, whilst some of these factors may not be applicable in all circumstances, we believe that most of them will be and that much of our analysis is useful in all of these areas.

We have based our analysis of the different factors on one central principle, that assurance is derived from comprehension of the complete procurement process. We believe that this conception is sound, and that it clarifies and guides the process of developing assurance measures. This principle can perhaps be expanded slightly:

> "Assurance on the part of technical staff arises from their comprehension of the complete procurement process, or their confidence that they have understood their part of the process, and that their colleagues have done similarly in their areas of responsibility."

> "Assurance on the part of the layman reflects confidence that the development team has properly understood the procurement process for the system, based on their ability to communicate their understanding (in terms of residual doubts)."

At best we have outlined a suitable basis for measures of assurance in a number of application domains. At worst we have identified the issues which have to be considered in producing standards for development and evaluation of high-integrity systems.

References

[Abdel-Ghaly1986]   A. A. Abdel-Ghaly, P. Y. Chan, and B. Littlewood, "Evaluation of Competing Software Reliability Predictions", *Transaction on Software Engineering* **SE-12**(9), IEEE (1986).

[Bell1976]   D. E. Bell and L. J. La Padula, "Secure Computer Systems: Unified

Exposition and Multics Interpretation", MTR-2997 Rev. 1, MITRE corporation, Bedford, Massachusetts (1976).

[Bishop1986]   P. G. Bishop, D. G. Esp, M. Barnes, P. Humphreys, G. Dahll, and J. Lahti, "PODS—A Project on Diverse Software", *Transactions on Software Engineering* **SE-12**(9), IEEE (1986).

[Boehm1981]   B. W. Boehm, *Software Engineering Economics*, Prentice Hall (1981).

[Bramson1984]   B. D. Bramson, "Malvern's Program Analysers", *RSRE Research Review* (1984).

[Brewer1987]   D. F. C. Brewer and D. H. Roberts, *Proceedings of an Invitational Workshop on Security Prerequisites*, DTI Commercial Computer Security Centre (1987).

[Carré1986]   B. A. Carré et al, "SPADE: Southampton Program Analysis or Development Environment", *Software Engineering Environments*, Peter Peregrinus, Ltd. (1986).

[Checkland1981]   P. Checkland, *Systems Thinking, Systems Practice*, J. Wiley & Sons (1981).

[Clark1987]   D. D. Clark and D. R. Wilson, "A Comparison of Commercial and Military Computer Security Policies", *Proceedings of the 1987 Symposium of Security and Privacy*, IEEE (1987).

[Dix1987]   A. J. Dix, M. D. Harrison, C. Runciman, and H. W. Thimbleby, "Interaction Models and the Principled Design of Interactive Systems", *Proceedings of ESEC '87*, Springer Verlag (1987).

[DoD1983]   DoD, "Trusted Computer System Evaluation Criteria", CSC-STD-001-83 (1983).

[Goguen1982]   J. A. Goguen and J. Meseguer, "Security Policies and Security Models", *Proceedings of the 1982 Symposium of Security and Privacy*, IEEE (1982).

[Good1984]   D. Good, "Mechanical Proofs about Computer Programs", Report No. 41, Institute for Computing Science, The University of Texas at Austin (1984).

[Green1984a]   T. R. G. Green, S. J. Payne, D. J. Gilmore, and M. Mepham, "Predicting Expert Slips", *Proceedings of Interact '84*, Elsevier (1984).

[Green1984b]   T. R. G. Green and A. J. Cornah, "The Programmer's Torch", *Proceedings of Interact '84*, Elsevier (1984).

[Halstead1977]   M. Halstead, *Elements of Software Science*, North Holland/ Elsevier (1977).

[Jahanian1986]   F. Jahanian and A. K. Mok, "Safety Analysis of Timing Properties in Real-Time Systems", *Transactions on Software Engineering* **SE-12**(9), IEEE (1986).

[Jones1986]   C. B. Jones, *Systematic Software Development Using VDM*, Prentice Hall (1986).

[Kampe1976]   M. Kampe, C. Kline, G. Popek, and E. Walton, "The UCLA Data Secure Unix Operating System", UCLA Technical Report, 9/76 (1976).

[Kemeny1979]   J. Kemeny et al, *Report of the President's Commission on the Accident at Three Mile Island*, Government Printing Office, Washington D.C. (1979).

[Kitchenham1986]   B. A. Kitchenham and J. G. Walker, "The Meaning of

Quality", *Software Engineering 86*, ed. P. J. Brown and D. J. Barnes, Peter Peregrinus (1986).

[Leveson1983]   N. G. Leveson and P. R. Harvey, "Analyzing Software Safety", *Transactions on Software Engineering* **SE-9**(9), IEEE (1983).

[Maibaum1986]   T. S. E. Maibaum, S. Khosla, and P. Jeremaes, "A Modal [Action] Logic for Requirements Specification", *Software Engineering 86*, ed. P. J. Brown and D. J. Barnes, Peter Peregrinus (1986).

[McCabe1976]   T. McCabe, "A Complexity Measure", *Transactions on Software Engineering* **SE-2**(4), IEEE (1976).

[McDermid1984]   J. A. McDermid and K. Ripken, *Life Cycle Support in the Ada Environment*, Cambridge University Press (1984).

[McDermid1987a]   J. A. McDermid, "Assurance Metrics for Secure Computer System: Rationale", C3158.27, Systems Designers (1987).

[McDermid1987b]   J. A. McDermid, "Assurance Metrics for Secure Computer Systems", C3158.15, Systems Designers (1987).

[Monk1986]   A. Monk, "Mode errors: a user-centred analysis and some preventative measures using keying contingent sound", *International Journal of Man Machine Studies* **24** (1986).

[Mullery1979]   G. P. Mullery, "CORE—a Method for Controlled Requirements Specification", *Proceedings of 4th International Conference on Software Engineering*, IEEE Computer Society Press (1979).

[Neely1985]   R. B. Neely and J. W. Freeman, "Structuring Systems for Formal Verification", *Proceedings of the 1985 Symposium of Security and Privacy*, IEEE (1985).

[Norman1984]   D. A. Norman, "Four Stages of User Activities", *Proceedings of Interact '84*, Elsevier (1984).

[Pease1980]   M. Pease, R. Shostak, and L. Lamport, "Reaching Agreement in the Presence of Faults", *JACM* **27**(2) (1980).

[Potts1986]   C. J. Potts and A. Finkelstein, "Structured Common Sense", *Software Engineering 86*, ed. P. J. Brown and D. J. Barnes, Peter Peregrinus (1986).

[Reason1979]   J. Reason, "Actions Not as Planned: The Price of Automatization", *Aspects of Consciousness*, ed. G. Underwood and R. Stevens, Academic Press (1979).

[Rouse1981]   W. B. Rouse, "Human-Computer Interaction in the Control of Dynamic Systems", *Computing Surveys* **13**(1), ACM (1981).

[Runciman1986]   C. Runciman and N. Hammond, "User Programs: a way to match computer system design and human cognition", *People and Computers: Designing for Usability*, ed. M. D. Harrison, A. F. Monk, Cambridge University Press (1986).

[Rushby1983]   J. M. Rushby and B. Randell, "A Distributed Secure System", *Computer*, IEEE (1983).

[Scott1984]   R. K. Scott, J. W. Gault, D. F. McAllister, and J. Wiggs, "Experimental Validation of Six Fault-Tolerant Software Reliability Models", *Proceedings of FTCS-14*, IEEE (1984).

[Sennett1987]   C. T. Sennett, "The Development Environment for Secure Software", Report No. 87015, RSRE (1987).

[Sheil1981]   B. A. Sheil, "The Psychological Study of Programming", *Computing Surveys* **13**(1), ACM (1981).

[Shooman1983]   M. L. Shooman, *Software Engineering*, McGraw Hill (1983).

[Walston1977]   C. E. Walston and C. P. Felix, "A Method of Programming Measurement and Estimation", *Systems Journal*, Vol. 16 No. 1, IBM (1977).

[Woodward1980]   M. R. Woodward, D. Hedley, and M. R. Hennell, "Experience with path analysis and testing of programs", *Transactions on Software Engineering*, IEEE (1980).

POSTSCRIPT

This material was first prepared in September 1987. Since that time some additional work has been carried out in this area, and this has led to a slight revision of our views. None of this subsequent work invalidates the principles and the concepts set out in this chapter; however the additional work does extend and enhance the principles on which our treatment of assurance is based. A recent paper, "Towards Assurance Measures for High-integrity Software" by J A McDermid, to appear in the Proceedings of Reliability 89 published by the Institute for Quality Assurance, sets out our current views on the topic of assurance. The interested reader is referred to this paper for a more up-to-date discussion of assurance.

11 Modelling real-world issues for dependable software

John Dobson, University of Newcastle-upon-Tyne

11.1 Introduction

The word "dependability" has been introduced by Laprie [Laprie1985] as a generic concept subsuming such system characteristics as reliability, availability, safety, and security. The usefulness of such a neutral word is shown by the realization that it leads to the discovery of interesting analogies. For example, Dobson and Randell [Dobson1986] advocate a new approach to secure system design based on considering security and reliability (concepts that are usually thought to be distinct) as different special cases of dependability. But as has been argued by a number of authors [Nessett1986, Chalmers1986], concentration on formal aspects of dependability fails to capture many of the real problems of achieving dependability in practice. Many current formal models do not make allowance for dependability factors related to the management of systems by more than one jurisdictive authority, for example. Nor do the models formally recognize the multiplicity of roles played by people in the overall scheme of the system operating in its environment.

As an illustration of the inadequacy of such models, consider a typical definition of a "safe" computing system as "one that should never kill anyone nor cause injury or damage to its users or environment". Although this is a sensible definition at a rather vague level, it is not at all clear how it would translate into a formal specification for the behaviour of programs; nor is it obvious how to analyse a failure with regard to the specification. What the definition does indicate is the importance of human-related issues in the specification of a system and its environment. There are similar issues too in the definition and analysis of systems that are intended to be "secure" in the sense of not revealing secrets entrusted to them. Both of these concepts can be encompassed by using the term "dependable" to mean the satisfaction of requirements such as safety and security which have connotations over and above mere conformance to a functional specification. Such connotations will include factors associated with the system itself and its relation to people, and will also include factors which relate the people in the environment to each other, as in an electronic funds transfer application where a computer message can be a legal instrument which creates a contractual obligation between the parties concerned.

But the system, and the methodology by which it is developed, must also allow for the uncomfortable fact that there are some people and organization who see their interests as being best served not by the correct operation of the system but by its misbehaviour. In principle, the intentions of the latter can be frustrated by the design and development of a system which is provably correct in all respects; but such a system is a system of the future, and probably always will be. It is not our intention to develop or design or even specify such a system; rather we are concerned with developing a model and a method which can be used to analyse a system with a view to determining its vulnerabilities.

Such a programme is ambitious, and it is not claimed that the approach described here solves all the very difficult problems involved. What is claimed is that in order to begin to attack these issues, a rigorous model, or more properly set of models, must be developed. The models must allow for the specification and analysis of real-world constraints and properties as well as the more usual computational model which allows formal reasoning and correctness proofs. There are many human factors which cannot be well expressed in current models designed only for reasoning about the correct operation of computer systems. In particular, the biggest single threat to dependable systems is human error and incompetence. We believe that a fully developed model must permit the expression not only of a failure in dependability but also identify the individual or organisation responsible for any liability which attaches to the failure.

The basic construct of our models is a *system* which exists in an environment of *relevant parties*. There are two kinds of relevant party, distinguished by the role that they play and their relation to the system. On the one hand there are those that are related to the system and to each other by a shared context involving wealth which can potentially be changed by system events (examples are network operators, VAN suppliers, and end-users; also spies and competitors); and on the other hand there are those parties who are relevant but disinterested (examples are lawyers who negotiate over disputes, arbitrators, and liability insurers). Instances of the former kind of interested party have, of course, a significant part to play in our model, and because it is admitted that they could well have secret or selfish purposes to promote in addition to their overt role in the system; we shall call them *axegrinders*. Relevant parties that are not axegrinders will be termed *disinterested parties*; such parties do not have a *direct* relation with the system, but only an indirect one by virtue of their relations to axegrinders. Strictly speaking, disinterested parties are disinterested only with respect to the domain of discourse under consideration; they may well also be axegrinders having their own policies and rules with respect to some other system. With respect to any particular system, only axegrinders can have dependability policies and publish rules, since policies and rules reflect an interest in the system.

The main motivation behind the proposed approach is that it should allow the explicit treatment of interested parties and the way they view the system. The expressive power and accuracy of the sociological model is as important as the formal correctness of the computational model. By "sociological model" we mean the relations between the interested parties, the differing roles that a particular party can play, and the different views of the system associated with each role. We are particularly concerned with the way in which the analyst might examine the system for potential weaknesses and provide assurance that actions and responsibilities following the exploitation of a weakness have also been analysed and defined as far as possible.

As mentioned earlier, we have tried to make our models rigorous and in principle capable of formal expression. For the purposes of this chapter, however, we have eschewed formality and have presented our definitions in what we hope is clear and correct English. It is crucially important to seek a clear definition of roles and their associated viewpoints and of dependability policies and rules, and to make a clear distinction between closely-related and oft-confused terms. Definitions and distinctions of this nature cannot be easily expressed in the low-level computation-oriented specification languages so widely used in computer science; something more abstract is required.

The structure of the rest of this chapter is as follows. Sections 11.2 and 11.3 describe the framework within which a set of models for the analysis of systems will be developed. The models themselves are described in sections 11.4 and 11.5. Sections 11.6 to 11.10 show how to use the models by means of a worked example of an Automated Teller Machine (ATM); sections 11.11 to 11.16 show how the analysis is applied to the models. The reader may find it helpful to keep referring to the final section (11.17) which provides an overview of the entire process.

11.2   The importance of policies

Two concepts are fundamental to our model: *policies* and *rules*. A policy is an often unstated and ill-defined set of objectives that an organization or individual appeals to as part of a decision-making procedure in cases where the topic is sufficiently important to preclude a mechanical method of choice. The reason for not explicitly stating a policy is not only that it might be difficult to capture except in the most general terms, but that it might involve secret or covert motives which the organization or individual would not wish to have fully exposed. Our method recognizes this and does not require a policy to be explicitly stated. However, a policy results in rules of construction, composition, and behaviour and guidelines for conduct. In the absence of a definition of the policy, these rules and guidelines can be taken as a (perhaps incomplete and inadequate) expression of it. Another way of putting this is to say that certain rules and guidelines are in conformance with a policy, and that certain other rules are not in conformance with the policy. When discussing this and similar issues in actual instances, it is important to be clear as to which policy is being referenced, since there may be a multiplicity of policies by virtue of the variety of organizations and roles, and rules that are in agreement with one policy might well not be in agreement with another. In such a case it might be necessary to define what resolution methods would be required to solve potential conflicts of interest.

The approach is based on an architectural set of models of a dependable communication system. By "architectural" we mean that the set of models is designed to show components and the relations between components rather than to act as an implementation specification. The architecture should incorporate the policy: certain externally imposed constraints have to be respected and fundamental decisions have to be made on the basis of political considerations which may override any technical ones.

Technical specifications and considerations are made on the basis of the rules (e.g. of construction, composition, or behaviour) which the system must observe or enforce; and a policy is a predicate over such a set of rules. It might be possible to say such things as a rule conform to a policy, or a set of rules is a complete statement of the policy, and so on. Examples of possible sets of rules will be given later on; for the moment the important thing is that although a policy need not be explicitly stated, the rules must be, in order for determination of whether or not the predicate applies.

It might seem that a policy in the way we have defined it is redundant, and that we are just identifying a subset of rules that satisfy some predicate. But this is not so for two reasons. The first is that there are potentially many policies and an important issue is to model the possible conflicts and resolutions concerning rules that satisfy some policies and not others. The second reason is that policies in practice change and the fact that a rule satisfied a policy yesterday does not necessarily mean that it will do so today. We wish to model the notion of a rule being tested against a policy to see if under the circumstances the rule should be suspended or is no longer applicable.

We are stressing the importance of communications systems in our approach, since we are interested in an environment which contains "distributed computing systems". We wish to model the nature of the communications between the various computers in the system, and in particular, the non-instantaneous nature of the communications medium and the fact that it and the computers are capable of failing independently of each other. But the problems of dependability have a wider domain than mere computers, and our real interest is in "distributed systems" which include people as well as machines.

An important feature of such interaction is that it is very frequently provided through a set of services supplied by an independent operator. This gives rise to a set of constraints and problems that are to some extent outside the scope of the communicating parties. In the case of communications networks, the network operator will not enforce any dependability policy other than his own. Thus in order for dependability policies to be formulated and enforced over domains that include networks, the rules under which the network operator provides services must be explicit and available for public inspection. It is then the responsibility of the service users to determine whether or not those rules are in conformance with their own dependability policy.

Differing policies may conflict. For example, it might well be that a particular organization has a security policy that results in a rule to the effect that it never reveals its encryption/decryption algorithms and keys to anyone not employed by the organization. On the other hand, the carrier may have a policy of wishing to assist in national security and therefore applies the rule that it will carry encrypted traffic only if it has previously been supplied with the decryption algorithm and keys, so that it could check that the traffic is not subversive. In this case, the user organization has to choose between not using the carrier's services for its encrypted traffic, or changing its own security policy.

The demonstration of dependability to a problem owner is achieved by an analysis of the rules and of the conformance of a system to the rules. The difficulty is that the problem owner wishes to be reassured that the system is flawless, or as near flawless as any real system can expect to be, when in fact the technology for the demonstration of such reassurance is either inadequate or incomprehensible except to a trained expert. Often therefore, the problem owner has no recourse but to translate the question "Is my system dependable?" into "Do I trust my advisor?". In many cases, the primary responsibility for problem definition and model building is in the hands of a system analyst who may well turn to specialists (e.g. on formal verification) on substantive aspects of the problem (according to the analyst's definition of it) without close involvement of the problem owner—and that in itself is of course part of the problem and not part of the solution.

Acting as an interface between the specialist's knowledge of a particular technical domain and the system being investigated or designed, the analyst's skill lies in using an appropriate formal calculus to capture an adequate representation of the problem. The longest established general modelling calculus is first-order predicate logic. However, in its standard form this is difficult to use in backwards inferencing from conclusions to assumptions—which is often what is required in order to investigate where a fault in the system might arise. Even if the clausal form of logic is used, which does permit both forwards and backwards reasoning, the structure of what is being represented does not always emerge in any clear way. Instead, there is a danger of the problem being represented as an unstructured sequence of apparently independent sentences with no indication of how the sentences should be grouped together in a higher-level recursively organized set of structures.

A recursive structure requires the definition of a conceptually rich set of relationship types which are in some sense complete, coherent, and consistent. They must exhibit *generality* (i.e. should support more than one function within the problem domain), *accessibility* (i.e. must be easily and unambiguously understood by the problem owner as the problem is developed or revised), and *extensibility* (i.e. must be capable of adaptation to the changing views of what needs to be modelled). The relationship types must match the decision-making processing capabilities of the human user and the languages used in employing those capabilities. In particular, the problem representation must not be so complex, and at such a low level of abstraction, that the problem owner cannot comprehend its capabilities. All this points to the advisability of partitioning the representation into a simple set of models, each model capturing a different aspect of the problem, such that a restricted calculus (not necessarily the same for each model) can be used to break down the analysis.

11.3 Multiple levels of representation

What we are trying to explain here is not a particular form of problem representation but a *framework for representations*. Since this framework is to be generic in nature and has to serve the purposes of both the problem owner and the problem analyst, the representation has to be capable of being recognized as suitable from both directions; the problem owner has to be convinced that the problem has in fact been correctly represented, which leads to a requirement for a certain degree of informality; whereas the problem analyst requires a certain degree of formality in order that the manipulations can be seen to be convincing. The question then arises: What are the principles on which such a framework can be constructed?

In order to develop such a framework, we shall consider the *cognitive operations* involved in the task of formalizing a problem. The framework we are proposing has been developed by Humphreys in connection with a theory of decision-making in the face of uncertainty [Humphreys 1984]. However, the framework seems to be a quite general cultural phenomenon and is, for example, fundamental to Piaget's concept of intelligence [Piaget 1978]. Thus, although we are trying to present the ideas from first principles, the principles are based on studies of human cognition rather than logic or mathematics. Five different levels of cognitive symbolization can be identified, each requiring a qualitatively different type of representation of the structure of the problem at that level, and each requiring a different set of cognitive operations on the representation. The framework incorporates three major formal features:

1) What is different at each level is *the set of cognitive operations carried out by the analyst in developing the problem representation*, rather than the formal content of the representation thus developed.
2) The *results* of the operations carried out at a particular level constrain the ways operations are carried out at lower levels.
3) The problem being analysed is represented at all levels simultaneously and it is necessary to examine how the problem is handled at each level in turn.

Briefly, the operations at each of the five levels are as follows.

Level 5   consists of operations to elucidate each problem owner's concerns and the rules which the system is desired to observe. The results are expressed in a set of unstructured natural language scripts. The cognitive operations here are probably beyond language.

We shall call this the *Linguistic Level*.

Level 4   is carried out by the problem analyst working in conjunction with the problem owner to determine from the scripts what are the features of the system that give rise to concern, and what kinds of model are required to represent those features. In general, more than one model will be developed, and relations between the models are explored. Operations at this level are essentially a cognitive activity of insight and synthesis.

We shall call this the *Conceptual Level*.

Level 3   Each model is separately formalized using an appropriate calculus which may well be different for each model. Relevant operations, representing real-world activities both legitimate and illegitimate, are defined in each calculus. This activity is undertaken by the problem analyst, possibly using advisers in specialist fields such as mathematics and formal logic. For example, a shared resource matrix or relational algebra database representation would be defined at this level. The cognitive operations here are essentially ones of model definition and refinement.

We shall call this the *Semantic Level*.

Level 2   The real-world interpretations of the operations in the calculus are defined and limitations on the scope of the operations are explored. For example, discovery of the difficulties of representing multi-level security within certain kinds of relational database [Denning1987] is a level 2 activity. The cognitive operations at this level are essentially analytic ones of hypothesis generation and testing in exploring the consequences of a model.

We shall call this the *Logical Level*.

Level 1   Implications of interpretation of the descriptive signs of the calculus are explored. For example, the message-passing protocols which implement a calculus of communications, or the encryption algorithms to be used, are defined at this level. The cognitive operations are ones of engineering and implementation decision.

We shall call this the *Descriptive Level*.

Before discussing in detail each of the five levels, we must stress again that we are trying to describe the *cognitive operations* that the analyst has to apply at each level rather than the facts to be represented or the rules describing relations between the facts. The procedural knowledge required to develop structure at each level is quite separate from the declarative knowledge represented within the structure to be developed. The structure of the declarative knowledge will be specific to the particular system being analysed, while the procedural knowledge is generic. Thus where our approach differs from others is, we claim, in the structuring of the human processes we employ and in the generic nature of the representational framework. We make no prescription for the actual methods or tools to be used; what we wish to do is to present a format into which the analyst can slot whatever methods and tools are thought best for the particular job in hand.

11.3.1 Level 5: Linguistic level

At level 5, aspects of the system are expressed, rather than structured, by an exploration in natural language of the features and concepts of interest in the system. The analyst is primarily attempting to discover what possible consequences of the system's construction and behaviour would be regarded as undesirable (in some dependability sense). This process can be regarded as an informal version of the failure mode analysis which is often carried out on the technical specification or implementation of a system, and its results are (loosely speaking) worries about the *vulnerabilities* of the system.

The major operation to be carried out at this level is the expression of the *rules* which each interested party wishes the system to observe, either in its construction or behaviour. Later, when the representation at the lower levels is complete, it will be possible for the analyst to ask "What enforces the rules?", and to evaluate the strengths or absences of the mechanisms by which the rules are enforced. These rules are the expression of desired behaviour as seen by a particular problem owner, and therefore reflect a partial viewpoint. In the context of a bank's teller function, for example, it would be appropriate to express concerns about authentication, authorization, correctness of information transfer, and the correct operation of the system (human or mechanical) that implements the teller function; whereas it would probably not be appropriate to express concern about the effect of floods or nuclear fallout on the system.

11.3.2 Level 4: Conceptual level

At this level it is necessary to produce a language for representing problem situations. It will have a vocabulary, a grammar, a set of rules and guidelines, and some limitations. The operations carried out at level 5 effectively set the constraints within which the analyst can choose a problem-structuring language to represent the various structures and models that will be used to analyse the system. The aim here is to exercise discretion in the selection and ultilization of models and calculi to describe substantive features of the system (e.g. communications threats, natural hazards, information leakage). The role of the problem-structuring language is to link together a number of different structural models representing different aspects of the system in order to assist the analyst in forming the judgements involved in analysing the system comprehensively. The problem owner's own language is the natural candidate for the role of the problem structuring language, and indeed is often employed for that purpose. However, some fundamental problems often arise when it is used to construct what is essentially a set of language primitives for building problem representations.

One way of developing a problem-structuring language is to treat the important aspects of the system (as seen at level 4) as *frames*, each of whose denotational meaning can be developed and explored separately through operations which develop structure within each individual frame. By the word "frame" here we mean a set of abstractions of real world entities, together with a set of operations on the entities and a set of relations between them. It differs from an abstract data type in that it does not necessarily contain a data representation, and in lacking any requirement that the operations be computable. However, the operations should be capable of representation in a calculus. Thus operations at level 4 define the analytical method separately for each frame. Within any particular frame, only part of the problem is processed, allowing the use of a restricted calculus which can be optimized for handling the type of content to which the frame is addressed.

To take once again the teller function, as implemented by an ATM, one choice of a set of frames would be for communications, messages, system composition, and system behaviour. The communications frame would enable discussion about the protocols and mechanisms at the human and system level within which issues of authentication and authorization could be formulated. The elements in the communications frame might include the generators and interpreters of communications, the shared context in which messages are interpreted, and any necessary relay functions in the transmission. Since communications is by means of messages, the communications frame would also include a set of references to the message frame. The message frame might include operations for the generation and deletion of messages, their reading and writing, and their interception, theft, and corruption. The system composition frame would contain a set of operations on components and links by which any rule concerning the way in which the system is put together could be expressed. The behaviour frame would include an appropriate model by which issues concerning the behaviour of the system could be formulated.

This is not necessarily a complete list of relevant frames. Other concerns expressed at level 5 might dictate additional frames to be considered: for example, if physical threats are a source of anxiety, it might be appropriate to consider a frame representing the physical act of designing and building the system and its resulting constructional attributes. The important point is that there is no "right" or "wrong" choice of frames. An idiosyncratic choice can prove quite valuable. What matters is that it is properly developed at the lower levels; it is no use, for example, choosing a "physical construction" frame if it is not known how to develop a calculus of physical construction.

11.3.3 Level 3: Semantic level

Operations at level 3 are concerned exclusively with developing structure within a particular frame identified at level 4 as modelling some important aspect of the system. This is done by selecting or inventing an appropriate calculus for the operations within the frame. For example, if the frame selected has the function at level 4 of modelling access control structures, then within this frame at level 3, development of structure implies some formal representation perhaps along access matrix lines [Kemmerer1983]. Or if the frame selected at level 4 has the function of analysing information flow leakage, then, within this frame, development of structure may imply a shared resource matrix definition.

Space does not allow us to give details of the calculi used in all the frames mentioned on our level 4 example. We shall summarize the operations on what is perhaps the simplest frame: that of messages. The semantics of reading and writing a message are well understood: they involve the additional notion of an agent (reader or writer). Generation and deletion are operations on a sequence of messages, and a theory of sequences is therefore required in the calculus. Interception and theft can be handled by representing a message as a tuple

$$< \text{sender, text, receiver(s)} >$$

Other calculi are of course possible; the choice of calculus is a design choice.

The result of the operations carried out at level 3 is a knowledge representation whose structure is fixed; the calculus of operations is in place, and the remaining two lower levels are concerned with the interpretation of the calculus. According to standard logic theory, this interpretation takes place in two stages: assigning conditions of use to the logical signs and assigning referents to the descriptive signs [Carnap1939]. These operations form level 2 and 1 respectively.

11.3.4 Level 2: Logical level

At level 2, the task is to determine, for each frame developed at level 3, the domain and scope limitations of the operations defined within the frame. At this level there is, for example, no longer any discretion over *which* information-bearing components are to be considered in a shared resource matrix, but some kind of sensitivity analysis may be employed to explore questions about changing degrees of coupling assumed between the components within the structure developed at level 3, in order to determine the most sensitive components. Hence at level 2 the content manipulated within the structure is not "facts" but hypotheses. At this level it is recognized, for example, that views or assignment of probabilities of certain events can vary between viewpoints and that certain parties can have interests and preferences that other parties may deem irrelevant.

The purpose of exploring the properties of the system at level 2 is that the resulting analysis may indicate areas of the system where change of viewpoint or assignment of value may make either very little or very great impact on the perceived dependability properties of the system.

As an example of the domain and scope limitations on the message frame, the analyst would ask, for each message identified in the system, under what circumstances it could validly be read, written, generated, or deleted. Theft, corruption, and interception would probably all be undesirable, and questions would be asked whether such operations could be invoked and with what degree of ease, and what preconditions would be necessary for such invocation.

11.3.5   Level 1: Descriptive level

Operations at level 1 are exclusively concerned with assigning denotations to the descriptive signs. The only degree of freedom left for the analyst is to decide on the "best available technology" for the implementation of the logical function of each item in the representation whose structure has now been completely fixed through the operations carried out at the higher levels. For example, assuming that level 2 has identified mutual authentication to be a sensitive issue in a certain part of the system, the level 1 issue becomes that of deciding whether appropriate authentication protocols have been employed. It is at level 1 that many of the security mechanisms that have been so widely studied (e.g. encryption) have their proper place in our problem representation framework.

11.4   Models for a communication system

This section will develop further the notion of "frame" by showing a set of frames that describe a communications system. There are in fact four models in our set: a model of system behaviour, a model of system composition, a model of messages, and a model of communication. Each of these will be described in a separate subsection, but all the models will be used for the same purpose, which is to provide the basis for a clear and well-defined terminology and to allow us to develop a taxonomy of types of dependability breach and to assist in the analysis of real systems with respect to their vulnerabilities.

Our modelling approach is thus to develop not a single model of a dependable system but a related set of models. Each model ignores detail irrelevant to its purpose and allows concentration on the set of features it is designed to exhibit. It is obviously important that the different models fit well together so that they can all be seen to be models of different aspects or facets of the same underlying entity. We shall now briefly describe our basic models of a dependable communications system.

11.4.1   Model of system composition

We need to begin this section with a preliminary remark on terminology. There are two aspects of building systems, which we distinguish by the terms construction and composition. Each of these activities may have its own sets of rules. *System construction* concerns the components themselves, of what kind they are and of what technological material they are made. An example of rules of construction is: "It shall employ a 68020 processor and shall be programmed in Ada". Such instructions are communications between the system specifier and the system builder but do not usually pass through the domain of the system itself; rather they form part of the context in which the system is built. *System composition* concerns the manner of connecting the components together and is topological in nature. An example of a system composition rule might be: "The peripherals shall not interface to the memory directly but must go through an I/O processor". Rules of composition are particularly important for networks where the problems are those concerning systems built from systems, and the issues that our models should address are those of putting systems together. This will have a number of implications for the statement of the relations between the axegrinders.

A system is composed of interconnected *components*, which can be given names. A component is a self-contained computational entity provided with *sockets*. No information may enter or leave a component except through one of its sockets. As seen from a component, its sockets are unidirectional (i.e. input or output). Either a component may be *atomic*, meaning that it has no internal structure visible at this level of abstraction, or it may be recursively composed of a set of interconnected smaller components. Components are interconnected by linking their sockets (with the obvious constraint as to gender). In the terms of this model, a conventional uniprocessor system is typically viewed as an example of an atomic component; a simple network can be regarded as a component that provides lots of sockets but rather limited computational power.

In order to apply this notion to dependability, it is convenient in addition to associate labels with sockets so as to distinguish between different kinds. This will enable us to model the provision of rules concerning system composition; for example "red-to-red and black-to-black", as used in the composition of secure systems. These composition rules should presumably be derived from the dependability policy of the system builder or of the system owner and may permit the ascription of the attribute "dependable" only if the system is constructed and composed according to the rules.

11.4.2 Model of system behaviour

The behaviour of a system or component can be described by a trace of the stimuli received by that system or component and the responses it exhibits. As previously described, stimuli and responses take the form of messages, and responses from one subsystem or component can act as stimuli to another. All possible modes of behaviour of the system can be given by a *trace space* formed by the association of stimulus and response messages with the externally visible sockets of the system. A system that has multiple sockets will have a parallel set of traces. At any instant in time, the current state of the system will be represented by a point in the trace space of behaviour up to that instant. We define a region in the trace space as bounded by a *selector*. A selector separates the traces that exhibit some property of interest from those that do not. We can describe the behaviour of any system component in just the same way by considering the trace space of the messages entering and leaving the sockets of the component. In what follows, however, we shall ignore the recursive composition of the system and treat it as if it were atomic.

A *vulnerability* is a point in trace space (and which therefore describes a possible mode of behaviour of the system) which is outside the region defined by the dependability selector. A *dependability breach* is a system event represented by the occurrence of a transition from a point inside the region defined by the dependability selector to a point outside. A *threat* is a stimulus that causes a dependability breach (or that could cause a possible security breach). A *dependability lapse* is an action (or inaction) of an axegrinder that permits the possibility of a threat. A lapse occurs when an axegrinder (or employee or servant) fails to conform to a behavioural specification appropriate for the role being performed.

Such a lapse need not immediately precede the threat. For example, a malfunctioning piece of equipment is not itself a lapse, though it may imply a lapse in the quality control of the equipment supplier. This definition does not require a lapse to be identified or even observed; all that is required is that a disinterested party could agree that an axegrinder has failed and that the system has exhibited a breach as a result. Since a breach is a transition from a point inside a dependability selector to a possible point outside, we can define a *countermeasure* as a restriction on trace space. The effect of the restriction is that certain modes of behaviour or breaches which were possible before the countermeasure was imposed are now no longer so. Countermeasures may also be probabilistic in nature; that is, they may merely serve to reduce the likelihood, rather than prevent the occurrence, of a breach. Thus the countermeasure increases the cost of perpetrating the threat and/or decreases the consequential benefit of the breach to the perpetrator.

11.4.3 Model of messages

The relation between axegrinders and the system is that the system acts as a communications medium between axegrinders. An axegrinder stimulates the system by creating and submitting a message, as a result of which the system responds by delivering messages to other axegrinders. In addition, there are certain external stimuli to the system that can be regarded as messages, albeit in a rather degenerate sense: an example is a bulldozer ploughing up and breaking a communications cable. We regard all intended stimuli as being associated with an axegrinder even if the connection is sometimes a little delayed or remote; thus accounting records for example can be regarded as deferred messages from the system builder. Unintended stimuli may or may not be associated with an axegrinder. The importance of this association is that should some stimulus be erroneous in some sense, one may wish to ascribe blame to someone.

Note that although we have used language that implies that the communicating axegrinders are separate parties as if to a telephone conversation, we recognize and include the common case of a single axegrinder using the system to assist in the activity of axegrinding. An example would be a safety officer monitoring and controlling the state of a plant through a terminal. In this case we would distinguish the roles of the same axegrinder acting as sender and as receiver of messages.

The standard form of a message in our model contains three fields:

> sender, message text, recipient set

The sender is the name of the component of origin and the recipient set contains the names of the destination components intended by the sender. At the outermost level, a system is a component with sockets. Messages arrive at the sockets from axegrinders and are delivered from the sockets to axegrinders. However, our model of a message insists that the sender and recipient fields name components and not axegrinders. Thus in the case of these messages that are sent and received by axegrinders, we have to associate a specialized component called a *portal* with the connection of an axegrinder to a system. Portals correspond to such things as keyboards and screens, and are provided with only one socket which can connect only to a system socket. We can now regard messages to and from axegrinders as naming the corresponding portals. For most purposes, however, the distinction between an axegrinder and the corresponding portal can be ignored.

Message text is *uninterpreted* in our model of messaging; thus a message is simply abstract syntax. Questions of interpretation and semantics will be discussed in the next subsection, on the communication model. It is because of our separation between the syntax and semantics of communication that the sender and recipients of a message are taken to be components and do not identify axegrinders. Acts of God can be modelled as messages from an unknown sender component.

11.4.4   Model of communication

Our definition of communication is somewhat broader than that often used in computer literature, where it is often restricted to issues of transmission of messages. We wish to extend the notion to include the human aspects, and consequently we stress the interpretation function. For the same reason, we also stress the essential role that the context plays in this process.

The model of communication deals with the interpretation of messages, and the fact that messages can be passed from one component to another. This leads to there being five kinds of entity involved in a communication:

generator, sender, transferrers, recipients, interpreters

The *generator* and *interpreters* are, by definition, axegrinders who share a common understanding in the context of which the interpretation of the message text is performed. The generator maps the semantics onto a sequence of messages which are transmitted from the sender component to the recipient components; at each of the latter another mapping takes place from the messages to their semantics. There are thus two *interpretation functions* performed: one at the generating end and one at the receiving end. These interpretation functions are difficult to characterize, but they involve the notion of a *context* which may include all previous messages between the parties. A context may also include messages transmitted by means other than the system of interest. Interpretation functions may also involve functions which change the internal state of the parties.

The role of *transferrers* in the communication model is potentially an important one. They represent the abstraction of components performing a message switching function or mail server. Although they are deemed to have no associated interpretation function, that is they act only on the abstract syntax of the messages they pass, there are obviously correctness proofs of invariance that they have to satisfy, and possible dependability breaches that result from invariance not being observed will have to be investigated.

One important aspect of a communication in the context of dependability, and of security in particular, is that of clearance and authorization. The interpretation function at a generator will yield a message which acts as an initial stimulus to the sender component. This message may have an attribute called *sensitivity* assigned to it by its generator. The *authorization* of an axegrinder in a particular context is the set of sensitivities of messages that can validly be generated or interpreted by the axegrinder in that context without causing a dependability breach. A *clearance* is a set of authorizations (and hence by implication a set of contexts) issued to or to be attributed to an axegrinder.

11.5 Dependability breaches

The models of messages and of communications may be used to develop a taxonomy of different kinds of dependability breach. A message contains three fields: sender, text, recipients. Since each of these may independently be corrupt or falsified, we have the following categories of breach:

forgery	Real Sender / Apparent Sender mismatch
text corruption	Real Text / Apparent Text mismatch

These are two cases of Real Recipient / Apparent Recipient mismatch:

eavesdropping	Real Recipients > Apparent Recipients
message loss	Real Recipients < Apparent Recipients

In terms of the communications model, we have the following categories of breach associated with the generators and interpreters:

impersonation	Real Generator / Apparent Generator mismatch
espionage	Real Interpreter / Apparent Interpreter mismatch
abuse	Real Generator not authorized
betrayal	Real Interpreter not authorized
	(the betrayal is perpetrated by the generator)

In addition, there are a variety of breaches that can arise from the fact that interpretation functions are invoked by generator and interpreter. For example, there are a number of sins associated with the deliberate application of a false context to the interpretation function ("rewriting history"). *Repudiation* is a particular case in which an axegrinder wishes to assert that a context contains a message trace less than that which it in fact contains. *Fabrication* is an attempt to assert that the message trace is greater than it actually is.

11.6 Outline of the ATM system

In this and the following sections we shall examine an application of the ideas presented so far. The example chosen is an automated teller machine (ATM). For the purposes of exposition, many aspects have been simplified compared with a real-world ATM; but even the simplification will reveal the possibility of a number of vulnerabilities which have in fact been exploited in the real world of theft and fraud.

The reader may well find it helpful from this point on to refer to the

Summary in section 11.17 which presents a step-by-step overview of the method. In section 11.6, we briefly describe the example system and identify the axegrinders associated with it, and define the communication pattern being analysed. Section 11.7 deals with the rules by which the axegrinders operate this pattern of communication. For each axegrinder, we shall state the rules by which he operates (and from which his policy can perhaps be deduced) and his view of the system. In section 11.8 we describe the various views of the system conformation associated with each axegrinder. These views are combined in section 11.9, producing a physical and a logical view of system conformation; the latter identifies the various message flows in the system. Section 11.10 describes the system in behavioural terms of processes and events. We are then in a position to do a vulnerability analysis of the system conformation and behaviour, which constitutes the remainder of this chapter.

We now briefly describe the Automated Teller Machine (ATM) system and its associated axegrinders. A high-level block diagram of the machine is shown in Figure 11.1.

The ATM is operated by a plastic Card inserted into a hole in the wall. The card is marked with a Magnetic Stripe containing an identification of the Account and a (perhaps encrypted) PIN (Personal Identification Number). The customer, following instructions presented on a Display, enters the Customer PIN on a Keypad. The Amount is then entered. (For the purposes of this simple example, we shall ignore the "Proceed" and "Cancel"

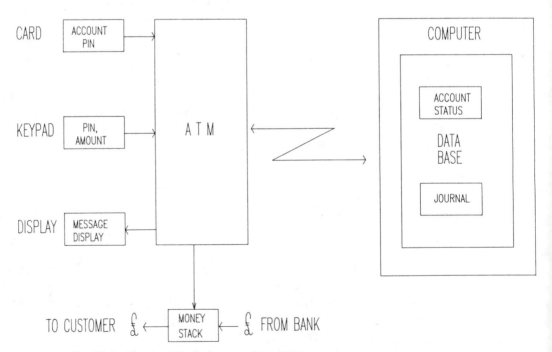

Fig. 11.1 High-level block diagram of the ATM

290

buttons.) A request is transmitted across the Communications Link to a database management system (DBMS) which interrogates the Account Status. If the account is in order, a confirmation is sent back over the communications link, as a result of which the Money Stack is instructed to deliver the banknotes (£).

The internal structure of the DBMS will be ignored except in so far as its operation and internal structure are relevant to the ATM. For the moment, all we need to know is that the DBMS manages a Database which contains all the accounts, and a Journal which records the details of all requests, responses, and transactions; the Journal also records any unsuccessful attempts to use the system together with their reason for failure. This view corresponds to the Bank's view of an account as a sequence of transactions, with the teller function being an implementation of a cash debit transaction.

11.6.1 Communications analysis

Given an application, our first task is to identify the axegrinders. We can identify five axegrinders in this system:

The Bank
The Customer
The ATM Supplier
The Communications Link Supplier (PTT)
The Database Supplier (DBMS)

There are, however, a number of less apparent interested parties, e.g. equipment suppliers to the PTT, field maintenance companies, software houses, and, most importantly, criminals. There are also some disinterested but relevant parties such as the legal profession and law enforcement agencies. This task is an iterative process, since examination of patterns of communication may yield new axegrinders, and analysis of policy (or at least of the rules expressing it) may yield new insights into the pattern of communication.

The enumeration of the rules under which each of these parties operates can be a burdensome task but is one that cannot be avoided. There are no formal tools available for the examination of the relationship between the sets of rules and the policy they purport to represent. At least the rules which are the external expression of policy must be represented in a formal language before such tools could be developed. For our purposes we would require a formalism which not only allows us to test the completeness of a set of rules with respect to a policy but also to test the compatibility of rules with policies and thus the compatibility between different policies. For the moment, however, we must rely on natural language and informal reasoning.

A service such as the teller terminal represents a context for a series of communications. Some of the communications associated with the service will take place when a failure has occurred and may involve additional axegrinders such as equipment manufacturers, maintenance companies, or even lawyers. Other aspects of the service are involved in the communication of PINs, which would need to be subjected to the same kind of analysis as we are proposing to apply to the cash disbursement communication act.

It is important to realize that this example is applicable only to the one pattern of communication being studied: a request from the Customer to the Bank and a response from the Bank to the Customer. The context of this communication is the series of transactions recorded in the Customer's account. Only those rules and system features relevant to this communication are mentioned (and not even all of them, for the sake of simplicity). But there are other patterns: the customer could simply issue an account status request, or enter a request for a new chequebook, or instruct the Bank to engage in some other financial transaction on his behalf. PIN mailing is another communication between the Bank and the Customer which has obvious security implications. Each of these patterns could be analysed in the same way as our example.

There are also other patterns of communication not directly involving the Customer. Examples are the mechanisms by which the Bank informs its suppliers that their service or product is broken and the protocols, both human and electronic, necessary to open the ATM in order to mend it. The communications patterns involved in taking the DBMS offline could be analysed. Again, if the Bank is informed that the ATM is "not working", what steps does the Bank take to verify and perhaps rectify the situation? All these patterns can be analysed in the way we propose.

11.7 Axegrinder rules

Each axegrinder has a set of rules, or specification of composition and behaviour. These rules constrain a particular pattern of communication, and are relative only to that pattern. Such a specification can be over the axegrinder's own equipment and procedures, or represent required behaviour of another axegrinder's equipment and procedures. We are not here trying to formulate each axegrinder's policy (e.g. "The Bank will make a profit") but the rules by which the axegrinder implements the policy (e.g. "The Bank may charge for its services").

11.7.1 Bank rules

1) To disburse money on request, provided
   i) There are sufficient funds in the account;
   ii) The Bank has Customer authority to debit the account;
   iii) The Bank is satisfied that it is disbursing to the Customer or an authorized agent.

2) Money disbursed is matched by an account debit, and amount debited is not less than amount disbursed.

3) Amount disbursed is not greater than amount requested by Customer.

4) There is a daily limit to the amount disbursed on each account.

5) The state of the account is taken as at the close of business on the previous working day.

6) Only the Bank supplies money for disbursement.

7) Only the DBMS inspects or modifies the account.

8) It is the Customer's responsibility to look after the card and not to use it if knowingly overdrawn without prior arrangement.

9) No guarantees are made that anything in the system works. However, in the event of failure, the above Rules will not be violated.

Notes on the above Rules

1) This looks like a statement of policy, but it is sufficiently formal that it is preferable to regard it as a rule. It is in fact a rule constraining the teller function generally and not just the ATM; this also applies to other Rules in this set. The underlying policy might be something like "To act in accordance with the common practice and regulations governing clearing banks".

2) This allows the Bank to charge for its services.

3) As well as its obvious use in refusing an overdrawn Customer, this rule allows the ATM to run out of money.

4) This rule protects both the Customer and the Bank by limiting liability.

5) This rule may be a procedural convenience for the Bank. However, the obvious implementation has several vulnerabilities.

6) This rule means that the ATM supplier has no independent access to the Money Stack.

7) This rule means that the ATM cannot bypass the DBMS in accessing the Database or Journal.

8) This rule forces the Customer to accept responsibility if a card is stolen and the Bank is not informed.

9) This rule is a general catch-all in an attempt to prevent unwarranted legal actions. It also reflects a fail-safe policy. Note the nice distinction between the informal use of the word "works", which implies satisfaction, and the formality implied by the word "failure", which implies a specification.

Note that Rules 1 to 5 voluntarily constrain the behaviour of the Bank, whereas Rules 6 to 8 attempt to constrain the behaviour of other axegrinders. Should the other axegrinders have policies which are in conflict with Rules 6 and 8, some negotiation between the parties concerned may be necessary to resolve the disagreement.

11.7.2 Customer rules

1) The amount disbursed is not less than amount requested.
2) The amount debited is not greater than the minimum of (amount requested, amount disbursed).
3) No account debits will be entered against an unauthorized transaction.
4) There should be no unreasonable refusal by the Bank to disburse on request.

Notes on the above Rules

1) This rule allows the Customer to profit from a beneficial mistake by the ATM.
2) The amount disbursed may be less than that requested. Note that if the Bank charges for its services under its Rule 2, a conflict of rules exists.
3) This rule attempts to constrain the behaviour of the Bank.
4) As does this rule.

11.7.3 ATM rules

1) To transmit to the Communications Link requests as received (except for encoding and encryption).
2) To disburse according to the response received from the Communications Link.

Notes on the above Rules
These rules absolve the ATM if the DBMS gets it wrong or the line is actively tapped.

11.7.4 PTT rules

None. The PTT does not guarantee a connection or delivery service.

Notes on the above Rules
The PTT might wish to observe that it has in the past maintained $x\%$ of connection establishments and correctly delivered $y\%$ of packets entrusted to its care, for suitably impressive values of x and y. Nevertheless, *caveat emptor* applies.

11.7.5 DBMS rules

1) To maintain the Database correctly most of the time, and to keep an accurate Journal, according to the information received from the Communications Link. The point here is that the Database can be out of date with respect to the Journal, but the Journal must always be up to date.

Notes on the above Rules

1) The DBMS wishes to be absolved in the case of a faulty ATM or active wiretapper. This rule should perhaps be supplemented by others because the difference in security characteristics (e.g. consequence of loss) between the Journal and the Database may well turn out to be very significant. Our justification for the acknowledged simplification is that in this exercise we are concentrating on the ATM side of the system.

11.8 Views of the system

In this section, we shall show the views of the system as seen by each of the axegrinders. Because of the nature of the axegrinders, some of these views

Fig. 11.2 Bank view of the ATM system

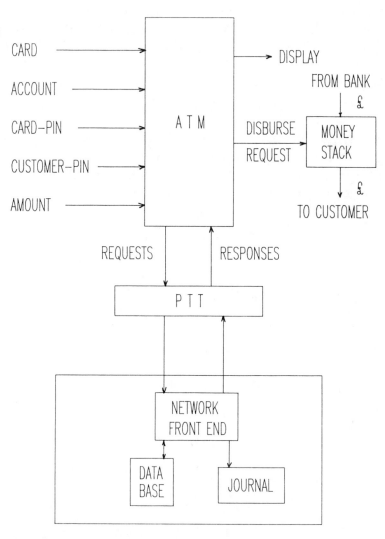

are logical and some physical. How these are combined is shown in the next section. These views are of the components involved, and not of their composition or behaviour, nor of the implementation of the components.

Bank view (Figure 11.2)   For the purposes of this security analysis, it is advantageous to treat the ATM supplied by the vendor as a black box. The Bank bolts on to the side of the ATM a Money Stack in which banknotes are placed. This Stack is not available to the ATM supplier, who knows only its external interfaces. The ATM system generates DBMS query messages to the PTT, and receives DBMS responses from the PTT. The Bank, though it may own the DBMS, does not know much about how it works. It is Bank practice to record all transactions on a Journal, which is kept on a daily basis. The Journal is used to update the Database overnight, when the ATM is offline.

Customer view (Figure 11.3)   The Customer sees only the physical external appearance of the system and the logical nature of the messages entered and displayed. The Customer knows that the system updates the account, and a sophisticated Customer might surmise that the account is interrogated before the request is honoured. Note that the Customer sees a "computer", and not anything as specific as a DBMS.

ATM view (Figure 11.4)   The ATM Supplier sees its box as a hardware device which executes programs supplied to it by the Bank, and with certain peripheral attachments. The latter include a special box for interfacing to a Communications Link.

Fig. 11.3
Customer view
of the ATM
system

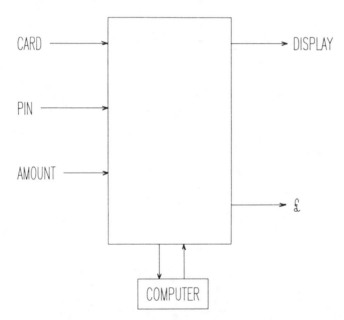

Fig. 11.4 ATM
view of the ATM
system

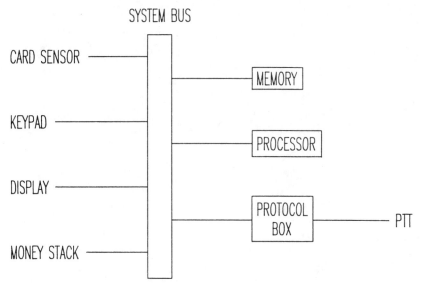

PTT view (Figure 11.5)   The PTT sees itself as providing a bearer service between Network Service Access Points. We have assumed a particularly simple switching topology.

DBMS view (Figure 11.6)   This view has been simplified quite a lot. There is a communications front end which embodies a Network Service Access Point (NSAP) and delivers queries and transactions, and receives responses for transmission back to the originator. The Database system is modelled as a Query Language Interpreter, which provides an interface to the externally visible state of the Database, and a transaction Journal which records the queries and responses and the financial transactions. The Query Language Interpreter is a software subsystem which executes on a hardware subsystem known as the Database Engine. The Database state is updated from the Journal. Thus the real information base is the Journal. The Database itself is only a convenient but slightly out-of-date representation of the state of the Journal.

Fig. 11.5 PTT
view of the ATM
system

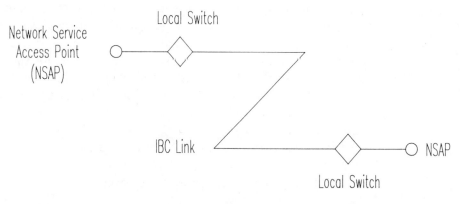

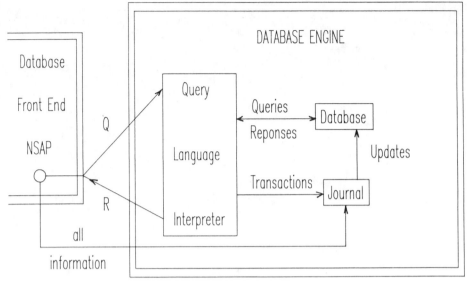

Fig. 11.6 DBMS view of the ATM system

11.9 Composite view of the system

In a sense, what we have done in the previous section is analogous to describing a set of database external schemas and we now wish to bring these together by building a single conceptual schema. But this cannot be done simply by plugging together the various views, since they are of differing logical levels of abstraction. We therefore need a methodological rule which tells us how to proceed.

In essence we wish to draw a series of "circuit diagrams" representing the equipment and interconnections used in the service. The elements which go to make up these diagrams may, however, be rather strange. A VDU includes a radio transmitter, which may be an important sender, and a buried cable is not just a connection between two points, but has its own peculiar input sockets by which the undesirable message from a misdirected mechanical excavator may be injected into the network.

The conformation diagrams allow us, at least in principle, to enumerate all the individual messages that the system is intended or capable of receiving or generating. It does this because it provides us with an enumeration of all imaginable senders and receivers, and can therefore provide a framework for the enumeration of the types of messages which may be transferred within the system. In addition we can make statements about the nature of the channels which carry the messages: for example, the cash in the dispenser represents the "text" of a particular class of message which passes via channels which are mechanical in nature. Note that we are not limited to purely electronic messages.

The interesting and extremely valuable feature of the diagrams we are looking for is that they should be capable of revealing to us not only the intended message channels but also the covert channels.

We draw two views of the conformation of the whole system. One is a *physical view*, in which the logical entities are bound to one or more physical components, and messages between the logical entities are shown as a set of message types along the physical links between the components. In the case of the automatic teller terminal, system conformation must express the physical divisions of the system: the "supplier-accessible" and "bank-accessible" partitions, the street-accessible parts of the system with their associated plugs and sockets, the communications link to the account centre, and the account centre mainframe. The second view of conformation is a *logical view*, in which each message type is represented as a separate channel between logical components. The second view can obviously be made recursive, but not even at the lowest level does it necessarily become physical.

Thus the two diagrams are bound together by means of the common messages represented in the differing ways.

11.9.1 Physical view of system composition

By "physical", we really mean "at the lowest level of abstraction". Thus the view presented in Figure 11.7 makes some simplifying assumptions and contains some abstractions. Similarly, when we present the various message types we shall ignore certain messages concerned only with the protocol structures. We shall also ignore most message types. In a real analysis, of course, we could not afford to do this.

The next section shows how the major message types map on to the links.

Fig. 11.7
Physical view of the ATM system conformation

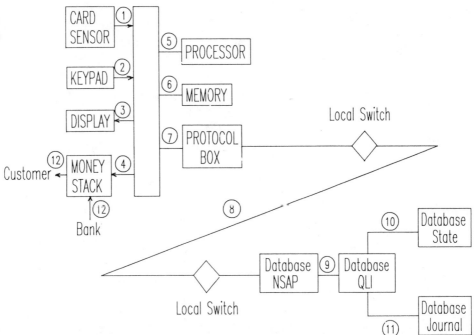

Message types on each of the links

    (1)   Between card sensor and ATM subsystem bus
         card inserted detector
         card removal detector
         account identifier on magnetic stripe
         PIN on magnetic stripe.

    (2)   Between keypad and ATM subsystem bus
         customer PIN
         amount.

    (3)   Between ATM subsystem bus and display
         instructions and error messages.

    (4)   Between ATM subsystem bus and Money Stack
         request to disburse banknotes.

    (5)   Between ATM subsystem bus and central processor
         data values representing message classes (1)–(4) above
         instruction sequences
         memory values
         communication protocol messages.

    (6)   Between ATM subsystem bus and memory
         instruction sequences
         memory values.

    (7)   Between ATM subsystem bus and protocol box (NSAP)
         communication protocol messages with embedded information.

    (8)   Between NSAP and NSAP
         communication protocol messages
         (any embedded information is not relevant to the PTT).

    (9)   Between Database NSAP and Database Engine
         communication protocol messages with embedded information.

   (10) Between Database Engine and Database State
         requests for state information
         responses containing state information
         updates to state information.

   (11) Between Database Engine and Database Journal
         transaction details
         Journal records of messages of type (10) above.

   (12) Between Bank and Money Stack
        and
        Between Money Stack and Customer
         banknotes.

11.9.2 Logical view of system conformation

Figure 11.8 shows the logical view of the system as a set of components and channels. Each channel is labelled with the type of the message it bears;

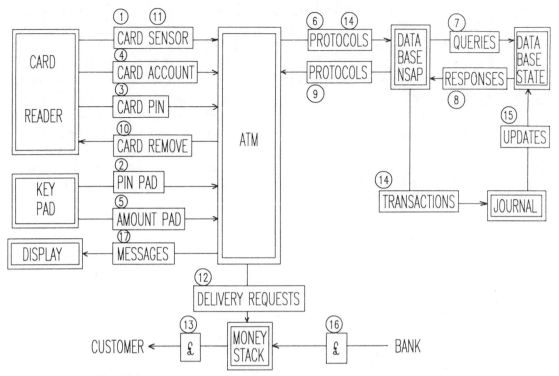

Fig. 11.8 Logical view of the system conformation

different message types are assigned to different logical channels even when connecting the same end-to-end components. Note that actual banknotes are regarded as messages.

The message channels are tagged with numeric identifiers used in the message analysis described below.

11.10 Behavioural model of the system

Physical conformation does not fully capture the state of affairs. There is an equivalent "logical" structure which relates to the sequence or order of behaviour. This sequence is expressed in a diagram (Figure 11.9) which is closely related to the standard functional specification diagram. The diagram differs from a conventional flowchart in that events or messages which occur logically in parallel appear in parallel. A correct diagram can only result from the examination of both the functional interdependence of the steps and their temporal relationships. This approach is needed to force consideration of a set of faults including:

i) The failure to complete an individual step.
ii) The different failure modes implied by permutations of individual failures of logically parallel steps.

301

The issuing of cash and the debiting of the account are examples of logically parallel operations in the teller terminal service. A specific implementation may choose to make them sequential with the latter conditional on the success of the former; whereas an alternative, functionally equivalent, implementation could reverse the operations. The actual choice of order has a direct effect on the nature of the consequences of a failure and also upon who will suffer them in the immediate and longer term. In the first implementation, it is the bank that suffers if the system fails in the middle of the transaction; in the second, it is the customer who suffers. This particular problem is usually solved using atomic transactions, but the point should be clear that in general there are ramifications associated with the ordering of logically parallel operations.

Fig. 11.9
Behavioural description of the ATM system

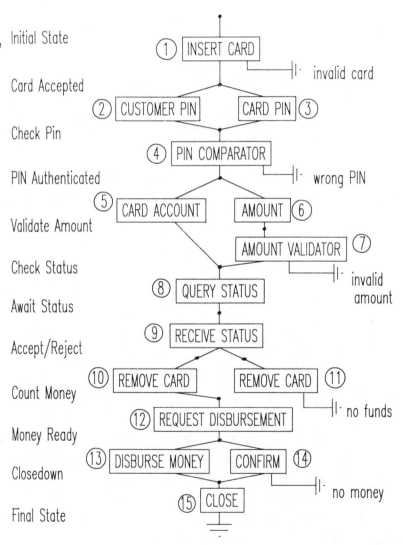

In this section, we shall try to model the abstract processes involved in the system. In realistic examples, the behavioural diagram will be too complex to fit on a single sheet of paper. For this reason, it is important to view the system in such a way that it can be decomposed into a number of pieces such that each piece can be treated as atomic at one level and then analysed separately at the next lower level of decomposition. The requirement to be able to do this places a number of restrictions on the formalism used to perform the decomposition and analysis which will not be discussed here. For the simplified example (Figure 11.9), we shall show how the analysis proceeds at a single level of decomposition. We shall do this by presenting the behaviour of the system in a table (Table 11.1) which could be translated into an event/process description language such as LOTOS. The direction of time is from top to bottom. Vertical parallelism represents concurrency. Blobs are events being offered to the processes identified by the boxes. The diagram is followed by a summary showing the (expected) inputs to and outputs from each process.

We can regard the behaviour of the system as having a tree-like structure but with rejoining branches at the points of synchronization. The root of the tree represents the initial state of the activity. The edges in the tree are labelled by the names of events or processes. In this way the labels on the outgoing edges of each node represent possible next steps of the activity. The tree structure thus represents activity behaviour as a sequence of possible choices ordered in time according to the depth of nodes in the tree.

We deal here only with the ATM. The DBMS and money stack processes are not shown, but could be subject to a similar analysis.

Table 11.1

#	Input State	Process	Output State
1	Initial State	INSERT CARD	Card Accepted
2	Card Accepted	CUSTOMER PIN	Check PIN
3	Card Accepted	CARD PIN	Check PIN
4	Check PIN	PIN COMPARATOR	PIN Authenticated
5	PIN Authenticated	CARD ACCOUNT	Check Status
6	PIN Authenticated	AMOUNT	Validate Amount
7	Validate Amount	AMOUNT VALIDATOR	Check Status
8	Check Status	QUERY STATUS	Await Status
9	Await Status	RECEIVE STATUS	Accept/Reject
10	Accept	REMOVE CARD	Count Money
11	Reject	REMOVE CARD	—
12	Count Money	REQUEST DISBURSEMENT	Money Ready
13	Money Ready	DISBURSE MONEY	Closedown
14	Money Ready	CONFIRM	Closedown
15	Closedown	CLOSE	Final State

11.11 Vulnerability analysis

In this section, we shall undertake a (rather superficial) vulnerability analysis based on the models of our system. This analysis is not meant to be exhaustive; it is merely indicative of how the analysis is to be performed on each of the diagrams we have constructed. The Vulnerability Analysis proceeds in five phases.

The first phase examines the individual acts of communication in the abstract script, and analyses them with respect to the possible communication breaches that can occur. This phase is described in section 11.12.

The second phase (section 11.13) takes the physical view of system conformation and asks questions about the relations between the axegrinders and the physical components and links. A number of heuristics can be applied to this diagram that indicate potential weaknesses.

The third phase (section 11.14) takes the logical view of system conformation and asks questions about the categories of message fault: forgery, corruption, message loss, eavesdropping. For each message channel, what are the assurances provided so that a vulnerability cannot occur or cannot be exploited?

The fourth phase (section 11.15) takes the behavioural diagram and attempts to identify the various failure modes of the processes and the nature of the assurances that the processes behave as expected. This phase also requires the analyst to ask questions concerning events that fail to occur or occur when they should not. Again, the assurances have to be stated and evaluated.

In the fifth and final phase, the analyst asks "What enforces the Rules?". It should be possible by now to take the various sets of axegrinder Rules and point to the mechanisms that are supposed to enforce them. The previous three phases of the analysis may well have exposed some weaknesses or dependencies in these mechanisms. At this stage, therefore, it should be possible to establish which Rules are more vulnerable to breach and which are less so. Section 11.16 attempts to supply such answers to the Bank Rules which were specified in section 11.7.

11.12 Analysis of communication

In section 11.5 we identified the following set of breaches based on the model of Communication:

Impersonation	real generator ≠ apparent generator
Espionage	real interpreter ≠ intended interpreter
Abuse	real generator not authorized
Betrayal	intended interpreter not authorized
Repudiation	generator context < interpreter context
Fabrication	generator context > interpreter context

Although the names of these types of breach are not always appropriate to the context of the ATM, since they may have a different set of connotations, the threats they represent are. We shall therefore use these names and expect the reader to make a suitable mapping from name to type of breach under consideration.

There are two acts of communication in our script: a request from the Customer to the Bank, and a response from the Bank to the Customer. We will deal with them separately.

11.12.1   Request communication

Impersonation of the Customer is a real threat, and it is one of the functions of the plastic card and the PIN to act as a countermeasure. *Espionage*, in the sense of the ATM appearing to be but not in fact connected to the Bank, is not secured against except by common-sense measures, such as the "hole in the wall" being in fact the wall of the Bank's premises, and so on. It would seem possible, at least in principle, to impersonate the Bank since the Customer has no independent means of knowing to whom the request, including in particular the card and the PIN, is being communicated. *Abuse* is supposed to be prevented by the plastic card and the PIN. *Betrayal* is perpetrated by the deliberate act by the Customer of providing the card and PIN to someone other than the Bank. Obviously it can occur, and is not prevented because it is unlikely to be in the interests of the Customer.

Repudiation and *Fabrication* (by the Customer) can occur. Repudiation does in fact happen, though whether it is ever in the Customer's interest to fabricate bogus transactions of the kind dealt with here is another matter.

11.12.2   Response communication

Impersonation is unlikely, since the communication act involves the generator handing out banknotes. *Espionage*, in the sense of the receiver of the notes not being the owner of the account as intended by the Bank, can and does occur. (For example, the criminal could wait until the genuine customer had validly initiated the request and then steal and run off with the money.) *Abuse* is not normally a problem for this communication act. *Betrayal*, in the sense of the Bank *deliberately* giving the money to someone else, does not occur, though the Customer has no obvious means of preventing it; the right to legal recompense seems to be the only countermeasure.

Repudiation and *Fabrication* (by the Bank) occur by accidental error, and are corrected (though it must be admitted that one is relying on good faith here).

11.13 Analysis of system conformation

11.13.1 Physical conformation

The vulnerability analysis of the system composition diagram (Figure 11.7) begins by grouping the physical components together into *Virtual Boxes*, such that a relation can be asserted between a Virtual Box and an axegrinder. Typically, a Virtual Box does in fact correspond to a real box with wires hanging out, such as a terminal, a point-to-point communication link, or a computer. Typical relations that might be involved are "uses", "maintains", "owns". All physical components must end up in at least one Virtual Box. Virtual Boxes can overlap. Each Virtual Box can be marked V or U for Verifiable or Unverifiable. "Verifiable" means that a system conformance test can be performed—that is, the actual system can be physically inspected to verify that it conforms to the specification of its physical composition. "Unverifiable" means that such is not the case.

The diagram so produced is termed the Virtual Box diagram. Figure 11.10 shows the component view of the Virtual Box diagram and Figure 11.11 shows the relations between the Virtual Boxes and the axegrinders.

The analysis proceeds by examining the diagram with a number of heuristics in mind. Examples of such heuristics are as follows:

1) A Virtual Box with more than one axegrinder having some relation to it

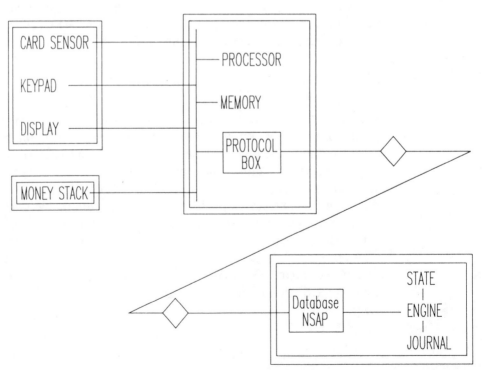

Fig. 11.10 Virtual box diagram for the ATM system (component view)

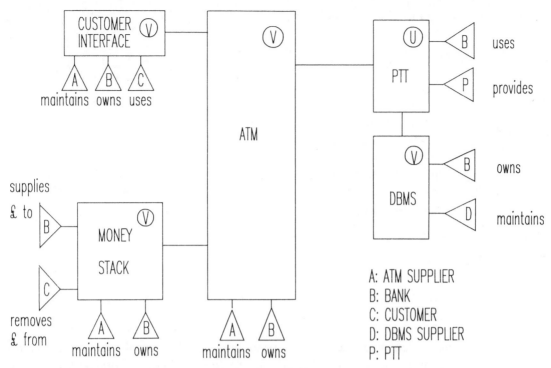

Fig. 11.11 Virtual box diagram for the ATM system (relational view)

is vulnerable to a conflict of interest. The most common example is where one axegrinder owns and another maintains. Is the maintainer trustworthy?

2) Two Virtual Boxes that are directly connected and that enjoy the same relation but with different axegrinders constitute a potential vulnerability. Suppose two adjacent boxes are each owned by a different party. Is the common boundary well defined and of zero thickness, or is there a possibility of territorial dispute?

3) There is an obvious vulnerability when two Unverifiable Virtual Boxes are directly connected, since it violates a basic security rule that constrains two untrusted components to communicate only via a trusted intermediary.

11.13.2   Vulnerabilities of the ATM system

Inspection of Figure 11.11 suggests that the following areas are potentially vulnerable:

By virtue of heuristic 1
All the Virtual Boxes are vulnerable to ownership/maintenance conflicts. In addition, the Money Stack and customer interface may be vulnerable to physical attack by Customers.

By virtue of heuristic 2

Ownership boundaries have to be clearly established between the ATM and the PTT link, and between the PTT link and the DBMS. The purpose is to ensure that the division of territory neither overlaps nor excludes anything.

The Customer must be prevented from gaining access to the ATM bus.

Care should be taken that the ATM has no direct physical access to the Money Stack.

By virtue of heuristic 3

Since the Communications Link is Unverifiable and hence potentially hostile territory, some method (e.g. encryption) should be used to protect data travelling across it.

11.14 Message analysis

The method we suggest for examining the messages in our system is to examine in a qualitative way the effect of forgery, corruption, message loss, and eavesdropping on each of the messages in our system. The purpose of the present exercise is to show the method of analysis, not to describe the system in full operational detail. For this reason, Customer error messages and messages concerned with instructing the Customer what to do are omitted. The analysis proceeds on the basis of the Logical View of System conformation shown in section 11.9.2.

Table 11.2

#	Sender	Text	Receiver	Class
1	CARD READER	card inserted	ATM	1
2	KEYPAD	number entered	ATM	1
3	CARD READER	card PIN	ATM	1
4	CARD READER	account ID	ATM	1
5	KEYPAD	amount requested	ATM	1
6	ATM	status request	DBNSAP	2
7	DBNSAP	status request	DATABASE	3
8	DATABASE	status response	DBNSAP	3
9	DBNSAP	response status	ATM	2
10	ATM	request to remove	CARD READER	1
11	CARD READER	card removed	ATM	1
12	ATM	request to disburse	MONEY STACK	4
13	MONEY STACK	banknotes	CUSTOMER	5
14	ATM	account, amount	JOURNAL	2
15	JOURNAL	account update	DATABASE	3
16	BANK	banknotes	MONEY STACK	5
17	ATM	information & errors	DISPLAY	1

We can see from Figures 11.10 and 11.11 that there are five classes of message (itemised in Table 11.2):

1) those contained entirely within the ATM subsystem and its external interfaces;
2) those that are transmitted across PTT lines;
3) those contained entirely within the DBMS subsystem;
4) those between the ATM and the Money Stack subsystem;
5) those entirely within the Money Stack subsystem and its external interfaces.

For each of these classes, the vulnerabilities to the various breaches are as follows:

1) Forgery: should not occur because of the mechanical construction of the ATM device (remember that because we distinguish the component from the axegrinder, we distinguish forgery from impersonation, which is a real vulnerability).

   Corruption, eavesdropping, message loss should not occur, for similar reasons.
2) All breaches are possible, since the PTT makes no guarantees and the operation of the PTT is unverifiable. Hence suitable protection mechanisms must be devised.
3) These messages should be protected by the DBMS subsystem.
4) These messages should also be physically protected since the ATM and the Money Stack are physically bound together.
5) These messages (banknotes) will also be physically protected.

11.15 Behavioural analysis

Essentially the behavioural analysis is a matter of asking two questions:

What are the possible failure modes of each process in the behavioural diagram?
What events may be gained (i.e. spontaneously generated) or lost?

In order to answer the first question, we need to state the behavioural predicates for each process and ask the nature of the assurance that each predicate will be satisfied. It follows that in order for this to be undertaken, some implementation decisions must have been made; for example, whether a certain function is to be implemented in hardware or software, or whether it is done locally or involves a remote operation, and so on. In the case of our ATM example, we will assume a simple and obvious implementation for the purposes of demonstrating the method.

To answer the second question, we note that the abstract events between processes can be modelled in a number of ways, depending on the

309

application being analysed and its implementation. For the ATM, the events are probably represented by state changes in the ATM processor and memory, or by the reception or transmission of messages inside the ATM subsystem. For other systems, events can be represented by the transfer of paper documents or the activity of human messengers. In all cases, however, we must ask ourselves: What assurance do we have that the events are neither gained nor lost? In the case of the ATM, this reduces to a question of confidence in the ATM software. In other cases the answer might be different.

11.15.1 Characterization of faults in systems

There are a number of general points to be made about our method for analysing behavioural faults. Faults are causes of system failures. The function of the vulnerability analysis is to predict or assume failure of the system's components and to determine the measure of assurance that the failure can be prevented or tolerated. Two generic classes of fault concern the "timeliness" and "expected value" as properties of a component's behaviour. The response of a component to a given stimulus will be said to be correct if the output value is not only as expected, but is also produced on time. This leads to the following generic types of fault:

1) A *timing fault* causes a component to produce the expected response to a given stimulus either too early or too late.
2) A *value fault* causes a component to respond within the specified time interval but with a wrong value.
3) A *commission fault* causes *any* violation from the specified behaviour. In particular, it includes the possibility of a component producing a response when no stimulus was applied.
4) An *omission fault* causes a component, for a given stimulus requiring a non-null response, not to produce a response. We can regard "not producing a response" as equivalent to "producing a null value on time", thus making it a special case of a timing fault. It may also be sometimes more convenient to treat it as a special case of a timing fault by regarding "not producing a response" as "producing a correct value at infinite time".

In our discussion of the various fault modes, we shall normally not explicitly mention timing or omission faults since they can always occur and therefore need to be dealt with globally rather than locally. We shall concentrate on the various value failures since the vulnerability and consequences may well critically depend on the exact value produced.

310

11.15.2   List of process failure modes

- PROCESS   INSERT CARD

  PREDICATES   valid card retained
                     invalid card rejected

  FAILURE MODES   valid card rejected
                     invalid card retained

  ASSURANCE   The process depends on the correct operation of
                     the card detection mechanism, the magnetic
                     stripe reader, and the associated software.

- PROCESS   CUSTOMER PIN

  PREDICATES   PIN obtained = PIN entered by Customer

  FAILURE MODES   value fault

  ASSURANCE   The process depends on the correct operation of
                     the keypad and its device driver. It may be
                     difficult to distinguish a timing fault in this
                     process from a timing fault in the Customer
                     process.

- PROCESS   CARD PIN

  PREDICATES   PIN obtained = PIN on card

  FAILURE MODES   value fault

  ASSURANCE   The process depends on the correct operation of
                     the magnetic stripe reader.

- PROCESS   PIN COMPARATOR

  PREDICATES   IF (customer PIN = card PIN) then TRUE else
                     FALSE

  FAILURE MODES   false positive
                     false negative

  ASSURANCE   This is a relatively simple function to perform
                     either by hardware or by software and should be
                     capable of verification.

- PROCESS   CARD ACCOUNT

  PREDICATES   account obtained = account on card

  FAILURE MODES   value fault

311

| ASSURANCE | The process depends on correct operation of the magnetic stripe reader. |

- PROCESS   **AMOUNT**

PREDICATES	amount obtained = amount entered by Customer
FAILURE MODES	value fault
ASSURANCE	The process depends on the correct operation of the keypad and its device driver. It may be difficult to distinguish a timing fault in this process from a timing fault in the Customer process.

- PROCESS   **AMOUNT VALIDATOR**

PREDICATES	if (amount requested is comparable with denomination of banknotes) then TRUE else FALSE
FAILURE MODES	false positive false negative
ASSURANCE	This is a relatively simple function to perform either by hardware or by software and should be capable of verification.

- PROCESS   **QUERY STATUS**

PREDICATES	value sent is correct and on time
FAILURE MODES	timing faults value faults
ASSURANCE	Logically, there is a need to ensure that a given message is placed on the network within a finite and specified time of its reception by the *send* process, and that the process does not spontaneously generate network traffic. Value faults can be checked using network encryption, but this does not insure against data corruption taking place immediately before, or during, the encryption process. One way to check might be to have the DBMS mention the value parameters explicitly in the reply; the *receive* process in the ATM could then check for a discrepancy between the intended and received values.

- PROCESS   RECEIVE STATUS

   PREDICATES   value received is correct and timely

   FAILURE MODES   timing faults
                                 value faults

   ASSURANCE   There is no obvious way for the ATM to check that the information given to it by the database is in fact correct.

- PROCESS   REMOVE CARD

   PREDICATES   card ejected

   FAILURE MODES   failure to eject card

   ASSURANCE   The process depends on the correct operation of the card ejection mechanism. This should be a comparatively simple mechanical device.

- PROCESS   REQUEST DISBURSEMENT

   PREDICATES   amount requested = amount authorized by DBMS

   FAILURE MODES   value fault

   ASSURANCE   The process depends on the correct operation of the Money Stack interface hardware and software.

- PROCESS   DISBURSE MONEY

   PREDICATES   amount disbursed = amount requested

   FAILURE MODES   value failure

   ASSURANCE   The process depends on the correct operation of the Money Stack hardware. This should be a comparatively simple mechanical device.

- PROCESS   CONFIRM

   PREDICATES   amount confirmed = amount disbursed

   FAILURE MODES   value fault

   ASSURANCE   See QUERY STATUS. But there is no mechanism for a secondary check in a response message.

- PROCESS   CLOSE

    PREDICATES   Initial state is re-entered

    FAILURE MODES   timing fault

    ASSURANCE   This is a relatively simple function to perform either by hardware or by software and should be capable of verification.

11.16   What enforces the rules?

In this section, we return to section 11.7 and examine each of the Bank Rules in the light of our study of the system. The examination is dependent on the implementation of the teller function as an ATM (as opposed to a human teller implementation).

1) To disburse money on request
   disburse—depends on ATM hardware
   money—depends on the Bank putting banknotes in (and not, for example, grocery coupons)
   on request—depends on the PTT and the database.
(i) provided there are sufficient funds in the account
   depends on the whole system, but primarily the DBMS.
(ii) provided the Bank has Customer authority
   depends on correct recognition of the card.
   [Note that the card has a dual role, since it contains both the PIN and the account number; here it is acting as a token of authority. It is interesting to observe that a sufficient (but not necessary) condition for the card to acquire these roles is participation in another pattern of communication, namely that of PIN and card distribution. Another point of interest is that a joint account such that both parties are required to authorize a transaction cannot be accommodated using the present ATM model.]
(iii) provided that the Bank is satisfied it is delivering to the Customer
   also depends on correct recognition of the card. Here the card is acting as a token of identification by virtue of its PIN.
2) amount debited $\nleq$ amount disbursed
   depends on the whole system and the DBMS in particular.
3) amount disbursed $\ngtr$ amount requested
   depends on correct operation of the Money Stack.
4) up to the agreed daily limit
   depends primarily on the Journal.
5) State is taken as at the close of business on the previous working day
   depends on the correct update of the Database State by the Journal.

6) Only the Bank supplies banknotes

    depends on the physical construction of the Money Stack.

7) Only the DBMS inspects or modifies the account

    depends on the construction of the Database Engine.

8) Customer not to abuse card

    depends on the behaviour of the Customer.

9) Fail-safe property

    depends on complex software and efficient dependability protection.

11.17   Final summary: the analytical method in outline

What we have done is observed the following sequence of steps:

1) Define the system and identify the axegrinders.
2) Communications Analysis

    define the pattern of communication and the relations between the axegrinders.

3) Rule Specification

    define the Rules by which each axegrinder operates in the context of this particular pattern of communication.

4) Views of the System

    define the view of the system as seen from the viewpoint of each axegrinder.

5) Conformation Model—Physical View

    define the physical components and links, and bind messages to these.

6) Conformation Model—Logical View

    bind each message type to a separate logical channel between logical components.

7) Behavioural Model

    model the behaviour of the system in terms of abstract processes and events.

8) Analysis of Communication

    examine the individual acts of communication in the script with respect to possible communication breaches.

9) Analysis of the Physical Conformation

    relate the physical components and links to axegrinders and look for potential vulnerabilities in the relations.

10) Analysis of the Logical Conformation

    examine the possibility, for each message type, of forgery, corruption, message loss, eavesdropping.

11) Analysis of the Behavioural Model

examine the process failure modes and the possibility of event loss or gain.

12) Analysis of Rule Enforcement

examine the mechanisms and assurances by which the Rules are enforced.

Acknowledgements

I wish to thank Mike Martin for the countless conversations which led to the ideas presented here, and Brian Randell for his many suggestions for improvement. I also wish to thank the editor for the extreme care which he exercised in reading and helpfully commenting on an earlier draft. Any remaining faults and infelicities cannot be attributed to him, and so must remain my own. This work has been funded by RSRE Malvern, and I am grateful to Derek Barnes for his continuing help and encouragement.

References

[Carnap1939]   R. Carnap, *Foundations of Logic and Mathematics*, University of Chicago Press (1939).

[Chalmers1986]   L. S. Chalmers, "An Analysis of the Differences between the Computer Security Practices in the Military and Private Sectors", *Proceedings of the 1986 IEEE Symposium on Security and Privacy*, pp. 71–74, Oakland, California, April 1986.

[Denning1987]   D. E. Denning, "Secure Databases and Safety: Some Unexpected Conflicts", *Proceedings of the 1986 CSR Safety and Security Symposium*, ed. T. Anderson, Blackwell Scientific, Oxford (in preparation).

[Dobson1986]   J. E. Dobson and B. Randell, "Building Reliable Secure Computing Systems out of Unreliable Insecure Components", *Proceedings of the 1986 IEEE Symposium on Security and Privacy*, pp. 187–193, Oakland, California, April 1986.

[Humphreys1984]   P. C. Humphreys, "Levels of Representation of Decision Problems", *Journal of Applied Systems Analysis*, vol. 11, pp. 3–22, 1984.

[Kemmerer1983]   R. Kemmerer, "Shared Resource Matrix Methodology", *ACM Transactions on Computer Systems*, vol. 1(3), pp. 256–277, August 1983.

[Laprie1985]   J.-C. Laprie, "Dependable Computing and Fault Tolerance", *15th IEEE International Conference on Fault-Tolerant Computing*, pp. 2–11, Ann Arbor, Michigan, June 1985.

[Nessett1986]   D. M. Nessett, "Factors Affecting Distributed System Security", *Proceedings of the 1986 IEEE Symposium on Security and Privacy*, pp. 204–222, Oakland, California, April 1986.

[Piaget1978]   J. Piaget, *The Development of Thought*, Blackwell, Oxford (1978).

12 Contractual specification of reliable software

C. T. Sennett, Royal Signals and Radar Establishment

12.1 The procurement process for high-integrity software

Within the context of this chapter, high-integrity software will be taken as meaning software which must satisfy the integrity requirements of an external body: this could be an aviation authority for safety-critical software in an aircraft, security authorities for software protecting classified data, or the safety boards in the various industries where computers are used to control hazardous processes. Procedures in these various fields are far from being fixed, let alone standardized, but inevitably there are factors which are common to the production of approved software for no matter what application. In particular, the roles played by the interested parties will be similar. As we are concerned with the contractual situation, there will always be a *procurer* and an *implementor* for the software. For high-integrity software, there must always be an *approver* who is responsible for allowing the system to be used. In most situations, neither the procurer nor the approver will have enough detailed knowledge about a system to decide whether it is trustworthy or not. Consequently, from the contractual point of view, the problem is not so much a question of producing high-integrity software as of demonstrating its integrity to the approver. The system must not only be trustworthy, but must be seen to be trustworthy in the approver's eyes. In cases where the public is at risk from the incorrect operation of software, accountability requires that approvers should be able to demonstrate their mechanisms of approval and the evidence on which a given approval was based.

For ordinarily reliable software, one may surmount the problem of lack of knowledge on the procurer's part by simply trusting the implementor, and supplementing this with acceptance tests and quality assurance checks on the implementor's means of production. As has been discussed in the chapter on assurance, this cannot give assurance that the software has no safety-critical errors. Indeed common experience is that delivered software, produced to ordinary standards of quality, will certainly have errors which will be missed

317

by acceptance testing. Note that the software testing is quite different from normal component testing: most items of hardware of complexity less than the simplest microprocessor can be understood by the procurer and tested by standard acceptance tests. Software is much more complicated and exhaustive testing is out of the question. If it is not possible to find exhaustive acceptance tests and if it is not acceptable to trust the implementor, there is no recourse but to have an independent assessment made, thus introducing the role of the *evaluator*. The task of the evaluator is to attain a similar degree of understanding of the system to that of the implementor and, on the basis of this understanding, to make a judgement as to the reliability of the delivered software. In making this judgement, the evaluator needs to be guided by criteria which specify the assurance level required and which ensure that the assurance levels given to different systems may be compared. The setting of criteria and assurance levels is clearly the work of a *policy authority*, who will be able to issue a certificate on the basis of the evaluator's evidence. The certificate and the relation it has to the purpose of the system then forms the basis for approval.

The introduction of the approval stage has resulted in a simple transaction between procurer and implementor being replaced by an interaction between at least five different bodies. This complication seems to be an almost inevitable consequence of the introduction of statutory integrity requirements for software, and an understanding of the relationship between the various bodies concerned is essential to both writing and responding to procurement specifications. To assist this understanding, an analogy drawn from the field of personnel management may be helpful. Suppose a department in a bank wished to recruit a manager. Part of the policy of the bank will probably be to require a given level of education, corresponding to the approval of the software for use. To satisfy the policy, it will be a requirement that a person may not be recruited without a certificate of educational attainment. The certificate is awarded on passing an examination in which the candidate submits evidence to the examiners in the form of written answers to questions. The examiner corresponds to the evaluator and the candidate's script to the evaluation evidence which the implementor will be required to submit to the evaluator. The examiner marks the script and the marked script, corresponding to the evaluation report, is given to the examining board which decides whether to award the certificate. The board also states the examination questions and ensures uniformity of marking, so it corresponds to the policy authority in its role of setting criteria and certifying. Finally, a decision to recruit or not will be made on the basis of the relevance of the certificate and the bank may have to weigh a certificate of ability in German, say, against one in French, which will be determined by the needs of the job in hand.

This highlights the first problem area in procuring high-integrity software, namely the criteria for evaluation: in terms of the analogy, what examination papers are to be set. In this area there is a clear conflict of interest between the procurer and the policy authority. As far as the latter is concerned, a safe system is one which does nothing at all, and the more nearly the system approaches this goal the better. The procurer of course desires flexibility, full functionality, the latest hardware, and all the other things which give policy authorities sleepless nights. The art in writing a procurement specification is to balance the operational needs against the feasibility of relying on trusted software.

Most systems requiring high-integrity software are bespoke. Again in terms of the analogy, it is not a question of choosing one of many candidates with varying qualifications, but rather that of having one candidate whose failure to pass would jeopardize the whole project. Because of this, the procurement specification must elicit candidate systems which have a very high probability of successfully completing the evaluation. This means the specification must make clear not only the evaluation criteria to be applied but may also specify the means of production and require the designs of the proposed systems to be presented in sufficient detail to judge whether the design has the potential to satisfy the assurance criteria.

The implementor will need to interact with the evaluator and it is necessary to make contractual provision for this. There are various policy stances it is possible to take on evaluation, ranging from a disinterested evaluation on completion of implementation to fully interactive design review. The requirements for the evaluator to access the implementor's premises and development systems will need to be specified accordingly, as well as the evaluation evidence to be produced for review. The evaluator may well be a software house or other commercial organization, so it will be necessary to specify the type of access the evaluator may have to the implementor's proprietary software.

One characteristic of high-integrity software which is rather unlike the examination analogy is the need for maintenance. Even high-integrity software is subject to change and it may well be embedded in a larger system which may be subject to considerable change. However the cost of evaluation is so great and the time taken to carry it out is so long that it is intolerable to have a system re-evaluated after every change of its configuration. It is important therefore to specify the means which will be used to carry out maintenance without prejudice to the integrity of the system.

Because of these various factors, the procurement of high-integrity software is quite different from the procurement of ordinary software and has many unexpected pitfalls. Experience shows that these pitfalls may be avoided by making clear exactly what the requirements are at the outset and it is the purpose of this chapter to go over some of the issues which must be considered when procuring high-integrity systems. Most of the discussion will be based on experience in the procurement of security-critical software, for which codes of practice are beginning to be established, but this experience seems to be equally applicable in the field of safety-critical systems. The issues which need to be addressed change during the evolution of the project and they will be discussed under the headings of *feasibility study*, *project definition* and *maintenance*. In addition, the important topic of *security policy models* will be addressed under a separate heading.

12.2 Procurement issues at the feasibility study stage

As far as the high-integrity aspects are concerned, the most important output from a feasibility study should consist of a clear policy statement of what the computer system is being trusted to do. Associated with this will be a preferred architecture which will give an indication of which components in the system need to be trusted to enforce the policy. The assurance level for each of the components in the system must be specified and the evaluation and certification policy stated. The feasibility study is concerned with questions such as whether it is feasible to trust the computer system at all and whether a given task ought to be undertaken by software or some other means. Consequently the activity of risk assessment, which should continue throughout the lifetime of the project, assumes central importance during the feasibility study stage. In carrying out this assessment it is helpful to have a methodology and Dobson's work, described in the previous chapter, gives a rather more structured approach than the simple checklist used in many current risk assessment methods and is more likely to lead to unexpected threats being identified.

High-integrity software tends to be associated with projects having a long lifetime. Usually there will be many changes of operational, procurement and implementation staff, and changes in the requirement itself and the hardware to carry it out. The trusted policy statement needs to be maintained throughout these changes in a traceable manner, that is with the reasons for a change recorded as well as its nature. It is particularly important to do this with the trusted policy because reliability is an invisible property as far as the users are concerned. Functional aspects of a project are the user's concern and will not be forgotten; safety and security policies restrict the user and are the concern of authorities at some distance from the project and so are more easily overlooked.

It is of the utmost importance to realize that the statement is absolutely central to the production of a trustworthy system. It is extremely unlikely that a system will be invulnerable to a threat which has not been explicitly considered, so the system can be no more safe or secure than the policy statement. Because of this property of defining the threats which the computer system is countering, the policy statement also defines the allocation of responsibility between the computer system and its environment. In particular, it indicates the requirements which will be made on the human world and responsibilities of the people who will ultimately operate the trusted system. The feasibility study must consider the question of whether the proposed policy is practical to operate and ensure that it does not make demands on the human element of the environment which are impossible to satisfy.

The importance of the policy statement has always been appreciated within the security world and it is frequently a requirement to formalize the statement into a mathematical security model. The development of a security model will normally take place during the project definition but on the basis of clear and complete policy statements produced during the feasibility study; techniques for the production of a security model are discussed below. The use of mathematics in this way is common in the security world, and there are articles in the scientific journals on the mathematical methods which may be employed. Formal mathematical statements of trustworthiness requirements are not encountered so frequently in the safety-critical world, mainly because the threats are much more diverse in the safety world and the techniques for countering them not so well codified. However, many of the techniques adopted in security could be generalized to safety applications. For example, separability, the property that outputs bearing a given label are only affected by inputs bearing the same label, could have applications in showing that certain actuators are only affected by certain sensors. In a similar vein, information flow techniques may be used to require that, in a fly-by-wire aircraft, the flap angle, say, is a function only of the angle selected by the pilot and the input from the air speed sensor and of no other input. For other cases it may be a requirement that the output is a monotonic function of the pilot's input, on the theory that this is the minimum requirement for controllability. In a banking system one may specify bounds to the size and number of transactions, so limiting liability. All of these requirements are readily formalizable, thereby gaining the advantage of a completely precise specification of the trusted properties required,

12.2.1 Developing security policies

The development of a security policy is mainly concerned with balancing threats and vulnerabilities: there is no point in strengthening a system to meet a non-existent threat; there is no point in strengthening a system to meet one threat to the exclusion of others equally likely; there is no point in strengthening a software system to meet a threat which could more easily be countered in the surrounding environment. For a security policy, the identification of the threat is straightforward: one is concerned to prevent unauthorized access to data. Within the military world this threat even has a crude measure in terms of the classification level of the data and the clearance level of the users with access to it. Consequently during the feasibility study it is essential to identify the data which will be stored in the system, to estimate the amount to be stored at each classification level, and to identify the authorities who control the data together with the handling rules which they will require to be imposed. Sizes and number of users clearly enter into the risk equation: the security threat must increase with the number of users who have access to the system, and the attractiveness of the target must depend upon the amount of data stored.

In many systems, the identification of the data is not immediately obvious and requires the consideration of hybrid items such as closed circuit tv channels and voice circuits as well as the more traditional items of data such as files, databases and messages. Particularly in the case of these exotic items, the functionality of access will play an important part in determining the level of the threat. A credit card authentication device, for example, both sends and receives data, so its use corresponds to an access of the account data stored at the credit card centre. However, the functionality of use is so primitive that the threat of illicit access may not be regarded as requiring strong countermeasures. For this to be the case, the primitive functionality must be imposed by the central system. Functionality is an important point in many command and control systems where the fact that the terminals are driven by dedicated software means that the ability to introduce and run unauthorized software is forbidden. On the other hand, command and control systems are often incorporated into networks and the extra functionality which this gives in the ability to export data considerably increases the threat compared with a stand-alone system with limited data output capability.

The questions of aggregation and inference will need to be addressed during the feasibility stage. *Aggregation* is concerned with the fact that a large number of items of data may warrant a higher classification than an individual item; *inference* with the fact that information which a person is unauthorized to see may be inferred from data which he may see. The codification of controls on inference and aggregation is difficult, partly because of the intrinsic difficulty of formalizing the subject, but mainly because the degree of aggregation which presents a significant threat is a question of judgement. The inferences which may cause problems are usually the ones which were unforseen. It is the task therefore of the feasibility study to make the judgement and explore the inferences possible within the framework of the data structure being proposed. The control mechanisms may take various forms. For example it may be simply a question of ensuring that large amounts of data may not be removed from the computer system and that the monitoring, audit and document control facilities may be effectively used to discover misuse of the system. In general the system design ought to take the problem into account by ensuring that each task carried out within the system only has access to the data it necessarily requires to carry out that task and that databases are structured to reflect the need of the individual users of the system to know the contents.

This introduces the sort of controls required in commercial systems where the problem is not so much a question of denying access to data, but rather a matter of ensuring that individuals do not exceed their authorization, are not allowed to falsify data and may not repudiate their actions. The controls required here have been discussed in a recent paper [Clark/Wilson1987], and focus on the ability to limit the capabilities of a program to handle data and to ensure that critical transactions necessarily require the intervention of more than one person, so that collusion becomes necessary to perpetrate a fraud. In fact, many of the mechanisms required in the commercial world are also required to ensure the safe maintenance of trusted software, so they will be discussed below. In particular, the question of integrity, which is concerned with the controls required to alter highly trusted data, will also be postponed to the section on maintenance.

Finally, a very important topic for consideration is that of *denial of service*. The problem is exemplified by recent networking incidents in which self-replicating programs monopolize network capacity, or in which imported software overwrites discs. Clearly, networks are particularly vulnerable to such attacks, but denial of service ought to be considered in any trusted system: after all, a trustworthy system will almost certainly need to have a high availability and this can be prejudiced by simple program errors such as looping or consuming all the resources on the machine. For very-high-integrity systems it may be necessary to employ the programming practices described by Currie in chapter 6 of this book which ensure that all programs are bounded in their consumption of resources. It will in any case be necessary to specify some measures to ensure that a process or user may not monopolize the system. At the higher level, denial of service may also be countered by requiring individual accountability (so that incidents may be traced to an instigator, even when introduced over a network) and by minimizing the ability of each process to consume resources or access data according to the task in hand. In trustworthy systems it is essential to specify the capabilities of jobs or processes introduced either from a network or from the outside world, and ensure that only these capabilities are made available to them.

12.2.2   Setting the assurance levels

As has been discussed in chapter 10, assurance is many-facetted. Many factors contribute to assurance and these may be combined together in complementary packages which may be arranged, somewhat crudely, into levels of increasing assurance. The feasibility study should be concerned with setting the assurance levels required in the implementation of the trusted policy. This is an extremely important decision as the assurance level will be a major factor in deciding whether the project is, in fact, feasible and will also be a major factor in establishing the cost and implementation time for the project. The overall assurance level will probably be arrived at very rapidly bearing in mind the risks to the system and the need to use a computer at all, both of which factors may well have been fixed at the outset of the feasibility study. Assuming therefore that the project is at all feasible, the question becomes one of balancing the assurance level against the trusted functionality. The trusted functionality must be reduced until the assurance level required by the risks can be met within the time, cost and performance constraints of the system as a whole.

An example of this process can be found in secure systems where one may be able to meet the access control requirements by having two separated systems for classified and unclassified data respectively and using physical control of access to each system to enforce the control of access to the data. In this case there is no reliance on software, but a system in which the separation was provided by software, or in which a one-way filter was used for interconnection, does have a very simple software element which could be implemented to a high degree of assurance. The policy of separation which systems of this nature enforce is probably a gross simplification of the user's ideal requirements and it is essential to establish that the mode of working enforced is operationally feasible. Nevertheless, the principle of removing dispensable functionality is an essential part of adjusting the policy to meet the assurance level required.

The process of simplification should include questioning the desirability of flexible policies which may be parameterized and altered in the operational system compared with preset policies fixed at compilation. It should question the need for exceptions and, a particularly important aspect in secure systems, it should question the granularity of the protection. *Granularity* is concerned with the size of the items requiring to be classified and is related to the hardware protection mechanisms which may be employed to encapsulate data. The more closely the data items are related to the computer's protection mechanisms, the easier it is to incorporate the checking mechanisms. So, for example, it is usually much easier to enforce a policy controlling access to files of data than it is to control access to individual items stored in a database.

A major element in the programme of adjusting the security policy will usually be the separation of the software into trusted and untrusted components. The aim will be to make the trusted part of the software a very small proportion of the whole, so reducing the costs of production and evaluation. However, it is to be noted that this approach changes somewhat the emphasis of the security policy. Whereas the system as a whole is required to obey the trust policy in the face of the threats presented by the physical environment, the trusted software must constrain the untrusted software, no matter what it is, to obey the policy. This element of universality presents a problem in developing a formal specification for the trusted elements, which will be discussed below in the section on formal policy models.

It will usually be worthwhile not making a simple black-and-white distinction between the trusted and untrusted code but instead establishing a spectrum of assurance levels to meet the various vulnerabilities in the system. Going back to the security example of two separated systems joined by a one-way filter, it would be possible to supplement the gross information flow policy which this enforces with a fine granularity access control policy within the separated systems, with the information flow policy being implemented to a much higher level of assurance than the more complex access control policy. Another example from the security world is concerned with the authentication mechanism used to start a user process. The password-checking algorithm, or whatever mechanism is employed, is required to be correct but may not need a very high degree of assurance if the software mechanism is supplemented by physical checks on access. On the other hand, one must have a high degree of assurance that the authentication mechanism is always invoked.

The development of a structure to the trust policy and the related spectrum of assurance levels should be addressed with some precision and it is interesting to note here the research of Neely and Freeman [1985] aimed at formalizing the structuring process. Whatever the structure developed, it will have the effect of imposing a preferred architecture on the final system and indeed the constraints of implementing the architecture will largely determine the trust structure. A major element in this will be the limitations and capabilities of hardware to enforce controls. Within a single computer, this usually boils down to the addressing mechanism which ensures process isolation and guarantees the integrity of the controlling software. Large modern computers usually have segmentation hardware in which protection mechanisms control the reading, writing and execution of segments of store. Microcomputers may have a much simpler mechanism, or no mechanism at all, simply relying on the use of read-only memory for protection. The hardware protection is the only mechanism which the trusted code has for maintaining its integrity and constraining code: if there is no hardware protection, all the software must be evaluated. The protection mechanisms therefore play a fundamental role in establishing the structure of trust within the system. One may note in passing that current technology results in a rather cumbersome structure, but that capability architectures offer the promise of protection mechanisms more suited to the needs of trust policies. (See, for example, [Wiseman1986] and [Karger/Herbert1984].)

Within a distributed computer system, the network architecture often offers opportunities for the incorporation of protection mechanisms, often in the case of security exploiting the use of encryption. By this means it is possible to incorporate separation features and one-way filters which enable the use of untrusted and off-the-shelf components. The Distributed Secure System, initially designed by Randell and Rushby [1983] and elaborated at RSRE [Wood1986], is an example of this approach. The use of trusted network components in this way is often highly desirable. It makes possible the re-use of trusted components from other projects, and one may expect to reduce the costs of developing the trusted elements in the system and make use of the results of previous evaluations. However, as with all highly trusted components, the functionality will tend to be simple and consequently the introduction of these trusted components may set quite rigid boundaries on the functionality of the system as a whole. It is important therefore for the feasibility study to identify the components which will become available during the course of the project, in order to decide whether the functionality provided is compatible with the desired trusted policy.

12.3   High-integrity considerations during project definition

The output from a project definition study should be a procurement document, specifying the requirements in sufficient detail for an implementation to be properly designed and costed. The system which is specified will be a major factor in determining the system which is delivered so, if the trusted aspects are not defined properly at this stage, the implemented system stands little chance of being trustworthy in operation. The output from a high-integrity project definition differs from a normal project in three main areas: the trusted functionality itself, the arrangements for evaluation and development of the software, and finally the architecture and design requirements needed to carry out the trusted functionality. When drawing up the contractual specification for the project definition itself, it is essential to require that each of these areas should be investigated in detail, particularly from the point of view of risk assessment and balance in the measures countering the threats to the system. The basic trusted functionality required will be peculiar to the project, but the considerations discussed in this section are actually common to most projects involving trusted software.

12.3.1   The specification of trusted functionality

The trusted functionality must be specified within the context of the use made of it, so it is essential to specify the organizational structure within which the trusted system will be used. Within that structure, each role defined must be accorded the minimum facilities needed to carry out the task associated with the role. This upholds the principle of least privilege and also the principle that individuals are accountable for their actions. Although this principle is applied mainly to security and commercial applications, it should be an important consideration within safety applications also. These should be equally concerned with minimizing trusted functionality and interfacing to the system of human responsibilities. It is most important that an individual who is accountable for some action should have complete control over it. In safety-critical systems this frequently leads to the need to distinguish testing, training and maintenance modes from operational use and requires a definition of the principles under which these activities can take place. In a secure system, one typically needs to distinguish the role of the security officer, who maintains the security status of the users and the audit records, etc.; the system manager, who has responsibilities for the configuration and the management of databases; and the operational users themselves. To each of these roles only the minimum facilities needed to carry out their tasks should be assigned.

The constraints on the trusted functionality should be given by the safety or security model and, while this may be similar for many projects, the detailed functionality will be peculiar to the individual project. In designing these functions it is important to bear in mind the strength of a particular function as well as the degree of trust required in its implementation. For example, one might design a password mechanism to carry out the trusted function of identification and authentication. In this case, the strength of the function would be determined by the length of the password. This could be set on the basis of what other mechanisms for identification and audit were provided, for example physical control of access to the terminals. Alternatively, as for example with credit cards, the maximum length of a personal identification number is determined by public acceptability, and in this case the complementary mechanisms, such as the forgeability of the credit card itself, must be designed to give an appropriate strength to the identification mechanism as a whole. Clearly, the decision on strength is a human one which cannot be supported by a formal method: it is not possible to prove that a password is long enough. In view of the notorious vulnerability of password mechanisms (see for example [Wood1977] and [Morris/Thompson1979]) it is worth emphasizing the necessity for designing an appropriately strong mechanism. Generally one requires passwords to be generated by the system rather than by the users, which requires them to be pronounceable and supplemented by operational procedures to ensure they are not written down. Passwords should also be subject to a maximum usage, and it will occasionally be necessary to make use of passwords which are valid for one use only.

Other cases where strength of mechanism is important occur in the safety world. When using redundant systems with majority voting it is important to decide what constitutes a majority and what techniques are to be employed to ensure diversity when doing redundant programming. Experience shows that in this area common mode errors are highly likely, so that the strength of this particular mechanism may not be so great as at first appears. (See chapter 3 for further discussion on these points.) A related question is concerned with interlocks, where, if a series of interlocks is used, they must be based on different mechanisms if they are to add to the strength of the mechanism. Where interlocks involve a human interaction, this needs to be particularly carefully designed. If a system requires a user to confirm every transaction with a "Do you really want to do X?" message, answering "Yes" rapidly becomes second nature and the interlock loses its strength.

Mechanisms which need to be considered within the context of human interactions occur frequently in high-integrity software. In the security world this commonly occurs with a mechanism called *trusted path*. This is invoked when users are carrying out transactions for which they are responsible, or in which they are particularly concerned with the identity of the other party to the transaction. An example of the former is a debit from a banking account. Only individuals authorized by the owner of the account should be able to make this transaction. An example of the latter case is logging in with a password mechanism where the typed password must only be handled by trusted code. In both of these cases a trusted path mechanism needs to be defined to ensure that the human side of the transaction is always involved and that the computer side of the transaction cannot be simulated. In some cases, for example self-contained systems, a relatively weak form of mechanism may be satisfactory; in others, for example wide-scale networks with potential public access, quite sophisticated trusted path mechanisms must be invoked.

The next common aspect which is frequently required in trusted functionality is to do with audit and monitoring. These are related functions although sometimes the distinction is made that audit is concerned with *recording* what has been monitored. Monitoring is carried out for two purposes, accountability and damage limitation. Accountability monitoring is concerned with recording events for which a given individual is responsible, for example the production of a hard copy of some classified information, or an authorization for payment of an invoice. The most obvious example of monitoring for damage limitation is an aircraft flight data recorder. In this case the data recorded is to establish the cause of some breach of trustworthiness with a view to making sure that it does not happen again, thus limiting the damage caused by a given vulnerability.

The monitoring facilities required for accountability should be fairly straightforward to define as they will be determined by the accountability structures external to the trusted computer system. This will determine what data is to be recorded for what events. The record itself will probably be sensitive and will need to be handled within a special role, the auditor or security officer for example, which in turn will determine the requirements for processing and archiving.

Monitoring for accountability is part of the trusted functionality, but this is not necessarily the case with damage limitation: it is not, for example, safety critical if a flight data recorder breaks down. Moreover the events recorded are probably of transient interest: if nothing has gone wrong on a flight, the data recorded is not needed for damage limitation. This obviously depends on the type of vulnerability which could in some cases manifest itself over an extended period of time. However, software faults are nearly always discrete and this requirement can often be satisfied by an online monitoring facility. Monitoring for damage limitation is more difficult to specify than that for accountability as it is not obvious what data should be recorded. In addition this branch of monitoring is also affected by performance-monitoring requirements so there is a tendency to record far more data than can reasonably be analysed. Where it is necessary to record data, the same mechanism will probably be used as that for accountability monitoring. This is because the data gathered may be sensitive, and a trusted mechanism may be necessary to gather it. However the processing of the event logs should be able to distinguish the two uses of the data and ensure that the minimum amount is stored for each purpose and that the accountability record is not swamped.

The final common factor in trusted functionality is the necessity for balancing the needs for simplicity in the trusted mechanism against the requirements for operational flexibility. A typical vulnerability occurs here when the peripheral configuration is allowed to be dynamic and certain peripherals are associated with certain critical functions; perhaps two serial interfaces, each controlling a printer, but one used for printing payable orders, the other for simple listings. With the ability to reconfigure dynamically, vulnerabilities are introduced which require extra trusted code and operational procedures to counter. In many cases it will be simpler and cause no great operational inconvenience to remain with a statically controlled configuration and produce different PROMs or system tapes for the various versions and modes of operation required. This does however bring with it the need to maintain tight configuration control over system tapes, discs and PROMs so the specification of the functionality required is not easy.

The demand for flexibility occurs often, and nearly always at the expense of complication of the trusted software. Another example is the requirement for users to assume more than one role, which tends to conflict with the principle of least privilege. While the ability to assume more than one role is almost certainly required, it is important that these roles should not be capable of being assumed simultaneously. If it is possible to change roles within one session, the conditions and re-initialization necessary for this to happen will need to be specified.

To summarize, the specification of the trusted functionality proceeds by the following steps:

1) Establish the basic functionality to carry out the trusted process.
2) Relate this to the role structure of the users, ensuring that each function is allocated according to the principle of least privilege.
3) Decide on the strength requirements for the trusted functions.
4) Define the requirements for audit.
5) Specify the flexibility allowed for each trusted function.

At each stage in this process, the impact the trusted functionality has on the software development costs, including the costs for evaluation, must be balanced against the operational costs and difficulties of living with the functionality thus specified.

12.3.2 The specification of the requirements for development and evaluation

The introduction of the evaluator complicates the procurement problem immensely, and raises some policy questions which must be addressed at the outset. Assuming the implementation and evaluation are both carried out in industry, with independent contractors, the following questions must be answered.

1) Will certification be part of the acceptance process, and will the implementor be responsible for rectifying faults found in evaluation.
2) Will the evaluator interact with the implementor to produce a satisfactory design during the whole process of evaluation, or will the system be handed over for evaluation when nearing completion.
3) Should the implementation contract be let first, allowing the evaluator to bid against a more clearly defined requirement, *or*
4) Should the evaluation contract be let first, allowing the evaluator to assess implementor's bids and allowing implementors the ability to judge who they will have to interact with, *or*
5) Should both contracts be let in parallel, with the possibility of incompatibilities and uncertainties leading to over-bidding and cost over-runs.

The possibilities for disputes in this process are clearly enormous. This lays a corresponding burden on the project definition study to make the responsibilities and roles perfectly clear. Two procurement documents have to be produced, one for the implementation and one for the evaluation, but a large part of the two documents will be the same and will consist of the assurance criteria to be used in evaluation. This part of the procurement specification must cover the roles of the interested parties and the evaluation and policy stances; the deliverables to be required for evaluation; and criteria for the methodology to be used for production. The design and architecture criteria will be discussed in the following section and the important question of control requirements in the development itself, including maintenance and configuration control issues, will be discussed in 12.4.

The prime role of interest to the implementor will be self-interest. It is clearly in the procurer's interest to make the acceptance of the system dependent on satisfactory certification. This should only be relaxed in cases where it is more important that the system should be operational early, even though dependent on human procedures for trustworthiness, than that it should be operational later but trustworthy within itself. Consequently the implementor should be responsible for delivering a certified system and for undertaking all the remedial work which will be necessary. Disputes will arise when the evaluator regards a feature lacking in the implementation as required by the criteria whereas the implementor regards it as not being required by the specification. The dispute can only reasonably be resolved by the procurer, possibly in consultation with the approver. Clearly the management and committee structures needed to make these disputes visible at an early opportunity and resolved reasonably needs to be established. This

330

is no more than good practice, but it is critically important to do this for evaluated software.

It is also important to start the evaluation process, or at least involve the evaluators, at the earliest possible moment. The evaluators should participate in design reviews and have access to the implementor's premises and development system. In this way problems can be spotted while it is relatively easy to rectify them. It is important to emphasize the fact that high-integrity software is not software with all the bugs removed, but software built according to high-integrity principles. High integrity in the design is a very important part of this. In a situation in which the evaluator is closely involved with the development process, questions of confidentiality of the implementor's proprietary information arise and the evaluator should indicate willingness to enter into whatever non-disclosure agreements the implementor might reasonably require.

The next thing to establish is the requirement for deliverables for evaluation. This should include, according to the degree of assurance required, the basic design documentation, source code, etc; explanation of the trusted facilities for the use of the evaluators; and a trusted facility user guide for the users. The first category of deliverable is the most difficult to specify, the amount of detail depending on the assurance level required. In most cases it would be inappropriate to receive this documentation in any other than machine-readable form and it is better to have access to the development machine than racks of out-of-date microfiches. Where a system has been evaluated already it may be possible to waive some of these deliverables in favour of the detailed report from the previous evaluation. It is wise, however, to retain the right to view all the evaluation evidence as the previous evaluation may be to differing criteria, and for a system with differing trust properties.

While on the topic of access to the development system, it is also wise to include the requirement to use it for the evaluator's testing. This will require access to the compiled system under development and any test harnesses necessary to run it in simulated mode.

Having established the basic contractual rules for the evaluation, it is now necessary to establish the requirements on the development methodology, which will be discussed under the two headings of languages and tools.

The question of languages is a rather vexed one as it is surrounded by a number of issues apart from those immediately concerned with the production of high-integrity software. This includes a number of highly subjective questions of the acceptability or otherwise of various language features. First of all, it is not altogether meaningful to ask whether one languge is inherently more reliable than another. If a given item of software can be realized in an error-free form, it can nearly always be translated into another language, which, if the translation were correct, would also be error-free. The prime example of this is machine code, that being the most error-prone form of programming language, which is inevitably used as a target by all language compilers. The question to be asked therefore, is how quickly can one detect and eliminate errors in one language as compared with another. In other words, a given high-level language may be specified not to achieve high integrity, but to achieve it at a reasonable cost. Taking the rapid elimination of programming errors as the overriding consideration leads to the use of a special-purpose language such as NewSpeak (see chapter 6) where the main intention has been to constrain the programmer to produce error-free code and to detect as many errors as possible at compile time. This is achieved at the expense of expressive power: there are some problems it is not possible to cast into a NewSpeak form, but it is possible to argue that these problems should form no part of a safety-critical system.

NewSpeak is appropriate for stand-alone, highly trusted system. For those systems in which the trusted code has to reside within a larger system containing untrusted components, a different language will be necessary as it will not be possible to program the whole system in NewSpeak. The next step down in the detection-of-errors scale will cover those languages with "good" control structures and strong typing. This is already a somewhat controversial statement as although one can make a good case for GOTO being harmful, one can also make a case for its entire elimination being harmful. Strong typing is undoubtedly beneficial in assisting in the detection of errors, but its use is sometimes constraining where the application is naturally polymorphic, for example in the case of a trusted operating system which needs to be able to handle objects of various types with one uniform trust mechanism. This perhaps explains the persistence of C in some trusted applications where its presence would otherwise be deprecated. On grounds of simplification one is often tempted to remove facilities such as references and pointers from language features, but this can be counter-productive. If the problem is of an inherently non-numerical nature, involving lists and trees and so on, it may well be less reliable to program these within a primitive language than one which supported the concepts properly. The language should not be made more primitive than the requirements of the problem.

Considerations such as these rapidly lead to the conclusion that no language is uniformly suitable for high-integrity work, which is a somewhat surprising remark to make decades after the definition of Algol60. One approach to this problem is to supplement existing languages with tools which impose some of the required discipline and structure. An example of this approach can be found in the work of Carré described in chapter 4 on subsets for Ada. However, even this is not the end of the story as there are other factors influencing the language choice apart from features supported by the language. A major factor is the trustworthiness of the compiling system. Does it support array bound and overflow checking, for example. Does type checking extend across modules? Does the system forbid the use of object code patches? These and many other low-level considerations should be mandatory requirements for compiling systems producing trusted code. Finally it should be observed that use of formal verification may require the use of a special-purpose implementation language, but this will be discussed further with the other tool requirements.

The language issues may be summarized as follows:

- It is preferable to specify the language to be used for implementation. Failing that, the language characteristics should be specified and the language definition either standardized or subject to a formal definition.
- Where a language is going to be used in a restricted mode the means and requirements for restriction should be specified.
- The integrity requirements for the compiling system itself should also be specified.

Turning now to tools, it will be assumed that the standard requirements for high-quality production have already been included. The additional requirements for high-integrity systems are that in order to meet the assurance requirements it will often be necessary to use special confidence-building tools, such as analysis techniques or formal verification. In most cases one will have the option of specifying either the tool or the technique. The former presents no problem from the procurement specification point of view, but the latter allows for competition. In this latter case the criteria for the tools must be given, which will take the form of the types of analysis to be supported, the relation to the language system for the implementation, the quality of the tools, and the access required to them for evaluators and for subsequent maintenance.

Program analysis is an almost essential tool for evaluation. If a particular tool-set is to be used by the evaluators, this may constrain the choice of language or may restrict the mode of use of the language, and this should be specified. Apart from its use by evaluators as a general investigatory tool, program analysis may be used to enforce certain properties of the implementation. In this case the implementor must have access to the tools as well as the evaluator. This is an important point for procurement specification. If the requirement for quality in the software to be produced is expressed in general terms, it is nearly always debatable as to whether the software actually meets the requirement or not. Consequently, if analysis is to be used it is also desirable to specify how it is to be used. Typical properties which could be enforced are as follows:

- A given level of test coverage.
- Data use anomalies (for example, two successive writes to the same variable) to be documented.
- All procedures to be supplied with input-output definitions which may be checked with information flow analysis.
- Programs to be well structured, as checked by control flow analysis.

The advantage of these particular properties is that they are easily achievable in implementation and easily checkable in evaluation. They ensure a quality level which may be adequate in itself, but which certainly forms a useful starting point for a more searching evaluation. Evaluation is often excessively drawn out because of the need to investigate trivial irregularities in the early stages.

Program analysis is a technique which may be fairly easily grafted on to existing production techniques; formal verification, on the other hand, demands a radical re-thinking of the entire production process. At the time of writing it must be admitted that the question of writing a fixed-price contract for the production of software to formally verified standards is somewhat academic. Existing technology is not adequately industrialized for the procurement to proceed in the way which will be described, so currently the production of formally verified software should be treated as a research exercise, with the contractual conditions allowing for review and direction by the procurers. However, looking forward to what one hopes will be the near future, the following requirements will need to be specified.

The first necessity, depending on the assurance level required, is to decide whether mechanical support to the theorem proving side of formal verification is to be a requirement or not. The second necessity, again depending on the assurance level, is the extent to which the formal verification is to be taken through the specification, design and implementation stages. And finally, and most important, the strategy for the use of the formal method must be specified, in the form of what formal properties are to be proved. Each of these necessities will now be considered in turn.

Writing a specification in a mathematical form confers many benefits in the way of greater precision and the removal of ambiguity; this is particularly important for evaluation. Formal proof is required: to verify certain properties of the specification, such as safety or security; to establish the consistency of the specification; and to show that a subsequent design is a refinement of the specification. The proof methods should be established for each of these cases and the main question is whether this should be an informal process or one supported by mathematical tools. The pros and cons of the two methods are debated elsewhere in this book, but both methods call for careful specification.

In the case of informal proofs, existing in documentation only, the main requirement is to identify the places within the documentation where the proofs are given and to make it plain that the proof has to be given in sufficient detail to convince an evaluator that it is in fact correct. The security or safety property proofs are peculiar to the application and may be complex, while the consistency proof is normally fairly trivial. Within a Z formulation, for example, one would normally be content to have the consistency arguments provided in the narrative accompanying the notation. The refinement obligations on the other hand are much more extensive and as a minimum the structure of the operation refinement should be given and the abstraction functions for data refinement should be exhibited.

For mechanical proof systems there are obviously requirements associated with the usability of the system and its general quality as a tool. These issues will not be discussed here. As far as the assurance is concerned the main requirements to be specified are the need to maintain consistency between specification and proof, requirements for display of proof, and requirements for soundness. A specification will normally be divided into modules, with independent amendment of the separate modules. Some mechanism is required to indicate when a change to a specification invalidates a proof and to indicate whether, for a given module of specification, proofs exist for all the proof obligations. The proofs will have to be evaluated and this means that the tool must provide some means of exhibiting the proof in a human-readable form; this is a very important part of the evaluation evidence for formally verified software. Finally one would expect the proof systems to be sound; that is, the underlying logic should not allow for incorrect theorems to be proved and the introduction of axioms should be controlled.

Given the proof technology, the next necessity is the specification of the extent to which formal methods should be carried through the software development process from specification to implementation. Ideally, the formality should be carried all the way through and it is certainly arguable that it is better to do this supported by informal proofs than to use mechanical proofs on some stages and abandon formality altogether for the rest. The Achilles heel in this is the implementation language as the standard languages have been defined without the requirements for formal verification in mind. Use of a standard language will nearly always require the use of restrictions, as discussed above, to enable the formality to be maintained.

The final necessity, and perhaps the most important one of all, is that if a formal method is to be used, it is important to specify what it is being used for. The normal use of formal methods is to prove correctness, that is that a program implements its specification. Technically, this allows a program to do more than its specification, which is probably contradictory with the safety or security policy, which is more concerned with what the system should not do. In fact, proving the negative aspects may be more important than establishing correctness and it is quite legitimate to have that as the objective of the use of the formal methods rather than correctness. In order to do this, it is however necessary to have a way of formalizing the negative aspects. Techniques for this are not well established. This topic will be further discussed below, in the section on policy models.

12.3.3 Architecture and design

The project definition will often need to define a preferred architecture for the system. The main reason for doing this is the need to define a trust mechanism for the minimization of the amount of trusted code. In addition, it may be necessary to use existing components or computer systems and the necessity for encapsulating these within the trust policy will constrain how that policy can be implemented. Another reason for defining an architecture is that the trust policy may be needed at differing levels of assurance. For example in a banking system with an online network of automated teller machines it will probably be useful to have at least two integrity domains; a low-integrity domain, connected to the network, in which accounts may be queried but not updated, and a high-integrity domain in which accounts may be updated on a controlled basis from the low-integrity journal. In this case the separation of the integrity domains is a simple function which may be achieved with a high degree of assurance, possibly even physically. The trust policy within the high-integrity domain may be implemented to a lower degree of assurance as a result, say, of limiting access to the bank's employees.

This indicates another way in which trust policies may influence architecture, namely in the interaction with the environment. Taking the banking example again, audit and accountability requirements will often lead to the requirement for a centralized system. This is because it will be desirable to unify the authentication mechanisms and centralize the audit logs, so that an individual's identification data are only held in one place and the audit trails may be more easily compared. This in turn will lead to the requirement for limited functionality in workstations. It is clearly a much more difficult task to maintain adequate records of updates to a database if portions of the database may reside in workstations with permanent storage. Similarly, confidentiality requirements may make it undesirable for workstations to have locally controlled hardcopy devices, or removable media such as floppy discs.

Thus the security requirement and the practical constraints will tend to force the software design to follow a certain architecture and it is the purpose of the project definition to specify this architecture in a sufficiently general way to allow the greatest possibility for differing designs. Within this framework it is necessary to require proposals produced in response to the specification to make manifest their design and to provide criteria by which the designs may be judged. The question of manifest design is a key issue in high-integrity software and is one of the distinguishing features of a high-integrity procurement. The difference arises as usual from the necessity for evaluation. The design will affect the ease and the cost with which it may be carried out and is therefore quite as important a factor as the external requirements such as performance and user interfaces. The overall requirement is that the trust mechanisms must be simple and the trusted code small and it is necessary in the procurement specification to elicit sufficient detail about the design to ensure that this is so.

This is probably best done in the form of statements of work, with questions similar to the following:

- Show how the design supports the separation into trusted and untrusted code and indicate the sizes required for the various components of the trusted software.
- Indicate how the hardware protection mechanisms will be used to protect the integrity of the trusted code and carry out the encapsulation of the objects protected.
- Give the flow of control throughout a typical transaction indicating the trust mechanisms invoked and how they are called into play.
- Show how the trust policy of the total system is enforced by the individual components, specifying what each component relies on and what each guarantees. In the case of previously evaluated components, show that what is guaranteed is provided by what has been evaluated.

The intention with each of these questions is to make the proposer invest sufficient effort in preparing, and committing to, a lean and spare design which can be confidently assessed for evaluation. In the descriptions it is particularly important to show how the control mechanisms resist subversion: as usual with trusted software it is much more important to establish that a mechanism cannot be bypassed rather than the precise form in which it is implemented. For this reason, the way in which the hardware protection mechanism is used by the software will usually be particularly important.

12.4   The development environment for trusted software

During the course of production of a trusted system the illusion often grows that development of the system will cease on technical transfer. This is far from the case. After evaluation the system will change: even an evaluated system will have bugs in the untrusted software; it is likely that the operational requirement will evolve and the system may need to change to meet the needs of new hardware or new versions of an underlying operating system. Change and development of the system call into question the original certification. But just as it is unrealistic to expect the operational system not to have to undergo some changes during its lifetime, it is equally unrealistic to expect the system to go through the complete evaluation process for every change, no matter how small. In the absence of any controls over maintenance, the only reasonable stance is to freeze the software, which will probably be unacceptable. It will be argued that, if the controls are to be effective, they must be present within the development environment used for maintenance. Consequently an essential part of procurement specification for trusted software must be a specification for the environment which will be used for its maintenance. This will no doubt be the environment used for the original development, but the considerations of the desirability of control over alterations apply equally during implementation. In addition, the development environment can provide features which support the role of the evaluator, so it is worth specifying these properties also to ensure trouble-free evaluation. As the question of integrity properties in development environments has not received much attention the position adopted will be justified in some detail.

First of all, there is an undoubted threat. The main problem is erroneous updating, occurring as a result of lack of knowledge, and of deliberate subversion. There are several published instances of malicious alterations in the form of fraud and of disgruntled employees attempting to hold firms to ransom as a result of illicit software planted into trusted code. Subversion may occur for frivolous rather than malicious reasons, but it is still a threat to the trustworthiness of the system. The vulnerability is that the trustworthiness of the software may depend on obscure features and so it is very easy for the consequences of alterations to be misunderstood or for subversion to be hidden. Maintenance of the system will not be done by the original developers: typically, one may suppose that it is undertaken by contract programmers, probably frequently changing. Personnel on short terms of duty cannot be expected to appreciate the subtleties of the setting of ring numbers or privilege bits or other equally obscure machine dependencies which may be absolutely crucial to the integrity of the trusted code, so it is necessary to protect against slips and errors arising as a result of lack of knowledge.

In discussing this vulnerability, the remark is often made that it is countered by a system of configuration control and the use of trusted programmers. This is not really an adequate approach. Most configuration management systems provide management tools which report the status of different versions and give the ability to assemble differing configurations, but do not exert adequate control. With many configuration control systems, the ability to alter a part of the delivered system implies the ability to alter the whole, so no matter how well the manual controls are applied there remains a substantial vulnerability. The problem is: supposing an old version of the system under development were to be assembled, what guarantees are there that the trusted parts remain as they were when evaluated? What guarantees are there that when a new version is produced, it has the same trusted properties as the old? Typically, a new version is produced to cure a bug, probably not relevant to the trust properties. The cure for the bug may however alter some property of the code which is relied on by the system to guarantee its integrity, and this property could be quite obscure. It is almost impossible to maintain, throughout the life cycle of a project, a team of programmers who totally understand the consequences which alterations of code may have, and it is quite possible for changes to be authorized which totally destroy the trustworthiness of the system.

The counter to the risk clearly requires the trusted code to be distinguished from the untrusted code, with appropriate handling rules for each. A counter to deliberate subversion is the introduction of accountability and constraints on maintainers and developers so that they may only alter

338

software they are responsible for. These counter measures are such that they may only be enforced within the development environment itself. It is not possible to introduce the concept of accountability without having the ability to audit operations which alter trusted software, and this can only be done by the development system itself. Trusted software is only vulnerable within the development environment; it cannot be altered outside the computer, only destroyed, so manual controls on alteration are ineffective as they are being exercised in an inappropriate environment. Quite apart from this, the scale of control required over many thousands of configurable items is entirely beyond human capabilities. Nor is it altogether believable that a manual system will not be circumvented from time to time as project deadlines draw nearer.

The requirement therefore is for the ability to label data stored within the environment and to control the overwriting of that data on the basis of the label and the individual initiating the action. In some cases, the action of overwriting will need to be audited, in others data may only be altered by certain tools or procedures. Expressed in this way, there are clear analogies with the type of control provided by a security policy such as that of Bell and LaPadula [1976], with integrity levels rather than security levels indicating the degree of protection to be applied to the data and integrity clearances indicating the level of trust to be given to a user. These analogies are in fact rather misleading as the policy required is not so much concerned with information flow as with processes and procedures. A workable integrity policy must be developed from the straightforward security analogy as follows. Consider a set of partially ordered integrity levels (where the partial order is associated with the degree of trust which is required in the control of overwriting), and associate a level with each item of data (an integrity classification) and each user of the system (an integrity clearance). Every operation initiated by the user which involves the overwriting of data is forbidden if the integrity clearance of the user does not dominate the integrity classification of the data. This is analogous to the simple security property in Bell and LaPadula and provides some of the control mechanism required. In particular this would allow for the auditing of write operations according to integrity level and the restriction of updates to designated personnel.

However, it does not provide for the limiting of update of trusted data to particular tools, and for this it is necessary to be able to attribute an integrity clearance to given tools and programs: an overwrite is allowed if the greatest lower bound of the clearances of the user and the tool being used dominate the integrity classification of the data being overwritten. Further control than this does not seem to be necessary and, in particular, the analogue of the Bell and LaPadula star property, namely that overwriting should be forbidden unless the integrity of all the data the process may read dominates that of the data to be overwritten, is not required. This is at first sight rather surprising, particularly when considering a compilation as the example operation; after all, the integrity of the object code cannot exceed the integrity of the source. The paradox stems from regarding the integrity of the data as stemming from some property of the data itself, rather than from the process it has undergone. This can be seen by considering a typical edit/compile/validate sequence during the development of a module of software. The validation process may consist of testing, analysis or human assessment; its output is the validated module which will be labelled high integrity; the input is the *same* module, together with other files of differing integrity. Use of an integrity flow constraint in this situation would be entirely inappropriate. It would also be inappropriate for the editing phase, the output from which can only be of low integrity. It is not necessarily appropriate for the compiler phase if the compiler makes use of low-integrity information for administrative purposes.

Thus the particular integrity changes from input to output vary according to the tool; so as far as the development environment is concerned, the simplest possible form of integrity control should be specified. This does of course presuppose that a tool is able to interrogate the integrity levels of its inputs so that it may provide an integrity check appropriate to the tool.

Integrity levels are somewhat controversial, so at the risk of belabouring the topic, it is worth answering some objections made against them:

"Integrity policies are difficult to operate in practice and all data tends to end up classified at high integrity or low integrity, which is pointless". This is a property of policies which implement the star integrity policy; removing it produces a policy which has substantially fewer operational problems and provides all of the controls required.

"Integrity policies are not necessary as all the controls required can be provided by standard operating system access controls". Standard access controls are *discretionary*, that is may be set or not at the discretion of the owner of the data. This is incompatible with the accountability objectives which require the limitations on access to be mandatory. In addition, the integrity level structure supports a hierarchy of auditing and handling rules as appropriate for the requirements of the project.

"Integrity levels are not required by a statutory body and therefore need not be implemented". This objection contrasts with the case of security where security levels are defined nationally and there is a statutory requirement to obey a handling rule appropriate to the level. Integrity levels relate to handling rules within a computer and the integrity policy is not required to interface to the people and paper world (although it is probably a good idea to have human-readable integrity labels, to remind developers they are handling trusted code). Integrity levels are required because *differing* handling rules are necessary for the data stored in a modern computer system. If all the data had as much effort invested in it as the evaluated software and had to be protected with the same procedures, there would be no need for integrity levels.

An integrity policy can be usefully supplemented by a system of type checking. By this is meant a system whereby items of data may be associated with types and programs are defined to operate on items of one type and produce items of another; indeed, the only way to produce items of a given type is by the use of constructor functions which are introduced when the type is defined. The type system may be used to bind together items of data, for example the source text of a module and its object code, and it may also be used to ensure that one is always dealing with objects with certain characteristics, such as formal proofs which have been machine checked.

Both of these uses of the type system are important in evaluation. An evaluator in assessing some code will normally be looking at the source text, rather than the loadable object code itself. This raises questions as to whether the object code actually corresponds to the source text and whether it will be the code actually obeyed in the operational system. By defining a type for modules with a constructor function which takes source text and compiled code as arguments, it is possible to build a trusted compiler which produces module values. In this way the evaluator does not have to be concerned with the consistency between the two: the fact that the object being handled is a module guarantees this. The same technique may be used to bind together a specification and its design, a verification condition and its proof, and in any other situation where items of data need to be consistent.

The other use of type constraints, namely the enforcement of certain characteristics, is a useful discipline in many areas and is a general technique for controlling the production of high-integrity software. The example chosen, namely its use to ensure that proofs have been checked by machine, may be used as a requirement for input to evaluation; the implementor is then constrained to produce the proof along with the specification and the evaluator is saved from being concerned with the status of proofs. Other uses which come to mind are those concerned with marking code which must reside in certain protection regimes, say a given ROM in a workstation, thus ensuring that a complex system may be correctly assembled.

Apart from the controls provided by the integrity policy and the type system, there exists the standard (discretionary) access control which will be available in most development environments, and the relatively simple tools which may be used to compare files of data for discrepancies and ensure that trusted code is unaltered. These various controls may be arranged in a hierarchy to give characteristics for development environments which exert progressively greater controls over the process of change. This hierarchy is as follows:

1) Discrepancy checking
2) Discretionary access control
3) Mandatory integrity control
4) Type checking

Each level in the hierarchy should be combined with the preceding levels to form a sensible combination of properties which a development environment must support. In specifying the particular level required, various external factors will need to be taken into account such as the attractiveness of the software to a potential attacker, physical access to the development system, and the degree of trust to be placed in the programmers. Note that, for this latter quantity, it is not simply a question of whether programmers are likely to be trustworthy, but also whether they are responsible and understand the nature of the system, so the degree of training is an important consideration. This is particularly the case in the maintenance phase of a project when the programmers are likely to be trustworthy but much less familiar with the system than the original developers. In view of this it is also helpful to categorize the types of change which may take place during maintenance according to the degree of understanding required, so that this may be balanced against the requirement for controls in the development environment. A possible categorization is as follows:

- Invariant software. No changes are allowed, the only maintenance being the production of back-up copies.
- Invariant trusted software. No changes are allowed in trusted code, but untrusted software may be undated.
- Anticipated changes. The only changes allowed in trusted software are those which have been predicted and taken into account in evaluation. These would be relatively simple changes such as alterations to configuration tables etc.
- Evaluated changes. Changes are allowed as a result of mini-evaluation which is able to correctly assess the impact of the proposed change.
- Major re-designs. This is equivalent to the original implementation.

Ideally, an evaluation certificate should state the category of allowed change which would not invalidate the certificate. The procurement specification should state the desired maintenance policy and specify the consequential requirements both for evaluation and for the development environment.

12.5 The formal specification of access control policies

One of the most important aspects of high-integrity software is the fact that the degree of trustworthiness can only be specified relative to some trust policy. A system cannot simply be trusted, it can only be trusted to do something. A failure in a system can often be attributed to a misunderstanding of what is being guaranteed by a given component, so it is essential that the policy should be specified precisely. Consequently, a formal statement of the trust policy is a requirement in many procurement documents. Most experience in the specification of trust policies has been obtained in the security field where the specifications of security policy are termed security models, and Landwehr [1981] gives a very good survey of possible techniques to employ. Unfortunately, the state of the art in this field is not entirely satisfactory. This is because, for procurements, the policy tends to be expressed in functional terms as the conditions under which access to files and other objects are allowed, rather than in terms of the fundamental security concept of information flow.

Ideally, the policy model ought to be expressed in terms which say what accesses and information flows are forbidden rather than the conditions under which they are allowed as this more accurately reflects the security requirement. Unfortunately the formalization of this negative concept is difficult and the most successful attempt which has been made at this may well be over-restrictive [Goguen/Meseguer1982, 1984]. This difficulty of formalization leads to the use of models containing security flaws called *covert channels*, that is information flows which are allowed by the model but forbidden by the policy. This is a rather curious notion given that the policy model is supposed to be a formal statement of the security requirements. However, provided the information flow through the channel is low enough, a covert channel may present no threat to security. Subject to this caveat, this section will be concerned with the formal specification of such policies in the kind of detail which will be necessary for a procurement document. By this stage, at the completion of the project definition, the overall structure of control within the system should be well established and it is helpful to have a specification of what that should be. The intention of this section is to present a number of techniques for specifying access control mechanisms which may be used or not as appropriate. In particular both security and integrity controls will be described. As the section is devoted to access control the techniques are mainly relevant to the security and commercial worlds, but the discussion contains some features relevant to safety also. The notation used will be the specification language Z, described briefly in chapter 2 (see also [Hayes1987] and [Sufrin1983]).

We are assuming therefore that the functionality of the system has been specified and that the requirement which the policy model should express is the security rules under which the operations may be invoked. The operations will obviously depend upon the particular system being specified so they are introduced here as a Z given set (OP) which may be instantiated or replaced as required. For the purposes of this example model the operations are classified as causing read, write or execute accesses to the objects they are applied to, because this covers the main features of information flow which are relevant to security. Differing security policies may require the identification of differing modes of access, such as a combination of read and write accesses, or a *control* mode of access for changes to security labels, or a *release* mode of access for sending messages and so on. The access rules for these modes of access may be formalized within this model framework.

The formalization of the classification of the operations is done here by simply defining *read*, *write* and *execute* to be subsets of OP, as follows:

[OP]

$$\underline{\qquad\qquad\qquad\qquad\qquad}$$

read, write, execute : $\mathbb{P}$ OP

$$\underline{\qquad\qquad\qquad\qquad\qquad}$$

⟨read, write, execute⟩ partition OP

The constraints in the definition above simply express the fact that every operation is a read, write or execute operation.

To express mandatory integrity and security policies, a set of security and integrity levels is required. Again, these are project-specific and will be introduced as given sets *Sy* and *Iy* respectively. To express the security policy it is necessary to have dominance relations and greatest lower bound (*glb*) and least upper bound (*lub*) operators. The dominance relation tests whether a given security level is "less than" or equal to another in the sense that an object classified to the given level may be inspected by a subject cleared to the other. The least upper bound of two security levels is the lowest level which dominates both: it is the security level which must be given to a document constructed from objects classified at the two security levels. The greatest lower bound is the opposite of this and is used, as will be explained below, to confine information at a given security level.

These operators depend on the structure of the security and integrity levels and so must be defined with them. For the purposes of this generic model, only the signature is given in the definition below, together with the security level *not_classified*, which represents the least of the security levels in the sense that it is dominated by all others.

[*Sy*, *Iy*]

$$\underline{\qquad\qquad\qquad\qquad\qquad}$$

$\_ \preceq_S \_ : Sy \leftrightarrow Sy$

not_classified : *Sy*

$(\_glb_S\_), (\_lub_S\_) : (Sy \times Sy) \rightarrow Sy$

$\_ \preceq_I \_ : Iy \leftrightarrow Iy$

$(\_glb_I\_) : (Iy \times Iy) \rightarrow Iy$

To express discretionary access policies it is necessary to formalize the concept of a user; this is usually associated with the concept of a *role*, which is associated with the particular jobs or roles a user is required to perform. It is a general principle that, in high-integrity applications, the users of the systems should have only the minimum access rights they need to carry out their particular function. Consequently, the discretionary access policies are usually expressed in terms of the roles rather than the individuals, although it will sometimes be the case that control is required at the individual level as well.

This security policy is expressed by requiring that a given user should be

344

associated with one or more roles, and that the roles should set the access rights for the job. Roles and users will again be introduced as given sets and the security policy is formalized by the existence of two functions, the mappings for which must be supplied by the security officer when introducing a new user to the system.

[*User, Role*]

allowed_roles : User $\rightarrow$ $\mathbb{P}$ *Role*

clearance : Role $\rightarrow$ *(Sy* $\times$ *Iy)*

Requirements will clearly differ in this area, and there are a number of different ways of formalizing the requirement. However, the user structure is an important part of the discretionary access control and should be formally specified.

The total security policy will specify which operations are allowed. The decision will be made on the basis of the current security and integrity levels, the user requesting the operation and the role to be adopted. These parameters are gathered together in the schema below, which defines the security relevant context of a process.

┌─ *Context* ──────────────┐
│ *hiso, losi : Sy; hisi : Iy*
│ *current_user : User; r : Role*
└──────────────────────────┘

The two security levels are used to enforce a security confinement policy and represent respectively the lowest classification of any object open for writing and the highest classification of any object open for reading. A read access will be permitted if the classification of the object is no greater than the first (*hiso* stands for highest source) while a write access is allowed if the classification is no less than the second (*losi* stands for lowest sink). The integrity level is used to enforce the simple integrity policy described in the section on development environments and the remaining fields control the discretionary access.

In keeping with the elementary access policy being specified, objects in the machine are simply regarded as stores of information. Consequently each object in the machine has a content which is called a *Value*, a given set. To express the security policy each object is associated with classifications for the mandatory policies and access control lists for the discretionary policies. This is represented by the schema definition below:

[*Value*]

┌─ *Object* ───────────────┐
│ *content : Value; class : Sy; iclass : Iy*
│ *access : (User* $\times$ *Role)* $\rightarrow$ $\mathbb{P}$ *OP*
└──────────────────────────┘

Use of the *access* field in the object will be discussed below. It is usual for the mandatory policy to vary according to the nature of the object, represented by the type of data stored in it. For example, objects such as output devices do not really have a content at all and it may be reasonable to have a different mandatory access control compared with a file access; similarly, a composite object, such as a disc volume, may require a different access control from the objects stored in it. For the purposes of this model, objects will be regarded either as primitive and indivisible, or as composite (that is, made up of other objects) or as programs. Composite objects, such as databases and program libraries, are extremely common and it is necessary to specify the handling rules appropriately. Programs, in this particular sample security model, are distinguished because the integrity policy chosen makes access dependant on the program being obeyed. If the integrity policy is not required, formalization of objects and values may be simplified. Programs are modelled as sequences of operations and names: the names are looked up in an environment to provide the object which the operation will act upon. The classification of values and objects into the categories of primitive, composite or program can be expressed by adding constraints on the set of values as follows:

[*Name*]

$$
\begin{array}{l}
data : \mathbb{F}\ Value \\
program : seq(OP \times Name) \rightarrowtail Value \\
composite : \mathbb{F}\ Object \rightarrowtail Value \\
\hline
\langle data,\ rng\ program,\ rng\ composite \rangle\ partition\ Value
\end{array}
$$

As before the constraint in this definition expresses the fact that the categorization of values is complete and mutually exclusive. In the definition above, *program* and *composite* can be regarded as constructors for values of that type, while *data* stands for all the primitive values.

The actual operation of the machine will be modelled as a series of state changes and initially the operations for one user only will be considered. As far as the model is concerned most of the changes in the actual state of the machine are irrelevant as it is only concerned with the security and the integrity aspects. For these purposes the state will be abstracted to a structure which contains only the context and an environment. The environment is a mapping from names to values which enables the execution of a program to be modelled. In some applications, this could be a filestore directory with names corresponding to character strings and values to filed objects. For other applications, more sophisticated name and value associations, such as an object management system, are provided but the essential features may all be captured by name and value mappings. The inclusion of an environment is an important feature of this model because it allows some of the assumptions about the nature of the data in the machine to be made explicit. In particular, the model has been developed to be appropriate for the situation in which the environment represents the stored permanent objects and operations govern access to them. The dynamic process environment which forms the process data space in the main store of the machine is ignored and implicitly treated as a black hole of values. When the model is generalized to cater for multiple users and processes, the requirement will be that each user's data space is isolated.

To simplify the formalism, the convention of having a distinguished object to represent the parameter of the current operation will be adopted. This will be the source or destination of data transferred to or from the user's data space in the case of read or write operations respectively. This is included within the state space associated with each user to give a definition for the security relevant part of the state as follows:

$$
\begin{array}{|l}
\hline
\textit{State} \\
\hline
\textit{Context} \\
\textit{Object} \\
\textit{env} : \textit{Name} \nrightarrow \textit{Object} \\
\hline
\end{array}
$$

The environment is only accessible as a result of obeying the program in the manner constrained by the model, which preserves security. Consequently the presence of a high-security object in the environment presents no threat. This allows, for example, an unclassified program to be run even if a user of a directory has a classified object in it. However, objects added to the environment by an operation must have at least the classification of data currently contained in the user's state space. This can be no more than *losi*. This constraint on the classification of objects added to the environment is applied to all state changes and therefore gives the security rule for the creation of objects. In addition, for discretionary security, the current user must remain invariant, although it may be allowable to change roles. These conditions on state transitions are expressed by the following schema:

$$
\begin{array}{|l}
\hline
\Delta \textit{State} \\
\hline
\textit{State; State}' \\
\hline
\forall \textit{obj} : \textit{Object} \mid \textit{obj} \in \textit{rng}(\textit{env}' \setminus \textit{env}) \bullet \textit{losi}' \preceq_S \textit{obj.class} \\
\textit{current\_user}' = \textit{current\_user} \\
r' \in \textit{allowed\_roles}(\textit{current\_user}) \\
\hline
\end{array}
$$

347

In the schema above, the \ symbol is the set difference operator, so

$$rng(env' \setminus env)$$

gives all the new objects in the changed environment.

The initial value for the state may be set at any time when the user's data space can be guaranteed to be empty of classified data and when no objects are being accessed. This will normally be at login or the start of a transaction. It is important to specify the latter if that is required, in which case it will also be necessary to specify the guarantees for ensuring that the user's data space is free of classified data. The initialization will be determined by the user and role adopted:

```
┌─ Initial_state ──────────────────────────────────┐
│ State                                             │
│                                                   │
├───────────────────────────────────────────────── │
│ r ∈ allowed_roles(current_user)                   │
│ hiso = fst(clearance(r)) ∧ losi = not_classified  │
│ hisi = snd(clearance(r))                          │
└───────────────────────────────────────────────────┘
```

The functions *fst* and *snd* in the schema above are the projection operators which give the first and second elements of a pair respectively.

The initial environment needs to be defined according to the needs of the system being modelled. For the user processes the initial environment will depend upon the role adopted. Supplying an environment purged of classified objects allows for a form of access control in which users are simply not aware of data they are not allowed to see, rather than having an error reported when they attempt to access it. Constraints on the environment may also be used to specify more subtle forms of access control. The set of objects accessible to a user is entirely determined by the environment and so it limits the capabilities a user may employ in a particular role. By this means one can develop suitable specifications for two-person rules and so on.

The sequence of state changes is governed by a function

$$obey : (State \times OP) \rightarrow State$$

which delivers the state resulting from the application of an operation within a given state. The remainder of this model consists of a partial specification for *obey* built up incrementally according to the type of operation and the nature of the object it is applied to. Thus the schemas which follow, each of which covers a different aspect of access checking, contain the signature $\Delta State$; $op : OP$ to represent the state before and after the application of the operation *op*. The model only constrains security aspects so the object in the new state and the values in the new environment are left unspecified.

The discretionary access check is the same for all operations:

```
┌─ DAC ────────────────────────────────────┐
│  ΔState;  op : OP                          │
├───────────────────────────────────────────│
│  op ∈ access(current_user, r)             │
└───────────────────────────────────────────┘
```

This specification allows for the most general form of control: specified in this way, using a function *access* to deliver the set of allowed operations, means that control may be exercised at the level of the individual operation. Note also that the access function has both the user and role as parameter. This is to allow control over access at the granularity of a single user, even though the main access control uses roles. The precise form required for the *access* function needs to be specified according to the project requirements. Usually, control would only be exerted according to the mode of access, in which case the result of the function would be one of the sets, *read*, *write* or *execute*, and the implementation could be simplified accordingly. Alternatively, the access function could be used to specify various forms of type control.

For the mandatory checks, the read operation has a different effect depending on whether the current object is composite or not. For read operations on simple objects, the effect is null if the current working clearance does not allow it. If it does, *losi* must be changed to indicate that the process potentially has high-security data in its data space and future write operations must be constrained accordingly. This is expressed by the schema *Sreadops* below:

```
┌─ Sreadops ───────────────────────────────────────┐
│  ΔState;  op : OP                                  │
├───────────────────────────────────────────────────│
│  op ∈ read                                         │
│  content ∈ data                                    │
│  class ≼_S hiso  ⇒   losi' = losi lub_S class      │
│                      hiso' = hiso ∧ hisi' = hisi   │
│  ¬(class ≼_S hiso) ⇒ θState = θState'              │
└───────────────────────────────────────────────────┘
```

The θ construction in the schema above is used to indicate the tuple value made up of the identifiers of the schema. (Without the θ, a schema identifier stands for the corresponding set.)

If a composite object is to be a meaningful entity, access to the constituent objects must be controlled as well as access to the composite object itself. In this case, access to the composite object may require no particular security check. For something like a disk volume, for example, a request to mount the volume could be treated as a read access. An alternative approach would be to have a *mount* mode of access which was applicable only to disk volume objects. In either case, the effect of the access may be modelled as the introduction of some or all of the constituent objects into the process environment without any change in the working clearances. This is expressed by the schema *Creadops* below. For this to be an allowable approach to the modelling of these operations, the constituent objects must be protected at least as well as any other object. For files on a disk volume this may be quite legitimate, but the protection of individual entities in a database may be more difficult to achieve for high levels of assurance as ordinary computer hardware does not protect items at this level of granularity. Similarly, it may be difficult to protect individual objects stored on a magnetic tape because of the difficulty of controlling rewinding and back spacing. In some applications therefore, it may be necessary to make more distinctions between objects than has been covered in this model, and develop access checks appropriate to each type of object.

Creadops _____

$State;\ State';\ op : OP$

$op \in read$

$content \in rng\ composite$

$rng(env' \setminus env) \subseteq composite^{-1}\ content$

$\theta Context = \theta Context'$

In the schema above, the constraints express the fact that the effect of a read operation on a composite object is being considered and that the only change allowed is that the new environment may differ from the old one only by having some or all of the objects it contains stored within it.

Write operations, either to a simple object or a composite one, are permitted if the object has a classification at least that of any object read. However, the integrity constraint must also be taken into account:

---
writeops _____

$\Delta State;\ op : OP$

$op \in write$

$content \in data \lor content \in rng\ composite$

$losi \preceq_S class \land iclass \preceq_I hisi \Rightarrow\ \ hiso' = hiso\ glb_S\ class$

$losi' = losi \land hisi' = hisi$

$\neg(losi \preceq_S class \land iclass \preceq_I hisi) \Rightarrow \theta State = \theta State'$

In this simple model, executable objects may be created or deleted, but not overwritten. In principle, there is no reason to forbid the overwriting of program, although it may be necessary to distinguish the integrity classification for overwriting the object from its clearance when being obeyed (see below).

After a write operation, subsequent read operations are constrained to a security level no greater than that of the object just written. This treats the write operations as being similar to open file operations in which it is assumed that once a file has been opened for writing, data may flow into it at any time afterwards. If this is not the case, *hiso'* can be left at the same value as *hiso*.

The integrity policy to be defined requires the integrity clearance of a process to change according to the program being obeyed. Programs may be obeyed from within other programs, so it is necessary to model the execution of programs. For this, it is necessary to have a function for the execution of sequences of operations:

$$obeyseq : (State \times seq (OP \times Name)) \nrightarrow State$$

$\forall s : State; \ ops : seq (OP \times Name)$
- $\#ops = 1 \Rightarrow obeyseq(s, ops) = s''$

  $\#ops > 1 \Rightarrow obeyseq(s, ops) = obeyseq(s'', tl \ ops)$
  where
  $s' \triangleq \mu \ State$
  $\quad | \quad env = s.env \land \theta Object = env(snd(hd \ ops))$
  $\quad\quad hiso = s.hiso \land losi = s.losi \land hisi = s.hisi$
  $\quad\bullet \ \theta State$
  $s'' \triangleq obey(s', fst(hd \ ops))$

This function is defined by induction on the sequence of operations and names which represents the program. The first operation in the sequence is applied to the object found in the current environment from the first name in the sequence. The state with this object present is represented by s'. Subsequent operations take place within the state changed by the preceding operations. Exceptions, such as overflows or break-in, have not been modelled for reasons of clarity, but the execution model may be easily extended to cater for this by allowing premature termination of the sequence. This function can now be used to define the constraints applied to execute operations (see schema at the top of page 352).

In this schema, $State_1$ is the start of the execution of the object, in which *hisi* is modified if necessary to be no greater than the clearance of the program, represented by *iclass*. In this model, any program may be executed, the control of access to the program itself being provided by discretionary security. This follows from the view that programs may only

$$\boxed{\begin{array}{l}
\underline{\textit{executeops}} \text{ \rule{6cm}{0.4pt}} \\
\Delta State;\ op : OP \\
\rule{13cm}{0.4pt} \\
op \in execute \\
content \in rng\ program \\
hisi' = hisi \\
\quad hiso' = hiso_2 \wedge losi' = losi_2 \\
\quad env' = env_2 \wedge \theta Object' = \theta Object_2 \\
where \\
\quad\boxed{\begin{array}{l}
State_1;\ State_2 \\
\rule{10cm}{0.4pt} \\
hisi_1 = hisi\ glb_1\ iclass \\
hiso_1 = hiso \wedge losi_1 = losi \wedge env_1 = env \\
\theta Object_1 = \theta Object \\
\theta State_2 = obeyseq(\theta State_1, program^{-1}\ content)
\end{array}}
\end{array}}$$

diminish clearances, so there is no point in having a mandatory access check to the program itself. *State₂* is the state after execution of the program. This is used to derive the final state after the completion of the execute operation in which *hisi* is restored to its initial value.

Finally the separate constraints may be combined together to give a specification for the security properties of *execute*:

$$ops \triangleq DAC \wedge (Sreadops \vee Creadops \vee writeops \vee executeops)$$

$$\forall\ \Delta State;\ op : OP \bullet \theta State' = obey(\theta State, op) \Leftrightarrow ops$$

The generalization to cover several users running simultaneously is probably best done informally, as otherwise a change of formalism is required to express the running of concurrent processes. The interaction is specified by defining how the environment of one user may change as a result of the actions of another. This will depend upon the inter-process communication allowed and the rules for simultaneous access of shared objects.

This completes the specification of the example model. The steps by which this may be converted into an application-specific security model may be summarized:

1) Define the security levels and dominance relations. (The greatest lower bound and least upper bound operations follow from this.)
2) Decide whether it is necessary to have an integrity policy and what it should be. In particular, decide whether it is necessary to keep the program execution model.

352

3) Decide on the information flow characteristics of the various operations in the system and classify according to how it is proposed to implement the mandatory security policy.
4) Decide on the access modes which will need to be controlled within the discretionary policy and the nature of the discretionary access control mechanism (that is, the form of the *access* function).
5) Decide the role structure or whatever other mechanism is required to give the discretionary access groups.
6) Define the nature of the objects to be treated within the system together with the corresponding rules for handling them.
7) Decide on the error-reporting strategy.

References

[Bell/LaPadula1976] Bell, D. E. and LaPadula, L. J., *Secure Computer System: Unified Exposition and Multics Interpretation*, Technical Report ESD-TR-75-306, Mitre Corporation, Bedford, Massachusetts, USA (March 1976).

[Clark/Wilson1987] Clark, D. D. and Wilson, D. R., "A comparison of commercial and military computer security policies", *Proc. 1987 IEEE Symposium on Security and Privacy*, Oakland, California, USA.

[Goguen/Meseguer1982] Goguen, J. A. and Meseguer, J., "Security policies and security models", *Proc. 1982 Berkeley Conference on Computer Security*, IEEE Computer Society Press (1982).

[Goguen/Meseguer1984] Goguen, J. A. and Meseguer, J., "Unwinding and inference control", *Proc. 1984 IEEE Symposium on Security and Privacy*, Oakland, California, USA.

[Hayes1987] Hayes, I. *Specification Case Studies*, Prentice Hall (1987).

[Karger/Herbert1984] Karger, P. A. and Herbert, A. J., "An augmented capability architecture to support lattice security and traceability of access", *Proc. 1984 IEEE Symposium on Security and Privacy*, Oakland, California, USA.

[Landwehr1981] Landwehr, C. E., "Formal models for computer security", *Computing Surveys*, **13**, 247 (1981)

[Morris/Thompson1979] Morris, R. and Thompson, K., "Password security: a case history", *Comm. ACM*, **22**, 11, 594 (1979).

[Neely/Freeman1985] Neely, R. B. and Freeman, J. W., "Structuring systems for formal verification", *Proc. 1985 IEEE Symposium on Security and Privacy*, Oakland, California, USA.

[Rushby/Randell1983] Rushby, J. M. and Randell, B., "A distributed secure system", *IEEE Computer*, **16**, pp. 55–67 (1983).

[Sufrin1983] Sufrin, B., "Formal system specification—notation and examples", *Tools and Notations for Program Construction*" (Ed. Neel), Cambridge University Press (1983).

[Wiseman1986] Wiseman, S. R., "A secure capability computer system", *Proc. 1986 IEEE Symposium on Security and Privacy*, Oakland, California, USA.

[Wood1977] Wood, H. M., "The use of passwords for controlling access to remote computer systems and services", *Proc. 1977 National Computer Conference*, AFIPS Press (June 1977).

[Wood1986] Wood, J., "A practical distributed secure system", *Proc. 2nd International Conference on Secure Communications Systems*, IEE, London (October 1986).

Index

355